Transitional Justice in Eastern Europe and the Former Soviet Union

During the last two decades, the countries of Eastern Europe and the former Soviet Union have attempted to address the numerous human rights abuses that characterized the decades of communist rule. This book examines the main processes of transitional justice that permitted societies in those countries to come to terms with their recent past. It explores lustration, the banning of communist officials and secret political police officers and informers from post-communist politic, ordinary citizens' access to the remaining archives compiled on them by the communist secret police, as well as trials and court proceedings launched against former communist officials and secret agents for their human rights trespasses. Individual chapters explore the progress of transitional justice in Germany, the Czech Republic, Slovakia, Poland, Hungary, Romania, Bulgaria, Albania, Slovenia and the successor states of the former Soviet Union. The chapters explain why different countries have employed different models to come to terms with their communist past; assess each country's relative successes and failures; and probe the efficacy of country-specific legislation to attain the transitional justice goals for which it was developed. The book draws together the country cases into a comprehensive comparative analysis of the determinants of post-communist transitional justice, that will be relevant not only to scholars of post-communist transition, but also to anyone interested in transitional justice in other contexts.

Lavinia Stan teaches at St. Francis Xavier University, Canada. A political scientist working on transitional justice, religion and politics, and post-communist democratization, she is the author of *Leaders and Laggards* (2003), co-author of *Religion and Politics in Post-Communist Romania* (2007), and editor of *Romania in Transition* (1997).

Transitional Justice in Eastern Europe and the Former Soviet Union

Reckoning with the communist past

**Edited by
Lavinia Stan**

Routledge
Taylor & Francis Group

LONDON AND NEW YORK

Transferred to digital printing 2010
First published 2009
by Routledge
2 Park Square, Milton Park, Abingdon, Oxon OX14 4RN

Simultaneously published in the USA and Canada
by Routledge
270 Madison Ave, New York, NY 10016

Routledge is an imprint of the Taylor & Francis Group, an Informa business

© 2009 Editorial selection and matter; Lavinia Stan; individual chapters,
the contributors

Typeset in Times New Roman by
Exeter Premedia Services Private Ltd.

British Library Cataloguing in Publication Data
A catalogue record for this book is available from the British Library

Library of Congress Cataloging in Publication Data
A catalog record for this book has been requested.

ISBN 978-0-415-77671-4 (hbk)
ISBN 978-0-415-59041-9 (pbk)
ISBN 978-0-203-88778-3 (ebk)

Contents

Contributors

Robert C. Austin (Ph.D. in History, University of Toronto) is a specialist in the history of Albania and Kosovo. His book *The Path Not Taken – Fan Noli and Albanian Democracy, 1920 – 1924*, which dealt with Albania's struggle to consolidate its democracy during the inter-war period, was subsequently published in two editions in Albanian in years 2000 and 2003. Austin was a Tirana- and Munich-based analyst for Radio Free Europe/Radio Liberty, a Slovakia-based correspondent for The Economist Group of Publications and a writer for the publicly-supported Canadian Broadcasting Corporation in Toronto. The author of numerous scholarly articles published in *ORBIS*, *East European Quarterly*, and *RFE/RL Research Report* and newspapers such as *The Globe and Mail*, Austin is currently teaching at the Centre for European, Russian and Eurasian Studies at the University of Toronto.

Gary Bruce (Ph.D. in History, McGill University) is currently writing the history of the Stasi in two East German districts, Gransee and Perleberg. He is the author of *Resistance with the People: Repression and Resistance in Eastern Germany 1945–55* (Harvard Cold War Studies, 2003), articles published in peer-reviewed journals such as *Contemporary European History* and the *Journal of Cold War Studies*, and several book chapters, Bruce is also the recipient of a Social Science and Humanities Research Council of Canada grant to examine the conduct of the Stasi at a local level, and has received substantial support from the German Academic Exchange Service (DAAD) for his work on the Stasi. The Federal Commission for the Documents of the former State Security Service of the GDR (the Birthler-Behörde) has invited him to contribute several chapters to their publications. He has presented at numerous scholarly conferences in Canada, the U.S., the United Kingdom, Poland, and Germany. He is currently teaching at the University of Waterloo, Canada.

Jonathan Ellison (B.A. in Russian and East European History, University of Toronto) expects to receive his JD from the University of Toronto's Faculty of Law in June 2008. Ellison spent one year working as a law clerk at the Moscow office of Baker & McKenzie and will be joining Proskauer Rose LLP in New York as a junior associate in September 2008.

Tamara Kotar (Ph.D. candidate in Political Science, Carleton University) is preparing to defend her doctoral thesis on liberalization in Slovenia and Croatia as seen through the vector of church and state relations. Kotar, who is of Slovenian descent, has delivered a number of papers at the annual conferences of the Canadian Association of Slavists, the American Association for the Advancement of Slavic Studies, and the Canadian Political Science Association, and has done research on Slovenian post-communist democratization with the Center for European Studies at Carleton University.

Momchil Metodiev (Ph.D. in History, St. Climent Ochridski University of Sofia, Bulgaria) is the author of *The Legitimacy Machine: The Place of the State Security in the Bulgarian Power Structure* (Sofia, 2008), the translator and editor of a selection of documents from the personal archive of the Bulgarian communist leader Todor Zhivkov, and the author of numerous articles published in Bulgarian academic journals and newspapers. From 1995 to 1996, Metodiev worked for the Bulgarian National Archives, while in 2002–2003 he was a research fellow with the Cold War International History Project, a program run by the Woodrow Wilson Center in Washington, D.C. Currently he writes for the Sofia-based *Christianity and Culture* journal, after working in the Bulgarian Ministry of Foreign Affairs and being affiliated with the Center for Liberal Strategies, recognized as the leading Bulgarian think-tank. Metodiev is among the selected few who have conducted systematic research into the archive of the Bulgarian Communist Party.

Nadya Nedelsky (Ph.D. in Political Science, University of Toronto) has done work on Czech and Slovak nationalism and transitional justice. Her dissertation focused on Czech and Slovak understandings of nationhood and their implications for both minority rights and democratization. Her publications include "Divergent Responses to a Common Past: Transitional Justice in the Czech Republic and Slovakia," in *Theory and Society* (vol. 33, February 2004, pp. 65–115), as well as articles focusing on Czech and Slovak politics in such peer-reviewed journals as *Nations and Nationalism*, *Ethnicities*, and *Ethnic and Racial Studies*. In addition, she has delivered a number of papers at conferences in Canada and the U.S. She is teaching International Studies at Macalester College in Saint Paul, Minnesota.

Lavinia Stan (Ph.D. in Political Science, University of Toronto) has worked on such aspects of post-communist democratization as religion and politics, social capital, institutional performance, and transitional justice. She is the author of *Leaders and Laggards: Governance, Civicness and Ethnicity in Romania* (2003), the co-author of *Religion and Politics in Post-Communist Romania* (2007), and the editor of *Romania in Transition* (1997). Stan contributed over 30 articles to peer-review journals such as *East European Politics and Societies*, *Europe-Asia Studies*, *Communist and Post-Communist Studies*, *European Journal of Political Research*, and *Problems of Post-Communism*, and wrote the Moldovan quarterly report for the *East European Constitutional Review* from 1997 to 2003. Her work has been generously funded by the Killam Trust Fund, and the Social Science and Humanities Research Council of Canada. Stan is currently teaching at St. Francis Xavier University in Nova Scotia, Canada.

Foreword

Truth, memory, and reconciliation: judging the past in post-communist societies

Vladimir Tismaneanu

Coming to terms with the traumatic past has turned out to be one of the thorniest, politically charged, and morally tantalizing experiences associated with the post-communist transitions. Like in other countries exiting dictatorial regimes (Latin America, South Africa, Greece, Spain, Portugal, etc.), the boundaries between victims, by-standers, and perpetrators have often been elusive, and efforts to bring perpetrators of crimes against humanity to justice have resulted in frustrating settlings of accounts and hollow rhetorical battles. This is not to say that the issue of political justice is irrelevant. On the contrary, as Lavinia Stan accurately points out in the first chapter of this most timely and profoundly illuminating book, "the experience of new democracies suggests that the process of assuming the dictatorial past represents the key to building a stable, legitimate democracy." Indeed, if properly pursued, transitional justice allows for rebuilding a democratic community established on trust, individual rights, rule of law, and respect for truth. After decades of organized forgetfulness or state-sponsored, ideologically-defined falsification of history, it is now finally possible to right the wrongs of the past. This cannot take place, however, via decrees from above. Society needs to participate in national conversations about the past. In order to avoid the birth of new mythologies (redemptive, self-aggrandizing narratives), one needs to take into account the institutional and human elements involved in the totalitarian and post-totalitarian stages of Leninist dictatorships. At the same time, political justice cannot be separated from moral justice as a continuous exercise in working through the past (to use Theodor W. Adorno's formulation). There is thus an urgent need to pierce through the long-held official stories and identify the main institutional and human instruments of the dictatorships. Those regimes were not run by extra-terrestrials. Crimes took place, they can be documented, and the guilty individuals can be brought to trial. Decades after the *guerra sucia* in Argentina or the student massacre in Mexico City, the cases against the fomentors and perpetrators remain valid.

The key issue in this context is the very trustworthiness, or better said the quality of the new democratic arrangements. If the former tormentors continue to benefit from impunity, if political justice is postponed *sine die* in the name of a politically-manipulated and self-serving understanding of reconciliation (e.g. Romania under former President Ion Iliescu), there is a growing feeling among the the population at large that the revolutionary changes as a whole were nothing but a smokescreen, a well-manufactured facade meant to protect and preserve the vested interests of the converted nomenklatura. Reconciliation in the absence of repentance is nothing but a mockery of national dialogue. This book offers a first comparative and comprehensive exploration of the dynamics of de-communization in East-Central Europe and the former USSR. The case studies provide excellent opportunities to engage in historical comparative discussions about the determinants of the speed, scope, magnitude, depth, and effectiveness of various de-communization strategies. Taking a relatively long historical perspective (1989–91 to 2007) the book explains why certain countries have been more successful than others in addressing issues related to what Germans call *Geschichtsbewältigung*. The authors also lucidly point to the relative meaning of the term success when it comes to political justice.

My own experience as chair of the Presidential Commission for the Analysis of the Communist Dictatorship in Romania has convinced me how explosive issues related to recent past can be. What Jürgen Habermas calls the public use of history is poignantly perceivable in the post-communist cultural and moral battles over the communist and fascist pasts. As Lavinia Stan emphasizes, in many of these countries it is hard to disentangle the communist from the pre-communist authoritarian, often Fascist experiences. Especially in the countries that belonged to the Axis during World War II, de-communization and de-Fascization are often intertwined and mutually conditioned. This is particularly striking in Romania where the Ceausescu dictatorship combined in its ideology motifs and obsessions of both far left and far right. I refer to this disturbingly puzzling phenomenon as *the Communist-Fascist baroque.* Add to this situation acute sensibilities derived from institutional memories of guilt, collaboration, and complicity. Quite often, former collaborators indulge in fantasies of victimhood and clamor for solidarity, empathy, and compassion. Think of the reactions of various religious hierachies in Germany and Romania to references made by historical commissions to past collusions between highly-placed members of the clergy and the communist party ideological apparatus or various branches of the secret police.

The authors avoid any one-dimensional, mono-causal explanation of the tribulations of de-communization in the countries they deal with. It is the merit of this path-breaking volume that it does justice to the complexities of political justice. The book is therefore coherent in its main hypotheses and compelling in its conclusions. De-communization has been decisively influenced by the willingness of the new (or not so new) political elites to initiate and assume judicial and political steps toward historical and legal accountability regarding a traumatic, violent, and brutal past. All the studies included in the volume examine carefully three levels of de-commmunization: 1) lustration as a means to temporarily ban from public office former members of the party bureaucracy and secret police officers and informers; 2) ordinary citizens access to their own files in secret police archives; and 3) trials and court proceedings launched against former communist dignitaries and secret police officers/agents charged with human rights abuses.

For many former communists, the very idea of political justice, even in the form of a scholarly report on the main institutions and methods that made possible the past crimes, is anathema. Their reproach to those who call for de-communization is that this would result in "witch-hunts."As a matter of fact, one of the most striking developments of post-communist times is precisely the absence of Jacobin-like mob campaigns for retaliation and revenge. Adam Michnik's legitimate fears that the former prisoners could turn into prison-guards have not been confirmed, and this is in fact good news about the moral and political self-control of post-communist politicians and intellectuals. On the other hand, as the situation in Poland has shown especially in 2005–2007, there is rampant discontent with the absence of a throroughgoing lustration. Many people consider preposterous the delays in implementing political justice and resent the fact the new elites are often recruited from the second echelon of the old ones. In Romania, Poland, Hungary, or Bulgaria, this trend indicates moral promiscuity and deliberate forgetfulness. In this respect, one may remember that Michnik has often said: "Amnesty yes, amnesia no." Reconciliation cannot be attained through the reproduction of lies. The marvelous Romanian film *12:08 East of Bucharest* (directed by Corneliu Porumboiu) captures this perplexing ambiguities. One of the characters (we hear his voice but do not see his face) is a former secret police agent turned into a most successful businessman. When hints are made during a TV talk show to his dirty past, the now "pillar of the community" threatens with a libel suit.

Cynicism, cronyism, and corruption are among the most dangerous pathologies of post-communism. Their antidotes are trust, truth, and tolerance. Superbly documented, carefully researched, and conceptually original, this book contributes significantly to our understanding of how to overcome the post-communist ethical morass and foster an honest democratic community.

Acknowledgments

An earlier version of Chapter 2 was published as Gary Bruce, "Lustration, Vetting, and Access to Secret Police Files in East Germany Since 1989," *German Politics & Society*, 2008, vol. 26, 82–111. Chapter 3 draws on Nadya Nedelsky, "Divergent Responses to a Common Past: Transitional Justice in the Czech Republic and Slovakia," *Theory and Society*, 2004, vol. 33, 65–111. Chapter 4 appeared as Lavinia Stan, "Transition, Justice and Transitional Justice in Poland,", *Studia Politica*, 2006, vol. 6, 257–284, and also Lavinia Stan, "The Politics of Memory in Poland: Lustration, File Access and Court Proceedings," *Studies in Post-Communism Occasional Paper*, no. 10, April 2006, while Chapter 5 was published as Lavinia Stan, "Goulash Justice for Goulash Communism? Explaining Transitional Justice in Hungary," *Studia politica*, 2007, vol. 7, 269–292. Finally, Chapter 8 appeared as Robert C. Austin and Jonathan Ellison, "Transitional Justice in Albania," *East European Politics and Societies*, 2008, vol. 22, 373–401.

Many people helped us to bring this project to completion. Gary Bruce gratefully acknowledges the assistance of Herr Detlef Niemann of the Schwerin Branch of the Stasi archives in setting up interviews, and the financial assistance of the German Academic Exchange Service (DAAD). Nadya Nedelsky wants to thank Samuel Abraham, Nishad Avari, Kevin Deegan Krause, Megan Metzger, Martin Schmutterer, Vladimira Sefranka, Zuzana Tomková, and Paul Wilson for their assistance. Her travel to Eastern Europe was supported financially by an ACM/GLCA/ACS Mellon Global Partners Project Central Europe and Russia Travel Grant, and a Wallace Travel and Research Grant.

Lavinia Stan thanks Maria Los, Pawel Machcewicz, Tibor Mandi, and Darius Stola for their insightful comments on earlier versions of Chapters 4 and 5. Ion Sebastian Chesches, Stefan Constantinescu, Ewa Zsuzsa Danielski, Robert Deptula, Sabina Stan, Razvan Zaharia, Rodica Milena Zaharia, and Bartolomiej Zdaniuk helped with data collection and interpretation for Chapters 4 and 6. Yuri Josanu and Alar Kilp provided valuable assistance for Chapter 10. Peter Hack, Reneo Lukic, Stejarel Olaru, Sabrina P. Ramet, Peter H. Solomon, Mircea Stanescu, Larry Watts, and Laurence Whitehead have provided support on more than one occasion, Richard Sakwa and Tom Bates have enthusiastically embraced the project, while Joseph Carens and Sarah Oates extended a helping hand in time of need. More importantly, Lucian Turcescu carefully read and re-read the entire manuscript, made numerous pertinent corrections and suggestions, and diligently prepared the bibliography. All are warmly thanked.

This volume benefited from the generous financial support provided by the Social Science and Humanities Research Council of Canada (SSHRCC) through the standard research grants program. The grant allowed Canadian team members to travel numerous times to Eastern Europe to meet with local academics, journalists, politicians, and representatives of the independent agencies mandated to effect transitional justice, and to attend a number of scholarly meetings in order to present the preliminary results of their work. Indeed, without the generous support of the SSHRCC, research for a project involving so many countries for so many years would have been practically impossible.

"'Transitional justice' is a phrase that embraces a wide variety of practices in new democracies, some of them more transitional than others, some not always entirely just. This thorough comparative assessment of the experience so far in all the countries of the former Soviet bloc examines the 'non-cases' as well as the more exemplary processes, and it takes into account not only policy intentions but actual difference in implementation (right up to the point when most of the countries in question joined the European Union). What emerges is a quite variegated picture, with pre-transition historical experiences and the specific correlation of forces between communist rulers and opposition challengers providing much of the explanation for the observed divergences. This is an important contribution to post-communist studies and to the comparative analysis of democratization in general. Experience from elsewhere suggests that unresolved conflicts in this area can continue to fester and may impede the stabilization of the democratic system despite generational change."

Laurence Whitehead,
Oxford University

"Coming to terms with unpleasant historical episodes is never easy for any society. The process has been especially difficult in the former Communist countries, most of which have failed to hold anyone accountable for the atrocious crimes of the Communist era. In some states, especially Russia, Belarus, and the Central Asian republics, officials who spearheaded the repression of dissidents during the Soviet era are back in high posts. In Central and Southeastern Europe, too, efforts to seek redress for the crimes perpetrated by Communist regimes have often been deeply flawed. The many obstacles to a full and fair reckoning with the Communist past are thoughtfully analyzed in this valuable collection of essays by distinguished experts. Lavinia Stan, the editor and lead author of the book, has assembled an excellent group of contributors. The comprehensive scope of the volume makes it a true comparative work. This book provides the most thorough and analytically sophisticated treatment yet available of this crucial topic."

Mark Kramer, Director,
Cold War Studies Program, Harvard University

"The question how countries deal with a difficult past is always intriguing but particularly so when several countries concurrently address the issue and the policies and the policy outcomes show significant variance. Such is the scenario in the former communist bloc in Eastern Europe and the Soviet Union. The in-depth country studies in this book provide the reader with up-to-date information and sound analysis while the analytical framework locates them in the broader body of literature and offers insightful cross-national comparisons. Timely and thought-provoking, this book is indispensable reading for scholars of transitional justice and democratization."

Helga A. Welsh,
Wake Forest University

"An outstanding, brilliant book that helps us to understand developments in post-1989 Eastern Europe. Lustration, the opening of secret police files and trials of communist perpetrators have marked political and intellectual debates in these new democracies, and constituted pivotal efforts to come to terms with the legacy of the communist dictatorship. The volume examines in detail the region's efforts to reckon with the recent past, and the theoretical explanations for country differences in the scope and pace of transitional justice. A 'must read' not only for Eastern Europeans, but also for students of transition to democracy in other parts of the world and other historical periods."

Pawel Machcewicz,
Institute of Political Studies, Polish Academy of Science

"Lavinia and her colleagues have produced a very good survey and explain why individual countries employed different models of coming to terms with their recent past. I specialize in Poland and know the literature on lustration– Lavinia's chapter is a concise analysis that would profit anyone interested in these issues. I will eagerly await publication of this volume, purchase it, and tell my colleagues and students that an English-language text has been published that reveals why dealing with the past in our part of the world is so complicated."

John S. Micgiel, Director,
East Central European Center, Columbia University

"In this pioneering new work, Lavinia Stan and her contributors have produced a theoretically coherent and empirically well-documented book that will be required reading in the field of post-communist transition in East-Central Europe and the Former Soviet Union. Rooted in an impressive understanding of transitional justice processes in the region, Stan's volume provides concise narrative about changes that occurred after the access to the communist secret files was partially granted to the citizens of former communist countries. This book will be appreciated by laymen and experts alike."

Reneo Lukic,
Laval University, Canada

"Why do some countries reckon with past repression by opening up the files of secret police, barring from office participants in the repressive regime, and prosecuting human rights abuses, while others, with similar abuses, do little to face their past? Tracing developments from 1989 to 2007, *Transitional Justice in Eastern Europe and the Soviet Union* provides fascinating, detailed case studies and a persuasive argument linking contrasting responses to past and present political alignments and to degrees of prior experiences with democracy and political pluralism. This will be a vital resource for understanding when and where transitional justice is pursued."

Martha Minow,
Harvard Law School,
and author of *Between Vengeance and Forgiveness*

"It is relatively rare in comparative social research that scholars conclusively demonstrate that they are both detail oriented and theoretically creative. The editor of this volume exemplifies both these qualities, identifying the specific provisions of lustration and de-communization laws across many post-communist countries, then evaluating disparate theories of transitional justice by advancing an innovative multivariate model. With an impressive cast of contributors, we now have a seminal work on East European de-communization."

Raymond Tarsas, Tulane University

1 Introduction

Post-communist transition, justice, and transitional justice

Lavinia Stan

Since the end of the Cold War, "de-communization," "transitional justice," the "politics of memory," and "political justice" have been among the terms and concepts commonly used to describe the wide range of inter-related processes of coming to terms with the recent dictatorial past in post-communist Eastern Europe and the former Soviet Union. As in other parts of the world, most notably South Africa, Southern Europe, and Latin America, in post-communist countries democratization has turned into an effort to envision a better future and to navigate an uncertain present as much as to investigate, reevaluate, and redress the mistakes of the *ancien regime*. Bit by bit, the touching personal testimonials of former political prisoners, the reserved memoirs of communist officials and secret agents, the testimonials of silent by-standers, and the independent research carried out in the newly-opened archives have lifted the veil of secrecy surrounding the activity of the communist parties hegemonic in the region, their privileged relationship with the ruthless secret political police forces, their alternate use of repression and cooptation to maintain monopoly of political power, and their victimization of countless individuals arrested, imprisoned, tortured, exiled, murdered or reduced to silence. Although much more work needs to be done in order to unravel the entire mechanism of communist repression and terror, and sort myth from truth regarding the identity and role of victims and victimizers, today we have incontestable proof for many human rights trespasses and violations we knew about only from unsubstantiated rumors prior to 1989. The challenge is to come to terms with these atrocities, while continuing to establish the truth and strengthen the rule of law.

This volume is the first to map the progress of three main transitional justice processes in post-communist Eastern European and former Soviet Union countries, explain why individual countries employed different models of coming to terms with their recent past at different times with different degrees of success, and probe the relative efficacy of country-specific transitional justice outcomes through the evaluation of the activity of state bodies in charge of moving the process forward. Finally, this study draws together this rich case-specific research into a comprehensive comparative analysis of the determinants of transitional justice in post-communist times.

Transitional justice: the broader context

The origins of the urge to reassess the past authoritarian regimes, to confront and to prosecute the victimizers, to rehabilitate the victims, and publicly to uncover the mechanisms of repression are identified with the post-World War II setting in Europe by some authors, the aftermath of the French Revolution by others, and 251 AD or even ancient Greece by still others. Bickford points to the International Military Tribunal at Nuremberg and the de-Nazification programs in Germany as representing the first efforts dedicated to assessing and redressing past injustice. Fitzpatrick places those first attempts much earlier and claims that they materialized as the purges and the revenge campaigns that followed in the wake of the French Revolution of 1789. For theology scholars, reconciliation first became important for the primary Church after the persecution sanctioned by Roman Emperor Decius in 250 AD, when Novatian and his followers refused readmission to communion to the lapsi, the baptized Christians who had denied their faith and had sacrificed to pagan gods. Elster discusses the politics of accountability carried out with the return of democrats to Athens in 403 BC after the rule of the Thirty Tyrants.[1] While different authors vacillate between different time periods when trying to pinpoint the first attempts at pursuing justice during times of regime change, they unanimously agree that the transitional justice framework gained in coherence, diversity, and importance only in the second half of the twentieth century. These developments emerged because "democratic activists and their allies in government sought to find new and creative ways to address the past,"[2] and further expanded the possibility of comprehensive justice during transition, relying on the idea of truth as an "absolute, unrenounceable value."[3] These efforts addressed the unprecedented genocide and regimes of tortures marking the twentieth century, and culminated in what Soyinka labeled "the end of millennium fever of atonement."[4] Each of the consecutive waves of democratization Huntington identified were accompanied by calls for holding the officials of the former authoritarian regime accountable for their many wrongdoings. The calls were heeded predominantly in those countries where the democratization process was not reversed, and the fragile new regimes did not succumb to a new wave of ruthless authoritarianism.[5]

The experience of new democracies suggests that the process of assuming the dictatorial past represents the key to building a stable, legitimate democracy. A number of political scientists and journalists have argued that democratization cannot be successfully effected without an honest reevaluation of the past that would bring justice to victims and closure to victimizers. According to O'Donnell and Schmitter, "it is difficult to imagine how a society can return to some degree of functioning which would provide social and ideological support for political democracy without somehow coming to terms with the most painful elements of its own past."[6] Tismaneanu reinforces the same point when writing that "to ask for a serious coming to grips with the past is not simply a moral imperative: none of these societies can become truly liberal if the old mythologies of self-pity and self-idealization continue to monopolize the public discourse."[7] Borneman similarly believes that "the relevance of retributive justice in the contemporary context goes far beyond the fate of individual crimes and victims; its increasing importance is part of a global ritual purification of the center of political regimes that seek democratic legitimacy."[8] For de Brito et al. reckoning with the past through truth telling can "address the social need for knowledge to become acknowledgement" and "bring victims back into the fold of society, by recognizing their suffering, providing a form of distributive or social justice, and giving out non-conventional resources such as social awareness, collective memory, solidarity, and the overcoming of low self esteem."[9] Transitional justice, Calhoun contends, provides a solid foundation for budding democracies because it constitutes the middleground solution between forgetting the past altogether and engaging in violent retribution, two unacceptable options that prevent new democratic regimes from gaining much-needed political legitimacy.[10] The experience of post-authoritarian countries reinforces Calhoun's position vis-á-vis the necessity of reexamining the past. During the last century only Spain opted to "forgive and forget" its former torturers working for Generalissimo Francisco Franco's dictatorial regime and to grant them the *carte blanche* of blanket amnesty that allowed them to prove their allegiance to the new democratic order. By contrast, all other democratizing nations chose to face the past more or less promptly, more or less vigorously, more or less effectively.

For some other authors, the stakes are more urgent, and they address specific goals that are key to a successful democratization process. "Forgetting the extermination is part of the extermination itself," Baudrillard said after World War II,[11] whereas Kundera voiced the Eastern European viewpoint when concluding that "the struggle against power is the struggle of memory against forgetting."[12] Rosenberg echoed that same position, explaining that "nations, like individuals, need to face up to and understand traumatic past events before they can put them aside and move on to normal life."[13] Beyond permitting a return to normalcy, transitional justice signals the break with the authoritarian past and the willingness of the political class and of the larger society to work together, rather than against each other, for the common good and in the national interest. Confronting the past honestly, vigorously, and constructively helps democratizing societies to bridge the great chasm dividing victims, victimizers and by-standers, and to reconstruct the national political community on firmer bases.[14] Transitional justice rebuilds trust among citizens and between citizens and the state, and in doing so allows the community and the state to come together and solve the problems of the nation. Trust, in its turn, leads to the accumulation of rich social capital reserves, the formation of vibrant voluntary associations, and the rebirth of a strong civil society able to hold the state accountable for its actions.[15] The South African experience proved that "no healing is possible without reconciliation, no reconciliation is possible without justice, and no justice is possible without some form of genuine restitution," as Beyers Naud argued.[16] Restitution is not limited to the return of abusively confiscated property, but can materialize as acknowledgement of past sufferings, the restoration of honor and dignity to long-silenced victims, or public knowledge of the repression mechanisms kept secret by the old regime. In the same vein, respect for human rights cannot be instilled as a quintessential value of new democracies if past injustices are left unpunished and unrecorded. When introducing the Truth and Reconciliation Committee, the South African Minister of Justice Dullah Omar reminded that "human rights is not a gift handed down as a favor by government or the state to loyal citizens [but] it is the right of each and every citizen."[17] Most of the killings, brutality, surveillance, and control were done in the name of political regimes keeping the state apparatus prisoner to their ideology of terror, not in the name of specific individuals or of distinguishable social groups. However, if perpetrators can hide behind the excuse that they acted at the command of their superiors rather than as a result of their own volition, then the repressive state is allowed to triumph over the captive society, even after the regime change is effected.

Confronting the past responds to genuine needs for justice, truth, and atonement, but it can also easily lend itself to political manipulation, and it can lead to new injustices if the rule of law is disregarded in favor of political expediency. In this respect, George Orwell's remark that "who controls the past controls the future" remains relevant in post-communist Eastern Europe and the former Soviet Union, where the memory of the past constitutes one of the most coveted prizes. There, "the battle for history is really a battle for the political culture of these new post-communist states," one which constitutes an important way for Eastern Europeans to compete for control of the present.[18] Albania engaged in extensive purges following each of its governmental changes of the early 1990s, and brought the family of dictator Enver Hoxha to trial not for his gruesome political crimes, but for living well in a country where most of the population barely made ends meet. In Romania few objected to the mock-trial and execution, commando style, on Christmas Day in 1989 of Nicolae Ceausescu and his wife Elena, who were singled out as solely responsible for communist abuses ironically by their one-time right-hand collaborator Ion Iliescu. The Baltic states of Estonia and Latvia marginalized former Soviet party officials and KGB agents by denying citizenship in the new state, thus depriving them of the important political rights of electing and being elected. Following her travels to Czechoslovakia, Poland, and Germany, lands still haunted by the ghost of their communist past, Rosenberg talks at length about the readiness with which post-communist political parties have embraced widely different myths about communism that are "constantly rewritten to fit the current political debate," to bring additional legitimacy to their initiators and to sully the track record of their political enemies.[19] Adopting a similar viewpoint, Tismaneanu includes the myth of de-communization among his "fantasies of salvation," describes it as a process of manifold mental, political, economic and legal dimensions with Jacobin propensities, and warns against the perils of reconciling legitimacy and legality through authoritarian methods in countries where the demarcation line between right and wrong remains utterly blurred. But to reduce the complexity of the politics of memory to the level of recognizing it only as a manipulating tool used in the cut-throat battles waged by power-thirsty political parties or to relegate it to the grey zone of illusory and unattainable myths ignores the Eastern Europeans' need to know the truth about the communist regime, to confront their own personal history, and to obtain justice and absolution.

The methods through which post-authoritarian countries have approached the cathartic quest for political justice differed widely, but they were generally divided into state-driven and society-driven solutions that can acquire either judiciary or non-judiciary characteristics. Post-authoritarian governments have supported truth and reconciliation commissions, court trials and amnesties, purges and screenings, public official apologies, as well as financial compensation, restitution and reparation programs. Initiatives proposed by human rights organizations, former political prisoners, religious denominations, political parties and other civil society groups, often pursued in parallel with government-sponsored solutions, have spanned acknowledging the past, rehabilitation, access to the governmental records detailing repression and persecution, the rewriting of official historical canons, and symbolic reparations in the form of commemorative monuments, new museums, name change for streets and localities, and official holidays celebrating important moments when the society stood up to the authorities. To these locally grown ways to confront the past and to seek justice during times of post-authoritarian transformation, one should add the solutions advocated by the international community, which have primarily included the international courts of justice hearing cases that involve genocide and crimes against humanity. As Elster explained, some of these political decisions were made "in the immediate aftermath of the transition and [were] directed towards individuals on the basis of what they did or what was done to them under the earlier regime."[20] The prime example here is the Nuremberg trial, which in the aftermath of World War II held accountable 24 top Nazi officials as war criminals. Other transitional justice methods were adopted a number of years after the authoritarian regime collapsed, when its officials had already lost much of their political clout. Taking post-Nazi Germany again as an example, the restitution of property abusively confiscated from Jewish victims of concentration camps is yet to be fully completed, although major accomplishments have been achieved during the last six decades. Transitional justice methods further divide in distinct categories in terms of their efficacy and effectiveness in providing justice, voice, atonement, and redress. Whether specific methods are more apt to provide efficiency depends less on the specific moment in time when they are adopted and more on the political will and resolve with which they are implemented.

The list of cases that could serve as models for post-communist Eastern Europe is impressive, testifying to the wealth of innovative solutions different countries have employed in order to conduct the politics of memory, prevent future abuse, and establish state–society relationships based on functioning and fair institutions. As comprehensive accounts of successive transitional justice cases were provided by Elster, Hayner, Barahona de Brito, and others, we will not embark on such an enterprise here, but instead we will highlight only the most important trends.[21] The end of World War II witnessed the launch of an array of different transitional justice methods in Germany, Japan, and countries that had been overrun by the Nazis like Austria, Belgium, and France. Top war criminals were tried in international tribunals, official historical accounts were reexamined in intense public debates, the Holocaust was acknowledged, documented, and condemned, and its victims

were called to provide moving testimonials, amnesties were granted to former collaborators in an effort to "normalize" the situation, confiscated property and assets
were returned to their initial owners, and the concentration camps were turned
into museums commemorating the plight of millions of innocent victims. The
court trials Greece and Argentina organized in 1974 and 1983, respectively, led
to the successful prosecution of former members of the bloody colonels' regime
and the military junta responsible for human rights abuses. The final report of
the Argentinean National Commission on the Disappeared, the best-seller *Nunca
Mas* (1983), the Chilean efforts to provide reparation to victims of the Pinochet
regime, and the truth commissions established in post-Apartheid South Africa
and twenty other countries in Africa (Zimbabwe, Uganda, Chad, Nigeria, Sierra
Leone), Asia (Sri Lanka and Nepal), Caribbean islands (Haiti), and Latin America
(El Salvador, Guatemala, Bolivia, Uruguay, Ecuador) have made significant contributions to establishing justice for victims of human rights abuses. By the time
the communist regime collapsed in 1989, the new Eastern European democracies and former Soviet republics could draw inspiration from a large array of
transitional justice methods adopted throughout the world.

Transitional justice in the post-communist world

In Eastern Europe and the former Soviet Union, calls for de-communization have
revolved around the Communist Parties and their feared instruments of repression, the secret intelligence services. The communist secret political police was
organized as an extensive repression apparatus of full-time officers and part-time
informers responsible for keeping dissent in check, discouraging anti-governmental opposition, censoring journalists and artists, and protecting the communist
party leaders, to which it was directly accountable. Its employment numbers were
vast. In the case of the Romanian Securitate, for example, they are estimated at
around 15,000 officers and between 400,000 and 700,000 informers in a total
population of about 23 million. In 1989 the East German Stasi employed some
90,000 officers and around 150,000 active informers in a total population of 17
million. It is believed that the Soviet KGB employed almost half a million agents,
but the numbers remain strictly guarded by authorities of the Russian Federation.
An informer became a collaborator when joining the Communist Party, then a
paid collaborator and finally a paid referent contemplating promotion to the rank
of political police officer with uncovered, partly covered or completely covered
identity. Monetary and non-monetary perks alike were available to informers if
they spied on and reported the whereabouts of their relatives, friends, workmates,
neighbors, and colleagues. Not all collaborations were voluntary, opportunis-
tic and revengeful, as many informers spied out of fear for themselves and the
well-being of family members, misplaced patriotism or blackmail. In such cases,
the informers' secret activity was neither rewarded financially nor resulting in
a speedier promotion, better living conditions, and permission to travel abroad.
The secret police kept files on Western visitors, pre-communist political leaders
and elite members, anti-communist dissidents, people suspected of pro-Western

sympathies and ordinary citizens alike. While the political police differed in numbers across countries, the recruitment, mission and general activity were remarkably similar. The extant archives attesting how some Eastern Europeans spied on others range in length from some 200 kilometers in the case of the Stasi to only 25 in the case of the Securitate.[22]

While omnipotent, controlling and pervasive, the much-feared secret political police remained nothing more than the obedient arm of the communist parties that dominated the region from the end of World War II until 1989. Those parties controlled the appointment to state positions and public offices, had virtual monopoly over policy making in most areas of life, imprisoned, tortured, and murdered thousands of pre-communist elite members, anticommunist dissidents and religious leaders, closely supervised mass media and literary and artistic productions to root out dissent and criticism of the leaders, the official policy and ideology, and curtailed basic human rights such as freedom of travel, expression, religion, opinion, and association. Career advancement depended on toeing the party line, submission to the communist leadership, and readiness to implement the official policy, however irrational, more than managerial skills and professional expertise. The secret police kept the general population under surveillance, but at the same time they deferred to the authority of the top party leadership, to which they were directly accountable. In each Eastern European communist country, the top party leaders decided the general mission, the tasks, and the individual targets of the secret police, and allocated the resources they needed for their daily operations. In the Soviet Union, those decisions were taken in Moscow, with only minimal input from republican leaderships. Communist Party leaders further maintained the pretence of socialist legality by obliging the judiciary to work closely with the secret officers to protect the identity of the secret informers, ignore the need to fair trials and vigorous defense, and obtain the legal evidence needed to convict dissidents, opposers, social parasites, and trouble-makers. The hierarchical relationship between the ruling party and the secret services was evidenced by the fact that the latter was permitted to freely recruit informers from among all social categories except party members, who could be approached only after the approval of the party leadership was secured (sometimes in writing) and whose collaboration was fiercely guarded as a secret according to standards not extended to regular, outside-party informers.

Given the extent to which both the Communist Party and its secret police controlled the lives of citizens in Eastern Europe and the former Soviet Union, it is not surprising that the collapse of these regimes in 1989 and 1991, respectively, prompted heated public debate over what should happen to secret police officers, informers, and communist officials, as well as their files. Some demanded that officials and secret informers be banned from politics and prosecuted for human rights trespasses, and that the secret police archives should be opened to the public. They argued that communist decision-makers should not be allowed access to state positions they could use to destroy the archives, and with them the proof of their past injustices. Many warned that democratization itself required not only accountable and representative political institutions, but also an honest attempt to deal with the undemocratic past that would bring some justice to its victims and lay the groundwork for greater respect for the rule of law.[23] Others, including not only former communists but also some former dissidents, argued that the files were not only full of lies and false accusations, but also that their integrity was in doubt, as interested parties removed, altered, and destroyed portions of them during the upheavals of the 1989 revolution. They pointed out that using deeply flawed materials to screen job candidates would violate the fairness standards of democracy and fuel politically motivated witch hunts. Allowing public access would also expose material wrenched from reluctant informers and trusted intimates and make public the private details of the lives of those spied upon, poisoning societal relations, and extending the secret police's influence over society into the post-communist period. While the debates throughout the region were contentious, those arguing in favor of lustration and file access gained ground as more former communist countries joined NATO, whose Western members were wary of former secret police officers getting access to sensitive military and intelligence data, and the European Union, where existing members felt apprehensive about high communist officials securing top leadership positions in Brussels.

Thus, by the year 2000 all Eastern European countries but war-torn Yugoslavia passed legislation providing for either the banning of communist officials and secret agents from post-communist politics or access to the secret files compiled by the communist state security services. The laws differed greatly, however, in terms of scope, stringency, and enforcement. In the Czech Republic, for example, high communist officials and individuals implicated by the secret files were banned not only from politics but also from such positions of influence as top academic posts and management positions in state-owned enterprises and joint-stock companies. By contrast, the 1997 Polish lustration law stipulated that, while public officials must declare whether they were knowing employers of, or collaborators with, the state security services, they may only be banned from office if their declarations were proven false by the Lustration Court. Hungary and Romania were still less severe, threatening public disclosure of one's past rather than mandatory exclusion from public office. On the far end of the continuum ranging from "prosecute and punish" to "forgive and forget," Slovakia allowed its Czechoslovak-era lustration law to lapse in 1996, never having enforced it seriously. Access to the secret police archives varies from state to state as well in terms of when laws granting access were passed, who may view the files, and how many files were made public. In 1991 East Germany was the first to grant access, whereas Albania reluctantly agreed to open some files only in 2006. Most Stasi files were made available to the public from the very beginning, compared with only a fraction of the Romanian Securitate archive, jealously protected by the post-communist state security services until 2006.

Overall, the former Soviet Union has lagged behind its Eastern European satellites in terms of lustration, access to secret files, and court proceedings. Because significant sections of the secret KGB archive were transferred to Moscow in the months preceding the collapse of the Soviet Union, most of the independent republics were unable to pursue the opening of secret archives as a method of reckoning with their recent past. Russia was the only successor republic with direct access to the bulk of the Soviet-era secret archival documents, but it lacked the political will to adopt that policy. There is much variation within the former Soviet empire with respect to lustration and court trials. The three Baltic states of Estonia, Latvia, and Lithuania have limited the political influence of former Communist Party officials and KGB employees, and have tried and convicted a number of Soviet-era KGB agents for their involvement in human rights abuses. At the other end of the spectrum, the societies and political elites of Belarus, Armenia, and Azerbaijan and the Central Asian republics of Kazakhstan, Kyrgyzstan, Tajikistan, Turkmenistan, and Uzbekistan have not seriously revisited their past, because local Soviet decision makers have retained significant political influence, these republics were rocked by violent ethnic and regional conflict, and their post-communist political systems are more dictatorial than democratic in nature. Russia, Ukraine, Georgia, and Moldova stand somewhere in between these two extremes, having discussed and rejected lustration bills, but having brought to justice no Soviet party official or secret agent.

While the variability in the transitional justice laws as they stand on the books is important in itself, a second and equally important question is how, in reality, these laws have been implemented. Taking investigations into the pasts of post-communist politicians as discussion points, the volume evaluates the success of the state bodies in each country charged with identifying the agents and informers, examines the frequency of contested findings, and investigates the factors responsible for mistaken verdicts. For example, previous examinations of the first verdicts on collaboration with the Securitate handed down in Romania in year 2000 by the National Council for the Study of Securitate Archives point to a mixture of factors explaining the low verdict accuracy. Some files were incomplete, while others remained out of reach for undisclosed reasons of "national security." Some file documents were original, others were modified sometime after 1989 by unknown hands. Retrieval of codified informer names was cumbersome, as spies used aliases to cover up their identity, and the card system matching code names to real identities remained out of reach. There were also numerous questions about the quality of information spies provided to communist secret services. Some spies had thick informer files, but provided only trivial details. Other spies played crucial police roles, but their files cannot be found or, if available, contain only little information potentially damaging to their victims. Then there were legislative loopholes opening laws to interpretation and allowing communist officials and spies to go unpunished. The Hungarian lustration law of 1994 provided for the screening of past collaboration with the domestic repression branch of Direction III, but not with the counter-intelligence and military intelligence departments. Though repeatedly screened, Premier Peter Medgyessy was deemed "clean" because his ties had been to the counter-intelligence, not the domestic, division. Finally, the activity of the independent agencies has been distorted by pressure from political parties and interest groups, absence of clear internal guidelines as regards the written documents that could attest to collaboration, and in-fighting among agency leaders.

After 1989, Eastern Europe's attempts to come to terms with its communist experience were sometimes viewed through the lens of the region's earlier efforts to deal with its Nazi or fascist past. During World War II, a number of Central European, Balkan, and Baltic countries were occupied by, or they aligned themselves with, Nazi Germany and fascist Italy, contributing troops and supplies to the Axis powers, supporting Hitler's or Mussolini's foreign policy, adopting racist legislation discriminating against ethnic and religious minorities, and organizing human transports to concentration camps located in Transnistria, Poland, Germany, and elsewhere. Lacking any significant long-term historical experience with democracy, the Eastern European and Baltic states rationalized their position at the time by claiming they had no real choice when trying to avert a possible fall into the Soviet sphere of influence. After communist regimes were installed in the region with support from the Soviet army, the new authorities embarked on a massive hunt of Nazi collaborators and sympathizers that soon was extended to target individuals critical of the communist ideology, policy choices or leaders. The purges carried out throughout the region during the first decade of communist rule were less concerned with the Nazi past and more with the communist present, as they aimed to consolidate the new regimes by weakening the social bases of pro-democratic political formations, silencing or co-opting the remnants of civil society, and mobilizing the citizenry behind the communist leadership. The memory of those purges, and of the numerous show-trials with predetermined outcome that allowed communist leaders to settle scores with their rivals both inside and outside the Communist Party, seriously affected the scope, pace, and aims of the post-communist transitional justice those countries envisioned after 1989. In the Baltic states, Hungary, and to a lesser extent in Poland, the process of dealing with the memory of the two totalitarian regimes that had gripped those countries during the twentieth century were linked together, thus recognizing that an honest reassessment must avoid reading history selectively, that is, condemning communism while ignoring fascism. Other countries drew parallels between the Nazi and communist regimes, admitting they were two sides of the same totalitarian coin, but failed to bring together the politics of memory corresponding to each of them into a single, unified and coherent process. In Bulgaria and Romania, for example, those who voiced support for dealing honestly with the communist past stopped short of calling on their fellow countrymen to reassess the country's pre-communist politics.

The volume's outline and contribution

While theoretically countries could embrace any method of dealing with the recent past, as long as the method of choice redresses some past injustice, in practice some solutions have been popular in some countries, but not in others. Despite proving their effectiveness in Africa and Latin America, truth commissions were never seriously considered in post-communist countries, although Eastern Europe and the former Soviet Union alike could greatly benefit from both truth telling and national reconciliation. In post-communist Europe, international tribunals were created to hear cases resulted from the Yugoslav wars of the 1990s, not to establish guilt associated with older or more recent communist-era crimes. As purges were reminiscent of the persecutions unleashed against democratic political actors during the early stages of communism, citizens in Eastern Europe and the former Soviet Union have been reluctant to reenact them *tel quel*, opting instead for alternative ways to reckon with the legacy of communist dictatorship. As such, this volume investigates the three most important transitional justice methods that have made an imprint on post-communist democratization. These methods include: 1) lustration, the banning of communist officials and secret political police officers and informers from post-communist politics and positions of influence in society; 2) ordinary citizens' access to the extant archive of the communist secret police; and 3) trials and court proceedings launched against former communist officials and secret agents for their human rights abuses. Taken together, these three methods reveal the complex tapestry that forms the background to the politics of memory in Eastern Europe and the former Soviet Union.

Given the wide variation in transitional justice strategies in those countries, the present volume has two central purposes: first, to offer in-depth country case-studies; and second, to identify broader patterns and address the question of what accounts for both similarities and differences between cases. To this end, we offer case studies on nine post-communist countries in Eastern Europe (the former East Germany, the Czech Republic, Slovakia, Poland, Hungary, Romania, Bulgaria, Albania, and Slovenia) and all 15 former Soviet republics looking at their historical background, the political negotiations leading to the adoption of specific methods, the enacted transitional justice legislation, the activity of the independent governmental agencies in charge of the secret archive, and relevant civil society initiatives. Our concluding chapter offers a comparative analysis of how these countries pursued the politics of memory. A substantial literature exists on the topic, offering a variety of explanations for country differences in dealing with the communist past. To date, theoretical frameworks were proposed by Samuel Huntington; John P. Moran; Helga Welsh; Kieran Williams, Brigit Fowler and Aleks Szczerbiak; Nadya Nedelsky; and Monika Nalepa. While all these frameworks offer valuable insight into country differences, none of them offers an analysis that is comprehensive in terms of cases, processes, or time span.

As such, our study contributes to the growing literature on transitional justice in general, and the politics of memory in Eastern Europe and the former Soviet Union in particular, in three important ways.

First, we survey all Eastern European and former Soviet countries that did not face prolonged war during the 1990s, the first decade of post-communist democratization. With this in mind, we have excluded Yugoslavia, but included tiny Slovenia, which seceded from the Yugoslav Federation in just seven days. Chapters 2 to 9 are the first to detail the progress to date in terms of lustration, file access, and court proceedings of these nine post-communist countries, to provide information on the organization, personnel, methods, and general goals of communist-era secret state security services, and to discuss the activity of the independent governmental agencies charged with effecting transitional justice in each Eastern European and former Soviet country.

Second, we examine the three most important transitional justice processes. Post-communist Eastern Europe was the first region that embraced lustration as a method of transitional justice. The first lustration law, adopted in 1991 in Czechoslovakia and prohibiting former communist officials and secret agents from participating in public life, regardless of their personal involvement in human rights trespasses, became a major focus of international attention and criticism for establishing what many viewed as collective guilt. Lustration has remained an important tool of de-communization throughout the region, so much so that most observers have employed it as the yardstick for measuring the progress of transitional justice in Eastern Europe and the former Soviet Union. Indeed, countries have been judged in terms of whether or not they adopted lustration legislation, and whether or not that legislation emulated the radical Czech model. Countries like Romania that failed to pass laws specifically aimed at lustration were often viewed as having done nothing to deal with their recent past. By contrast, countries like Hungary that passed a mild lustration law that did not lustrate anybody were still regarded as pioneers in transitional justice. The focus on lustration has overshadowed efforts to deal with the communist past by other means, such as court proceedings, and has ignored the fact that lustration itself depends a great deal on access to the secret archives compiled by the communist-era political police. Only by studying lustration together with court proceedings and file access can one properly understand transitional justice in the post-communist context.

Third, we have included a longer time span for our analysis. The volume is the first to discuss transitional justice processes effected from 1989 to 2007. The time period begins with the collapse of the communist regime, although we do not ignore the negotiations that immediately preceded the transfer of political power from the communist rulers to the pro-democratic opposition in Czechoslovakia, Poland and Hungary. The time period ends in January 2007 with the acceptance of Romania and Bulgaria into the European Union, two years after their Central European and Baltic neighbors were admitted as full members. There are no plans for the accession in the near future of any other post-communist country, and therefore year 2007 will remain a landmark for the eastern enlargement process for years to come. Accession into the European Union is important because, with it, the new member states turn their attention to the future of integration and away from the legacy of communism. As many citizens in Eastern Europe and the Baltic states have proudly remarked, post-communist transition ended once their country joined the Union. Surely political transformation and economic transformation will probably continue even after 2007, but accession signifies recognition, on the part of the initial European Union member states, that Eastern European and Baltic efforts to democratize and construct fully functioning market economies have been successful.

Notes

1 L. Bickford, 'Transitional Justice', in D. Shelton (ed.) *The Encyclopedia of Genocide and Crimes against Humanity*, New York: Macmillan, 2004. Online. Available

HTTP: http://www.ictj.org/static/TJApproaches/WhatisTJ/macmillan.TJ.eng.pdf (accessed 4 January 2008), S. Fitzpatrick and R. Gellately (eds) *Accusatory Practices. Denunciation in Modern European History, 1789–1989*, Chicago: University of Chicago Press, 1997, pp. 1–21, and J. Elster, 'Coming to Terms with the Past: A Framework for the Study of Justice in the Transition to Democracy', *Archives Europeenes de Sociologie* 1998, vol. 39, 9–13. I thank Lucian Turcescu for pointing out to me the theological point of view on reconciliation and transitional justice.

2 Bickford, 'Transitional Justice', p. 6.

3 J. Zalaquett, 'Introduction to the English Edition', in The Chilean National Commission on Truth and Reconciliation, *Report of the Chilean National Commission on Truth and Reconciliation*, trans. P. Berryman, South Bend: University of Notre Dame Press, 1993, p. xxxi.

4 W. Soyinka, *The Burden of Memory. The Muse of Forgiveness*, Oxford: Oxford University Press, 1999, p. 90.

5 S. P. Huntington, *The Third Wave: Democratization in the Twentieth Century*, Oklahoma: University of Oklahoma Press, 1993.

6 G. O'Donnell and P. C. Schmitter, *Transitions from Authoritarian Rule: Tentative Conclusions about Uncertain Democracies*, Baltimore: Johns Hopkins University Press, 1991, p. 30.

7 V. Tismaneanu, *Fantasies of Salvation. Democracy, Nationalism and Myth in Post-Communist Europe*, Princeton: Princeton University Press, 1998, p. 116.

8 J. Borneman, *Settling Accounts. Violence, Justice and Accountability in Postsocialist Europe*, Princeton: Princeton University Press, 1997, p. viii.

9 A. Barahona de Brito, C. Gonzalez-Enriquez and P. Aguilar (eds) *The Politics of Memory. Transitional Justice in Democratizing Societies*, Oxford: Oxford University Press, 2001, p. 25.

10 N. Calhoun, *Dilemmas of Justice in Eastern Europe's Democratic Transitions*, New York: Palgrave Macmillan, 2004.

11 Cited in J. E. Young, *The Texture of Memory: Holocaust Memorials and Meaning*, New Haven: Yale University Press, 1993, p. i.

12 M. Kundera, *The Book of Laughter and Forgetting*, New York: Knopf, 1980, pt. i.

13 T. Rosenberg, *The Haunted Land. Facing Europe's Ghosts after Communism*, New York: Vintage Books, 1995, p. xviii.

14 T. E. M. Wong, 'The Truth and Reconciliation Commission. A Brief Analysis', unpublished paper, 1996, p. 1.

15 R. Putnam, *Making Democracy Work. Civic Traditions in Modern Italy*, Princeton: Princeton University Press, 1993.

16 M. Hay, 'Grappling with the Past: The Truth and Reconciliation Committee of South Africa', *Accord. African Journal on Conflict Resolution* 1999, vol. 1, 29–51.

17 D. Omar, 'Introduction to the Truth and Reconciliation Committee', in H. R. Botman and R. M. Petersen (eds) *To Remember and to Heal*, Cape Town: Human and Rousseau, 1996, pp. 24–36.

18 Rosenberg, *The Haunted Land*, pp. xviii and xiv.

19 Ibid., p. xiv.

20 Elster, 'Coming to Terms with the Past', p. 15.

21 Ibid., pp. 9–17, also P. B. Hayner, *Unspeakable Truths. Facing the Challenge of Truth Commissions*, New York: Routledge, 2001, and de Brito, Aguilar and Gonzalez-Enriquez, *The Politics of Memory*, pp. 1–39.

22 K. Persak and L. Kaminski, *A Handbook of the Communist Security Apparatus in East Central Europe, 1944–1989*, Warsaw: Institute of National Remembrance, 2005, pp. 163–220 and 285–328, T. Garton Ash, *The File. A Personal History*, New York: Vintage Books, 1997, and L. Stan, 'Access to Securitate Files: The Trials

and Tribulations of a Romanian Law', *East European Politics and Societies* 2002, vol. 16, 55–90.
23 J. Linz and A. Stepan, *Problems of Democratic Transition and Consolidation: Southern Europe, South America and Post-Communist Europe*, Baltimore: Johns Hopkins University Press, 1996, K. Dawisha (ed.) *The Consolidation of Democracy in East-Central Europe*, Cambridge: Cambridge University Press, 1997, and R. Teitel, *Transitional Justice*, Oxford: Oxford University Press, 2002.

2 East Germany

Gary Bruce

In August 2007, the Stasi Archive[1] made global news when it revealed that the East German secret police, the Stasi, had standing orders to shoot East German border guards who were attempting to flee East Germany. The most sensational line in the document from 1 October 1973, splashed across CNN, read: "Do not hesitate to use your weapon even when women and children are present. The traitors often exploit them for their own purposes."[2] In an ill-advised move, Marianne Birthler, the federal commissioner for the Stasi files, used this document to underscore the importance of the Stasi archive, to emphasize that there is much more research that needs to be done, to raise the issue of bringing individuals involved in the repression apparatus to justice, and to end discussion on whether the Stasi Archive should be closed. When it was revealed that the Potsdam historian Matthias Judt had uncovered a fundamentally similar document 10 years ago, Birthler's claims of the continued need for the Stasi archive rang hollow. She sheepishly admitted to the *Berliner Zeitung* that she had not been aware of the earlier document.[3] Debate then raged in German newspapers as to whether it was finally time to dismantle the Stasi Archive. Leading Cristian Democrats like Reinhard Grindel and Arnold Vaatz criticized Birthler and called for the end of the Stasi Archive on the basis that its integration into the federal archive would end the more or less research monopoly that the Archive currently enjoys.[4] Wolfgang Thierse, a Social Democrat leader and the vice-president of the Bundestag, argued vociferously that an integration of the Stasi archive into the federal system would reduce access to the files as the Stasi files would no longer be exempt from the privacy rules that govern access to other files.[5] Given fears that East Germans may not as easily be able to view files the Stasi kept on them, Thierse proposed keeping the Stasi Archive as it is until at least 2019 by which time the vast majority of East Germans would have had sufficient opportunity to view their files. In a telling comment, Thierse pleaded: "The [Stasi Archive], the fruit of the 1989 Fall revolution, does not deserve this second-class burial."[6]

The call for the end of a special commission for the Stasi files and the documents' integration into the federal archive is not new. Beginning in December 2005 with the so-called "Nevermann-Papier" and continuing in June 2007 with a proposal of the German Culture and Media Ministry (where the Stasi Archive is housed), the Stasi Archive has been targeted as an institution that has outlived its usefulness.[7] Those who back this proposal generally point out that two of the archive's main functions – vetting and assisting in court trials – are now more or less at an end, leaving the remaining task solely that of providing access to files for Stasi victims (and others, but predominantly victims). The Stasi Archive was, however, conceived *primarily* for this latter duty, the crowning triumph of the demonstrators who demanded secret file access – access that would be jeopardized if the files were transferred to the federal system in the immediate future.

In light of this most recent controversy, a review of the history of the Stasi Archive and the development of the extraordinary Stasi Files Law is very much in order. This chapter, based in part on interviews with prominent German politicians, activists, and Stasi officers, traces the history of access to secret police files in Germany since 1989. Such an undertaking reveals the intimate relationship between the revolution that swept aside the East German regime and the subsequent history of the Stasi Archive and makes clear that Thierse's comment about the Archive being the "fruit of the revolution" was not simply political hyperbole. At key junctures since 1989, such as German unification and the controversy regarding former Chancellor Helmut Kohl's files, access to the Stasi files has been challenged – yet successfully resisted by reiterating the aspirations of the demonstrators who took to the streets in 1989. I also deal with two other key components of reckoning with the past (*Vergangenheitsbewältigung*) which involved the Stasi Archive: vetting of public officials for prior involvement with the Stasi, and trials of those responsible for the repression apparatus. The brief overview of these aspects reveals two processes that have had less-than-satisfying outcomes. What is important to stress, however, is that these outcomes do not reflect poorly on the work of the Stasi Archive, which acted solely in a support capacity and was not responsible for verdicts.

Access to secret police files

As time marches on, both scholars and the general public could well make the mistake of thinking that the East German revolution of 1989 ended with the fall of the Berlin Wall. Although the dramatic images of East and West Berliners dancing on the Wall and bewildered border guards helpless to stop them seem to capture the peak of the revolution, in many ways these events represented the beginning of a delicate and volatile few months. Racked by a plummeting economy, an uncertain government, and a still militarized society, the German Democratic Republic teetered toward the new year. In the quest to understand the subsequent history of the East German secret police, the Stasi, and access to its staggeringly large collection of documents, the course of the revolution in the fall of 1989 is of vital importance.[8]

Unlike the first revolution in East Germany of 17 June 1953, when a mere handful of Stasi offices were stormed out of roughly 200 that existed in the country,[9] Stasi buildings formed a focal point of unrest in 1989. Stasi workers received orders to keep the office blinds shut so that demonstrators outside the buildings would think that the workers had gone home, and to clear the front of the buildings of any rocks that could be thrown. By the fall of 1989 it became common practice for Stasi workers to have to sneak out at night and clear the candles from the front of their offices. Joachim Gauck, a Rostock pastor who was an active participant in the revolution and who would become the first Federal Commissioner to oversee the Stasi archives in the united Germany, describes how demonstrators simply had to point to the Stasi building.[10] No words needed to be spoken, or elaborate justification provided. A simple finger point summarized years of repression and a morally bankrupt regime. East Germans completely dismissed Stasi efforts in the fall of 1989 to portray themselves as an important contributor to East German society who busied themselves with scientific and industrial research, including improving washing machines. Upon hearing this justification for continued Stasi existence, demonstrators in Plauen dumped a broken washing machine on the steps of the local district Stasi office.[11]

For our purposes the fall of the Wall is of less importance than the occurrences of the first week of December and early January. Stasi officers were not the dreamers, as one Stasi officer put it to me, who thought that somehow East Germany could be saved, that some form of reform Socialism could be instituted.[12] Almost immediately after the fall of the Wall, Stasi workers began a systematic destruction of documents – a terrible historical loss that is often overlooked considering the mammoth collection that remained. In some instances the destruction was complete. In the district of Schwerin, for example, Stasi workers burned and shredded the entire collection of Department XX which dealt with underground opposition. Finding that the burning of documents was taking too long, Stasi workers turned to shredding the material. When the new federal commission to oversee the Stasi files was brought to life, the newly minted workers were shocked by the 17,200 sacks of shredded material that they found,[13] a repository that keeps an entire section of the archives busy to this day, the workers of which are affectionately known as the "puzzlers." It was precisely this destruction of material that led to citizens storming the regional offices of the Stasi in the first week of December, as small flecks of paper floating in the air of East German cities and the smoke blowing from Stasi offices led them to the obvious conclusion. On 15 January 1990 a dramatic occupation of the main Stasi office on 22 Normannenstrasse in Berlin by an East German citizens' committee secured the primary archival holdings. The citizen committees that oversaw the process of securing the archives were not appointed by parliament, nor did they have democratic approval in any real sense. Their legitimacy came from the "street," from the fact that they had stormed and secured the documents themselves.[14]

This part of our story is not an unimportant one. Without the background of the revolution it becomes impossible to understand the subsequent history of access to the Stasi files. In many ways, the specter of the Stasi drove the revolutionaries. It became understandable, then, that these same revolutionaries and their elected officials would consider the legacy of the Stasi in the form of its files as a crucial element to be addressed. The question of access to the Stasi files begins with crowds of ordinary East Germans pointing their fingers at Stasi buildings during the 1989 revolution. Tobias Hollitzer put this succinctly: "The liberation from the

state security service was a central issue in the Fall of 1989."[15] Individual access
to files was, of course, at the forefront of the revolutionaries' minds, rather than
scholarly examination of the East German past.[16] Indeed, this aspect of the East
German revolution is a remarkable one. As several noted historians of the Stasi
have said, "Citizens occupying a still-intact secret service in order to oversee its
work is historically unprecedented."[17]

Lothar de Maziere, the last Minister President of East Germany, and the first
freely elected government leader in the history of East Germany, came to power
at the head of the Christian Democrat-led "Alliance for Germany" coalition in
March 1990. Soon, de Maziere would negotiate the terms of German unification and he would fade in the public view as Helmut Kohl took centre stage. The
first freely elected East German parliament (*Volkskammer*) should not simply be
glossed over, however, as a short-lived caretaker, or worse, an absurdity on the
rapid path to German unification. This parliament undertook several important
initiatives in dealing with the Stasi. Shortly after its election, it established a committee that would oversee the breakup of the Stasi. Additionally, it drafted a bill
that dealt with access to the Stasi files that was passed in August 1990 as the
"Law on the Securing and Use of Individual-Based Data of the former Ministry
for State Security/Office for National Security."[18] On the day that the bill was
passed, Joachim Gauck gave an emotional speech on the need to access the documents, and sharply criticized the view held by many in West Germany, including
prominent figures like Interior Minister Peter-Michael Diestel, who had promoted
destruction of the documents.[19] Although the law was hardly put into effect before
German unification occurred and the law itself lost force, those East German
parliamentarians paved the way for a Stasi law that was passed by the German
parliament in 1991.

Amidst the painful discovery of the East German past that has occurred since
the opening of the files, many observers began to see a Machiavellian West
German plot behind the relatively free access to the documents. The law governing
access to the Stasi files from 1991, according to this theory, was a result of West
Germany wanting to expose the sinister East German regime for what it was and
thereby show West Germany to have been "the better Germany." This approach
entirely ignores the fact that a largely similar law was passed by a freely elected
East German parliament. In fact, the Stasi file access law of 1991 changed but a
few points from the law passed by the East German parliament, one of the key
of which was that the initial law did not foresee citizens and researchers viewing
actual documents, nor photocopies.[20] Rather, these individuals would be informed
by a case worker of the information that the files contained on them.[21] As a conse-
quence, the issue of whether Stasi collaborators would be made known to victims
was not addressed in the Volkskammer law: citizens had a right to information,
not to documents.[22] Nevertheless, the goals and basic principles of the two laws
were very similar and, indeed, this issue was addressed in the Unification Treaty
which stated that the new all-German parliament was to pass a law on Stasi file
access that would "take into consideration the principles" of the Volkskammer
law.[23] Although it seems self-evident now that individuals affected by the Stasi

would be able to access material the Stasi kept on them, discussions in 1990 about file access ranged from an organized and systematic destruction of the documents, to the handing over, permanently, of files to Stasi victims.[24] The image of revolution often involves people storming buildings and throwing papers or file cabinets into the streets. Burning the documents could well have seemed to many of the participants in 1989 a euphoric victory act.

Access to the Stasi files today is governed by the *Stasi-Unterlagen-Gesetz*, or Stasi Files Law, which was passed by the first all German parliament in December 1991 and came into force on 1 January 1992.[25] The files themselves are administered by an agency with the unwieldy name *Bundesbeauftragte für die Unterlagen des Staatssicherheitsdienstes der ehemaligen Deutschen Demokratischen Republik* (The Federal Commissioner for the Files of the State Security Service of the former German Democratic Republic – BStU). Parliamentarians involved in the committee to draft the law insisted that access to Stasi files be regulated by a law emanating from the German parliament, rather than by government policy, and that it have support across the political spectrum[26] (except for the *Partei des Demokratischen Sozialismus*, the reformed Communist Party, which did not support the process). Although the political consensus on access to Stasi files broke down amidst the controversies regarding Helmut Kohl's files, it is worth remembering that it existed when the law was enacted. In many ways, what was at the heart of the East German revolution of 1989 is captured in the opening section of the Stasi Files Law which sets out the law's purpose. First and foremost, the primary purpose of the Stasi Files Law is to allow the individual access to information stored by the Stasi about himself or herself, so that he or she can judge the influence of the Stasi on their life. This individual reckoning with the past is paramount in the Stasi Files Law. Second, the law is designed to protect the impairment of personal rights arising from use of information stored by the Stasi. German law-makers were extremely concerned lest the archival material be used anew for repression. Third, the law is to ensure and promote historical, political, and legal analysis of the activities of the Stasi, a category that applies to the vast majority of foreign researchers, is but a trickle in the deluge of applications that the Stasi Archives receives. From the over 5 million applications to view Stasi files received by 2003, roughly 14,000 were from researchers.[27] In order to support this activity, the German government authorized the Stasi Archive to establish a Research and Education Department. One of the major criticisms of the Stasi Files Law is that it provides the Federal Commission with a research monopoly. Whereas external researchers are only permitted to view files once they have been vetted and all personal information blacked out, researchers employed by the Stasi Archive are allowed to see original files. They must, however, exercise due diligence in maintaining privacy rights in their publications.[28] Finally, the federal commissioner for the Stasi files is also mandated to put at the disposal of public and private institutions the information required for the purposes specified in the law. Of note is that the Stasi Files Law gave exclusive authority to the Stasi Archive for the registration, the safe-keeping, the administration, and the use of the Stasi files. In other words, no individual or government office should be in possession of original Stasi documents, and risk punishment if they are.[29]

What we see in these key provisions of the Stasi Files Law is the relationship, often at odds, between the first two elements which deal primarily with personal rights, versus the second two elements which deal with the rights of the general public. It is this tension between an individual's right to privacy and the public and individual's right to information and to know the past that makes for such an interesting dynamic. Because the law leans toward the individual's right to know rather than right to privacy, the names of informants and Stasi workers can be released to the public. It is no wonder that Hansjörg Geiger, a legal expert on data protection, was among the first employed in the Gauck Agency in 1990.[30] The privacy issue has been extremely contentious in the united Germany. How could it be that information that was gathered on an individual in a manner "contrary to the dignity of the individual" – and almost all of it was gathered in some underhanded way[31] – be archived? The West German privacy law calls for the destruction of such material, not its preservation for future generations.[32] The fact that the general public is permitted to know the names of those who cooperated with the Stasi, be it officially or unofficially, has also been the subject of much controversy since it suggests that in agreeing to work for the Stasi, that individual somehow forewent their right to privacy.[33] Hansjürgen Garstka, the Data Protection Commissioner for Berlin, has defended this course of action when he stated that: "We recognized that right of access to personal files was a categorical right for the victim, for the one affected by the Stasi, in order to come to an understanding, to a catharsis, but that in order to do so there would be groups of individuals who would have to have their rights reduced."[34]

The issue came to a head in the so called *Aktenstreit* or File Debate of 2000–2005, which revolved around transcripts of tapped telephone conversations of Chancellor Helmut Kohl that the Stasi archive located at the beginning of 2000 – a fraction of the nearly 7,000 pages in Kohl's Stasi file.[35] Journalists had applied to the Stasi Archive to see the documents on Helmut Kohl, hoping to find information that would shed light on the issue of whether there had been illegal political contributions to Kohl's Christian Democratic Union (CDU). Kohl himself applied to see his files and was granted access in September 2000.[36] Interestingly, although the law had been in existence for nearly 10 years, this was the first time that it had been challenged on the basis of infringing privacy rights.[37] By the end of the year Kohl had sued the Federal Commission for the Stasi Files – ironically, an organization that Kohl was instrumental in establishing – so as to prevent the commission from releasing documents containing information on him. The *Bundesverwaltungsgericht* (Federal Administrative Court) upheld a lower court decision in support of Kohl, ruling in March 2002 that "public individuals," like Kohl, are fully within their rights to limit access to their information. Furthermore, since Article 10 of the Basic Law of the Federal Republic of Germany guaranteed postal and telephone privacy, the Stasi Files Law seemed incompatible with the basic law of the land.[38] Effective immediately such files could be viewed only by the individuals, or by researchers who had received permission to view the files – the same criteria for the individuals *affected* by the Stasi. The Stasi Archive, and in particular the Federal Commissioner for the Stasi Files, Marianne Birthler, lashed out at this decision, arguing that this could effectively terminate serious historical scholarship emanating from the documents, or make the time lag such as to be an insurmountable barrier. We see here clearly both the conflict of the right of the individual as set against the right of the public to knowledge about its past, and the nature of the East German revolution. In the German parliament, the Social Democrats and the Greens took the initiative arguing that the court's decision was incompatible with article one of the Treaty on German unification which guaranteed a "political, historical and judicial dealing with the activities of the former Ministry for State Security."[39] Consequently the German parliament passed an amendment to the Stasi Files Law on 6 September 2002 which allowed documents relating to holders of public office to be released for the purposes of historical research or for media purposes, *provided that the information in the documents relates to their public life.*[40] Information on their private persona remains inaccessible to researchers unless the individual in question provides express permission to view this information. Furthermore, the paragraph in the Law relating to this issue, paragraph 32, was adjusted to make clear that information in the documents could not be released if the information was obtained in a manner that infringed on human rights (such as torture), or if there was an overwhelming need for that individual's protection. A new paragraph was added to this section that requires the Stasi archive to inform the individual in question when documents related to them are being prepared for researchers.

The majority of the Kohl debate revolved around Paragraph 32, which read:

> The Federal Commissioner shall provide the following records for research related to the political and historical reappraisal of the activities of the State Security Service and for political education: ...

records containing personal data regarding:

> contemporary historical personages, political office-holders or public-law officials while in office, unless they are data subjects or third parties.[41]

Because of the intense debate surrounding these last eight words, it is perhaps surprising that key figures involved in drafting the law could not recall how the clause had been adopted.[42] In fact, the qualification was somewhat strange considering that the very fact that they were mentioned in Stasi documents would make them, on some level, a victim or third party of the Stasi. According to the law, a "Betroffene," which is very awkwardly defined as a "data subject", but is best thought of as someone who was affected by the Stasi, was "a person about whom the State Security Service collected personal data by deliberate, [sic] including secret, information-gathering or spying."[43] For some observers, Kohl could not have been an affected person by this definition since he was not the targeted subject of an operation, but rather the Stasi engaged in his general monitoring. Others sympathized with Kohl. How could it be, they argued, that one could be a victim of the Stasi twice? Once during the East German regime, and once afterward?[44] Moreover, in purely technical terms, the release of documents to a parliamentary committee investigating a spending scandal was not permitted under paragraph 32 because this was not for the purpose of "political and historical reappraisal of the activities of the State Security Service and for political education."[45] This is not to say, of course, that the material could not be accessed by researchers or media investigating other, related, topics.

The most recent decision in the Kohl case took place in June 2004, when the presiding judge Hans-Joachim Driehaus of the Federal Administrative Court in Leipzig announced that the release of documents to researchers and journalists regarding public figures should be the "exception, not the rule."[46] Whereas the Berlin daily *Der Tagesspiegel* praised the decision in an editorial entitled "Chancellors also have rights,"[47] Joachim Gauck criticized the decision, saying that lawyers were taking into account the privacy rights of individuals today while ignoring the fact that the law had been drawn up in part so that East Germans could deal with the fact that their privacy rights had been violated for 40 years. He believes, and this relates again to the history of the enactment of the Stasi Files Law, that the judges did not sufficiently honor the political process that gave rise to the law in the first place. In many ways, these are difficulties that occur when judges and lawyers settle political questions, as Gauck explained. It would have been, and would still be, very unsatisfactory for people to be turned away from seeing their own files based on the strictest interpretations of individual privacy rights.[48] Gauck was also concerned that East Germans who were "contemporary historical personages" but not part of the Stasi apparatus can hide behind the new decision, a fear echoed by the historian Hubertus Knabe, head of the former Stasi prison memorial site at Berlin-Hohenschönhausen, who suggested that Margot Honecker, wife of the East German leader Erich Honecker, could claim that her files should not be released because she too had been spied on by the Stasi.[49] According to Knabe, even the files of the deceased could theoretically be protected by the latest Kohl decision.[50] The fact that some files relating to Helmut Kohl were released in March 2005 – and more importantly, that Kohl has withdrawn his objections against their release – suggests that the Kohl controversy may have indeed slowed the process to view files, but it has not closed access completely.[51]

Another aspect of the decision in the Kohl case that was roundly criticized in Germany was the distinction between journalists and researchers. Essentially, the court determined that researchers could be given slightly more access to files than journalists, a decision that suggested journalists were irresponsible. A parliamentary member of the Free Democratic Party found this decision to be untenable: "The difference between Academics and Journalists, and the disadvantaging of Media to Research purposes, is neither justifiable nor sustainable."[52] The Social Democratic Party member Dieter Wiefelspütz, one of the main authors of the Stasi Files Law, was shocked at the decision stating that the law makers never intended for there to be a difference between academics and journalists in terms of access.[53] The decision also made clear that a researcher was not an average curious citizen. A researcher, to have access to Stasi files, was to be associated with a research institution, such as a university, or an individual with a well-conceived research plan which the Stasi Archive would carefully examine for suitability.[54]

The public–private dynamic also plays out in the four categories of individuals involved with the Stasi outlined under the law. The first category are those "affected" by the law (data subjects), a group that has come to be known in common parlance as "victims" although the terminology in some cases is too harsh. The law-makers purposely avoided the terms "victims" and "perpetrators" in the law since these have moral undertones, opting for terms that were more factual.[55] "Affected" individuals were those that the Stasi monitored, arrested, or controlled in some fashion, such as denying them a place at university. They were above all the objects of a targeted operation. Until 2006, files of "affected" individuals could only be viewed by the affected individuals themselves, by researchers who had received the permission of the affected individual to view his or her file, or by researchers who receive photocopies of documents with personal information (including identity) blacked out. When the Stasi Files Law was amended in December 2006, access to files was improved somewhat. Files of those "affected" by the Stasi can now be viewed without permission or blacking-out if the individual has been deceased for 30 years, or 110 years after the individual's birth.[56] For the first time, the amendment also permits, under certain (still vague) circumstances, for researchers to view documents that have not been blacked-out provided that the researcher swears an oath of secrecy.[57] The second category of individuals falls also largely within the "victim" category and is known as a *third party*. These are individuals on whom there is information in the Stasi files although they were not the targets of specific information-gathering operations. This tends to be a catch-all category for those mentioned in the files who do not fall under the other three categories.

Two categories comprise the 'perpetrators,' again, a term that in some cases is too harsh and has a strong association with the Holocaust. The first of these categories is the *collaborators*, a group that encompasses both the official Stasi employees (*Mitarbeiter*) and the unofficial employees, or informants, known in Stasi jargon as the *Inoffizielle Mitarbeiter*, literally Unofficial Coworkers.[58] Official Stasi workers are considered to be "figures of contemporary history" and, as such, the information on them is fully accessible. Researchers have complete access to the individual's work history with the Stasi and to their signature on various documents. Former Stasi workers have access to their own files with the important qualifier that they are not permitted to view reports that they authored containing information on "affected" individuals unless there is a compelling legal reason. Informants are treated the same as official workers in terms of privacy. Their names and activities can be made available to researchers, including to affected individuals. In other words, a "victim" is allowed to know the identity of his or her "perpetrator" whether that individual was an official or unofficial worker.

The greatest fear of the parliamentarians who brought forth the Stasi Files Law was that families would be ripped apart by revelations that family members reported family activities to the secret police, and that East German society would be overrun with vendettas as victims exited the archives to hunt down their perpetrators. In matter of fact, neither has happened. Rare has been the case of a family member reporting on another family member, and in the 15-year history of the Stasi Files Law not one case of individual retaliation has been reported.[59]

The final category of individuals is known as *advantaged persons*, those individuals who received substantial advantages from the Stasi usually in the form of material or career gain. In short, the law is designed to differentiate the rights of individuals in the above categories. Broadly speaking, the "victims" are entitled to greater rights of access and privacy than the "perpetrators."

Two important issues have arisen with regard to the above categorization. The first is that there were many individuals who worked for the Stasi who do not fall under these categories. It was not uncommon for the leader of the local Stasi district office to telephone his contact in the regular police force, in the factory, or high school and receive an oral briefing, often many times a day. One Stasi officer I interviewed became irate recalling how he was drummed out of town after the revolution while his many informal contacts, who helped monitor the population, continued in their jobs.[60] These individuals no doubt greatly assisted the Stasi in its efforts to control the population but are immune from the effects of the Stasi Files Law, one of the key results of which is that these individuals have found their way into the public service, a particularly troublesome occurrence given the fact that one of the purposes of the Stasi Files Law was to restore confidence in the public sector by assuring that no former collaborators with the Stasi would find their way into the public sector. In fact, recent research has revealed just how *integral* the *Kontaktpersonen* (informal contacts who were neither informants nor full-time employees) were to Stasi work.[61]

The Stasi Files Law applies strictly to the Stasi; there was no attempt to deal with other instruments of repression such as the regular police or the dominant Socialist Unity Party (known as the SED). When I asked Herr Gauck about this, he replied that their thinking at the time was that individuals had no protection against the secret police, precisely because it worked "in the dark."[62] The party and the Volkspolizei were visible manifestations of power, which citizens could take note of, and act accordingly. Secret relationships were more damaging, in Gauck's view, than the open authoritarianism of the SED.[63] David Gill, who stormed the Stasi central office in Berlin in January 1990 and then partook in overseeing its dismantling as chair of the Citizens' Committee, echoes this sentiment. Since party members were known to the public and their buildings were not secretive, Gill describes the party apparatus as "*berechenbarer*" (more able to be calculated with).[64] The Stasi Files Law was, therefore, not a de-communization law as in the Czech Republic, but a specific de-Stasinization instrument. Gauck now believes that this path was somewhat flawed, and that regional party leaders who were in a position of authority over the Stasi should also have been considered in the law. The latest progress report of the Stasi Archive admits that there were a number of people like school principals who were complicit with the Stasi, but who were not held accountable because of the narrow definition of "collaborator" provided in the Stasi Files Law.[65] Rolf Schwanitz, a parliamentary member of the committee responsible for drafting the initial law, points to another reason that the Stasi, rather than other branches of the regime, was the focus of legislative efforts in 1991: unlike the Volkspolizei which was also involved in normal criminal investigation, the Stasi was exclusively a dictatorial instrument of repression.[66]

A second issue that has arisen with the categories of individuals affected or involved with the Stasi is that of overlapping categories. As a matter of course, the Stasi attempted to recruit the targets of its operations for informant work. In one case, an East German female student who caught the Stasi's eye because she was corresponding with a West German prisoner was observed and monitored for a time, before she was approached by Stasi officers with a veiled threat that she would find it difficult to obtain her sought-after architecture study spot unless she agreed to engage in undercover work for the Stasi. She then became an informant.[67] This individual is both a victim and a perpetrator and the law provides that if she were to access her documents, she would fall under the appropriate category for her given relationship. She would be able to view documents that the Stasi kept on her as part of their targeted operation, but as an informant she would not be able to view the documents that she authored on other individuals. According to Gauck, this was one of the most difficult issues to tackle in the process of drawing up the law. Stasi documents have revealed that informants were often coerced or even blackmailed into working for the Stasi, yet this would no doubt be a refrain of those willingly complicit with the regime.[68] It was vital that those who were coerced into being informants be allowed to prove their innocence, while at the same time holding willing informants accountable for their actions.

Justice

The East German dissident Bärbel Bohley famously, and cynically, once said: "We expected justice, but we got the Rechtsstaat [state ruled by law] instead."[69] Debates raged in Germany shortly after reunification as to how a Rechsstaat was to deal legally with former high-ranking Socialist Unity Party leaders and their subordinates who engaged in murderous activity like shooting would-be escapees at the Berlin Wall. Finding such individuals guilty not under their own laws, but under a "higher moral justice" suggested a victor's justice[70] and a major affront to one of the principal underpinnings of justice: *nulla poena sine lege*, that is, "an act could be punished only if it was an offense against the law before the act was committed."[71] If this approach had been taken, as it was at Nürnberg, it would have been difficult for West German political leaders, including Helmut Kohl, to explain the relatively decent relationship between West Germany and East Germany since the 1970s. After all, Erich Honecker, who was put on trial, had been accorded red-carpet treatment on his visit to West Germany just two years before the fall of the Wall. Given these complications, Germany opted for a different approach. Klaus Kinkel, the Minister of Justice, recommended that East Germans be tried under *East German* law. As he stated, "even the criminal code of the GDR treated manslaughter, bodily harm, false imprisonment, and violations of the peace as punishable offenses. In numerous ways, the GDR's rulers disregarded and infringed upon their laws, and thus they can be prosecuted today according to the criminal code of the GDR."[72] This approach did not prove easy to put into practice. At the first borderguard trial, which began on 2 September 1991 and led to the conviction of two soldiers for killing Chris Gueffroy at the Wall on 5 February 1989, the presiding judge, Theodor Seidel, waved off the guards' claims to be following orders: "Shooting with the intent-to-kill those who merely wanted to leave the territory of the former GDR was an offense against basic norms of ethics and human association."[73] The next border guard trial took place in 1992 and dealt with a 1984 shooting death at the Wall. This time, the presiding judge determined that the border guards had committed an act that was illegal even during East Germany's existence, by their *excessive* use of force. The East German code, she noted, required that the "means employed to prevent a crime be proportionate to the crime being committed."[74] In this precedent-setting case, the judge found both defendants guilty but suspended their sentence arguing that their actions were not completely independent, but were bound with the political and military circumstances of East Germany. Partly as a result of this decision, only two border guards of the many tried in the early 1990s served jail time.[75]

The question, then, was of responsibility for creating these political and military circumstances. In May 1992, the Berlin Prosecutor General's office charged with manslaughter Erich Honecker, Erich Mielke, Minister-President Willi Stoph, Defense Minister Heinz Kessler and his Chief-of-Staff Fritz Streletz, and Suhl District Party Secretary Hans Albrecht, all of whom were members of the East German National Defense Council.[76] Apart from Admiral Dönitz, the last leader of Nazi Germany, the last German head-of-state to be put on trial was Henry the Lion over 800 years previous.[77] Honecker was tried with maintaining a state based on force (*Zwangsstaat*) and with ordering the killing of defenseless and innocent people.[78] Less than a year later, Berlin's Constitutional Appeals Court stopped the proceedings on the grounds that Honecker's liver cancer had advanced to a point where he was not expected to live much longer. Rather than let the trial become an "end to itself," they allowed Honecker to leave the country. He arrived in Santiago, Chile shortly thereafter.[79] Honecker was, then, never really brought to trial – an important difference from having been found innocent.[80] The trial against Kessler, Streletz, and Albrecht, however, continued and resulted in all three receiving jail terms. In upholding the lower court decision, the *Bundesgerichtshof* (Federal Court of Justice) made it clear that these three were as responsible for deaths at the Wall as border guards, perhaps even more so.[81] In many ways, the approach to justice adopted by the new German government with regard to East German crimes was vindicated by the European Human Rights Court in Strasburg that heard the appeal of the decision in the case of Egon Krenz, who briefly served as the leader of East Germany in 1989 before the end of the communist rule. The European Court upheld the German ruling, confirming that Krenz had been involved with a regime that used mines, automatic firing devices and the order to shoot on the border, all of which were contrary to Articles 19 and 30 of the East German constitution and were against the humanitarian principle of the dignity of the individual.[82] Krenz's six-year prison sentence ended in 2006, three years after he was released from prison and allowed to quietly retire.

On 26 October 1993, the Berlin Regional Court sentenced the 85-year-old Erich Mielke, leader of East Germany's Ministry for State Security from 1957 to 1989, to six years in prison for murder in two cases.[83] Mielke was found guilty of complicity in the murder of police officers Anlauf and Lenk on Bülow Square (now Rosa Luxemburg Square) in Berlin on 9 August 1931. Remarkably, the man who guided the Stasi for 32 years was sentenced for a crime that he committed 62 years previously when he was a 23-year-old communist in Weimar Germany.[84] This, although Mielke was also accused of: 1) incitement to manslaughter at the Berlin Wall and the German–German border; and 2) abuse of trust, disloyalty, and incitement to perversion of justice, including the illegal ordering of telephone taps and assisting in electoral fraud in 1989; 3) mistreatment of a prisoner in 1950; and 4) wrongful deprivation of individual liberty of an individual in 1950.[85]

Former spies, including the long-time head of East Germany's foreign espionage, Markus Wolf, were tried in the early 1990s, but the Federal Constitutional Court ruled in 1995 that they could not be prosecuted for their activities on behalf of East Germany.[86] Wolf's sentence of six years in prison for treason was overturned. Markus Wolf died on 9 November 2006 continuing that date's pattern of fateful events in German history.

The volume of cases that have been heard by the courts is shockingly large. Of the 23,000 cases dealing with various crimes committed in East Germany (from doping of athletes to mistreatment of prisoners, but excluding any cases involving death or murder), by 2000 some 16,494 had been heard in which a sentence was handed down.[87] The investigation of these middle-range crimes came to an end on 3 October 2000,10 years after unification, when the statute of limitations passed.[88]

Vetting

One key aspect of the Stasi Archive work was to assist in vetting the individuals entering civil service, a process known as vetting, although the actual term is rarely seen in German literature. Germans refer to *Überprüfung*. Vetting and private viewing of files were the lion's share of Stasi Archive duties, followed by academic research.[89] The catastrophe of 11 September 2001 had an impact on this aspect of Stasi Archive work, as the German federal Minister for Transport, Construction, and Housing issued changes that required vetting of some 17,000 involved in air transportation.[90] Vetting is perhaps most simply defined as "the screening of groups of people for previous acts of collaboration under the communist regime (especially acts of collaboration with the secret police) and in turn disqualifying members of these groups from holding high-level government positions in the public sector."[91] In justifying vetting in East Germany, Gauck eloquently summarizes:

> Why did East Germans decide to embark upon this [vetting] process in 1989? It was not a quest for vengeance; there was no majority in the Volkskammer for such vindictive action. On the contrary, the MPs recognized the following problem: In East Germany from 1933 onwards (i.e. the start of the Nazi dictatorship), the entire public administration government, and parliament had been largely comprised of people who, to a greater or lesser extent, had

collaborated with the antidemocratic rulers. They included judges, lawyers, police, teachers, university professors, and other representatives of the federal and regional legislature and executive offices. If, after more than fifty-five years of Nazi and Communist dictatorship, citizens were to trust elected officials under the new democratic system, it was important that those officials be trustworthy. The intention was not to remove former Communists (members of the Socialist Unity Party, the SED) from all posts, but rather to respond to the East German people's minimal demand that persons who had conspired with the regime, unbeknown to their fellow citizens, should be deemed unsuitable for public positions of trust.[92]

And, indeed, the *Volkskammer* opted for a vetting of all members of parliament for informant work very early in the unification process, well before it drafted a law on access to the Stasi files.[93] Vetting was, then, the first of the "reckoning" activities to take place after the fall of communism in East Germany and began even unofficially in the summer of 1990 when certain members of parliament informed regional police offices of former Stasi officers on their staff (based on very early, and often incomplete opening of the archives), and these were then systematically laid off.[94]

Vetting related specifically to those who had collaborated with the Stasi and not to those in the party, in the regular police, or in other branches of government. The German Unification Treaty explicitly states that "A justifiable reason for dismissal is then, when an employee had been in the employ of the former Ministry for State Security/Office for National Security."[95] With over two million party members (in contrast to the 93,000 Stasi officials and 178,000 part-time informants), many of them simply opportunists, the law makers of the day thought it would be too unfair to remove from public service anyone who had been a member of the Communist Party. Gauck admits that from today's point of view, they acted somewhat erroneously and should have placed the Communist Party leaders on the same level as Stasi officials: "The members of the district leadership, the regional leadership and of course the leadership of the SED are more responsible for repression than a single informant."[96] The Stasi was not a state-within-a-state but rather an *ausführendes Organ,* an instrument that executed the orders given it by the Socialist Unity Party. Gauck also makes clear that vetting was not meant to judge guilt in a legal sense, but it simply dealt with the question of trust. Was an individual who had worked with a secret police trustworthy enough to assume a position in the civil service? Many who had worked only in passing and in non-destructive ways with the Stasi were permitted to continue. In some branches of the civil service, more former informants continued than were fired. In Berlin, for example, there were more teachers who continued in their professions than teachers who were dismissed.[97] Although the Stasi Archive has often been vilified as a "witch hunter," in reality the Archive did not pronounce judgment on whether the individual should be dismissed. The Archive simply told the potential employer what was in the documents related to the employee. It was, as one author has said, the technical go-between between the Stasi documents and the employer.[98] In a press release of 12 September 2003, Birthler said clearly: "The Federal Commissioner neither decides who will be vetted nor has any influence on the procedure, criteria or the results of the investigation – a wise decision of the law-makers, as experience has demonstrated."[99]

Employers in the civil service had the right to ask for a screening of an employee for a Stasi background, although they were not obliged to. Generally, the candidate was permitted to continue in the job if their collaboration with the Stasi ended prior to 1975 (unless they were involved in crimes against humanity), if it ended before the candidate was 18 years old, or if their association occurred during compulsory military service and strictly involved guarding Stasi installations.[100] Although vetting was to come to an end on 28 December 2006 as agreed to in the terms of German unification,[101] the Stasi Files Law was amended on 15 December 2006 by a wide parliamentary majority to allow further vetting for five years of individuals in leading positions in state and society, including members of *Land* and federal governments, parliamentarians, heads of federal agencies, judges, certain sports representatives, and soldiers in high-ranking positions.[102] Anyone dealing with the Stasi files in an official capacity, such as employees of the Stasi Archive, may be vetted indefinitely.[103] Although vetting has dealt primarily with the civil service, the law also allowed for background checks and dismissals of church administrators and those in leading positions in industry.[104] It has been exceptionally difficult to determine how many German citizens were dismissed because of association with East German instruments of repression. By 1996, these estimates ranged from 60,000 to 100,000.[105] In a 1999 survey of 16 government departments, the percentage of those examined for Stasi involvement who had in fact worked for the Stasi in some fashion ranged from 3 percent to 18 percent.[106] In total, the Stasi Archive has received roughly 1.75 million vetting applications.[107]

The vetting process has not been without its difficulties, the greatest deficiency being the lack of a nation-wide standard. It was up to individual provinces, and to individual employers, to set the standard for what level of involvement with the Stasi would be grounds for dismissal.[108] There have also been major differences in the level of vetting across East German provinces. The federal *Länder* of Thüringen and Saxony undertook systematic vetting of civil servants, as did Sachsen-Anhalt, but to a slightly less degree. *Land* Brandenburg vetted much less, and Mecklenburg-Vorpommern undertook token vetting.[109]

Conclusion

This overview of some of the salient features of the Stasi Files Law and its recent history, justice, and vetting in East Germany permits some tentative conclusions. First, the course of the revolution must occupy a key place in understanding the subsequent process of access to secret police files, even though access occurred over two years following the revolution. The Stasi was both a catalyst of the revolution and an impulse to continue revolutionary activity. It should not surprise, then, that the first freely elected German parliament passed a law on access to

Stasi files, or that in the Kohl controversy parliamentarians reiterated the need to understand the Stasi past which was of such importance that it found its way into the German Unification Treaty.[110] As a government minister said to me, had the Stasi documents not been opened but sent to Koblenz and placed under restricted access like other documents, the majority of East Germans would have seen this as a betrayal of their desires expressed on the streets in the fall of 1989.[111] Similarly, Gauck relentlessly pursued the handing over of *Herrschaftswissen* – the knowledge that a regime has and uses to repress its own population – to the repressed.[112] The Stasi documents have stayed in regional archives in part so that they remain closer to the people. Second, the most important dynamic in the Stasi Files Law is the relationship between privacy rights and personal and societal rights to know the past. This delicate relationship has been the subject of major court cases and subsequent amendments to the law, and represents the kind of engagement that only a country steeped in legal traditions can undertake. Joachim Gauck rarely missed an opportunity to argue that only a state ruled by law (*Rechtstaat*) could have issued the Stasi Files Law.[113] West Germany had an administrative and judicial apparatus in place with some 40 years of experience – the single greatest difference between access to files in the East German case compared with other countries of Eastern Europe.[114] There was an efficient administrative and legal system available immediately after 1989, one that enjoyed basic popular confidence.[115] The Federal Commissioner for the Stasi Archives has solid evidence that the people of Germany view access to the files as orderly, necessary, and above all, legitimate given the fact that over five million applications have been received since 1992. In fact, applications to see files rose 20 percent from 2005 to 2006, an unexpected trend after 15 years of archival access.[116] Driven partly by a need to establish confidence in the public sector, and partly by the need of individuals to come to a complete understanding of their past, the Federal Commission has opened certain files to the public and allowed for public identification of those who collaborated with the Stasi. In a survey of citizens who viewed their files conducted in the early 1990s, 95 percent of respondents considered it "right" that they should view their files. Equally importantly, 64 percent of them discussed the Stasi with their friends and families,[117] something that the Stasi Archive considered important because of the Stasi Archive's mandate for political education outlined in the Stasi Files Law.[118]

Apart from the legal infrastructure that was in place, financing played a major role. East (and West) Germans interested in maintaining access to the files had the good fortune of having a wealthy German government. Shortly after unification, the Stasi Archive grew to some 3,000 employees (as of June 2006, the agency had been pared back to 2,025)[119] and the total budget for the Stasi Archive in 2006 was €88,539,000.[120] Part of the reason for the huge apparatus is that for each person interested in seeing files, 13 separate steps were necessary, from evaluating the legality of viewing the document, to the return of the documents to the archive. Since almost every Stasi victim wants to have copies of their documents, it is no wonder that in 1992 alone, nearly 10 million copies were prepared by Stasi Archive workers, an enormously time consuming task since all of those documents had to be vetted for personal information and, where appropriate, that information had to be blacked-out.[121]

Restorative justice in East Germany has focused on bringing to trial East Germans not on the basis that East Germany was an *"Unrechtstaat,"* as Nazi Germany has been described, where the whims of those in power could become law, but by the fact that East Germany did have a deliberate, codified law. The truth is, however, that only a handful of those complicit with the regime ever served time, and then only briefly. Regular Stasi officers, many of whom had seriously disadvantaged the lives of East Germans by their informing and by their actions, proved almost impossible to bring to trial for these actions. Supporting the repressive instrument of a dictatorial regime is not in itself a crime. For whatever dissatisfaction Bohley and others in East Germany may have had with the trials, it is worth remembering that justice is only one way to deal with the past. The opening of the archives has provided another very important path to catharsis.

The vetting process has generally been orderly but it has not been perfect. Stasi collaborators who did not fall into the category of informant or full-time worker were exempt from vetting, the party, the Stasi's political master, was also exempt, nation-wide vetting standards were never developed, and West Germans who worked for the Stasi generally had nothing to fear. Private sector vetting was spotty (only the most senior positions could be vetted) and inconsistent. Public television employees, for example, were vetted whereas private stations and print media employees were not.[122] Vetting was, however, never a witch-hunt, but a vital process to restore confidence in the public sector, something that East German deputies recognized in the first freely elected parliament in that country's history. Although aware of the shortcomings, the Stasi Archive maintains its positive position vis-à-vis vetting: "The vetting process has demonstrated that it is possible to remove politically-tainted individuals without jeopardizing the functioning of public administration or the stability of society."[123]

As we look to the future of the Stasi Archive, major changes loom large. The vetting process will end in 2011 and in the foreseeable future the last victim of the Stasi will apply to see his/her files. The future of the Stasi Archive will clearly revolve around historical research. Here, however, is the greatest criticism that can be leveled against the Stasi Archive – there is no compelling reason for in-house researchers to have privileged access to the files. This is by no means to disparage historians like Ilko-Sascha Kowalczuk, Jens Gieseke, and Roger Engelmann, who are among the finest German historians of any era, but the fact that they have instant and unfettered access to the files is difficult to justify. To be sure, research on contemporary history is still possible for external historians, but the hurdles are daunting. It is not unusual for the Stasi Archive to vet material for months before making it available to researchers, and it is virtually impossible to follow-up a documentary lead on-the-spot because of the need of archivists to vet the material. The latest efforts to speed access, modest as they are, are therefore to be welcomed. Because the Stasi Archive will increasingly be involved in "typical" archival work, and because of research lapses like the "sensational" revelation of a shoot-to-kill order in August 2007 that bring into question the

Archive's research quasi-monopoly, some observers, including politicians of both the left and right, have called for its integration into the existing Federal Archive. It must be remembered, however, that the Stasi Archive was established by East German parliamentarians reflecting the wishes of revolutionaries who demanded special access to files that would otherwise be under much stricter rules of access in the federal system. As much as integration into the federal archive would level the playing field among historians, it would hinder file access for Stasi victims.[124] The time to dismantle the Stasi Archive, the "fruit" of the revolution, will come only when East Germans have had sufficient opportunity to view their files and to come to a certain historical understanding of their content. The current date proposed by the Stasi Archive of 30 years after the fall of the Wall seems a reasonable time frame in which healing can take place. As Gauck has eloquently summarized: "We will be in a position to forgive and forget only if we are given enough time to heal our wounds, to calm our anger, and, yes, to curb our hatred."[125]

Notes

1 The official name of the Stasi Archive is the *Bundesbeauftragte für die Unterlagen des Staatssicherheitsdienstes der ehemaligen DDR* but for simplicity will be referred to as the 'Stasi Archive' here.
2 'Birthler-Behörde in der Kritik', *die tageszeitung*, 13 August 2007.
3 Ibid.
4 R. Grindel, 'Ist die Stasibehörde noch nötig? Nein!', *die tageszeitung*, 15 August 2007.
5 W. Thierse, 'Ist die Stasibehörde noch nötig? Ja!', *die tageszeitung*, 15 August 2007.
6 Ibid.
7 Knut Nevermann, a state secretary working under the federal Culture and Media Commissioner Christina Weiss, issued a discussion paper on 1 December 2004 calling for the end of an independent commission for the Stasi files and the integration of the files into the federal archives. See *Erinnerungspolitisches Konzeptes zu den Gedenkstätten der SED-Diktatur in Berlin*. Online. Available online: http://www.havemann gesellschaft.de/info193.htm (accessed 22 January 2008).
8 The best recent account of the revolution in East Germany after the fall of the Wall is G. Dale, *The East German Revolution of 1989*, Manchester: Manchester University Press, 2006.
9 G. Bruce, *Resistance with the People: Repression and Resistance in Eastern Germany*, Lanham: Rowman and Littlefield, 2003, ch. 5.
10 J. Gauck, 'Dealing with a Stasi Past', *Daedalus*, 1994, vol. 123, 277.
11 Interview with Rolf Schwanitz, former member of East German parliament, Berlin, 23 June 2004.
12 Interview with former Stasi Captain, 8 August 2003.
13 *Erster Tätigkeitsbericht des Bundesbeauftragten für die Unterlagen des Staatssicherheitsdienstes der ehemaligen Deutschen Demokratischen Republik*, Berlin: BStU, 1993, p. 4.
14 Three Stasi generals assisted the citizens' committee in deciphering and cataloguing the documents. Interview with David Gill, former member of Berlin citizens' committee, Berlin, 26 August 2004.
15 T. Hollitzer, *Wir leben jedenfalls von Montag zu Montag: Zur Auflösung der Staatssicherheit in Leipzig*, Berlin: BStU, 2000, p. 58.
16 Interview with Gunter Weißgerber, former member of East German parliament, 13 August 2004.

17 David Gill and Ulrich Schröter, as quoted in Dale, *The East German Revolution of 1989*, p. 154.

18 M. Haas, 'Vor zehn Jahren: Kontroverse Debatte um die Öffnung der Stasi-Akten', *Deutschland Archiv*, 2000, vol. 33, 998.

19 N. Robers, *Joachim Gauck: Die Biografie einer Institution*, Berlin: Henschel, 2000, p. 131. Only one deputy voted against the law.

20 *Fünfter Tätigkeitsbericht des Bundesbeauftragten für die Unterlagen des Staatssicherheitsdienstes der ehemaligen Deutschen Demokratischen Republik*, Berlin: BStU, 2001, p. 10.

21 H. Garstka, 'Freiheit für meine Akte': Die Öffnung der Archive – Das Gesetz der Volkskammer über die Sicherung der Nutzung der personenbezogenen Daten des ehemaligen MfS/AfNS', in D. Unverhau (ed.) *Das Stasi-Unterlagen-Gesetz im Lichte von Datenschutz und Archivgesetzgebung*, Münster: LIT, 1998, p. 47.

22 Ibid., p. 49.

23 J. Gauck, 'Das Erbe der Stasi-Akten', *German Studies Review*, 1994, vol. 17, 189.

24 Haas, 'Vor zehn Jahren', 998.

25 The most detailed overview of the origins of the Stasi Files Law is *Vernichten oder Offenlegen? Zur Entstehung des Stasi-Unterlagen-Gesetzes*, Berlin: BStU, 1997. On its subsequent application, see A. J. McAdams, *Judging the Past in Unified Germany*, Cambridge: Cambridge University Press, 2001.

26 Interview with Rolf Schwanitz, Berlin, 23 June 2004.

27 *Sechster Tätigkeitsbericht der Bundesbeauftragten für die Unterlagen des Staatssicherheitsdienstes der ehemaligen Deutschen Demokratischen Republik*, Berlin: BStU, 2003, p. 19.

28 J. Weberling, *Stasi-Unterlagen-Gesetz: Kommentar*, Berlin: Carl Heymanns Verlag, 1993, pp. 104–105.

29 *Zweiter Tätigkeitsbericht des Bundesbeauftragten für die Unterlagen des Staatssicherheitsdienstes der ehemaligen Deutschen Demokratischen Republik*, Berlin: BStU, 1995, p. 104, and *Sechster Tätigkeitsbericht*, p. 18.

30 Interview with David Gill, Berlin, 26 August 2004.

31 One of the most illuminating books on Stasi tactics is S. Pingel-Schliemann, *Zersetzen: Strategie einer Diktatur*, Berlin: Robert Havelmann Gesellschaft, 2002. A useful overview in English is M. Dennis, *The Stasi: Myth and Reality*, London: Pearson, 2003.

32 H. Garstka, 'Stasi-Unterlagen-Gesetz (StUG) – Bewährung oder Mißachtung der informationellen Selbstbestimmung', in T. Hollitzer (ed.) *Einblick in das Herrschaftswissen einer Diktatur – Chance oder Fluch?* Opladen: Westdeutscher Verlag, 1996, p. 156.

33 Ibid., p. 157.

34 Ibid., p. 158.

35 J. Müller-Neuhof, 'Vorteil Kohl', *Der Tagesspiegel*, 24 June 2004, 4. There was a case involving access to Stasi documents and SPD politicians in Schleswig-Holstein that was remarkably similar to the Kohl case, but has received far less attention. E. Benda, 'Persönlichkeitsschutz und Stasi-Akten', in E. Benda, R. Bachmeier, and P. Busse, *Persönlichkeitsschutz und Stasi-Akten*, Berlin: Broschürenreihe der Konrad-Adenauer-Stiftung, 2000, p. 5.

36 Müller-Neuhof, 'Vorteil Kohl', 4.

37 K. W. Fricke, 'Das StUG ist auch ein Aufklärungsgesetz:' Interview mit Marianne Birthler', *Deutschland Archiv*, 2001, vol. 34, 14.

38 R. Bachmeier, 'Datenschutz und Umgang mit Stasi-Akten', in Benda, Bachmeier and Busse, *Persönlichkeitsschutz und Stasi-Akten*, p. 13.

39 *Sechster Tätigkeitsbericht*, p. 10.

40 P. Maddrell, 'The Revolution Made Law: The Work Since 2001 of the Federal Commissioner for the Records of the State Security Service of the Former German Democratic Republic', *Cold War History*, 2004, vol. 4, 158.

41 Weberling, *Stasi-Unterlagen-Gesetz*, p. 104. In this outstanding commentary on the Stasi Files Law, Weberling is noticeably silent on the complications that could arise from the disclaimer 'as long as they are not affected or third parties.' The Stasi Files Law has been translated into English and is available from the BStU.

42 Key individuals that I interviewed who were involved with the drafting of the law (Joachim Gauck, David Gill, and Rolf Schwanitz) could not remember precisely how this wording had been adopted.

43 *Act Regarding the Records of the State Security Service of the Former German Democratic Republic,* Section 6.4. The original German is 'Personen, zu denen der Staatssicherheitsdienst aufgrund zielgerichteter Informationserhebung oder Ausspähung einschliesslich heimlicher Informationserhebung Informationen gesammelt hat.' See W. Ullmann, 'Das Stasi-Unterlagen-Gesetz. Eine Demokratie-initiative der Friedlichen Revolution', in S. Suckut and J. Weber (eds.) *Stasi-Akten zwischen Politik und Zeitgeschichte: Eine Zwischenbilanz*, Munich: Olzog, 2003, p. 60.

44 Interview with Joachim Gauck, Berlin, 25 June 2004.

45 Benda, 'Persönlichkeitsschutz und Stasi-Akten', p. 11.

46 Müller-Neuhof, 'Vorteil Kohl', p. 4.

47 'Auch Kanzler haben Rechte', *Der Tagesspiegel*, 21 June 2004, 10.

48 Interview with Joachim Gauck, Berlin, 25 June 2004.

49 'Historiker und Medien kritisieren Stasi-Aktenurteil', *Der Tagesspiegel*, 25 June 2004, 4.

50 Ibid.

51 Pressemitteilung *Die MfS-Unterlagen zu Dr. Helmut Kohl werden morgen herausgegeben* 23 March 2005.

52 R. Birnbaum and R. von Rimscha, 'SPD und FDP kritisieren Stasi-Urteil', *Der Tagesspiegel,* 26 June 2004, 4.

53 Birnbaum and Rimscha, 'SPD und FDP', 4.

54 'Statement der Bundesbeauftragen Marianne Birthler', 3 August 2004, Presseinformation der BStU.

55 Interview with Joachim Gauck, Berlin, 25 June 2004. Thomas Lindenberger in particular has been critical of the moral categories of "victim" and "perpetrator" for East German history. See T. Lindenberger, 'Everyday History: New Approaches to the History of the Post-War Germanies', in C. Kleßmann (ed.) *The Divided Past*, New York: Berg, 2001, p. 53.

56 'Birthler: Neue Impulse für die Aufarbeitung der SED-Diktatur durch novelliertes Stasi-Unterlagen-Gesetz', 15 December 2006, Pressemitteilung der BStU.

57 *Achter Tätigkeitsbericht des Bundesbeauftragten für die Unterlagen des Staatssicherheitsdienstes der ehemaligen Deutschen Demokratischen Republik*, Berlin: BStU, 2007, p. 14.

58 The best work on the full-time Stasi officers is J. Gieseke, *Die hauptamtlichen Mitarbeiter der Staatssicherheit*, Berlin: Ch. Links, 2000, on the informants, H. Müller-Enbergs, *Inoffizielle Mitarbeiter des Ministeriums für Staatssicherheit*, Berlin: Ch. Links, 2001.

59 *Sechster Tätigkeitsbericht*, p. 5.

60 Interview with former Stasi Captain, 8 August 2003.

61 G. Bruce, "Wir haben den Kontakt zu den Massen nie verloren:' Das Verhältnis zwischen Stasi und Gesellschaft am Beispiel der Kreise Perleberg und Gransee', in J. Gieseke (ed.) *Staatssicherheit und Gesellschaft*, Göttigen: Vandenhoeck & Ruprecht, 2007, pp. 365–379.

62 Interview with Joachim Gauck, Berlin, 25 June 2004.

63 Ibid.

64 Interview with David Gill, Berlin, 26 August 2004.

65 *Achter Tätigkeitsbericht,* 12.

66 Interview with Rolf Schwanitz, Berlin, 23 June 2004.

67 BStU-Potsdam, AOV 898/79, 93. 26 February 1979. Vorschlag zum Abschluss des OV 'Student'.

68 Interview with Joachim Gauck, Berlin, 25 June 2004. A fascinating overview of the myriad reasons for collaboration with the Stasi is found in B. Miller, *Narratives of Guilt and Compliance in Unified Germany*, New York: Routledge, 1999.

69 A. J. McAdams, 'The Honecker Trial: The East German Past and the German Future', *The Review of Politics*, 1996, vol. 58, p. 53.

70 This is, of course, the refrain of many East Germans tried for crimes committed during the communist era. See the odious *Siegerjustiz?* Berlin: Kai Homilius Verlag, 2003.

71 McAdams, 'Honecker Trial', 3. In truth, this principle of justice has been broken repeatedly in instances of regime change. See N. Becker, 'Strafprozesse gegen Funktionäre der ehemaligen DDR', *Neue Justiz*, 1998, vol. 7, 353. Most recently, it was deemed inapplicable for Nazi crimes. J. Arnold, 'DDR-Vergangenheit und Schranken rechtsstaatlichen Strafrechts', in J. Arnold (ed.) *Strafrechtliche Auseinandersetzung mit Systemvergangenheit*, Baden-Baden: Nomos Verlagsgesellschaft, 2000, p. 108.

72 McAdams, 'Honecker Trial', 3.

73 Ibid., 4.

74 Ibid., 4.

75 Ibid., 8.

76 J. Arnold, 'Einschränkung des Rückwirkungsverbotes sowie sorgfältige Schuldprüfung be den Tötungsfällen an der DDR-Grenze', in Arnold, *Strafrechtliche*, p. 131.

77 C. Schaefgen, 'Der Honecker-Prozeß', in J. Weber and M. Piazolo (eds.) *Eine Diktatur vor Gericht: Aufarbeitung von SED-Unrecht durch die Justiz,* Munich: Olzog, 1995, p. 89.

78 Ibid., p. 90.

79 McAdams, 'Honecker Trial', p. 6.

80 Schaefgen, 'Der Honecker-Prozeß', p. 99.

81 McAdams, 'Honecker Trial', p. 7.

82 Ullmann, 'Das Stasi-Unterlagen-Gesetz', pp. 58–59, B. Jahntz, 'Die juristische Aufarbeitung der SED-Herrschaft', in S. Suckut and J. Weber (eds.) *Stasi-Akten zwischen Politik und Zeitgeschichte: Eine Zwischenbilanz*, Munich: Olzog, 2003, p. 322.

83 P. Jochen Winters, 'Der Mielke-Prozeß', in Weber and Piazolo, *Eine Diktatur*, p. 110.

84 P. Jochen Winters, 'Erich Mielke – der falsche Prozeß?', *Deutschland Archiv*, 1993, vol. 26, p. 1347.

85 Winters, 'Erich Mielke', 1349; Winters, 'Mielke-Prozeß', p. 113.

86 McAdams, 'Honecker Trial', p. 9.

87 Jahntz, 'Die juristische', p. 325.

88 Ibid., p. 333.

89 Fricke, 'Das StUG ist auch ein Aufklärungsgesetz', p. 16.

90 'Die Bundesbeauftragte Marianne Birthler anlässlich der Vorstellung des 6. Tätigkeitsberichtes am 12.9.2003', 12 September 2003, Pressemitteilung der BstU.

91 H. Appel, 'Anti-Communist Justice and Founding the Post-Communist Order: Lustration and Restitution in Central Europe', *East European Politics and Society*, 2005, vol. 19, 383.

92 Gauck, 'Dealing', pp. 278–279.

93 J. Gauck, 'The German Way of Dealing with a Stasi Past', in M. Mertes, S. Muller and H. A. Winkler (eds.) *In Search of Germany*, London: Transaction Publishers, 1996, p. 297.

94 Interview with Joachim Gauck, Berlin, 25 June 2004.

95 F. Arendt, 'Die MfS-überprüfung im öffentlichen Dienst am Beispiel des Freistaates Sachsen', in Weber and Piazolo, *Eine Diktatur*, p. 159. There was, however, the proviso that each case would be examined to determine the extent of this collaboration. Ullmann, 'Das Stasi-Unterlagen-Gesetz', p. 54.

96 Interview with Joachim Gauck, Berlin, 25 June 2004.

97 In the Bundesland of Saxony, 25 percent of the teachers were fired. Appel, 'Anti-Communist Justice', p. 384.

98 H. Both, 'Rechtliche und sachliche Probleme bei Mitteilungen zur Überprüfung von Personen', in Suckut and Weber, *Stasi-Akten zwischen Politik,* p. 294.

99 BStU, Press Release, 12 September 2003.

100 Both, 'Rechtliche', p. 297.

101 Fricke, 'Das StUG ist auch ein Aufklärungsgesetz', p. 15.

102 *Achter Tätigkeitsbericht,* pp. 10–11.

103 'Birthler: Neue Impulse für die Aufarbeitung der SED-Diktatur durch novelliertes Stasi-Unterlagen-Gesetz', BStU Press Release, 15 December 2006.

104 Both, 'Rechtliche', p. 291.

105 McAdams estimates that by 1997 the number of Stasi dismissals was roughly 55,000. McAdams, *Judging the Past,* p. 73.

106 Both, 'Rechtliche', p. 304.

107 *Achter Tätigkeitsbericht,* p. 11.

108 F. Arendt, 'Die MfS-überprüfung im öffentlichen Dienst am Beispiel des Freistaates Sachsen', p. 165.

109 *Achter Tätigkeitsbericht,* p. 11.

110 *Sechster Tätigkeitsbericht,* p. 10.

111 Interview with Rolf Schwanitz, Berlin, 23 June 2004.

112 Interview with Joachim Gauck, Berlin, 25 June 2004.

113 J. Gauck, 'Die politische Aufklärung nicht beschädigen', in T. Hollitzer (ed.) *Wie weiter mit der Aufarbeitung? 10 Jahre Stasi-Unterlagen-Gesetz,* Leipzig: Evangelische Verlagsanstalt, 2002, p. 20.

114 A useful overview of the abysmal manner in which Romania has dealt with the secret police is L. Stan, 'Spies, Files, Lies: Explaining the Failure of Access to Securitate Files', *Communist and Post-Communist Studies,* 2004, vol. 37, pp. 341–359. Although the essays contained in it are uneven, a good source nevertheless comparing the records of East European countries in dealing with the secret police is K. Persak and L. Kaminski (eds.) *A Handbook of the Communist Security Apparatus in East Central Europe 1944–1989,* Warsaw: Institute of National Remembrance, 2005.

115 J. Miller, 'Settling Accounts with a Secret Police: The German Law on the Stasi Records', *Europe-Asia Studies,* 1998, vol. 50, 19.

116 *Achter Tätigkeitsbericht,* p. 9.

117 *Zweiter Tätigkeitsbericht,* p. 17.

118 *Dritter Tätigkeitsbericht der Bundesbeauftragten für die Unterlagen des Staatssicherheitsdienstes der ehemaligen Deutschen Demokratischen Republik,* Berlin: BStU, 1997, p. 6.

119 *Sechster Tätigkeitsbericht,* p. 8.

120 *Achter Tätigkeitsbericht,* p. 16.

121 Gauck, 'Das Erbe', p. 194.

122 *Achter Tätigkeitsbericht,* p. 11.

123 *Achter Tätigkeitsbericht,* p. 12.

124 I.-S. Kowalczuk, 'Was den Stasi-Unterlagen im Bundesarchiv droht', *Frankfurter Allgemeine Zeitung,* 8 January 2005.

125 Gauck, 'Dealing', p. 5.

3 Czechoslovakia and the Czech and Slovak Republics

Nadya Nedelsky

On the continuum of East European transitional justice strategies, Czechoslovakia sits with East Germany nearer the "prosecute and punish" than the "forgive and forget" pole. Most notably, the Czech and Slovak Federative Republic pioneered post-communist lustration, passing a tough and wide-ranging law in 1991. This vigor conforms nicely to patterns that scholars have identified regarding three factors that appear to shape how states in the region have approached transitional justice: the nature of their communist regime, transition type, and the balance of power between former communists and their opposition in the subsequent regime. Beginning with the first factor, Gustáv Husák's Soviet-backed "normalization" regime (1969–1989), which sought to retrench Communist power after the liberalizing period of the 1968 Prague Spring, was an excellent example of repressive and ideologically inflexible "bureaucratic-authoritarianism." Allowing people neither the possibility of "voice" through dissent nor "exit" through emigration, its repressiveness produced a pressure-cooker situation, stoking the kind of societal resentment which, in the aftermath of regime collapse, is typically supportive of rigorous transitional justice policies. And collapse the regime did: having "resisted reforms on the Hungarian or Polish model to the bitter end, the communist leadership in Prague was in an exceptionally weak position to stem the tide of protest that swept all the East European capitals."[1] The ten critical days of 1989's Velvet Revolution, which began with a student demonstration on 17 November and built up to a millions-strong general strike on 27 November, so undermined the deeply unpopular regime that "the outcome of negotiations reflected almost wholly the preferences of the opposition."[2] Thus, Czechoslovak Communist leaders were in no position to demand the kinds of concessions that, for example, their Polish counterparts were able to gain from Solidarity through the Roundtable Agreements earlier that year. As a number of theorists argue, such a transition is unfavorable for elites hoping to encourage forgiving and forgetting. And finally, unlike in Romania, for example, the first elections brought a real change in leadership, with members of dissident-led umbrella parties (Civic Forum in the Czech Republic and the Public Against Violence in Slovakia) replacing Communist elites at the highest levels of the state.

In light of this combination of factors—all of which, according to powerful scholarly argument and evidence, are supportive (though perhaps not determinative) of more thorough-going justice policies—the Federal Assembly's passage of a stringent lustration law is not surprising. Things get a bit more complicated, however, as the story continues. Over the course of 1992, negotiations between Czech and Slovak leaders over how to restructure the post-communist federation unraveled rapidly. During this remaining year of common statehood and since setting up independent states on 1 January 1993, the Czechs and Slovaks diverged sharply in their responses to the communist regime's former high officials and secret police agents, files, and collaborators. The Czech Republic continued to pursue lustration, which is still in effect at this writing. The Czechs also allow broad public access to the secret police files and have set up institutions for investigating and prosecuting crimes committed by the previous regime. In Slovakia, by contrast, lustration was never seriously enforced and the law expired at the end of 1996. Far fewer prosecutions have been carried out, and Slovakia lagged behind most states in the region – including Romania and Bulgaria – in opening the secret police files to the public.

Returning to the continuum of transitional justice strategies, it would appear that while the Czechs do sit near their prosecuting and punishing German neighbors, the Slovaks have situated themselves much closer to the forgive and forget end. This distance between the former partners throws into question the relationships posited between these three factors and transitional justice policies and requires us to assess whether the three factors discussed above were the same for both the Czechs and Slovaks.

Of the three factors, the type of transition from communist to successor regime is arguably the easiest to pin down. By transition type, I am not referring to the broader consolidation of democracy, which may take many years, but rather to the process by and terms under which Communist leaders surrendered their party's monopoly on power and other, non-communist players were able to enter the political sphere, with the goal of effecting regime change. On this count, it is possible to conclude that the Czechs and Slovaks did share a transition, as they were both governed by a powerful federal government that essentially crumbled in the face of the opposition over the short course of the Velvet Revolution. The question of whether the nature of the Communist regime was the same for both nations is, however, more complicated, and the issue of the balance of power between former Communists and their opposition is clearly relevant beyond the period of common statehood, up to the present.

In the following sections of this chapter I explore the relationship between these factors and the two nations' transitional justice policy choices. I begin with a brief overview of the Czechoslovak communist political police's history and nature. In discussing this aspect of the regime's repressive apparatus, I also address the question of whether the Czechs and Slovaks lived under the same regime type during the final twenty years of communism. Next, I consider the development of and debates over Czech and Slovak policies on lustration, file access, and prosecutions, attending particularly to how they have related to both ideological principles and the narrower concerns of power competition between former communists and their opposition. Finally, I explore how a number of Czech and

Slovak government and civil society leaders perceive and retrospectively assess transitional justice's goals and outcomes ten to 15-plus years after the Velvet Revolution. This final section has two key purposes. First, it seeks to further "unpack" transitional justice's relationship to communist regime type, transition type, and post-communist political competition. It is easy to see the role that power considerations and self-interest could (and do) play in all of these factors. It is also easy to conclude that this is *the* central issue—that "justice" is primarily or even exclusively pursued for power advantages extrinsic to the ideals of justice in itself. By looking at these Czech and Slovak perspectives, and particularly at the criteria by which they judge the legitimacy of the policies' goals and outcomes, it may be possible to get at other important reasons why these three factors are related to justice policies. And finally, this section seeks to draw on these same perspectives for practical lessons from the Czech and Slovak experiences relevant not only to scholarly observers, but also to current and future states undergoing regime change.

The Czechoslovak political police

The Czechoslovak State Security (*Statní bezpečnost*, or StB) predates the communist regime. It was set up shortly after the Czechoslovak state's reestablishment after World War II as a section of the Ministry of the Interior's National Security Corps. Over the next three years, it came increasingly under the control of the communists, the strongest postwar party in the Czech lands. The communists used the StB to undermine their competition by planting informers in their offices, gathering compromising materials on their members, sending out bogus correspondence on their stationery, and using agents to act as provocateurs at their rallies.[3]

After the communists completed their takeover the state in February 1948, they consolidated control over the StB with a thorough purge. Over the next 41 years, the StB's structure underwent repeated reworking. Sometimes the changes were superficial; other times they were instituted to streamline the command or, alternatively, to enhance the autonomy of different StB departments.[4] One of the more dramatic restructurings came in 1950, when, following the Soviet model, the StB was de-linked from the Ministry of the Interior and put under a new Ministry of National Security. This greatly enhanced the StB's power to take on its key tasks, via six sectors, of conducting counter-intelligence against both foreign and internal enemies, combating economic sabotage, installing intelligence equipment, undertaking investigations, reading mail, and following and arresting people.[5] The secret police relentlessly persecuted those deemed the regime's enemies in these early years, and as the policy of terror spiraled upward in 1951, many of the StB's top officials were caught up and devoured by the political trials that they had helped orchestrate. Under new leaders, the secret police grew even more powerful, until both Stalin and his Czechoslovak counterpart and minion Klement Gottwald died in 1953. Thereafter, the StB remerged with the Ministry of the Interior, where its powers were scaled back and again reorganized.[6]

Concerted de-Stalinization came somewhat later to Czechoslovakia than many other communist states, but by 1963, the StB's role in the crimes and excesses of 1948–53 came under scrutiny, as did its continuing role in society. A performance review concluded that it was wastefully focusing more than three-quarters of its personnel's efforts on searching for the "enemy within."[7] Still, its task continued to include exposing the workings of "both the external and internal enemy for political and ideological subversion."[8]

A much greater challenge to the StB's role as political police came five years later, when during the Prague Spring new Interior Ministry leaders sought to dramatically downsize the StB's officer corps, restrict its authority, cease most domestic political surveillance, and submit its workings to parliamentary rather than strictly party oversight. Not surprisingly, these reform efforts did not survive the Soviet-led invasion of Czechoslovakia in August 1968. The "normalization" regime purged 73 percent of the StB's command and quickly reactivated the sections tasked with combating political and ideological subversion in the spheres of religion, culture, science, youth, social class, and the former "reactionary" political parties and "bourgeois" state structures.[9] Federalization of the state, the only major Prague Spring reform to proceed after 1968, led to a new Federal Ministry of the Interior, within which the Czech and Slovak Republics gained some influence over the StB, but by 1974, control was largely recentralized. While it was further reorganized over the last 15 years of the communist regime, the StB's role as the intimidating guardian of a repressive regime was not challenged again until 1989.

When one takes a broad view of its history, the StB generally fulfilled the role of guardian less by overt terror and more by appearing omnipresent in citizens' lives.[10] As was common in Eastern Europe, Czechoslovakia's secret police had one officer per 1,200–1,700 people; with a population of 15 million, it generally had 9,000 regular employees.[11] Recruitment was problematic. At the regime's outset, most of the secret police members were young blue collar workers with very little education. The StB tried to correct this over time, in part by sending them on study trips to Moscow. Still, in 1956, 35.6 percent of the Ministry of Interior personnel had not even completed elementary school, and ten years later, at the end of 1966, 45.1 percent of StB personnel had only an elementary education. Relatively low education levels continued throughout the communist period.[12] Recruitment was further complicated by the StB's prestige level in society: in the late 1960s, a classified poll showed that the only profession held in lower esteem than the security service was sewer cleaner.[13]

Thus, to cultivate the impression of seeing and hearing all, the StB needed to develop a wide network of informers.[14] In the regime's early and most terrifying years, there was actually little recruiting, "since emphasis fell instead on finding convenient victims and torturing them into confessing to whatever the StB had scripted."[15] Thereafter, according to Williams, the StB primarily motivated its informers through sympathy for the regime and fear (especially by blackmailing people with evidence of previous crimes, sexual behavior, and wartime collaboration) rather than outright coercion. In 1954, the first year with comprehensive data records, the StB recruited 30,000 people; thereafter, the numbers rose and fell alongside the mood and orientation of the regime, falling with the thaw in 1956, rising with the re-hardening from 1957–1961, and then falling again during the period leading up and into the Prague Spring.[16] Precise figures on the agent network from 1970 to 1989 are not available at this time, but Ministry of Interior records registered 29,192 collaborators with the StB counter-intelligence in mid-1989.[17]

In the regime's early years, the main targets of informing and surveillance were members of former political parties, nationalists, churches, former representatives of the capitalist system and the "class dictatorship" (here including members of the judiciary), and people involved in espionage and sabotage.[18] Many of these groups were dealt harsh blows during the show trials. In the mid-fifties through the 1960s, the focus began to shift to surveillance of the workplace and defectors.[19] Available figures suggest that the StB "surveyed" at least 125,000 people between 1951 and 1968, though investigators subsequently took up only 10 to 15 percent of these cases.[20] From 1978 until the end of 1989, a Ministry of Interior directive required that persons "threatening the internal order and security of the state" be registered according to four levels of dangerousness in the spheres of the mass media, education, industry, ideology and culture, agriculture, health care, transport, services and trade, science and research, and other areas. As of October 1989, there were 7,261 "registered persons," though all their files were destroyed that December.[21]

Though imprecise, available figures give a sense of the StB's impact on the lives of Czechoslovak citizens. Between 1948 and 1989, at least 250,000 people were sentenced for political reasons, not quite half of whom were condemned *in absentia*. 22,000 were sentenced to forced labor, and 243 were executed. Somewhere between 3,000 and 8,000 people died in the brutal conditions of prisons, labor camps, and uranium mines[22] (mostly during the 1950s), and an estimated 320 to 400 people who tried to leave the country were killed crossing the border. Approximately 7,000 people were imprisoned in psychiatric institutions.[23] The first six years of "normalization" involved sending 1,142 people to prison. The StB also continued to monitor society's mail, "checking," for example, 55,681,000 parcels in 1982. During the regime's final decade and a half, StB efforts zeroed in on the human rights community Charter 77. Via Operation *Izolace* (Isolation), the StB sought to divide and conquer the Chartists by exploiting ideological differences between their members and to more generally undermine them through surveillance, infiltration, and the use of compromising materials. These efforts were buttressed by Operation *Asanace* ("slum clearance" or "decontamination"), which involved relentlessly harassing dissidents, threatening them with death, beating them, searching their homes, and interrogating them with the goal of driving them into exile.[24]

Clearly, then, the communist regime ramped up the StB's repressive role during its last twenty years. At the same time, it is important to note that repression levels were not the same in the two parts of the federalized state, in large part due to the different political orientations and projects that Czechs and Slovaks took up during the Prague Spring. Broadly speaking, Czech reformers wanted to liberalize and democratize the state, while in Slovakia leaders were much more focused on enhancing Slovak national sovereignty through federalization, a long-standing goal that was far less threatening to communist power and in fact conformed to the Soviet model.[25] After the invasion, then, the purges were much more sweeping in the Czech Republic, where almost 42 percent of party members were expelled, compared to only 17 percent in Slovakia, where cadres were considered by and large more "ideologically sound."[26] The purge of Czechs (many of whom were demoted to positions like street sweepers and stokers) offered Slovaks career opportunities that were much broader than would have been produced by federalization alone.[27] This greater hand in government helped propel Slovak economic development during the 1970s, building upon the significant modernization that Slovakia had undergone since the 1950s. The Czech Republic, by contrast, stagnated. Former dissident and post-communist Czech Prime Minister Petr Pithart estimates that more than 1.5 million people in the Czech lands had their career possibilities curtailed during normalization.[28] This period thus alienated not only dissidents from the regime; many technocrats demoted after 1968 became "internal exiles," avoiding both dissidence and cooptation, and instead retreating into the private sphere.[29] "Within a few years," Pithart observes, "Czech society was intellectually and culturally decimated."[30]

The difference in the two republics' experience with the normalization regime was reflected in dissidence levels. Charter 77, which never gained a widespread societal following anywhere in Czechoslovakia, was nevertheless predominantly Czech. Ninety-five percent of state-suppressed dissidence occurred in the Czech lands during the late 1970s, and while the Slovak percentage grew to 13 percent by the mid-1980s, it still fell well below the proportion of Slovaks to Czechs in the state. This difference cannot be simply ascribed to greater Slovak satisfaction with the regime; the StB intimidated Slovaks (as well as many Czechs) by threatening the security, families, and careers of those who dared to oppose or criticize the regime.[31] Still, Slovaks had "more to lose, and more to hope for" than the Czechs during the regime's final 20 years.[32] Indeed, many of Slovakia's technocrats, nationalist intellectuals, and enterprise managers saw their relationship to the regime as supporting national progress.[33] This view is more broadly reflected in opinion polls from the 1970s and 1980s, in which Slovaks consistently held a more positive view of postwar economic and social developments than the Czechs and, up to the end of 1989, were significantly more optimistic about the country's future.[34]

These different national relationships to the regime return us to the question, raised at the outset of this chapter, of whether the Czechs and Slovaks experienced the same regime type during the last 20 years of communism. Even from this brief overview of that period, it appears that they did not.[35] While the Czechs clearly lived under bureaucratic authoritarianism, the government in Slovakia ensured societal compliance with its rule through strategies more typical of national-accommodative communism (stressing cooptation rather than repression) and patrimonial communism (using a combination of repression and cooptation into

vertical clientelist networks). As we turn to the post-communist period, it is helpful to keep in mind that despite the long period of common statehood, the regime
type to which Czech and Slovak transitional justice responds is, in fact, different
in important ways.

This said, the way the Velvet Revolution toppled communist rule was characteristic of the demise of bureaucratic-authoritarian regimes, which tend to end
through massive capitulation. This came as something of a surprise to the StB,
which had expected that the country's relatively high living standards would keep
citizens from joining in the wave of uprisings sweeping the region in 1989. When
the catalyzing student protest happened on 17 November, the StB responded brutally (there were untrue rumors that they killed a student), prompting conspiracy
theories to which I will return in the following section. In reality, the StB waited
for the Communist Party command to activate emergency measures, which never
came, and when it became clear that the government was negotiating with the
opposition, the secret police began destroying its files.[36] Unfortunately for the
progress of transitional justice, even as the opposition Civic Forum rapidly gained
negotiating leverage, it was slow to demand that the StB leadership be removed,
allowing its officers, under communist General Alojz Lorenc, to shred and make
off with files until the middle of December. At least a third of the active files disappeared during this time. It was only at the end of the year that the new president,
former dissident Václav Havel, put a non-communist, Richard Sacher, in charge
of the Interior Ministry. Though Sacher proved to be a controversial figure, he did
set about disbanding the Secret Security units. By 15 February 1990, the StB was
history[37]—though its influence lived on, as events quickly made clear.

Lustration

Early screenings and the November 17th Commission

In the spring of 1990, President Havel invited the country's new array of political
parties to use Sacher's ministry to screen their candidates for StB connections.
Most parties did this (though a few, including the Communists, declined), but
none disclosed the results and no repercussions were required. The StB legacy
soon began to disrupt Czechoslovak politics, however, with two developments in
particular prompting demands for a more systematic approach to dealing with the
files. The first was a series of scandals fueled by the sensitive information they
contained. Minister of Interior Sacher himself was widely suspected of allowing
certain files to go missing and others to find their way into public knowledge.[38]
Some high officials also unilaterally screened their employees, and Deputy Minister of the Interior Jan Ruml went on television to accuse a prominent party leader
of working for the StB for 15 years.[39] Though Sacher stepped down in the mid-
1990 and was replaced by Jan Langoš, these and other scandals led to demands
that "wild" screenings be replaced by an orderly legal process.

A second factor prompting movement toward the lustration law was the widespread rumor that key aspects of the 17 November events were part of an StB

conspiracy to change the government on the secret police's own terms. Parliament set up a "17 November Commission" to investigate. According to Petr Toman, the Commission's first spokesman and eventual co-author of the Lustration Act, this investigation familiarized the Commission with the StB files, which turned out to contain many well-known names, including people highly placed in government and Parliament.[40] The Commission reported this to the Federal Assembly, which passed a resolution authorizing the Commission to screen all Federal Assembly deputies, employees of the Offices of the Prime Minister and of the Federal Assembly, and federal ministers and their deputies for StB collaboration. The Commission members checked the files to see if evidence existed that the person knew he or she was considered an informer, had hand-written a report or signed an agreement, and was named in more than one file. In cases where the Commission agreed unanimously that a Federal Assembly Deputy had collaborated, it gave the person 15 days to resign. According to Toman, only a few took this option, and they were allowed to claim health or other reasons for departing. If they refused to step down, their names would be disclosed to the Assembly. All other implicated (non-Deputy) employees had the choice of leaving voluntarily or being dismissed.

On 22 March 1991, Toman presented the Commission's report, covering both the events of November 1989 and the screening results, in a televised Federal Assembly special session. Toman stated that "[t]he only way to prevent blackmail, the continued activity of the StB collaborators, and a series of political scandals that could surface at crucial moments is to clear the government and legislative bodies of these collaborators."[41] He then read aloud the names, registration numbers, categories of collaboration, secret code names, and dates of service of ten deputies who had declined to step down. Two names were added later.

The televised session provoked a mixed reaction. Many deputies celebrated the Commission's work: for example, Federal Deputy Prime Minister Pavel Rychetsky declared that the naming was a necessary purge, and Deputy Chairman of the Civic Democratic Alliance Daniel Kroupa offered to give up his own mandate if the ten named did so as well.[42] Others were more critical. Parliament First Deputy Chairman and Charter 77 signatory Zdeněk Jičinský questioned the screening's legality, and Federal Assembly Chairman and former Prague Spring leader Alexander Dubček argued that disclosing the deputies' names diminished the Parliament's prestige, stating, "I am still convinced that those whose names were read should not only have the chance to defend themselves but primarily the presumption of innocence should apply to them."[43]

The Czechoslovak press echoed some of these concerns, with many journals weighing in with fairly strong criticism. *Mladá fronta dnes* wrote that final judgment of the ten needed to await proof beyond any doubt that they were conscious agents, adding that if any were wrongly accused, the "credibility of the whole parliament will be put in doubt." The leftist *Rudé pravo* wrote, "It is certainly right and necessary to purge political life of StB collaborators, agents or staff. However, the guilt or innocence of every person should be weighed on the apothecaries' balance and innocence must be preferred in the case of the slightest doubt." The

Slovak daily *Národná obroda* as well expressed concern about the presumption of innocence, observing that the investigation had lacked human decency. *Smena*, a youth daily, argued that screenings needed to differentiate between levels of guilt, adding that high officials in the StB and Communist Party had not even been the Commission's main concern. It concluded that "a law-abiding state received several slaps in the face yesterday." *Pravda* argued that those in favor of screening had "fallen victim to the disease of mistrust and suspicion," and *Prace* denounced the process as "unconvincing witch burning."[44]

The 1991 Lustration Law

Critics of the Commission's screening efforts did not, however, necessarily oppose screening itself, and demands grew for a legal process to govern it.[45] The Federal Assembly obliged in October 1991 through Law 451/1991, known as the Lustration Law.[46] It applies to persons who, between 25 February 1948 (the Communist takeover) and 17 November 1989, were members and agents of the State Security, Communist Party officials from the district level up, knowing StB collaborators, People's Militia members, political officers in the Corps of National Security, members of purge committees in 1948 or after 21 August 1968 (the Soviet invasion), students at KGB schools for more than three months, and owners of StB "conspiration apartments." For the following five years, these people could not be employed in: most elected or appointed positions in the federal and republican levels of government (though, importantly, it did not include the position of Member of Parliament); rank above colonel in the army; management positions in state-owned enterprises and joint stock companies; the official press agency; top positions in Czechoslovak, Czech, and Slovak Radio and Television; top academic positions; and the Supreme Court, judgeships, and prosecutorial posts. Employees and applicants for employment would have to be certified by the Ministry of the Interior or be dismissed, demoted, or rejected for employment. Citizens 18 years and older could ask to have their files reviewed, though could not see them personally. Political parties, publishers, and radio and television producers could have an employee "who takes part in the shaping of the intellectual contents of the communication media" screened if the staff member consented, and the results could not be publicized unless the person agreed.[47] Anyone could prompt the investigation of a senior official for a deposit of 1000 crowns (around $35 at the time), which they would lose if the official's record was clean. The law was set to expire on 31 December 1996.

A long, heated debate preceded the law's passage. Roman David combed the parliamentary records to identify both how deputies articulated the law's goals and how frequently they voiced support for them. The most common goal—expressed by 50 percent of deputies—was "personnel discontinuity and minimal justice."[48] This responded to the communist regime's policy of reserving the prestigious and influential positions in society for those who met certain ideological criteria. The justice lustration provides is "minimal" because it does not criminally prosecute those responsible for injustices in the previous regime, but does exclude them from influence in the new one. Twenty-one percent of deputies who spoke in support of the bill talked about the second goal, "national security and public safety," which focused on the threat to the democratic transition posed by old elite networks, as well as the potential that the previous regime's collaborators would be vulnerable to blackmail. "Protection of rights and the need for legal regulation of the process"—especially in response to uncontrolled and arbitrary screenings—and "truth revelation" tied for third place, with 14 percent of deputies approving of each of these during the debate. Truth revelation, according to David, "was a precondition of establishing democracy in the transitional countries. It could help people gain confidence in political candidates, regain trust in public institutions, disclaim rumors and gossip, and ease the tight atmosphere in society."[49] Finally, three percent of deputies offered "protection of territorial integrity" and three percent offered "trust" as goals of the law. David does not elaborate on this final motivation, but President Havel's explanation of his decision not to block the law despite certain misgivings (discussed below) gives a sense its potential role in building trust in the new government: "I must bear in mind that society needs some public action in this regard because otherwise it would feel that the revolution remains unfinished ... Our society has a great need to face [the] past, to get rid of the people who had terrorized the nation and conspicuously violated human rights, to remove them from the positions that they are still holding."[50]

On the other side, the bill's opponents offered three main arguments. Fifteen percent argued that it violated human rights and particularly compared it with Czechoslovakia's excessively retributive actions after World War II and to McCarthyism; 5.5 percent of deputies supporting the law disputed this. Twelve and a half percent argued that it was motivated by vengeance, calling it "legal violence," an "inquisition," and a "proxy for the inability to prosecute communist crimes."[51] Some also argued that it was based on the principle of collective guilt and imposed unfair punishment.[52] President Havel shared the concern about collective guilt and proposed that the law should provide an impartial hearing that considered mitigating circumstances and the "specific circumstances of the individual case."[53] (Parliament never did amend the law to conform to Havel's suggestions.) Eleven percent of deputies on the other side denied these charges, and 4 percent of deputies argued that the law was based on political rivalry; no deputies took debate time to dispute this.

It is also important to note that after its passage, the law was modified by a November 1992 Constitutional Court ruling that nullified the law's application to "category c" collaborators, which included "candidates" for collaboration. Under the law, people falling into this category could appeal to an Independent Lustration Commission, which would check to see if the person had in fact gone on to become an informer. In 1992, of 600 cases, the Commission found evidence in only 3 percent of the cases that the candidates actually collaborated. Thus, the Chairman of the Independent Commission, Jaroslav Bašta, joined 99 lawmakers in successfully asking the Constitutional Court to remove candidates from the law's purview.[54] With this category gone, the avenue of appeal is the civil court system. In its ruling, the Court also rejected a number of other challenges to the law, stating:

A democratic State has not only the right, but also the duty to assert and protect the principles on which it is based. It cannot be inactive in the situation in which the leading posts on all levels were staffed on the basis of political criteria ... In democratic societies the requirements imposed on the employees of the State and public organs ... include also the compliance with certain prerequisites of State citizenship which can be characterized as loyalty to democratic principles on which the State is based ... Such restrictions may concern also certain groups of persons without these persons being assessed individually ... [The Law] is not a retaliation against individual persons or groups of persons ... Every State, the more so that which had been obliged to suffer the violation of basic rights and freedoms by the totalitarian power for more than forty years, has the right to apply such legislative measures [for] the establishment of a democratic system [and aimed] at the foiling of the risk of subversion or return of the possible relapse of the totalitarian system.[55]

The vote on the law, before 300 federal deputies, came down to 148 in favor, 31 against, 22 abstaining, 29 boycotting, and 80 absent. This vote reflected partisan differences: all the deputies of the predominantly Czech center-right Civic Democratic Party (ODS) voted for it, and all the deputies from the nationalist-populist Movement for a Democratic Slovakia (HZDS) voted against it. This particular partisan division is important, because it would soon develop into the major fault line not only between right and left, but between Czechs and Slovaks, with important repercussions for transitional justice.

In June 1992, the Czech and Slovak Federative Republic held federal elections. The ODS won the Czech vote overwhelmingly and the HZDS the Slovak. Having displaced the dissident-led umbrella parties that had captained the first phase of regime change, the two parties became the key negotiators of the state's future. This future was not promising, as the ODS and HZDS in many ways could hardly have been more different in their makeup, political orientation, and view of the former regime. The ODS was largely made up of monetarist technocrats and conservative intellectuals and led by Vaclav Klaus, formerly the new state's Finance Minister and a vocal fan of Milton Friedman and Margaret Thatcher. The HZDS was strongly nationalist, economically left-leaning (with goals of a "third way" system), and comprised largely of former Communist cadres and enterprise managers.[56] Their leader was the charismatic but highly controversial Vladimír Mečiar, who had been the post-communist Slovak Minister of Interior and then Slovak Prime Minister until his ousting in early 1991. The reasons for this dismissal (which caused widespread public protests in Slovakia) are relevant here: in early 1992, the Parliamentary Committee on Defense and Security investigated allegations that as Interior Minister, Mečiar and his staff had taken advantage of his position to make sure certain files disappeared, while using others "to manipulate

Slovak politics to their advantage."[57] He was also accused, as Prime Minister, of having unfairly forced the new Minister of the Interior to resign because he had dismissed a number of former StB agents that Mečiar had appointed. The Parliamentary Committee found that these allegations were true, and further concluded that sufficient evidence survived to prove that Mečiar had himself collaborated with the StB since 1976. The Slovak National Council accepted the report, and Mečiar lost his position as Prime Minister. Still, the Slovak media "remained fairly quiet" about the StB issue, and the report clearly did not prevent Mečiar and his party from achieving a massive electoral victory that June.

Once the two parties took up their positions, negotiations over restructuring the federation soon became something of a showdown. Among the non-negotiable demands the HZDS placed on the table (which also included rejecting Havel as President) was the revocation of the Lustration Law. The power-political considerations here are obvious, given the high proportion of former communists in the HZDS compared to the ODS. There is likely, however, an added dimension to the way these parties saw the issue, with roots in both the nature of the previous regime and the party members' relationships to it. As Eyal argues, many Slovaks saw the communist past, and especially the normalization-era projects of enhancing national autonomy and rational planning, *not* as something to be "erased or purified; on the contrary, its remembrance was part of the work of imagining the nation."[58] Indeed, many Slovaks saw the post-communist project as building on the best aspects of reform communism, and therefore "[l]ustration was the direct symbolic antithesis of the ideological package of the left in Slovakia, and threatened it with symbolic annihilation."[59] The ODS—which rejected the HZDS demand to end lustration—had a very different view of the previous regime: "the idea of lustration expressed what the dissidents had in common with the monetarists, even if they differed on questions of method and authority – the rejection and condemnation of the past."[60] These elites saw communism as entirely unredeemable, and viewed reform communists as no better than communists "without adjectives."[61] Without getting into the complexities of the breakup, it is safe to say that, overall, the ODS and HZDS could agree on neither a common vision of the past nor of the future, and by the end of that year, the Czech–Slovak union was over.

Lustration in the Czech and Slovak Republics

Slovakia never seriously enforced lustration, either before the state's breakup or after (federal legislation left over from the Czech and Slovak Federative Republic remained in force in both new states unless expressly overturned). In 1994, the Mečiar government petitioned the Slovak Constitutional Court to reject the Lustration Law as unconstitutional and incompatible with international human rights agreements. The Court declined to do so, but the new state never invoked the law, and it was allowed to expire at the end of its five year life-span. Interestingly, even after Mečiar's HZDS and its ally, the (formerly Communist) Party of the Democratic Left (SDL') lost their dominant position in the state in the 1998 elections to an (admittedly shaky) coalition of moderate, center-right parties, the post-Mečiar governments have not shown any particular interest in pursuing lustration, either.

In the Czech Republic, by contrast, Parliament has extended lustration's life-span twice, both times overriding President Havel's veto. In 1995, the law gained five years via Act no. 245/1995, and in the autumn of 2000 Parliament used Act no. 422/2000 to extend it indefinitely, until after the passage and implementation of new civil service and security laws, as yet uncompleted. It also exempted people born after 1 December 1971. Here, it is worth noting that while the 1995 extension was passed during the period of center-right ODS domination, the Klaus-led coalition collapsed in 1997 amid major scandal, and power has since been much more balanced between the center-right and center-left, the latter represented most strongly by the Czech Social Democratic Party (ČSSD).

In addition to prolonging the law's validity, the Parliament has also specifically rejected proposals to end it, most recently at the end of 2005. This latest proposal, put forward by the Czech Communists (KSČM), sparked particular controversy, as for the first time it received support from a Prime Minister, Jiří Paroubek (ČSSD). Paroubek defended his position by arguing that he followed such former dissidents as Havel, Jičinský, and Petr Uhl in finding that the law is based on the principle of collective guilt. Indeed, Jičinský, also of the ČSSD, spoke out in favor of repealing the law as well, calling it "a black mark on our legal order."[62] The repeal was strongly opposed, however, by the senior opposition ODS and the two junior government parties, the Freedom Union-DEU (US-DEU), and the Christian Democrats (KDU-CSL).[63] Paroubek's support stirred up a fair amount of negative press, and newspapers quoted KDU-CSL Chairman Miroslav Kalousek as warning that "the ČSSD will have to choose whether it wants to work with the Christian Democrats, or the former StB members."[64] Under fire, Paroubek switched his position and supported the law's continuation, saying no change was necessary "for at least a year or two."[65] Ultimately, only a third (60 of 180) of the deputies present in the Parliament voted to abolish the law, which included a minority of ČSSD members. It thus remains unclear how long the law will last. Paroubek argued that the issue should be settled before the new civil service law took effect in early 2007, while ČSSD representative Zdeněk Koudelka suggested that it should remain in force until 17 November 2009, consistent with the idea of a 20-year statute of limitations for certain criminal acts.[66]

The Czech Republic thus has the longest record of lustration in Eastern Europe. From 4 October 1991, the date the Lustration Law went into effect, until the beginning of November 2005, the Ministry of Interior issued 451,000 lustration certificates.[67] Of these, approximately 2.03 percent were positive, meaning that that the verdict found that a person was in fact registered under one of the law's specified categories. The extent of collaboration is not examined. During this same time period, there were 870 suits in civil law courts contesting the verdict. In most cases, the courts decided that the StB's registration of the person was unjustified; in other words, they found for the person challenging the verdict. According to Pavel Brunnhofer, Assistant Director of the Ministry of Interior Archives, a major reason for the high verdict turnover rate is that the courts accept only original paper evidence, not records transferred to microfiche (which was done with much StB documentation) as signatures cannot then be verified. Because many paper records were destroyed or have gone missing, and because the Ministry of Interior has the burden of proof, this rule works overwhelmingly to the advantage of those challenging verdicts.[68]

The validity of some lustration-*negative* certificates has also been contested. In June 2001, Czech Interior Minister Stanislav Gross alleged that during the early 1990s, over 100 StB agents had received fake lustration clearances and used them to hold on to government jobs. As a result, Gross stated that the Ministry would review roughly 150,000 lustration clearances.[69] Such scandals have nevertheless continued intermittently over the years; for example, in February 2007, the Czech head of Interpol was exposed as an StB collaborator. He had obtained a clear lustration certificate by slightly changing the spelling of his name. Two months later, further scrutiny prompted by this case uncovered 15 former collaborators, also previously lustrated, at Czech police headquarters.[70]

Thus far, I have focused on the perspectives and policy choices of dominant Czech and Slovak political elites, which were clearly quite different from one another with regard to the nature of the previous regime and the proper response to it. In the interests of discerning whether transitional justice policies are driven not only by political power considerations, narrowly construed, but also by understandings of justice, it is important to take note of the extent to which political parties were representing their constituents' perspectives. And, in fact, polls taken during the 1990s do show that Czechs and Slovaks differed on three important things. First, Slovaks tended to see the communist regime more favorably, and the post-communist regime less favorably, than Czechs did.[71] Second, a Central European University survey conducted seven times between 1992 and 1996 consistently showed a statistical difference between Czech and Slovak responses to the question of their agreement with the goal of "removing former communists from positions of influence," with the Czechs indicating a substantially higher agreement.[72] Finally, analyzing survey results from the Institute of Sociology at the Czech Academy of Sciences, Kevin Deegan Krause found that the "question of decommunization" was "significantly less relevant to Slovak than to Czech party competition."[73] There is a certain harmony, then, between elite and broader views, and lustration policy choices should be assessed in this context – a task to which I will return in the final section of this chapter.

File access

Czechoslovakia: the Cibulka lists

Though the post-communist Czechoslovak state took an early lead on lustration, it was less forthcoming with public access to the secret police files. According to estimates, the secret police had files on some 600,000 people.[74] As Brunnhofer notes, however, many files were destroyed, and other "disappeared," though the list of names in the register of files is more complete. In part to keep the remaining materials safe from further manipulation, the 17 November Commission requested that the Federal Government declassify and publish all the names of the StB members and collaborators.[75] The response was Federal Premier (and former high Communist official) Marian Čalfa's explanation that "the government is convinced that the publication, at a time when democratic institutions and habits are not yet consolidated, would expose these persons and their families to harassment, and would therefore be an ill-considered step."[76] Some, however, did not agree that much more time needed to pass. The following year, before the June 1992 elections, former dissident and political prisoner "turned freelance StB hunter" Petr Cibulka published the names of roughly 200,000 alleged StB officers and collaborators.[77] The list was entirely unauthorized and unofficial, and included the above-noted "category c" candidates for collaboration. Still, according to such well-placed sources as Jičinský and Toman, the list turns out to have been very accurate in relation to the StB registers, leading Toman to conclude that someone simply took the register out of the archive and copied it.[78] Not surprisingly, the "Cibulka Lists" rocked Czech and Slovak politics, prompting a hostile reaction to those named. Many on the lists also argued that the situation was extremely unfair because with the files themselves still off-limits to the public there was no way for them to defend themselves by pointing to exonerating or mitigating contextual documents.[79] According to Jiří Pehe, a political analyst and former advisor to President Havel, this situation eventually made it necessary to open the files because "it would not be just to have just the names of people with no background information."[80] For both the Czechs and Slovaks, this opening did not happen until after the breakup of the common state.

File access in the Czech Republic

Although the Social Democrats, with Interior Minister Ruml, introduced a bill to open the archives in 1993, a law allowing this did not pass until three years later. President Havel had voiced some trepidation about the law, arguing that "[c]hildren will be ashamed of their parents, families will break up, people will treat those who they find were informers as they would treat poison."[81] Such disclosures, he argued, would be "one of the StB's greatest successes." Still, Havel was willing to sign the law (Act no. 140/1996), which allowed citizens to examine their own files, with names of third parties blacked out. The law's passage prompted "little fanfare" because all parties except the communists and the extreme right-wing Republicans were in favor of it.[82] The following year, a center opened in the Czech town of Pardubice where people could view their files.

Six years later, a new bill came up for a vote that allowed much broader access, allowing citizens to access not only their own files, but also those of StB collaborators, StB personnel files, and entries recorded with intelligence technology and monitoring. Files that could endanger human lives, foreign agents, or the state's security interests would remain closed. The files would also remain closed to foreign citizens, including Slovaks who had previously been Czechoslovak citizens.

In addition, after one year, a list of all StB collaborators would be published.[83] The bill's initiator, ODS Senator Dagmar Lastovecká, explained that its intention was to allow "Czechs to know their history."[84]

The proposal for broader access prompted a fairly sharp debate. The Communist Party declared that such a law would provoke hatred in society. Some members of the ČSSD and former dissident community (in several cases, overlapping categories) also criticized the bill. In particular, the ČSSD argued that the bill contradicted other legislation, such as that on the protection of personal information, and Vice-premier Pavel Rychetský (ČSSD) expressed concern that the files would reveal more about the StB's victims than its collaborators.[85] For his part, Jičinský argued that the law would prolong the StB's influence over society.[86] Fellow Charter 77 signatory and Czech Government Commissioner for Human Rights from 1999 to 2001 Petr Uhl, as well, wrote in *Pravda* that the bill's "most problematic aspect" centered on the

> protection of personal information. It is not clear what information about persecuted individuals will be blacked out – after all, the agents' reports were composed of information about their activities, contacts with other of the regime's opponents, and intimacies, the bedroom not excepted. If we blacken out the majority, what will remain in the file will be the sums paid to agents and reflections on their effectiveness and reliability. I am not sure whether such reflections about people who were often acting under pressure can be made public. Even former secret collaborators enjoy the protection of the law.[87]

Still another fellow Chartist, former dissident and ex-Foreign Minister Jiří Dienstbier, warned that the files are full of lies, accusations made by neighbors, and fabrications. Thus, he argued, "I think they should be accessible to experts who can really evaluate them. Otherwise, it will be the final victory of the defeated state security which once again is able to disseminate disinformation about various people in this society."[88] Cibulka criticized the bill from a different angle, arguing that it was "deceptive" because the volumes that contain the names of people who performed or perform high functions in the Czech state would not be made public.[89]

Despite these criticisms, the Chamber of Deputies approved the bill by a vote of 102 to 33, and the Senate followed with a vote of 42 to 11. The communists were the only party to vote in a unified bloc against the bill, and a majority of ČSSD members voted against it as well. Havel overcame his reservations and signed the legislation (Act no. 107/2002), arguing that "the importance of the truth is higher, that it surpasses all the rest."[90] He also concluded that "his signature was one step toward the purification of the nation."[91] On 20 March of the following year, the Czech Interior Ministry posted the names of over 100,000 StB spies and informants on the internet.

In 2004, the Parliament opened the files one step further through a new Archive Act (499/2004), which stipulates that the protection of personal data does not apply to documents created by the StB before 1 January 1990. Since the beginning of 2005, when the law came into effect, it has been possible for people to ask for files not only of collaborators and agents, but also of those hostile to the regime, and to read all personal information contained therein. This means that a fair amount of compromising material gathered against, for example, dissidents and church officials, including details of their love lives and sexual indiscretions, is now available for public viewing. Not surprisingly, this has generated fairly significant controversy as well, with a number of former dissidents speaking out against the invasion of privacy.[92]

Under this set of laws, it is now possible for a person to come to the Archive and find out a great deal from the files. The Archive has about 60,000 files and 22 kilometers of written documents, including not only the StB materials but also other security files, such as those kept by the border police.[93] To access the files, one makes a written or oral request and fills out a research card to study the materials. In compliance with Acts 140/1996 and then 107/2002, the Archive has provided about 5000 files to applicants, consisting of roughly 1 million pages. There were requests for about 10 times as many, but either there was no file on the person requesting it or it has not been preserved. If a person asks within the intention of Act 107, he or she will receive a digitalized version of the file where the data of third persons is illegible, but if the request is according to Act 499, he or she can get it in either original or in copy, without anything blacked out. Since early 2005, most requests have been according to the terms laid out in Act 499. One may also, for a fee, bring a copy of a file home.

File access in Slovakia

Slovaks have also debated file access, though later not only than the Czechs, but also than most of Eastern Europe. The Slovak debate gathered momentum in the fall of 2001, around the time the journal *Kritika & Kontext* put out a special issue on the "Phenomenon of the StB in Slovakia." The authors attended particularly to reasons for the "silence" in the country regarding the secret police. According to Miroslav Kusý, a prominent Slovak social scientist and one of the few Slovak signatories of Charter 77, not only was the general public uninterested in the StB, there was also "insufficient interest of the expert community, historians, political scientists, opinion makers."[94] In explaining this, many of the authors point to the lack of Slovak opposition to the regime during the normalization period. For example, Olga Gyárfašová, referring to a 2001 poll showing that 59 percent of Slovaks felt they had lived better under the pre-November regime than its successor, questions whether there was much impetus for the Slovaks to either oppose the communist regime or explore the StB past in the post-communist period. Given the increases in standards of living in Slovakia from the 1950s onward, the smoothness of normalization, and the small numbers of dissidents, about whom many people knew little, she asks, "for which Slovaks was the StB phenomenon actually something real?"[95]

The issue nevertheless appeared on the political agenda that same autumn, when former Federal Minister of the Interior Ján Langoš and former post-communist Slovak Prime Minister Ján Čarnogurský—both prominent former dissidents who spent time in communist jails—submitted proposals for laws opening the files to the citizenry. Not surprisingly, the HZDS and SDL' gave them a particularly skeptical reception. Chairman of the Constitutional Committee and SDL' representative Ladislav Orosz dismissed Langoš's proposal as legally confused and in contradiction with several laws, including those on public order and on archives.[96] Čarnogurský's proposal encountered copious criticism as well, including that: it contradicted both domestic rules and international agreements; the StB materials were too incomplete; the materials had been outside of Slovak control (in Prague) for a while and may have been manipulated or tampered with there; it was too broad, allowing non-victims access; it could endanger the workings of the current secret service by disclosing its methods; and insufficient time had elapsed since the events under consideration.[97] On a different note, an "unnamed expert" warned *Pravda* that "[d]isclosing the materials is only a political gesture and will not have any use. The big fish escaped and the little ones are unimportant."[98]

Čarnogurský's proposal also received some very positive reactions. In a survey of several deputies, *Národná odbora* found support from members of the governing coalition. Some argued that it was overdue, pointing out that all of Slovakia's neighbors had already passed such legislation and so it was "high time" for the country to do the same. Ján Budaj, leader of the Liberal Democratic Union (LDÚ) also told *Pravda* that "real 'decommunization' had not yet occurred in Slovakia," and that opening the archives would be a step in that direction.[99] A number of editorials were more strongly supportive, arguing that file access was a moral imperative and expressing frustration that both political leaders and the broader public seemed to lack the "political will" for "this step."[100] For example, Marek Vagovič writes that "the principle is indisputable: every nation has the right to know its own past."[101] Observing that the SDL' had begun to "concoct the most manifold excuses," he argues that their claims that international agreements and security concerns place barriers to opening the files are untenable, given that all of the state's neighbors had opened their files without encountering any such disasters. Milan Stanislav, as well, writes that the proposed law has an important informative effect, producing a situation where the "people who made life hell for others, and it doesn't matter the size of the fish, would not live among us anonymously and would not pretend that they are innocents."[102] Writing in *Národná odbora*, Peter Vavro observes that in Slovakia, lustration "is considered a witch-hunt, and the opening of the StB volumes to public access as the opening of old wounds."[103] People are uninterested, even though the "witches" continue to fulfill "high public functions." Finally, Ivan Bača writes that, "even in the underworld, which has its own moral understanding, stoolpigeons, narks, [etc.] ... belong to the most despised. Nevertheless, the leaders of the mature socialist society relied on their services."[104] After 1989, people hoped "that they would learn who belonged to the moral dregs of society." He concluded that such hopes had been repeatedly dashed.

In this case, however, they were not. Langoš's bill passed in July 2002, even with some support from the HZDS. According to Čarnogurský, this success was partly made possible by the SDL's pre-election weakness as well as the fact that it offered somewhat broader file access than his own bill.[105] President Rudolf Schuster then vetoed the law, but Parliament overrode it. The law not only opened the files, but also set up an Institute for National Memory (under Langoš's leadership) where citizens can read their own files and those of conscious collaborators, upon written request. The Institute is also charged with gathering documents on crimes committed during both the communist period and the Slovak state that existed under Nazi tutelage during World War II. Files that could "pose a threat to human life and public interest," those kept on foreign nationals, and the personal data of persecuted individuals remain classified.[106] Initially, the Institute had trouble getting the actual files from the SIS (the new Slovak security service), which stalled for quite some time in turning over some 60,479 files of the former state security and other security agencies. The handover finally got under way, and up to the end of January 2006, the Institute registered 6,200 requests for access to the files, and of these located some 1,500 files.[107] Following the Czech example, the law stipulated that the names in the StB registers be made public, which the Institute began in November 2004 (a full year after it was originally scheduled). Going region by region, over the course of several months, it published the names of agents and collaborators.

In June 2006, the Institute suffered a terrible blow when Langoš was killed in a car crash. For several months thereafter, the Institute remained without a director, as Parliament failed twice to elect a replacement. During this time, some in the new government (a coalition of Prime Minister Robert Fico's "Smer" Party with Mečiar's HZDS and the far-right nationalist Slovak National Party) also publicly questioned the Institute's value, and even whether it should continue its operation as an independent institution.[108] In January 2007, it was unexpectedly evicted from its space in the Bratislava District 1 Court building, which had undergone expensive renovation to suit the Institute's purposes, and given six months to find new quarters, though its budget had no room for such expenses.[109] The reason given was a need for courtroom space. Later that same month, Parliament finally elected a candidate for director nominated by the SNS, Ivan Petranský. A 30-year-old historian, Petranský had previously worked for the strongly nationalist state cultural organization Matica Slovenska, known (in part) for its controversial celebration of the Nazi-allied wartime Slovak state. Given the Institute's mandate, many have questioned the appropriateness of this choice. Under his leadership, in any case, the Institute has continued to publicize darker elements of the communist past; for example, in mid-2007, it published a list of the notorious StB counter-intelligence corps, the "XII Division."[110]

Interestingly, although Slovakia's two most tireless advocates of file access—Langoš and Čarnogurský—both expected that it would allow citizens to understand the truth about past, they envisioned some of its other purposes differently. Although the law does not mandate any repercussions for those linked to the StB, Langoš hoped that when the Institute for National Memory notified state authorities that they had implicated persons highly placed within their ministries and organs, they would be prompted to "purify" their ranks by voluntarily demoting them. He calls this "lustration without legal consequences."[111] Čarnogurský, by contrast, found that "now lustration as such has no sense," particularly because unofficial lists of collaborators (such as those Cibulka published) have long been available on the internet. In his view, "if even someone who was listed as a collaborator would be nominated by a political party to some position, if this political party is strong enough to appoint the man, that means he has to be appointed."[112] Čarnogurský's hopes centered rather on the possibility that file access will provide the necessary context for making sense of the lists of collaborators, as it allows some people to prove that they cooperated under duress or gave only, in their view, innocuous information. Thus, Lángoš envisioned effects that would be both somewhat retributive and protective of democracy, while Čarnogurský stressed file access's role in promoting societal reconciliation.

Such differences in perspective were evident in other spheres of society, as well. For example, with the first official internet publication of the StB registers, the journal *Sme* interviewed prominent Slovak artists about the issue. The introduction to the piece notes that an appointee of the Czech Premier, who had a role in abusing demonstrators in 1989, had been successfully pressured by Czech artists to step down. Thus, the Slovak artists were invited to exercise their influence as well. Some of those interviewed echoed Čarnogurský's concerns; for example, Emília Vášáryová observed that while "we must come to terms with our past," publishing the names did not offer sufficient basis for "condemning people," since it is not fully clear what the people did.[113] Oľga Feldeková, as well, argued that context is necessary for moral judgment, pointing out that it makes a difference whether people became collaborators during the 1950s, and if they did it under threat or voluntarily and/or with the goal of furthering their own careers. Miro Noga, by contrast, took a view more similar to Lángoš's, arguing that "regarding people in public functions, I would immediately propose that they resign." Boris Farkaš agreed, stating somewhat ruefully,

> Of course, they [the names] would have to be made public, and of course, people ought not to be in functions. With us, no one is heading to the streets for the sake of this ... because there is no lustration law. Our citizens are accustomed to this. They are also accustomed to the fact that it is normal that such people are in office ... If we had lustration law, then not only the government, but also the parliament would fall apart. In the Czech Republic, a lustration law exists, they live with it; we live in a different reality.[114]

As Farkaš pointed out, file access in the absence of lustration may affect society quite differently from one in the process of being lustrated.

Interestingly, the internet publication of names has sparked some self-lustration, as well as some scandals. The lists included several cabinet members, Members of Parliament—including the Speaker—and bishops and archbishops.[115] Some resigned, complying with Slovak President Ivan Gašparovič's suggestion that "[t]hose who really did actively cooperate with the StB should leave of their own accord."[116] Others have fought the accusation, denying that they collaborated with the StB and seeking legal recourse. These revelations have met a mixed reaction in the broader Slovak public as well; like the political and cultural elites surveyed above, some think that those implicated should quit positions of authority, while others take the view of one Bratislava secretary, who argued, "Some of these people may have done something wrong but bringing it all up and punishing them by forcing them out of their jobs isn't going to undo that wrong."[117] One analyst placed the indifference of many Slovaks in the context of recent opinion polls which found that only 20 percent of Slovaks find the current political and economic system in the country superior to the communist system.[118] Ultimately, the political will for opening the StB files to the public was lower in Slovakia than in the Czech Republic, but both countries have struggled with the moral ambiguities inherent in making public the records of an organization built upon deceit, blackmail, and treachery.

Prosecutions, criminals, and criminality of the communist regime

Czechoslovakia

Ruti Teitel has observed that "[t]he defining feature of the rule of law in periods of political change is that it preserves some degree of continuity in the legal form, while it enables normative change."[119] Of course, legal continuity with a preceding regime severely complicates the prospect of prosecuting its officials, to the extent that their actions—though unjust or illegal by the new regime's standards—were legal under the old. During the first years after the Velvet Revolution, then, the Czech and Slovak Federative Republic, which recognized legal continuity with its predecessor, prosecuted few former officials. Still, it did bring charges against several high-ranking individuals for repressing demonstrators during 1988 and 1989 in ways illegal even under the former regime. Former Communist Party leader Miroslav Stepan was tried and convicted of abuse of power in 1990 and spent 15 months in prison. Courts martial of former Interior ministers Frantisek Kincl, former Chief of Counter-espionage Karel Vykypel, and former Deputy Minister Alojz Lorenc (the General who presided over the shredding of the StB files) for using illegal methods against dissidents followed in October 1992. Kincl and Vykpel were both imprisoned, but Lorenc escaped to his native Slovakia and when the state split, he was not extradited back to the Czech Republic. In 2001, a Slovak military court gave him a suspended 15-month sentence after convicting him of similar offenses, though it found that far fewer specific instances of illegal detention could be proven.

The Czech Republic

While the Czech–Slovak split was a blessing for Lorenc, the new Czech state quickly became a less friendly place for the communist regime's former officials.

In 1993, Parliament passed the Act on the Illegality of the Communist Regime and Resistance to It. In Article 2, it declares the Communist regime "criminal, illegal, and contemptible" and the Czechoslovak Communist Party "a criminal and contemptible organization." The Act also exempts crimes committed during the regime from statutes of limitation if the perpetrator was not convicted or had charges against him dismissed for "political reasons incompatible with the basic principles of the legal order of a democratic state." The Czech Constitutional Court upheld the Act when 41 Parliamentary Deputies challenged it as retroactive, affirming in its ruling the previous regime's illegitimacy.

Having laid the groundwork for investigating and prosecuting certain of the previous regime's actions, Parliament set up the Office for the Documentation and Investigation of the Crimes of Communism (ÚDV) in 1995. The ÚDV merged two pre-existing offices: a Ministry of Interior commission tasked with initiating criminal proceedings against StB members, and the Center for the Documentation of the Unlawfulness of the Communist Regime, which had only a documentary function. The ÚDV is part of the Czech Police, governed by the Direction of the Minister of the Interior No. 5/2001. The documentation portion of its mandate spans from 1 January 1945 to 29 December 1989, and contributes to a number of publications, including educational materials distributed in the schools. The investigation mandate covers the period from 25 February 1948 until 29 December 1989. The actual filing of charges and prosecution is done by the state attorney, and the courts decide the guilt or innocence of the accused. Facilitating this work, in December 1999 Parliament extended the statute of limitations for serious crimes committed under the communist regime, allowing the ÚDV to continue investigating cases.

During its first twelve years (1995–2007), the ÚDV investigated over 3,000 such cases. As of 1 January 2008, these investigations had led to the prosecution of 192 people in 98 criminal cases.[120] These charges led to 30 final judgments resulting in prison terms ranging from six months to five years (the sole five-year sentence went to 85-year-old Jaroslav Daniel, an especially brutal StB agent). Of the crimes prosecuted, the most frequent was "abuse of powers of a public official," with 119 such offenses. The next most frequent were bodily injury, with 22 offenses, and murder and high treason, each with 13.[121] The most common positions held by those prosecuted at the time of the offense are Chief of the State Security (StB), Investigator of the State Security (StB), soldier of a border patrol, and member of the StB. The years when the most prosecuted offenses occurred were 1978 (35 offenses), 1968 (14), and 1950 (14), and the most common age of the prosecuted persons at the time they were notified of the accusation was between 69 and 75 (the range was between 30 and 87).

The three years with the highest number of offenses—1950, 1968, and 1978—correspond to the three most repressive periods in Czechoslovak history: the Stalinist terror, the invasion and repression of the Prague Spring, and the normalization-era persecution of the dissident movement. Teitel observes that in post-communist Eastern Europe, transitions "are haunted by a pervasive sense of occupation, analogous to postwar defeat," and therefore that "[s]uccessor trials are conceived around defining juncture points, drawing the line between freedom and repression, resistance and collaboration."[122] In Teitel's view, the crushing of the Prague Spring was such a juncture point in the former Czechoslovakia. The investigation and prosecution of Czech Communists who invited Soviet troops into their country have, however, mostly failed to produce convictions. Over the course of the 1990s, 11 leading communists who aided the invasion—including Miloš Jakeš, the former Communist Party General Secretary, Karel Hoffman, former head of telecommunications, and General Karel Rusov, the Army Chief of Staff who ordered Czechoslovak troops to remain in the barracks when the country was invaded—were investigated, but the Czech courts (often under communist-era judges) repeatedly sent cases back to prosecutors citing procedural errors or the statute of limitations.[123] In late 2001, after having their cases returned to them twice, prosecutors indicted Jakeš and Jozef Lenárt, a Communist-era Prime Minister, on charges of treason and trying to subvert the republic by collaborating with the Soviet invaders. Both were eventually acquitted for lack of evidence. Finally, in 2003, Karel Hoffman was convicted of sabotage for blocking a radio announcement made by the Central Committee of the (Prague Spring) Czechoslovak Communist Party declaring the Soviet invasion "a violation not only of relations between socialist countries but also of international law."[124] Hoffman began his four-year sentence in 2004, at age 80, as the only top Czech official to be sentenced for actions related to the 1968 invasion. Many speculate that he may also be the last.

Prosecutors have made better headway in bringing charges against individuals involved in the infamous anti-dissident Operation *Asanace* (discussed above), and a number of officials from both the Interior Ministry and the StB have been sentenced. These cases included charges that the secret police choked one dissident with a wet towel until he lost consciousness, broke into another's house and physically attacked her, and shoved a vinyl record into the mouth of still another, threatening to hang him, and beating him with an iron bar. The punishment for such crimes has ranged from suspended sentences to four years in jail. These results prompted one Radio Prague reporter (among others) to ask, "Is it enough, given how few were brought to justice overall?"[125]

While observers of transitional justice have praised the ÚDV for documenting past human rights abuses, the results of its criminal justice efforts are generally seen as disappointing. It has had to drop more than 2000 cases. According to ÚDV Deputy Director Pavel Bret, the challenges it faces are significant.[126] The passage of time has damaged many cases, as often the victims are no longer alive, there are few to no witnesses, and original materials have been destroyed. Further complicating the situation, many of the accused were originally policemen, prosecutors, judges, and high political officials who had professional knowledge of how to eliminate evidence. In addition, many crimes were committed in buildings owned by the state police, when victims were in investigative custody, detention, or prison, minimizing the number of witnesses and making it more likely that the crimes would never be exposed. Officials falsified the cause of death on medical records, and people pled guilty under unacceptable conditions, still giving the appearance of being convicted according to the law. Bret offered the failed 2001 prosecution of former Prime Minister Lubomir Strougal as an example. Strougal was charged with covering up the murders of three anti-Communist activists, who secret police tortured and shot in 1949, but sufficient evidence of his order simply did not exist.[127] In such cases, Bret observed, the outcome must always favor the accused, and law and power must not be intermingled, as it was before 1989.[128] Thus, in an irony typical of transitional justice, the requirements of Czech due process often preclude the prosecution of those who violated due process in the past.

Slovakia

Like its Czech counterpart, the Slovak Parliament passed a law on the immorality and illegality of the communist regime. The final version of the 1996 law modified the original bill, changing the description of the Communist Party from "a criminal organization responsible for violating human rights and spreading terror" to "a party which did not prevent its members from committing crimes."[129] The main support for the bill came from two staunch political rivals, Mečiar's HZDS and the Christian Democratic Movement (KDH). Petr Brnak of the HZDS congratulated the Parliament containing "92 former communists" for passing such a bill.

In late 1999, then Justice Minister Ján Čarnogurský set up a Department for the Documentation of Crimes Committed by the Communist Regime within the Ministry to provide legal advice to people seeking to be restituted or rehabilitated after incarceration or persecution by communist authorities. Most of the claims it received sought compensation for job or property loss, and the office made rather slow progress on these. According to Slovak *Pravda*, the Minister's original plans were more expansive: he had "tried to set up an Office for the Documentation of the Crimes of Communism, but did not find support from his coalition partners, and the office turned into just a two-member department of the Ministry of Justice"[130] staffed by Čarnogurský, who has since gone back to private legal practice, and Marian Gula, who went on to the Board of Directors of the Institute for National Memory.

The Slovak government has shown little interest in prosecuting former officials. As noted above, a Bratislava military court did convict Lorenc of abuse of office and gave him a suspended sentence (he became a successful businessman in Slovakia). Charges were also brought against former high Czechoslovak official Vasil Bilak for treason (for signing the letter that invited the Warsaw Pact to invade Czechoslovakia in 1968) and for violating foreign-currency regulations. In 2001, a regional court returned the case to the prosecution, citing "serious shortcomings." The Prosecutor-General appealed, but the Slovak Supreme Court upheld the regional court ruling in 2002, when Bilak was already 84 years old. Langoš stated that he expected that the Institute for National Memory would request the indictment of certain StB officers based on their findings in the files, and in late 2007 the Institute's documentation department announced it was preparing five proposals for prosecution.[131] To date, however, Lorenc is the only high official to have been brought before a Slovak court for offenses committed under the communist regime, and none has served jail time in Slovakia. Thus, though both the Czech and Slovak Parliaments denounced the previous regime as "illegal," the Czech Republic did so in stronger terms and the ramifications have been different. And while the Czech system is often criticized for its few successful cases and light sentences, the contrast between the countries on this issue—which should not be overstated—is nevertheless real.

Assessing transitional justice's goals and outcomes: Czech and Slovak perspectives

Having offered a broad overview of the development of and debates over transitional justice in Czechoslovakia and its successor states, in this section I narrow my focus to how several lawmakers, transitional justice officials, and former dissidents and political prisoners (in some cases these categories overlap) assess the goals, means, and outcomes of transitional justice at a distance of roughly 15 years from the Velvet Revolution. In interviewing them, I found lustration to be by far the most controversial issue; no one expressed deep reservations about file access (though some see the Czech Archive Law 499/2004 as unjustly invading StB victims' privacy) and people seldom lingered on the issue of prosecution, though no one was particularly impressed by its results. Following this emphasis, my discussion focuses on three lustration goals (both official and alleged) and their outcomes that, across the course of my interviews, appeared to me to be the subject of particular concern and disagreement. These lustration goals are protecting state security, gaining a power advantage over political rivals, and drawing a moral distinction between collaborators and non-collaborators. I conclude with a brief overview of the key challenges to transitional justice my sources identified and the lessons they drew from their countries' experiences.

The first of the three lustration goals—the protection of state security—is one that Toman, as one of the law's authors, identified as its central purpose. He justified it according to the government's right to decide who exercises its powers and to exclude from this exercise those who pose a risk to its security. He added that the 17 November Commission had found people with StB links "everywhere" in the new democratic institutions, and that protecting the state from them was a temporary, "revolutionary standard." Many I spoke to agreed with, or at least understood, this justification, given the uncertainty of the transition's early days. Others, however, were highly critical of it; Ján Kavan (who was one of the ten deputies named by on television in 1991 by Toman, but challenged the charges in a long court battle that he won) argues that the regime was on "sandy legs and rotten to the core already by 1989. It collapsed like a deck of cards here."[132] It was therefore ludicrous, in his view, to argue the old regime was capable in 1991 of challenging or toppling the democratic transition. Jičinský offers a similarly strong rejection of the security threat argument used today, observing that returning to communism is simply not a possibility now that the Soviet Union is gone, the Czech Republic is part of the EU and NATO, and the country has a market system linked into the global economy.

While views vary on the legitimacy of state security as goal of the lustration law, there is broader agreement that one of its outcomes was to encourage many compromised elites to move into the newly private economic sphere. Pehe argued that they "simply used their connections, contacts, networks, and probably even money they had stashed away in Swiss banks to start very nice careers in the economy, and they are now very rich and very influential as a result."[133] He further observed that while it is preferable not to have an StB agent in the government, the same agent probably would have even more influence as, for example, the Chairman of the Board of a large Czech chemical company, a position that allows him to "hold hostage" many a politician needing money.[134] While no one suggested that the private sphere should also be lustrated, the powerful presence of these elites in the economy disconcerted many.

This raises a second of lustration's controversial outcomes: that, in defining the categories that constitute a threat to the state, it netted "small fish" and let the "big fish" go. As Hubert Procházka and Čestmír Čejka of the Confederation of Political Prisoners of the Czech Republic (KPV) observed, if an informer became a member of the Communist Party, they were deregistered by the StB, meaning that the lists are of non-communist informers of lower function.[135] Kavan, as well, argues that the law targeted those who collaborated under personal pressures "rather than the people who created those files, the big cheese who gave the orders, the top guys of the secret service. They didn't create files for themselves. So it's true – there are no files on them. But does that mean that they are less guilty? Those who made the decisions?"[136] Flowing from the first outcome noted here (that old elites are thriving in the economy), there is a pervasive view that, in lustration's wake, the big fish are living the "good life"[137] while laughing at the little ones left struggling.[138]

While most agree that post-communism has not been too hard on the former high officials, it is worth noting that some do not find that this outcome undermines transitional justice. I asked ÚDV Deputy Director Pavel Bret how valid he finds the "big versus little fish" criticism, as it is also often levied at his office. He compared the situation to Nazi Germany, where many argued that responsibility for the Third Reich's crimes fell only on Hitler, or perhaps also his top officials. Bret argued that as in Germany, the crimes would not have been committed without executioners willing to take up the task, and that co-responsibility must also be attributed at the lower levels.

The second lustration goal—that of gaining a power advantage over political rivals, particularly by the Right over the Left—was never an official goal, but is one that lustration's opponents (as well as many scholarly observers) argue is clearly at work. Kavan suggests that his own case was an example of this goal's outcomes, as he believes he was targeted by the 17 November Commission in part because he was critical of the economic transition based on rapid privatization favored by many in the new government. Jičinský made a similar allegation, arguing that in the broader struggle over the state's future, and in particular over the extent to which capitalism will have a "social" nature, the issue of the past (including lustration) is often used instrumentally by the Right to undermine its rivals.

Quoting Orwell, he noted that who controls the past, controls the future. Others, however, strongly dispute that one of lustration's outcomes has been to seriously undercut the Left, and particularly the Communist Party. According to the KPV representatives, despite lustration, Communists continue to influence Czech society, spreading lies just as they did before 1948. Pavel Bret similarly observed that even though Parliament passed a law declaring the Communist Party a criminal organization, it still functions. And Pehe, a critic of lustration, agreed, arguing that lustration is simply easier than actually "doing something about the Communist Party." It is also important to note that in Slovakia, both Langoš and Čarnogurský saw the strength of the *anti*-lustration and file access positions throughout the 1990s as both an outcome of, and a support for, the HZDS and SDL' power advantage (both parties include many former communists).[139]

While the goals of state security and power advantage (and their outcomes) were controversial, the most heated disagreement among my sources surrounded a third lustration goal: distinguishing morally between collaborators and non-collaborators. This distinction of course falls far short of a criminal judgment or punishment; still, there was quite a difference of opinion on its ramifications. The first outcome that some identify is the ascription of collective guilt, a charge familiar from every debate over lustration since 1991.[140] In essence, they argue that it is impossible to determine moral responsibility sufficient to justify lustration simply from someone's falling within the law's broad categories, without knowing the individual circumstances of the case. Several sources offered a number of examples where moral condemnation would be difficult when one takes circumstances into account, such as the case of a woman contact of Charter 77 signatory Jiřína Šiklová (herself one of the StB's main targets), who acted as a "cover" author for Šiklová's translations and put her address at the disposal of several dissidents. When the StB came after this woman, Šiklová counseled her to cooperate in benign ways and to report back to her, allowing the dissidents' productive relationship with the woman to go forward. After the revolution, the woman was accused of collaboration and faced difficulty getting a particular job. Another of Šiklová's friends, a poet, became suicidal when he was named as a collaborator; Šiklová knew that he had only given authorities her name with her express consent while he was ill and in prison and had withheld much information that could have harmed others. The law makes no allowance for such mitigating circumstances, and many people suffered terribly from being categorized as collaborators.

Others, and in particular Toman and the KPV spokesmen, countered that the law requires that there be proof that *each* person did, in fact, collaborate. Moreover, the lustration act's specified categories are composed of people who chose their fate, even if under some kind of pressure, as opposed to being born into it. Toman said that he understood why people made the decisions they did, especially when their children's education was at stake. Still, he argued that having made that choice, they also needed to understand that among the many and great possibilities in life, the option of being a civil servant would be closed to them for a time. The lustration law itself also does not make the names of those affected public, making the consequences of falling within its scope relatively mild.

Many also argued that the file access laws, by making available necessary contextual information, have mitigated the problem of insufficient assessment of collaborators' individual responsibility, at least in the broader eyes of society. At the same time, both file access and lustration depend on the records of an unsavory and treacherous group. Some, including Toman, the KPV representatives, Brunnhofer, Langoš, and Čarnogurský nevertheless expressed confidence in the reliability of the information contained in the remaining StB files. According to Brunnhofer, the StB operated within a system of controls that required that collaborators meet not only with an overseeing agent, but also occasionally with this agent's boss (though Brunnhofer did state that some controls may have slipped at the very end of the regime), making it difficult to include innocent people in the lists of collaborators. Pehe, on the other hand, expressed serious doubts about the files' trustworthiness. He offered the example of a friend who had gone to Pardubice to see her file, checked it against her diary, and found that the agent following her had reported that she had been in the spa town of České Budějovice over a weekend when she had been elsewhere. Pehe guessed that the agent had simply wanted to take a little vacation, and warned that "there is simply no reason to believe that in a corrupt regime, the secret police was not corrupt." For his part, Čarnogurský, found the state's official use of the files distasteful (though necessary), as in a sense the democratic legal order thereby "renewed" the secret police's "unjust criteria" for assessing people.

A second outcome of the moral distinction underlying the lustration law is that many people have conveniently interpreted it to mean that those *not* falling within its categories have been cleared of responsibility for the previous regime's injustices. According to several sources, this is an entirely illegitimate conclusion. Šiklová observes that the regime succeeded in making almost everyone complicit; for several years after the 1968 invasion, for example, everyone who wanted to keep their job was required to sign a declaration stating that the occupation was not in fact an occupation. Šiklová views this act as qualitatively the same as those who signed collaboration agreements with the StB, which precludes the moral exoneration that many would like to take from the lustration law. Making a similar point, Pehe observes that the law does not apply to communists below the district level. No one, however, attempted to recruit such people to become informers, partly because no one would trust them and partly because it was already part of their job as a Party member to inform. In practice, this places the ordinary communist and the informer in the same position, but only one falls on the far side of the law's moral divide. Pehe thus argues that the law "was an administrative measure that artificially divided society into 'bad people' and 'good people,'" allowing people to avoid honestly and inclusively discussing the difficult issue of responsibility for the regime's injustices.

This brings me, finally, to a point of agreement among those I interviewed: not a single person thought that either the Czechs or Slovaks had come close to adequately dealing with the past (a view further reflected in a November 2007 poll showing that most Czechs feel that the country has not come to terms with former members of the StB[141]). My sources spoke of the profound difficulty of the project, and identified several particular challenges. One is that there is not just "one past." Those who lived through the Stalinism had a very different experience from those who only knew the normalization regime, and the KPV spokesmen, Šiklová, and Jičinský all stressed that the political prisoners of the 1950s were subjected to a very different level of repression than the dissidents of the 1970s and 1980s. Thus, "settling accounts" means different things to different generations and to different segments of society.[142] Second, both Šiklová and Jičinský told me that the Velvet Revolution was a time of great uncertainty and many dissidents felt unprepared for leadership (especially given the lack of broadly organized opposition in the country) and very unsure about the regime's ability to reassert itself.[143] This complicated their ability to make the necessary quick and assertive decisions regarding the state security service and its files. And third, the nature of the wrongs committed under the previous regime makes responding to them extraordinarily difficult. Bret observed that the problems they produce are in a sense too deep for a criminal law response alone. Toman agreed, arguing that the issue in many cases is not criminal guilt, but a "human guilt" which defies weighing and measuring.[144] Defining a proper response is further complicated by the dramatically shifting moral standards that accompany such a transition; as Šiklová argues, such transitions result in a state of anomie. Pehe adds that it is difficult to condemn one's own past, comparing it to "amputating part of your personality." Finally, bringing the issue to a personal level, Brunnhofer admitted to simply not knowing what it means to "settle accounts"; he himself was dealing with the fact that a friend had informed on him, which he only found out after the friend died. His own questions face the entire society on a grand scale, and defy ready answers: "How can you cope with this? How can you come to terms with this?"[145]

Having identified formidable challenges, several sources also drew specific lessons from the Czech and Slovak experiences with transitional justice. Both Šiklová and the KPV spokesmen argue that in order to protect the files and their information from being falsified or manipulated, the government should have published the list of people involved with the StB quickly, along with a full explanation of the state security hierarchy and how the system worked. The KPV representatives further argued that all StB documents should have been rapidly declassified. Beyond this, the KPV argued that there should have been legal continuity with the First Republic (1918–1938) rather than the communist regime, so as to avoid its distortions and more easily prosecute its criminals. Like the KPV, Kavan found significant fault with the post-communist judicial system, arguing that transitional state leaders should make it a top priority to construct an independent judiciary capable of responding to the human rights violations of the previous regime. He acknowledged that justice would be a longer-term process than that offered by Czech lustration, but would avoid the pitfalls of "revolutionary justice."[146] Finally, for his part, Pehe drew lessons from other countries' experiences, arguing that the Polish approach to lustration is preferable to the Czech, as it avoids the problem of collective guilt; that a South African-type truth commission would be helpful for prompting people to discuss and confront the past; and finally, as in Germany after World War II, it would likely be the sons and daughters of perpetrators and victims who would first be capable of reckoning with the past. This last argument is another key point of agreement among these sources; almost all of them expected that coming to terms with the past will take at least one and likely more generations.

Conclusion

Given the fact that the Czechs and Slovaks were citizens of the same regimes for most of the twentieth century, the contrast between their records on transitional justice is quite striking. The Czechs quickly undertook and continue to pursue relatively strenuous lustration (even if one takes into account the criticism leveled at its outcomes), while the Slovaks never engaged in the practice seriously. The Czech Republic has also offered progressively greater file access to its citizens, beginning much earlier than Slovakia and today allowing substantially broader investigation of the archives. And finally, while neither state has engaged in much successful "prosecution and punishment," the Czechs investigated more cases and both prosecuted and sentenced to prison significantly more members of the communist regime. In this final section, I return to the question of the extent to which these policies have been shaped by the factors of regime type, transition type, and the relative power of former communists and opposition.

The evidence offered in this chapter indicates that the Czech and Slovak cases conform most strongly to patterns associated with regime type: during the last twenty years of communism, the Czechs lived under bureaucratic authoritarianism and the Slovaks under a combination of national-accommodative and patrimonial communism. Theories focusing on this distinction correctly predict that transitional justice would be stronger among the Czechs and weaker among the Slovaks. Transition type is a good bit more problematic: according to regional patterns, the Czechoslovak regime's capitulation would indicate a higher likelihood of strong transitional justice, which of course did not happen in Slovakia. And finally, the relative power of former communists versus their opposition does seem to be related to the progress of transitional justice in the two states. In the Czech Republic, the center-right was dominant until 1997, and continues to be fairly strong, though it is well matched by the center-left. In Slovakia, the populist-nationalist-left (including many former communists) was dominant until 1998, and since has been fairly well matched by a shaky coalition that leans somewhat to the center-right (the coalitions are ideologically fractious, however). Thus, during the early-to-mid 1990s, things went as one would expect: strong transitional justice under the Right in the Czech Republic, and weak justice under the formerly communist Left in Slovakia. Things become less straightforward, however, in the period after Klaus and Mečiar's dominance: the Czech Republic under the center-left continued with strong transitional justice, and while file access was finally made possible under the center-right in Slovakia, most of its leaders did not otherwise show interest in more vigorous policies.

It appears, then, that these cases also offer several deviations from expected patterns: transition type was not predictive for Slovakia; prosecution numbers are fairly low in the "prosecuting and punishing" Czech Republic; and the shift in the balance of power between right and left in the two states in the later 1990s did not produce a particularly strong reorientation of transitional justice policy. I would further argue that these puzzles may be at least partially explained if we focus on a factor that is embedded but not explicit in the three larger factors: the normative orientation of dominant elites. If we recall Eyal's analysis of elites in the normalization-era Czech and Slovak Republics, we find a large number of Slovak elites invested in and co-opted by the regime, and a large number of Czech elites alienated or internally exiled. Not long after the Velvet Revolution, these same elites, with their very different orientations, became dominant in each of the two republics. The elections that made this possible overrode the importance of the transition type in Slovakia: the former communists do not need major concessions from the opposition during the transition itself if they are able to move right back into power via the ballot box. (Indeed, given the quite different relationship between regime and society in the Slovak Republic, it seems possible that if it had not been part of a federation with the Czechs, it might well have undergone a different transition type, more similar, perhaps, to that in Hungary.) It is also worth noting here that the regime's rapid collapse did not prevent its officials from destroying large numbers of files, thereby undermining its successor's ability to undertake stronger transitional justice. Based on my discussions with former dissidents and lawmakers involved in the revolution, it appears that massive capitulation, in a state where the opposition had almost no political experience, can lead to massive confusion among those newly taking up the reigns of power. In other words, the regime's weakness does not necessarily lead to strong leadership on the part of its rivals, and the benefits of being on the winning end of capitulation may therefore be overrated.

Moving into the post-communist period, I would argue that the normative orientation of dominant elites not only helps explain transitional justice choices in the early 1990s, but also in the post-Klaus and post-Mečiar periods. Here, the overview of elite perspectives on goals and outcomes that I offered in the preceding section may be instructive. The Czechs I interviewed spanned the moderate political spectrum, and included both strong supporters and strong critics of lustration. Interestingly, the grounds on which they assess the legitimacy of lustration's outcomes were, across the board, consistent with liberal democratic principles. They judged the outcomes of compromised elites in the economy and the escape of the "big fish" according to the principles of moral accountability for bad acts and for fairness in the economic marketplace. On the issue of the use of lustration for power advantages, the left-leaning critics again expressed a concern for fairness (or procedural justice, to use Noel Calhoun's term[147]), while those who leaned to the right stressed the need for accountability (or substantive justice), particularly for the communists that they see as morally equivalent to Nazis. And with regard to the question of distinctions between collaborators and non-collaborators, everyone—both those decrying the principle of collective guilt and those defending against that charge, as well as those calling for a broader societal reckoning—stressed the importance of *individual* responsibility, a cornerstone of liberal political philosophy. Thus, their normative orientation was, by and large, supportive of the moral reasoning of transitional justice.

The Slovaks I interviewed fell within this philosophical rubric as well, and it is clear that others, such as the Slovak artists interviewed by *Sme* and the authors surveyed by *Kritika y Kontext*, share their views. Based on voting records and polling data, as well as impressionistic accounts by various commentators, however, it appears that their perspectives on transitional justice's importance are not the *dominant* ones in Slovakia. That the state policies reflect popular preferences, at least to some degree, is in a sense a testament to the strength of both Czech and Slovak democracy. At the same time, it would appear that liberalism is a good bit more powerful among Czechs than Slovaks, and helps to explain why in the Czech Republic even under governments led by the center-left, we find relatively strong continuing support for transitional justice, while under the center-right in Slovakia we do not.

This is certainly not to argue that most or all Czech elites are principled liberals or committed democrats. As Calhoun points out, during times of transition and after, many former communists understand well that they "can use the language of democracy to ensure their future right to participate in the government, while invoking liberalism's limitations on state powers to safeguard themselves against future retribution."[148] It would be naïve and dangerous to overlook the role that rational calculation plays in political rhetoric. This point may, in fact, offer insight the Czech Republic's low prosecution rates, as roughly half of its judges are communist-era elites, educated under that system and, one would expect in at least some cases, invested in it to some extent.[149] Given their ties to the regime, the normative orientation that they bring to transitional justice may be less supportive than that of some other elites. At the same time, the fact that they have learned the language of liberal democracy may work to the advantage of defendants who, in the past, operated under rules that always favored the state. This is certainly not a full explanation for the low rates of successful prosecution, and the difficulties that Pavel Bret identified are clearly important here as well. Still, it points to the role that normative orientations may play in shaping not only the construction of policy, but also its implementation. Ultimately, in the Czech and Slovak cases, the dominant normative orientations of elites help to link the three broader factors of regime type, transition type, and the relative electoral strength of former communists and their opposition by offering a thread of continuity, in the midst of change, in people's understanding of the nature and purposes of political power.

Notes

1 M. Kraus, 'Settling Accounts: Postcommunist Czechoslovakia', in N. Kritz (ed.) *Transitional Justice: How Emerging Democracies Reckon with Former Regimes,* vol. II, Washington, D.C.: United States Institute of Peace, 1995, p. 544.
2 Ibid.
3 K. Williams, 'The StB in Czechoslovakia, 1945–89', in K. Williams and D. Deletant, *Security Intelligence Services in New Democracies: The Czech Republic, Slovakia and Romania*, New York: Palgrave, 2001, p. 28.

4 Ibid., p. 30.
5 P. Blažek and P. Žáček, 'Czechoslovakia', in K. Persak and Ł. Kamiński (eds) *A Handbook of the Communist Security Apparatus in East Central Europe 1944–1989*, Warsaw: Institute of National Remembrance, 2005, p. 89.
6 Ibid. for a comprehensive account of the StB's many restructurings.
7 Williams, 'The StB in Czechoslovakia', p. 31.
8 Blažek and Žáček, 'Czechoslovakia', p. 94.
9 Williams, 'The StB in Czechoslovakia', p. 32, and Blažek and Žáček, 'Czechoslovakia', p. 94.
10 Williams, 'The StB in Czechoslovakia', p. 32.
11 Ibid.
12 Blažek and Žáček, 'Czechoslovakia', pp. 106–7.
13 Williams, 'The StB in Czechoslovakia', p. 32.
14 Though StB terminology changed over the course of the regime, Kieran Williams identifies six categories of collaborators, the first four of which are considered "secret co-workers," usually involving a written agreement and sometimes payment: agent, the "top class of informer," trusted to infiltrate both foreign and domestic groups; informant, a lower form of agent, tasked with getting information from those close to foreign and domestic groups; resident, go-betweens between case officers and five to eight informants; occupant of safe house, a person who either allowed the StB to use their apartment or posed as the occupant of an Interior Ministry property; confidant, an ambiguous designation where no formal agreement or assignments were involved; according to Williams, the "information provided was probably highly anecdotal and unsystematic, relating largely to morale in strategic enterprises," and it was not always clear if the person understood that he or she was communicating with the StB; and candidate, a person the StB hoped to recruit as an agent. Williams, 'The StB in Czechoslovakia, 1945–89', p. 33.
15 Ibid., p. 34.
16 Ibid., p. 35.
17 Of these, 9,399 were targeting the "internal enemy," 4,852 the "external enemy," and 10,723 the protection of the economy. There were also 1,456 registered safe houses. Blažek and Žáček, 'Czechoslovakia', p. 130.
18 Ibid., p. 112.
19 Williams, 'The StB in Czechoslovakia', pp. 37–8.
20 Blažek and Žáček, 'Czechoslovakia', p. 114.
21 Ibid., p. 116.
22 Williams, 'The StB in Czechoslovakia', pp. 25–26, and R. David, 'Lustration Laws in Action: The Motives and Evaluation of Lustration Policy in the Czech Republic and Poland (1981–2001)', *Law and Social Inquiry*, 2003, vol. 28, 396, fn 22. David's figure of 8,000 includes those killed trying to leave the country. Some survivors barely made it out alive. A member of the Confederation of Political Prisoners of the Czech Republic I interviewed told me that when he left the uranium mines, he weighed about 40 kg.
23 'Czech Informers' Names Published', *BBC News*, 20 March 2003. Online. Available HTTP: http://news.bbc.co.uk/2/hi/europe/2868701.stm (accessed 27 January 2008).
24 Williams, 'The StB in Czechoslovakia', p. 42.
25 One of the Slovak reformers' key slogans was "Federalization first!," meaning, before democratization.
26 C. Skalnik Leff, *National Conflict in Czechoslovakia: The Making and Remaking of a State, 1918–1987*, Princeton: Princeton University Press, 1988, p. 261.
27 'Češi, Slováci, a federace', p. 24.
28 P. Pithart, 'Towards a Shared Freedom, 1968–1989', in J. Musil (ed.) *The End of Czechoslovakia*, Budapest: Central European University, 1995, p. 211.

29 G. Eyal, *The Origins of Postcommunist Elites: From Prague Spring to the Breakup of Czechoslovakia*, Minneapolis: University of Minnesota Press, 2003, p. 28.
30 Pithart, 'Towards a Shared Freedom', p. 211.
31 K. Zlobina, 'Slovensko: impresie a depresie', *Listy*, 1978, vol. 8, 45.
32 H. G. Skilling, *Charter 77 and Human Rights in Czechoslovakia*, London: Allen and Unwin, 1981, p. 57.
33 Technocrats found hope in reform communism, nationalist intellectuals in historical reinterpretation, and managers felt linked to the success of state enterprises. Eyal, *The Origins of Postcommunist Elites*, p. 103.
34 V. Průcha, 'Economic Development and Relations, 1918–1989', in Musil, *The End of Czechoslovakia*, p. 75.
35 For a more in-depth consideration of this question, see N. Nedelsky, 'Divergent Responses to a Common Past: Transitional Justice in the Czech Republic and Slovakia', *Theory and Society*, 2004, vol. 33, 65–111.
36 Williams, 'The StB in Czechoslovakia', pp. 46 and 48.
37 Some of the StB's functions were immediately inherited by seven new agencies, including the Bureau for the Protection of the Constitution and Democracy (ÚOÚD). The ÚOÚD faltered badly, and was renamed the Federal Information Service in late 1990. The FIS was, in turn, replaced by the Federal Security Information Service (FBIS) in May 1991, which lasted until the end of the common statehood in December 1992. Thereafter, the Czech Republic set up the Security Information Service (BIS) and Slovakia the Slovak Information Service (SIS), infamous for its illiberal activities under Slovak Prime Minister Mečiar in the mid-1990s (for example, it was involved in the strange abduction of the son of the Slovak President, who was Mečiar's rival). For details, see Williams and Deletant, *Security Intelligence Services in New Democracies*, chapters 3–5, and J. Obrman, 'New Minister Dissolves State Security', *Report on Eastern Europe*, 16 February 1990, p. 11.
38 Whether with Sacher's knowledge or not, a substantial number of files fell into the hands of people interested in blackmailing the new elites. Jiřina Šiklová, a prominent Charter 77 dissident, personally talked with new, high-placed officials who had been approached in these early months by people who had evidence, for example, of their marital infidelity and hoped to use this information from the files to blackmail them. She was also told by a secret police officer that people were selling the files to one another. Interview with Jiřina Šiklová, Prague, 20 October 2005.
39 P. Sustrova, 'The Lustration Controversy', *Uncaptive Minds*, 1992, vol. 5, 130.
40 Interview with Petr Toman, Prague, 18 October 2005.
41 For the text of the parliamentary commission's report, see 'Collaborators Revealed', *Uncaptive Minds*, 1991, vol. 4, 9.
42 'Vetting of Parliament a Necessary Purge, Civic Movement', CTK, 22 March 1991, and 'Ten Collaborators of Former Secret Police in Federal Parliament', CTK, 22 March 1991.
43 Ibid.
44 All citations in this paragraph are from Press Survey, CTK, 23 March 1991.
45 In response to the 17th November Commission's screening efforts, eight political organizations (the Socialist Party, the Farmers' Movement, the Agrarian Party, the People's Party, the Self-government Democracy Movement-Society for Moravia and Silesia, the Greens Party, the Obroda Club and the Social-Democratic Party) wrote a letter to Havel pointing out that cooperating with the StB had not been illegal, but also calling for screening legislation. 'Eight Parties Believe Collaboration with StB is No Crime', CTK, 31 January 1991.
46 For an English translation of the law's text, see Kritz (ed.), *Transitional Justice*, vol. III, pp. 312–321.
47 Article 21, Ibid., p. 320.

48 A 1991 poll showed that 50 per cent of Czechoslovak respondents thought that state office and enterprise personnel situations would benefit from the lustration law. Cited in David, 'Lustration Laws in Action', 394.
49 Ibid., p. 405.
50 Quoted in R. Boed, 'An Evaluation of the Legality and Efficacy of Lustration as a Tool of Transitional Justice', *Columbia Journal of Transnational Law*, 1999, vol. 37, 357–402.
51 Quoted in David, 'Lustration Laws in Action', p. 406.
52 Both Zdeněk Jičinský and Ján Kavan (who was one of the ten deputies named by Toman, but challenged the charges in a long court battle that he won) said that the most important reason they opposed the law was its reliance on the principle of collective guilt. Interviews with Zdeněk Jičinský, Prague, 13 October, and Ján Kavan, Prague, 28 October 2005.
53 Quoted in Boed, 'An Evaluation of the Legality'.
54 Williams, 'Czechoslovakia 1990–2', p. 76.
55 The Constitutional Court Decision on the Screening Law of 26 November 1992 was reprinted in Kritz, *Transitional Justice*, vol. III, pp. 350–1.
56 Eyal, *The Origins of Postcommunist Elites*, p. 143.
57 J.Obrman, 'Slovak Politician Accused of Secret Police Ties', *RFE/RL Research Report*, 12 April 1992, p. 14.
58 Eyal, *The Origins of Postcommunist Elites*, p. 13.
59 Ibid., p. 105.
60 Ibid., p. 161.
61 Ibid., p. 175.
62 N. Adamičková and M. Königová, 'Lustrace se rušit nebudou', *Právo*, 8 December 2005. Online. Available HTTP: http://pravo.newtonit.cz/default.asp?cache=617992 (accessed 8 February 2006).
63 'Lustration Laws Further Valid, Lower House Decides', *CTK/Prague Daily Monitor*, 27 December 2005. Online. Available HTTP: http://www.praguemonitor.com (accessed 23 March 2006).
64 Quoted in K. Tylová and P. Kolář, 'Paroubek chce konec lustrací', *Lidové noviny*, 24 November 2005. Online. Available HTTP: http://www.lidovky.cz/paroubek-zruseni-lustraci-pocka-do3-/ln_domov.asp?c=A051124_144702_ln_domov_lvv (accessed 28 January 2008).
65 Quoted in I. Lamper, 'Respekt Weekly Roundup Nov 26th', *Respekt Weekly Roundup*, 28 November 2005. Online. Available HTTP: http://www.prague.tv/articles/respekt/respekt-26-11-2005 (accessed 28 January 2008).
66 'Lustrace zrušme v roce 2009, říká docent Zdeněk Koudelka', *Právo*, 28 December 2005. Online. Available HTTP: http://www.pravo.newtonit.cz/default.asp?cache=822124 (accessed 8 February 2006).
67 The statistics in this paragraph were provided to me on 1 November 2005 by Dr. Josef Veselý of the Czech Ministry of the Interior's Security Division (*Bezpečností odbor*).
68 Interview with Pavel Brunnhofer, Assistant Director of Archives, Czech Ministry of the Interior, Prague, 19 October 2005.
69 J. Pitkin, 'Influence of Former Communists Ruffles Political Feathers', *The Prague Post*, 13 June 2001. Online. Available HTTP: http://www.praguepost.cz/news061301f.html (accessed 28 January 2008).
70 'Check uncovers 15 former secret police collaborators at Czech police headquarters', Radio Prague News, 18 April 2007. Online. Available HTTP: http://www.radio.cz/en/news/90506#5 (accessed 26 January 2008).
71 I. Radicova, 'The Velvet Divorce', *Uncaptive Minds*, 1993, vol. 6, 51–52.
72 Nedelsky, 'Divergent Responses to a Common Past', p. 93 and Appendices A and B.

73   K. Deegan-Krause, 'From Another Dimension: Public Opinion and Party Competition in Slovakia and the Czech Republic', paper presented at the American Political Science Association conference, Boston, 5 September 1998. Online. Available HTTP: http://www.la.wayne.edu/polisci/kdk/papers/apsa1998p.htm (accessed 28 January 2008). The statement used by the survey was "It is right to forbid certain positions to people with a Communist past."

74   Williams, 'The Czech Republic Since 1993', p. 114.

75   'Screening Commission Wants Names of StB Agents Made Public', CTK, 22 May 1991. Also, interview with Pavel Brunnhofer, Prague, 19 October 2005.

76   'Government Sees Public Naming of StB Collaborators as Imprudent', CTK, 24 May 1991.

77   'Spies Caught in the Web', *Time Europe,* 24 March 2003. Online. Available HTTP: http://www.time.com/time/magazine/article/0,9171,433236,00.html (accessed 28 January 2008).

78   Interviews with Zdeněk Jičinský, Prague, 13 October 2005, and Petr Toman, Prague, 18 October, 2005.

79   I spoke to more than one person in Slovakia who felt that their career and honor were irreparably damaged by the lists, including one person who had a very promising political future in the early 1990s.

80   Interview with Jiří Pehe, Prague, 17 October 2005.

81   Comment made in 1993, quoted in M. Korecký, 'Havlův podpis odtajnil agenty ŠtB', *Lidové noviny,* 14 March 2002. Online. Available HTTP: http://www.lidovky.cz/tisk.asp?c=L063A01A&r=atitulni (accessed 25 March 2002).

82   Williams, 'The Czech Republic Since 1993', p. 114.

83   For the law's details, see the Czech Ministry of the Interior, 'Zpřistupnění svazků vzniklých činností bývalé ŠtB'. Online. Available HTTP: http://www.mvcr.cz/agenda/labyrint/svazky.html (accessed 28 January 2008), B. Janík, 'Havel podpísal zákon o sprístupení zväzkov ŠtB', *Pravda,* 14 March 2002. Online. Available HTTP: http://www.pravda.sk/spravy/2002/03/14/svet/article.34918.html (accessed 29 March 2002), and.Korecký, 'Havlův podpis'.

84   Janík, 'Havel podpisal'.

85   L. Navara and D. Steiner, 'Havlův podpis odmekl archivy ŠtB', *Mladá fronta dnes/idnes,* 14 March 2002. Online. Available HTTP: http://zpravy.idnes.cz/havluv podpis-odemkl-archivy-stb-d46-/domaci.asp?c=A020208_213018_domaci_pol (accessed 28 January 2008).

86   B. Janik, 'Otvorenie Pandorej skrinky vyvoláva v Česku obavy', *Národná obroda,* 11 Februrary 2002. Online. Available HTTP: http://195.168.40.176/20020211/08_006.html (accessed 1 April 2002).

87   P. Uhl, 'Několik argementů pro Havla', *Právo,* 11 March 2002, p. 7. Online. Available HTTP: http://pravo.newtonit.cz/tisk.asp?cache=797095 (accessed 25 March 2002).

88   Quoted in J. Naegele, 'Czech Republic: Bill Would Open Communist Secret Police Files to General Public', *Radio Free Europe/Radio Liberty*, 13 February 2002. Online. Available HTTP: http://www.rferl.org/features/2002/02/13022002085655.asp (accessed 28 January 2008).

89   Janik, 'Otvorenie Pandorej skrinky'. KDU-ČSL representative Josef Janaček also observed that "Fond Z" has been kept from the public since 1989.

90   Quoted in Korecký, 'Havlův podpis odtajnil'.

91   Janik, 'Otvorenie Pandornej skrinky'.

92   Author's correspondence with Charter 77 signatory, Professor Jiřina Šiklová.

93   Statistics in this paragraph are from author's interview with Pavel Brunnhofer, Prague, 19 October 2005.

94   Kusý's response to written questions from the journal's editor, 'Dedičstvo ŠtB na Slovensku', p. 30. Kusý contrasts the lack of Slovak interest to that of the Czechs: "In the Czech lands the young generation of historians has pounced on the topic of recent

history, write professional essays and popular articles on this, publish books. With us it is still only a couple of people who are professionally engaged with this."

95 O. Gyárfašová, 'Fenomén ŠtB v širšom Kontexte', *Kritika & Kontext*, 2001, vol. 2–3, 33.
96 'Orosz označil Langošov zákon o pamäti národa za právny galimatiaš', *Pravda*, 17 October 2001. Online. Available HTTP: http:/www.pravda.sk/spravy/2001/10/17/slovensko/article.900.html (accessed 29 March 2002).
97 L. Živnerová, 'Podporíte odtajnenie zväzkov ŠtB v parlamente?', *Národna obroda*, 30 October 2001, J. Borčin, 'Dokedy bude štát občanmi skrývat' spisy ŠtB?', *Národná obroda*, 21 February 2002, and M. Vagovič, 'Tiene minulosti', *Pravda*, 2 November 2001. Online. Available HTTP: http://www.pravda.sk/dennik/2001/11/02/nazory/01/article.5309.html (accessed 29 March 2002).
98 Quoted in P. Ďurišková, 'Eštebákom hrozia problémy', *Pravda*, 30 October 2001. Online. Available HTTP: http://www.pravda.sk/dennik/2001/10/30/slovensko/01/article.5566.html (accessed 29 March 2002).
99 M. Vagovič, 'Najvišší čas diskuovat' o zločinoch komunistckého režimu', *Pravda*, 16 November 2001. Online. Available HTTP: http://www.pravda.sk/dennik/2001/11/16/slovensko/01/article.14559.html (accessed 29 March 2002).
100 Borčin, 'Dokedy bude štát'.
101 Vagovič, 'Tiene minulosti'.
102 M. Stanislav, 'Osvieženie pamäti', *Pravda*, 7 November 2001. Online. Available HTTP: http://www.pravda.sk/dennik/2001/11/07/nazory/01/article.2819.html (accessed 29 March 2002).
103 P. Vavro, 'Preverení', *Národná obroda*, 22 February 2002.
104 I. Bača, 'Udavači, mate zelenú', *Národná obroda*, 12 February 2002.
105 Interview with Ján Čarnogurský, Bratislava, Slovakia, 2 June 2003.
106 'Slovak Parliament Overrides Presidential Veto', *RFE/RL Newsline*, 21 August 2002. Online. Available HTTP: http://www.rferl.org/newsline/2002/08/3-CEE/cee-210802.asp (accessed 28 January 2008).
107 Ústav pamäti národa, 'Disclosure'. Online. Available HTTP: http://www.upn.gov.sk/?page=disclosure (accessed 28 January 2008).
108 'Slota indifferent to National Memory Institute', *The Slovak Spectator*, 25 September 2006. Online. Available HTTP: http://www.spectator.sk (accessed 25 January 2007).
109 T. Nicholson, 'Nation's Memory Institute Evicted', *The Slovak Spectator,* 8–14 January 2007. Online. Available HTTP: http://www.slovakspectator.sk (accessed 1 August 2007).
110 '764 more StB officers ousted', *The Slovak Spectator*, 14 May 2007. Online. Available HTTP: http://www.spectator.sk (accessed 25 January 2008).
111 Interview with Ján Langoš, Bratislava, Slovakia, 22 May 2003.
112 Interview with Ján Čarnogurský, Bratislava, Slovakia, 2 June 2003.
113 'So zverejnením zväzkov ŠtB slovenskí umelci súhlasa', *Sme*, 25 November 2004. Online. Available HTTP: http://www.sme.sk/clanok.asp?cl=1835468 (accessed 28 January 2008).
114 Ibid.
115 J. Kunicová and M. Nalepa, 'Coming to Terms With the Past: Strategic Institutional Choice in Post-Communist Europe', January 2006. Online. Available HTTP: http://www.sscnet.ucla.edu/polisci/cpworkshop/papers/Kunicova.pdf (accessed 28 January 2008), and A. Purvis, 'Dredging Up Bad Memories', *Time Europe*, 4 April 2005. Online. Available HTTP: http://www.time.com/time/magazine/article/0,9171,1042420,00.html (accessed 28 January 2008).
116 'Ghosts of Communist Past Haunt the Present', Bratislava: IPS/GIN, 25 January 2005. Online. Available HTTP: http://ins.onlinedemocracy.ca/index.php?name=News&file=article&sid=4600&theme=Printer (accessed 28 January 2008).
117 Ibid.

118 L. Kubosova, 'Slovakia: Pandora's Box Online', *Transitions Online*, 16–22 November 2004. Online. Available HTTP: http://www.ciaonet.org/pbei/tol/tol_2004/nov16-nov22/nov16-nov22e.html (accessed 28 January 2008).

119 R. Teitel, *Transitional Justice*, Oxford: Oxford University Press, 2000, p. 21.

120 Statistics in this paragraph conform to The Office for the Documentation and the Investigation of the Crimes of Communism (ÚDV), 'Information about Cases', 1 January 2008. Online. Available HTTP: http://www.mvcr.cz/policie/udv/english/pripady/index.html (accessed 27 January 2008). See also K. McKinsey, 'Czech Republic: Documenting Crimes of the Communist Past', *Radio Free Europe/Radio Liberty*, 9 July 1998. Online. Available HTTP: http://www.b-info.com/places/Bulgaria/news/98–07/jul09b.rfe (accessed 28 January 2008).

121 The other offenses, in declining order of frequency, are: abuse of office or professional authority (12), grievous bodily harm (11), sabotage (8), prohibited acquisition and possession of firearms (5), subversion against the Republic (4), deprivation of personal freedom (4), breach of responsibility of a public official (3), common threat (2) homicide (2), restriction of personal freedom (2), breach of the sentry duty (1), preferential treatment (1), blackmail (1), and expulsion abroad (1).

122 Teitel, *Transitional Justice*, p. 37.

123 F. Harris, "Velvet Justice' for Traitors Who Crushed 1968 Prague Spring', *The Telegraph*, 23 August 1998. Online. Available HTTP: http://www.telegraph.co.uk/html Content.jhtml;jsessionid=V5SUIAXYEKSMTQFIQMGCFF4AVCBQUIV0?html=/archive/1998/08/23/wcze23.html (accessed 28 January 2008).

124 'Former Hard-line Communist Sentenced for Role in 1968 Invasion', *Radio Prague*, 9 June 2003. Online. Available HTTP: http://archiv.radio.cz/ (accessed DATE), and B. Kenety, 'Top Communist, Aged 80, Begins Prison Sentence for Radio 'Sabotage' which Aided 1968 Soviet-led Invasion', *Radio Prague*, 9 August 2004. Online. Available HTTP: http://www.radio.cz/print/en/56873 (accessed 28 January 2008).

125 J. Velinger, 'Asanace – the Communists' Infamous Clearance Operation – Left Indelible Stain on Dissidents' Lives', *Radio Prague*, 31 August 2004. Online. Available HTTP: http://www.radio.cz/en/article/57645 (accessed 28 January 2008). Also 'Two Former StB Officers Charged with Torture', CTK, 14 September 2005.

126 Interview with Dr. Pavel Bret, Deputy Director of the Office for the Documentation and Investigation of the Crimes of Communism, Prague, 19 October 2005.

127 P. Green, 'Czech Communists Face Treason Charge in '68 Soviet Invasion', *The New York Times*, 20 December 2001, Online. Available HTTP: http://query.nytimes.com/gst/fullpage.html?res=9807E2DA133EF933A15751C1A9679C8B63&scp=1&sq=Czech+Communists+Face+Treason+Charge+in+%9268+Soviet+Invasion%92&st=nyt (accessed 28 January 2008).

128 Interview with Pavel Bret, Prague, 19 October 2005.

129 Cited in S. Fisher, 'Slovak Parliament Approves Anti-Communist Law', *OMRI Daily Digest*, 5 February 1996. Online. Available HTTP: http://archive.tol.cz/omri/restricted/article.php3?id=4117 (accessed 28 January 2008).

130 'Langoš predkladá zákon o zločinoch nacizmu a kommunizmu', *Pravda*, 12 October 2001. Online. Available HTTP: http://www.pravda.sk/spravy/2001/10/12/slovensko/article.669.html (accessed 29 March 2002).

131 'Slovak Supreme Court Returns Bilak Case to Prosecution', *RFE/RL Newsline*, 13 March 2002. Online. Available HTTP: http://www.hri.org/news/balkans/rferl/2002/02-03-13.rferl.html (accessed 28 January 2008), and Ľ. Lesná, 'Eighteen years after the revolution, no justice', *The Slovak Spectator*, 19 November 2007. Online. Available HTTP: http://www.spectator.sk (accessed 25 January 2008).

132 Interview with Ján Kavan, Prague, 29 October 2005.

133 Interview with Jiří Pehe, Prague, 17 October 2005.

134 Hubert Procházka and Čestmír Čejka of the Confederation of Political Prisoners of the Czech Republic (KPV) point out that given how many files were allowed to go missing during the Revolution's early days, many elites know their file exists somewhere, and thus can be blackmailed, extending the security threat in individual cases. Interviews with Hubert Procházka and Čestmír Čejka, Prague, 19 October 2005.

135 Ibid.

136 Interview with Ján Kavan, Prague, 29 October 2005.

137 Interview with Jiří Pehe, Prague, 17 October 2005.

138 Interview with Eugen Gindl, Bratislava, Slovakia, May 2003.

139 Interviews with Ján Langoš, Bratislava, Slovakia, 22 May 2003, and Ján Čarnogurský, Bratislava, Slovakia, 2 June 2003.

140 Ibid.

141 'Poll: most Czechs of opinion country has not come to terms with StB collaborators', Radio Prague, 16 November 2007. Online. Available HTTP: http://www.radio.cz/print/en/news/97688 (accessed 26 January 2008).

142 Interview with Zdeněk Jičinský, Prague, 13 October 2005.

143 Šiklová observes that the army was clearly in the hands of the socialist state, hundreds of police officers were waiting for instructions, and several hundred thousand Soviet Army troops were on the territory. Interview with Jiřina Šiklová, Prague, 20 October 2005.

144 Interview with Petr Toman, Prague, 18 October, 2005.

145 Interview with Pavel Brunnhofer, Prague, 19 October 2005.

146 Interview with Ján Kavan, Prague, 29 October 2005.

147 N. Calhoun, *Dilemmas of Justice in Eastern Europe's Democratic Transitions*, New York: Palgrave Macmillan, 2004, p. 170.

148 Ibid., p. 24.

149 This is a point the KPV representatives emphasized.

4   Poland

Lavinia Stan

Poland adopted limited transitional justice almost a decade after its neighbors Germany and the Czech Republic, but de-communization has been one of the most divisive issues in the political life of this young democracy. Poles remain divided about the communist past, its effects on nation-building and political culture, and the way in which the post-communist state should deal with it. Some agree with their country's choice for the Spanish model, where transition to democracy is effected without granting public access to secret archives, prosecuting communist leaders for human rights trespasses and blocking *ancien regime* officials from accessing positions of power and responsibility. Others believe that Poland's soft stand toward communist repression provides the wrong moral example for younger generations, and allows former communists to succeed in the market economy and open electoral competition. Curiously enough, in Poland the strongest case against comprehensive transitional justice was made not by former communists, but by former dissidents fearful of what it would reveal about the opposition movement, while the hostility towards the old political elite was caused not by its opposition to market economy and democracy, but by its successful adaptation to these new conditions.

The Polish political police

After the October 1956 de-Stalinization, the Polish communist secret political police, *Sluzba Bezpieczenstwa* (SB), replaced the Ministry of Public Security (*Ministerstwo Bezpieczenstwa Publicznego*, with its local offices, *Urzad Bezpieczenstwa*) as the political police, intelligence, counter-intelligence, personal protection, and confidential communications agency. The SB, meant to protect "the democratic people's system established by the Constitution of Polish People's Republic and the national interest against enemy espionage and terrorist activity,"[1] was part of the Ministry of Internal Affairs and included departments on intelligence, counterintelligence, combating hostile activity and organized opposition, surveillance of religious organizations, industry, transport, communication and farming, operational technology, correspondence control, radio counter-intelligence, and protection of the party leadership. The total number of full-time agents grew steadily from around 10,000 in 1957 to 25,600 in 1985, in a total population of some 37 million. The agents' profile also changed. Whereas at the beginning of the communist rule most officers were brutish and uneducated, by the late 1980s a majority of them had secondary education and a middle-class background.[2]

The SB was independent of other state administrative organs, but never more than an tool of the Polish United Workers' Party (*Polska Zjednoczona Partia Robotnicza* or the PZPR), which decided the agents' hiring and promotion. After 1956, the party leadership and particularly General Secretary Wladyslaw Gomulka, a former prisoner of the political police, treated the secret services with reserve and made efforts to underline the party's supremacy. In 1960, SB officers were prohibited from recruiting PZPR members as secret collaborators, but exceptions were permitted with the approval of the local party leadership. Despite the order, the secret police continued to use party members as operational or official contacts, even in the absence of the standard signed pledges required to initiate collaboration. The SB was dominated by PZPR members, but party membership was not a prerequisite to join the secret police. Party membership among SB functionaries decreased steadily from 84 percent in 1957 to 69 percent in 1983.[3]

The SB maintained an active network of secret collaborators for information gathering and as "an instrument of terror," because "people were recruited to be broken" and mass recruitment meant "humiliating people, creating an aura of fear ... a way to keep people dependent."[4] In 1948, 65 percent of agents and 33 percent of informers were recruited using compromising materials (reports of theft, embezzlement, improper sexual inclination or having relatives in the West). The information network included a steady 10,000 agents until 1968, when the demand for informers grew rapidly at a time when major events – the Church's Millennium celebrations, the 1968 student protests, and the workers' revolt on the Baltic Coast in 1970 – had to be supervised. After the imposition of the martial law in 1981, the network continued to grow, reaching a record level of 98,000 informers in 1988. The entire state administration was obliged to cooperate with the SB, which deeply infiltrated it. The most penetrated areas included the northern and western regions, the last to be incorporated into the country, and the Bialystok and Gdansk regions, known for their strong anticommunist underground and frequent social unrest. Larger informer networks were planned within the clergy, the judiciary, the social elite, and the political opposition groups.[5]

As other communist political police, the SB had to protect the party's control over the country, crack down on dissent and opposition, and ensure acceptance of official ideology, policies, and leaders. Its victims included pre-communist state dignitaries and party leaders, industrialists, merchants and agricultural landowners, and intellectuals and workers who openly opposed or criticized the communist regime. According to a 1979 report of the Ministry of Internal Affairs, from 1944 to 1956 the security apparatus arrested 243,066 persons, with four-fifths of the arrests occurring in the late 1940s. Around two million Poles, including Jaruzelski and his parents, were deported to the Soviet Union during or immediately after World War II. The statistics do not include preventive custody, excesses during arrests, torture in interrogation, extermination in prison as result of extreme harsh conditions, death sentences, and cases of murder in prisons disguised as suicides.

While mass terror began to subside in 1954, an additional 5,600 people were detained and dozens were killed in the mid-1956 mass protests in Poznan, the 1960 riots in Nowa Huta, the 1968 student strike, and the 1970 and 1976 strikes and demonstrations on the Baltic Coast.[6]

Once the martial law was imposed in December 1981, country leader General Wojciech Jaruzelski and his army collaborators acquired growing power in the party-controlled political system. The state administration was increasingly staffed with military and secret service agents, and the country's command was taken over by a military council.[7] Jaruzelski's protégé Czeslaw Kiszczak, who helped with the preparation and introduction of the martial law, became the first army officer to be appointed Minister of Internal Affairs. Although he extended the secret informer network within opposition ranks and designed the repression measures, Kiszczak successfully transmogrified from a hard-line communist personally responsible for the regime's crimes into a key negotiator of the communist side during the Roundtable talks. The PZPR's 1989 electoral defeat led to the SB's funeral as a repressive political police, but its destruction was controlled. As Deputy Premier and Minister of Interior in the Mazowiecki government, Kiszczak was able to destroy the most sensitive parts of the secret archive and camouflage the SB's worst activities. The reforms led to the sudden collapse of the information network, which was almost halved in the second part of 1989. By the end of the year, the dying secret service still maintained 52,000 informers. From 1989 to 1991, almost half of the intelligence officers left the service.[8]

In April 1990, parliament replaced the SB with a new organization, the State Protection Office (*Urzad Ochrony Panstwa* or UOP). Two months later Krzysztof Kozlowski became the first post-communist Minister of Interior. The destruction of the old institution clearly demarcated the past and the future, and allowed for SB documents and property, but not personnel, to be transferred to the UOP. SB agents were re-hired by the UOP if they successfully passed a verification procedure. Each district formed a qualification commission, which reviewed applications from SB agents who wished to work for the UOP and determined whether the candidate fulfilled the moral qualifications for service. SB agents who had violated the law, had infringed on human rights or had used their position for private gain were disqualified. The verification process was uneven among districts, prompting charges of gross unfairness and even "procedural nihilism."[9] Of the 14,500 individuals who sought appointment, around 8,000 were approved for further employment in the Ministry of Interior and about 4,000 of them ended up working for the UOP. The rest found employment with the police and private security agencies. More than two-thirds of those rejected appealed to the central commission for a review of their cases, and the ombudsman received complaints from 589 people regarding these verification procedures. The procedure was never substantially revised, despite the many complaints.[10] Following this initial vetting, politicians were reluctant to approve further screening of the secret services and the armed forces, on grounds that it would weaken national security by depriving the country of skilled intelligence professionals.

In order to become a Western-style intelligence service, the UOP was prohibited from monitoring the activity of the political opposition and launching surveillance operations without court approval, and instead was called to gather intelligence material in the fight against terrorism, organized crime, and corruption. In May 2002, the Polish secret services were redesigned as an intelligence community formed by the Foreign Intelligence Agency (*Agencja Wywiadu*), whose head was also the head of the intelligence community, and the Internal Security Agency (*Agencja Bezpieczenstwa Wewnetrznego*), constituted on the basis of the UOP. In the 2005 electoral campaign, the Catholic center-right Law and Justice party (*Prawo i Sprawiedliwosc*) accused the intelligence services of becoming a tool in the hands of the leftist government, and refusing to uncover the corruption of government members and leftist party leaders. After the party won the poll, the government announced sweeping reforms of the intelligence community and plans to dismantle the military intelligence services, all in an effort to help Poland to break with its communist past. It remains to be seen how far the promised reforms will go.[11]

From mild to radical lustration

Premier Mazowiecki explicitly rejected pursuing lustration, both because he wished to honor the spirit of the Roundtable Agreements and because, as the first non-communist premier in Eastern Europe, he wanted to reassure Moscow that his government sought no revenge against communist leaders. On 24 August 1989, in a speech that set the tone for how Poland would (not) come to terms with its communist past, Mazowiecki announced that a 'thick line' (*gruba kreska*) would be drawn between the past and the present. Past loyalties were not grounds for discrimination, and everyone, including communist officials, could start a new life if ready to embrace the new democratic order. Satisfied that the new government would not reprimand them, the PZPR leaders accepted the new order, many of them renouncing politics after the party dissolved itself in January 1990. Its legal heir, the Union of Democrat Left (*Sojusz Lewicy Demokratycznej* or the SLD), broke with the principles of democratic centralism, encouraged internal debates, and formally embraced parliamentary democracy and free market economy.[12] Both its young leader, Aleksander Kwasniewski, a communist apparatchik who became a key architect of the Roundtable Agreements, and intellectual and Solidarity activist Adam Michnik stressed their commitment to the Spanish way, ignoring the question of its relevance and applicability to post-communist transformations.[13]

The "thick line" policy allowed Poland to avoid bloodshed and effect a smooth transition to democracy, but inhibited government from pursuing lustration as a component of transitional justice, gave victims wronged by the old repressive regime no voice, and reflected no wide public consultations. While catchy, the phrase was never fully explained, and people were not told where exactly the line was drawn. The policy divided the public into two camps with opposite views on lustration. Over the 1994–1999 period, a clear majority of Poles favored vetting key political officials for their links with the SB, while only one in three Poles opposed lustration. From 1996 to 1999, around 45 percent of Poles supported, and as many opposed, the exclusion of PZPR officials from public office.[14] Clearly, the policy reflected the popular mood only in the early 1990s, if at all, and helped Poles to postpone dealing with their past honestly, not to put it behind them. Since then, the country has been rocked by numerous scandals exposing top politicians as former SB agents. Each time, supporters of the "thick line" policy reaffirmed its merits, but the usually defiant attitude and repeated denials of the former secret agents, coupled with their uncanny ability to take advantage of communist-era networks to turn their old political power into economic power, prompted many Poles to question the virtues of the "amnesty but not amnesia" (*amnestia, nie amnezja*) option.[15]

As early as 1989, influential politicians denounced the "thick line" policy as a cowardly moral compromise or a "clever communist manipulation, serving the interests of the nomenklatura who wanted to enrich themselves while continuing to rule the country indirectly behind the scenes."[16] Among these critics were politicians for whom a compromise with the communists was unacceptable, and Solidarity members embittered by their marginalization at the Roundtable talks and the new government's failure to offer them a satisfactory share of power as a reward for their sacrifices as underground militants. In the face of demands for decommunization mounted by such groups, in September 1991 President Jaruzelski asked parliament to prepare presidential elections based on direct popular vote. In the poll, Solidarity leader Lech Walesa easily defeated Mazowiecki, who had lost popularity as a result of the shock therapy reform program.

Even after it explicitly rejected lustration, Poland was forced to reform its state structure to make it more apt to effect post-communist transition. A key candidate for reform was the judiciary, which had close and visible ties to the SB. With some exceptions, communist judges and prosecutors were obedient instruments of the repressive apparatus, detaining opponents without legal basis, orchestrating show-trials with pre-determined outcomes, fabricating evidence, and sending thousands to prison for their political opinions. Instead of the Czech lustration model, Poland used a novel approach to decide which judges and prosecutors could continue their careers. It absolved tainted individuals who confessed to their crimes, however gruesome they were. Confession was not public, but written, as prosecutors had to provide signed declarations describing their communist-era activities. If the Ministry of Justice deemed the declaration false, the prosecutor was not reappointed. While avoiding costly, lengthy, and disruptive disciplinary procedures, the procedure allowed for the dismissal of only the prosecutors providing false declarations, not those who had violated human rights with impunity but fully disclosed their activities. After such verifications, only some 10 percent of all prosecutors and one-third of the staff of the General Prosecutor's Office were dismissed, though it was widely believed that many more had infringed human rights and collaborated with the SB. Solidarity representatives claimed that the screening of the prosecutors stalled democratization by disregarding the rule of law and violating the prosecutors' civil rights.[17]

Following the 27 October 1991 first fully free general elections, Jan Olszewski formed a short-lived minority government with the support of a volatile center-right coalition rejecting compromise with the communists and supporting radical lustration. In February 1992, center-right deputies asked parliament to condemn the communist regime, but legislators refused, wary that a completely new beginning would bring legal chaos and anarchy, and rob them of their many privileges. Shortly afterwards, on 28 May, the Sejm accepted a decision obliging the Minister of Interior to disclose publicly the names of all current senior public officials occupying the rank of provincial governor upwards who had collaborated with the SB. A special investigation bureau had to compile a list of such collaborators based on the secret archives. Compelling the Ministry of Interior to unmask former spies from among public officials had an obvious advantage. The ministry, as secret archive custodian, could operate the most accurate identification. But the process was opened to political manipulation, since the quality and quantity of revelations depended on the minister, a political figure representing the government. The appeal procedure was not formally laid down, an oversight disadvantaging the opposition over the government, whose representatives could use informal channels to pressure the minister. There were no clear instructions as to whom the bureau should release the information, and the one-week deadline to release the list made errors likely. Leftist representatives denounced the initiative for breaching "state secrets" and pursuing partisan aims, and argued that lustration was incompatible with democracy because it violated the principles of inclusiveness and due process, and the bans on retroactivity and collective punishment.[18] While the principle that public officials should have clean pasts was reasonable, the opposition denounced its practical implementation as "morally questionable and politically dangerous."[19]

Those fears were confirmed when Minister of Interior Antoni Macierewicz presented parliament with the names of 64 persons who allegedly figured in the SB archives as informers, not least Walesa and some former dissidents advocating lustration.[20] The list was so hard to believe for some that it sparked a public scandal. On 23 July, the Sejm accepted the view that only 10 of those named could be suspected of collaboration, and only six of the 10 had signed compromising documents.[21] Faced with criticism from all corners, the minister admitted that the SB unsuccessfully tried to recruit some of those named. Instead of apologizing for damaging those persons' reputation he asked them to come forward and "tell the whole truth" to thereby restore their credibility. Michnik rejected the manner in which individuals were unmasked as informers, noting that the "logic of the guillotine" would demand the blood of all "traitors," including the premier and the Minister of Interior.[22] In the end, not those named, but the minister saw his credibility shattered. The Olszewski cabinet lost the confidence of parliament, after pro-lustration legislators reconsidered their position. On 19 June, the Constitutional Court ruled the lustration decision unconstitutional, thus blocking its further implementation.[23] More importantly, the name disclosure compromised the lustration effort. By coming across as a battle for power among politicians, it showed how lustration could be manipulated to shape the politics of the present more than to address the injustices of the past.

In the coming years, parliament debated six bills on how to deal with former informers, but none advanced. Between 1992 and 1993, the government of Hanna Suchocka, a member of Mazowiecki's Democratic Union (*Unia Demokratyczna* or the UD), focused on economic transition, and neglected the politics of the past. After the SLD and the Peasant Party, the direct successor of the communist satellite, won the late 1993 elections, lustration was hardly mentioned in parliament, but did not entirely disappear from public life. Anticommunist intellectuals and politicians complained about the stolen revolution, deplored the lack of political will to condemn communist mistakes and horrors, and denounced the "thick line" policy. The SLD leaders insisted that employment or secret collaboration with the communist secret police could not be held against anyone, since these structures were legal state organs. The prevailing popular mood contradicted this view. A 1994 opinion poll found that 75 percent of respondents believed that SB collaborators should not occupy senior state posts.[24]

Lustration did not come to the forefront until late 1995, when the so-called Oleksy Affair tilted the balance in favor of publicly disclosing the politicians' ties to the SB. In view of the presidential elections of that year, incumbent Walesa ran an aggressive campaign deploying sharp anticommunist rhetoric against his contender, SLD leader Kwasniewski. After his electoral defeat but before leaving the presidency, a bitter Walesa claimed that Poland's security was endangered by SLD Premier Jozef Oleksy, who had been and still was a Russian spy. After the Minister of Interior repeated the accusations, parliament set up special committees to investigate the affair. Oleksy forcefully declared his innocence, but had to step down before the military prosecutors dismissed the charge and anticommunist dissidents Kuron and Karol Modzelewski accused the secret police of interfering in politics. According to them, the allegations against Oleksy were prepared by a secret officer who compiled evidence against them in the 1980s. A former PZPR official, Oleksy was friends with a KGB man and, according to former Minister of Interior Krzysztof Kozlowski, failed to notice that "in 1989 Poland became a sovereign state and the contacts that in the 1980s were not de facto treated as spying have now changed their meaning ... Formerly, nobody in the party saw anything wrong with them. On the contrary, for the party activists it was a chance to speed up their career."[25] A decade later, when a court found that he hid his collaboration with the communist military intelligence, Oleksy had to step down as parliament speaker. The decision indirectly vindicated Walesa by establishing Oleksy's collaboration with the Polish military intelligence, not the KGB.[26] After the issue of collaboration had brought down Oleksy's leftist government, in addition to Olszewski's rightist one, Poland learned that the refusal to adopt lustration imposed costs on parties on both sides of the political spectrum. It was in this context that the center-left Freedom Union (*Unia Wolnosci* or the UW), the Labor Union (*Unia Pracy* or the UP) and the Peasant Party came to see the merits of "mild" lustration.[27]

Kwasniewski's apology in parliament to "all those who had experienced injustices and wickedness of the [communist] authorities and the system before 1989" and his pledge to "finish the process of coming to terms with the past" were deemed insufficient by the pro-lustration camp, and his 1995 electoral triumph over Walesa added more fuel to complaints about the stolen revolution.[28] To direct attention away from the Oleksy Affair, protect his tainted SLD allies, honor his pledge to distance Poland from its repressive past, and personally control the screening process, on 1 February 1996 Kwasniewski unexpectedly sent parliament a modest lustration proposal, which called on a newly created Commission of Public Confidence to vet public officials for their SB ties. According to the president, the process aimed to protect the state against former secret agents and help innocent people defend themselves against false accusations. The "conscience of the Polish Left," deputy Aleksander Malachowski, was to chair the commission, made up of senior judges appointed by the president. The house turned down the proposal, after the pro-lustration coalition complained that it only affected the secret part-time informers (the muscle), but not the full-time agents or party activists overseeing the activity of the secret political police (the brains).

The house adopted the three-party coalition's counter-proposal in April 1997 as the Lustration Law. According to the initiators, lustration was needed because it allowed citizens to know the background of their public representatives, ensure that public officials were not vulnerable to blackmail on account of their past collaboration with the SB, and de-politicize the issue of collaboration by subjecting it to a judicial process.[29] The SLD refused to support the proposal, unless intelligence and counter-intelligence agents were excluded from the provisions of the law, collaboration was narrowly defined as "conscious participation in actions against the church, the independent trade unions, the nation or creating a threat to civil liberties and property of others," and low-level public officials were included among lustrated categories. The house rejected all these amendments, which made the proposal unworkable.

Inspired from the 1989 vetting procedure of the prosecutors, the law was directed not against all former PZPR officials, but only those with links to the SB. The law did not apply collective guilt retroactively, as it did not impose automatic sanctions for past collaboration. All elected state officials from the rank of deputy provincial governor upwards to the ministers, the premier and the president, as well as the barristers, judges, prosecutors, and public mass media leaders, were required to submit written declarations stating whether or not they consciously worked for or collaborated with the SB between 1944 and 1990. A 21-judge Lustration Court headed by a prosecutor checked the declarations' accuracy. As clarified by the Constitutional Court, collaboration had to be conscious, secret, and connected to the SB's operational activities. Simply having submitted a declaration of intent to collaborate was not sufficient proof of collaboration, as there had to be proof of actual activities undertaken by an agent or informer, in the form of information reports. The public office holders and candidates to such positions making false statements were banned from politics for 10 years and had their names published in the State Gazette. By contrast, the political careers and public image of former SB agents who acknowledged collaboration were not affected, as they retained their posts and were shielded from public condemnation. In the case of elected officials, it was up to the voters to decide if they wanted to support individuals with a tainted past. The

Lustration Court was granted access to the archives of the UOP and the Ministries of Defense and Interior, and its verdicts were subject to appeal within 14 days. The decision of the appeal court was binding, and anyone found guilty had to resign the office immediately. If the Supreme Court overturned the decision of the appeal court, the lustration process was re-opened.

The greatest impediment to the implementation of the law was the judges' unwillingness to serve on the Lustration Court. While judges and prosecutors were among the first to be lustrated in Poland, few were banned from their positions. Those who did continue their careers were part of the old system, thus unwilling to expose SB collaborators, become involved in a process calling them to hand down political judgments, and implement a controversial law. Despite attempts to recruit the 21 required judges, in the end only 11 agreed to serve on the Lustration Court. In June 1998, parliament recognized the Warsaw District Appeal Court as the Lustration Court (thus circumvented the problem of finding judges willing to conduct lustration trials), transformed the lustration prosecutor from the government's representative in lustration trials to the key figure conducting the process, analyzing declarations, collecting information and interviewing witnesses, and allowed parliament members to initiate lustration procedures through "parliamentary denunciation."

A year after his reelection in 2000 President Kwasniewski submitted to parliament changes inspired from his 1996 lustration proposal which significantly limited the applicability of the Lustration Law. First, persons who collaborated with the intelligence, counter-intelligence and border guard units were exempted from the law, although historians argued that all Ministry of Interior departments, including the SB, functioned as a repressive apparatus, and thus it was senseless to single out some departments as purportedly "harmless" components of the political police. Second, the lustration prosecutor had to notify persons suspected of having lied in their statements in advance of their lustration trial, and the Lustration Court had to pass a clear guilty or not guilty verdict, and no longer set cases aside for lack of evidence. Third, the definition of collaboration was changed to include only the spying actions that harmed church organizations, the democratic opposition, trade union or "the nation's aspirations to sovereignty," though such consequences were difficult to establish indisputably. The SLD-UP parliamentary majority hailed the changes for preventing parties from using lustration against political rivals, but the opposition accused the government of trying to shield its allies from being declared lustration liars. At the time, the Lustration Court was hearing the cases of three SLD leaders suspected of having lied about their collaboration. After the Sejm approved the amendments in early 2002, the opposition petitioned the Constitutional Court, which found the amendments unconstitutional, thus allowing some 20 lustration trials to resume.[30] On 15 October 2002, President Kwasniewski signed amendments to the Lustration Law decried as an attempt to "strip the law of its small significance," and "block the way to the truth."[31]

Afterwards the Lustration Court adopted a cautious stance toward unmasking tainted public officials. By mid-1999, only 300 of all 23,000 officials asked to provide lustration statements admitted to their secret collaboration. According to the Lustration Law, statements were first checked by the lustration prosecutor, and then sent to the Lustration Court for scrutiny, if deemed questionable. The lustra-tion prosecutor Boguslaw Nizienski sent only seven statements to the Lustration Court because, he said, only those were "sure" cases which would result in lustra-tion verdicts. The press charged that it will take Nizienski some 1,333 years to check all statements, based on the slow pace of his work.[32]

The law should have applied to the 1997 presidential elections, but the Lus-tration Court was not constituted in time. Knowing that their statements would not be properly verified, only 11 candidates admitted to having served as secret agents.[33] Subsequent presidential polls were marked by public revelations about the candidate's tainted past. In 2002, commentators lamented the fact that voters had to choose between former SB agent Andrzej Olechowski and a former com-munist minister suspected of having been a secret informer, Kwasniewski. In his lustration statement, Olechowski admitted that he was a SB agent for two decades, but insisted that he dealt only with economic intelligence.[34] Presidential candidates Kwasniewski and Walesa also faced court trials designed to clear alle-gations that they were SB agents, a collaboration they denied in their lustration statements. Kwasniewski stood for re-election once cleared of past collaboration. After reviewing secret documents on the activity of an agent code-named Alek and interviewing former SB officers, the Lustration Court ruled that Kwasniewski was not a secret collaborator while Minister of Sport in the last communist gov-ernment, without completely ruling out the possibility that Kwasniewski was Alek.[35] The next day Walesa rejected accusations of having collaborated with the SB in the early 1970s. According to the secret documents the court studied, false evidence was produced in the early 1980s to block Walesa's Nobel Peace Prize nomination. The plans succeeded partially. In 1982, Walesa's name was crossed off the list of nominees, but he received the prize a year later, after Western intelli-gence services dismissed the allegations. The documents were used again in 1991, when Walesa figured on Macierewicz's list, and in 1993, when Jaroslaw Kaczyn-ski reiterated the accusation.[36] While rejecting the charges brought against him-self, Walesa was confident that Kwasniewski had cooperated with the SB without having to sign a collaboration pledge, because he was "one of them." After being cleared of collaboration charges, the former president lamented that the ruling convinced no one, since "those who believed me, will continue to believe me, while those who believed I was an agent will continue to believe that, too."[37]

The law affected other political luminaries. Because lustration and appeal pro-cedures were slow, the verdicts were often handed down long after politicians who misrepresented their past ended their public mandate. Thus, even when the Lustration Court branded an individual a lustration liar, the verdict did not result in the loss of position, if the individual no longer occupied a public office. Not surprisingly, most of those accused of having lied in their lustration statements appealed the verdict and defended their innocence, but only in 2002 in the case of Marian Jurczyk did the Supreme Court overturn a decision of the Lustration Court.[38] In 1999, Minister of Interior Janusz Tomaszewski resigned in protest to the Lustration Court's decision to check his statement. The case was important because, as Minister of Interior, Tomaszewski had jurisdiction over the secret archives which the Lustration Court used to verify the statements. After the press alleged that the minister had gathered intelligence to discredit opposition politicians and used the secret archives to settle political accounts, observers took issue with the fact that the secret files and the identity of SB agents remained known only to a handful of high-ranking politicians not subject to parliamentary supervision.[39] As a result, an independent institute gained custody of the secret archive (see below). In 2002, the court cleared SLD leader Jerzy Jaskiernia of being a lustration liar by not disclosing his ties with SB in the 1970s, but found that former head of Walesa's Presidential Office Tadeusz Kwiatkowski failed to disclose that he was formally registered as an SB agent in 1974–75, and delivered information to the SB without being a registered agent in 1969–1970.[40] That year, the Polish commissioner for European Union integration Slawomir Wiatr admitted that he "willingly and covertly" collaborated with the SB, but the Sejm's European Integration Commission allowed him to keep his post.[41] In 2005 Premier Marek Belka was asked to resign over allegations of past collaboration with the SB. Secret documents showed that, before undertaking a study trip to the United States in 1984, Belka agreed to inform the SB if approached by foreign intelligence officers and to seek potential informers for Poland, but provided SB with information of "no importance" on his return home. Scholars leaving communist Poland were sometimes approached by SB officers ahead of their trip abroad.

Polish lustration might have continued to drag its feet if the 2005 elections were not won by Lech and Jaroslaw Kazynski, who became President and Prime Minister with the support of the conservative Law and Justice Party. In December 2006, the Kazynski brothers delivered their promise of radical lustration in the form of a law that required an estimated 700,000 citizens in some 53 positions of authority – including academics and teachers, journalists, and state company executives born before 1 August 1972 – to declare in writing whether they collaborated with the SB.[42] The Institute of National Remembrance (see below) had to verify the statements' accuracy on the basis of the extant secret archives. Individuals found to have lied could lose their positions and be subjected to a ten-year professional ban. The law was controversial because it required the verification of individuals holding positions in the private sector, and it cast the net too wide, risking to overwhelm the Institute and to render it inefficient. Bitter opposition came from former Solidarity leaders unwilling to revisit the Roundtable Agreement and punish the former communist spies. Tadeusz Mazowiecki and Bronislaw Geremek refused to sign such declarations.[43] This renewed lustration effort was stopped in its tracks in May 2007, when the Constitutional Court rendered key provisions of the law unconstitutional. After Jaroslaw Kazynski lost the premiership in November 2007, lustration was not revived by the new cabinet.

Access to secret archives

As long as tainted politicians will refuse to publicly acknowledge their former ties to the SB, Poland will continue to face lustration scandals when information contained in the secret archives becomes available to the public by other means. As any other communist political police, the SB kept detailed records of its activities, and compiled files on both its victims and informers. The fate of the secret archive became a bone of contention immediately after the collapse of the communist regime, and has represented a subject of heated debates ever since.

There is controversy with respect to the total number of files the Polish communist secret police compiled. A ministerial instruction issued in 1949, when the record already contained files on 1.2 million people, listed 23 social categories to be automatically included, from prisoners and members of illegal organizations, to pre-war landowners, party activists, industrialists and foreign currency dealers. By 1953, some 5.2 million Poles (in a total population of 26.5 million) had secret files. Following the 1955 thaw, some documents were removed from the archive, which still contained files on 1.6 million people. A central card system allowed searching the database for those under surveillance and for secret informers without knowing their names. Secret collaborators could be found according to their home address, workplace, professional environment, code name or foreign language command. The SB took great care to prevent leaks of sensitive information by restricting access to the catalogue to a specific department, whose agents each had access only to different parts of the card system. By 1987, the catalog totaled 3.1 million cards. The SB started to computerize the archive in 1969, but it is unclear how many files were available electronically by the end of the communist regime.[44] According to historians, the extant secret archive totals some 90 linear kilometers of documents, including records on more than 98,000 secret spies.[45] In 1999, 80 meters of "lost" archives, including signed declarations of cooperation and payment receipts, were discovered in a cellar of the former SB headquarters in Warsaw.[46]

To keep operations secret, agents started to destroy selected materials as early as August 1989, when it became clear that the PZPR had lost its grip on power. By the end of the year, students stormed the PZPR buildings and found equipment for destroying incriminating files and sacks of shredded documents. In response, they called on the state to take over and preserve the SB and the party archives. The government condemned the students' unlawful occupation of party buildings, but began to take the question of the secret archives more seriously. On 31 January 1990, after Sejm deputies asked for guarantees for the safety of the archive, Minister of Interior Kiszczak issued an order to halt file destruction, and allowed historians and intellectuals to access the archives and report on their content. No external monitoring commission ensured compliance with his order.[47] After Kiszczak's removal and the dismantling of the SB, the Deputy Prosecutor General asked the UOP to investigate the file destruction. The service revealed that from August 1989 to February 1990 many SB secret documents were destroyed, including the files of high-ranking post-communist politicians and operational materials on 1,200 informers and materials documenting the infiltration of church and opposition circles.[48] Since the document destruction had been ordered in violation of standard protocol, prosecutors brought charges against the SB leaders. The Lodz district court heard a case against three officials who allegedly ordered the destruction of files on the clergy and the Solidarity, but the hearing

was abandoned in 1995.[49] A year later, a military court handed down short suspended sentences to five officers found guilty of destroying from 30 to 50 percent
of the military intelligence secret archive. In 1993, the parliamentary commission
on constitutional responsibility began investigating the destruction of the summa-
ries of the Politburo and Central Committee Secretariat meetings of 1982–1989,
ordered by Jaruzelski and carried out by Kiszczak. Two years later the case was
dropped when the commission became dominated by SLD members.

In Poland's negotiated transition, the Ministry of Interior was reluctant to open
the secret archives and expose its network of informers, while Solidarity wanted to
prevent the violence that could have followed revelations potentially devastating
for the unsuspecting families and friends of the secret informers. However, there
were rumors that selected politicians close to the Minister of Interior and prominent intellectuals were allowed to see their personal files.[50] The lack of procedure
for file access reinforced the feeling that the archive was regarded as a powerful
tool to settle political disputes. Repeated leaks of secret archival documents and
the circulation of damaging rumors forced victims of these allegations to undertake
expensive and lengthy libel suits to clear their names. While most Solidarity successors feared that the archives could not be opened without violating due process
and civil rights, the closure of the files imposed heavy costs on innocent people. In
addition, the former communists' victory in the 1993 parliamentary poll gave rise
to sobering reflection among Solidarity heirs, who feared that the new rulers would
destroy valuable archival documents to cover up their past activities. As a result,
in 1997 parliament agreed to partly open the secret archive to the public.[51] Access
to personal files was granted to those "wronged" by the communist regime, but not
to informers. After the Tomaszewski scandal, the Institute of National Remembrance
(*Instytut Pamieci Narodowej* or IPN) became the archive custodian.

The Institute was set up in late 1998 to investigate Nazi and communist crimes,
gather evidence to prosecute the perpetrators of such crimes, inform and educate
the public with respect to Poland's recent past, and give citizens access to their
own secret files. The Lustration Law also charged the IPN with helping to investigate claims of collaboration, vetting the background of public-office seekers, and
granting file access to researchers, historians, and dissidents wishing to conduct
their own searches. The Institute employs about 2,000 researchers working in
the Committee for the Prosecution of Crimes against the Polish Nation, bureaus
for archival research and public education and local chapters. It began its work
in June 2000, when parliament named independent senator Leon Kieres as the
IPN head for a five-year term. Kieres pledged to gather together the secret files
dispersed among institutions and provide "careful" access to secret files in order
to avoid "irreversible damage and harm through fast but chaotic activities that
would discredit the institute." Kieres further promised to grant access to all those
pursued by the SB and ensure that "everyone has an equal chance of access to
personal materials."[52] By 2005, some 14,000 Poles read their files.[53]

The pace at which files were made available and the IPN's failure to fulfill
its mandate to publicly name secret agents and informers apparently prompted
journalist Bronislaw Wildstein to "steal" from the Institute a working list of some

240,000 names of former SB agents, military intelligence, secret covert informers, prospective candidates to informer positions and victims, and post it on the internet in February 2005. The list did not distinguish between perpetrators and victims, thus exposing all those named to the suspicion that they had collaborated and arousing concern that the incomplete data may be used for political purposes or personal vendetta. Prosecutors launched an inquiry into the case, but were unable to identify the IPN employee who helped Wildstein. Refusing to name his accomplice, Wildstein defended his action as legitimate, since "this is not our past, this is our present. Those people are present and play important roles in our reality." Roman Catholic priest Jozef Maj, whose name appeared on the list, saw the leak as a "blessed offense" that could help Poland reach the truth in public life.[54] But Kieres accused Wildstein of being irresponsible, and Prime Minister Belka asked the UOP to ensure that agents on active duty were not affected by the revelations.[55] Many of those on the list asked the IPN to allow them to read their secret file, regardless of whether they were victims or informers.[56]

The list's publication increased pressure on Polish authorities to open up the secret archives. However, file access could prove necessary but not sufficient to find the truth about secret collaboration and communist repression. Many historians insist that, since the files were intended for internal use only, secret officers had no reason to fabricate them. But a recent case showed the discrepancy between communist reality and its reflection in the files, and suggested the possibility that officers could have generated records of collaboration under pressure to support their promotion, prove their usefulness in the repression apparatus, cover up inefficiency in intelligence work or complement dwindling networks of active informers. In 2005, Malgorzata Niezabitowska, a former *Solidarity Weekly* reporter, was accused of collaboration. According to her, accusations were traceable to her only encounter with SB agents on 15 December 1981. Although interrogated for seven hours without food or water, she refused to tell them anything other than information they already knew. According to her secret file, Niezabitowska ultimately gave in to pressure, acted as an informer under the code name Nowak, and met her contact officer 10 more times. She maintained that her activity as an anticommunist opposition member belied the accusation of collaboration, and insisted that political police agents should not be allowed to write the history of communism.[57] Historians believe that archives hold the keys to historical puzzles, but the case suggests that archival documents should be complemented by personal interviews and oral histories.

Trials against communist officials

As other Eastern European countries, Poland has struggled to bring charges against communist officials and political police agents, while differentiating between crimes subject to the Penal Code (torture and killings), and offences legal when committed whose prosecution could be construed as politically motivated (spying for the SB). Attempts to bring justice by means of criminal law have focused on crimes against humanity, although it was recognized that communist-era human rights abuses took the form of mass surveillance not mass killings. The number of trials has remained low because of flagrant political interference and manipulation, the difficulty to build strong cases resulting in convictions, the legal chicanery employed to prolong or stale the proceedings, intimidation of witnesses, prosecutors and judges, and the judges' unwillingness to take up such cases. Unable to convince judges to support transitional justice, in 1998 parliament allowed judges of the 1944–1989 period to be brought before a disciplinary court and removed from service if it was proved that they had issued unjust sentences or obstructed the defendant's right to a defense. Afterwards, the Council of Judges cancelled the retirement pensions of seven Stalinist-era judges, and announced that the past activity of 16 other judges was closely scrutinized (Poland has around 25,000 judges in total). Judges saw these decisions as punishment for their lack of co-operation with the Lustration Court and unwillingness to hear criminal cases related to transitional justice.[58]

To date, court proceedings have referred to crimes committed either during the Stalinist or the martial law periods, with the cases the courts heard first not being the cases involving higher repression levels. The only case falling outside these broad categories investigated the military's use of force in the suppression of the Gdansk strikes in 1970. Opened in 1990 at the request of Minister of Justice Aleksander Bentkowski, the case later faced the opposition of those seeing it as a distraction from the more pressing task of judicial reform. The court took four years to investigate the case, not because of lack of documents but because of the excessively voluminous documentation (90 volumes of 200 pages each) presented to it. The trial, considered the Polish equivalent of the Nuremberg trial, began on 28 March 1995 in Gdansk. Some 12 defendants – among them then Minister of Defense Jaruzelski, Minister of Interior Kazimierz Switala and Deputy Prime Minister Stanislaw Kociolek – were accused of ordering the police to shoot at protesting workers, killing 44 and wounding about 200. The order to shoot was given by Gomulka and Politburo members Kociolek and Zenon Kliszko, no longer alive. In 1996, the court discontinued proceedings against Jaruzelski, but the Court of Appeals overturned that decision, allowing the General to face trial. Court proceedings against four defendants, including Jaruzelski, were suspended and the opening of the trial of the remaining defendants delayed because it proved impossible to gather all of them for a formal reading of the charges. All claimed they were unable to appear in court for heath reasons. Jaruzelski denied responsibility, and at the trial's opening session told the families of those killed that he could not forget the hundreds of wounded policemen and soldiers.[59] The protest of the Gdansk shipyard workers, resulting from steep price increases two weeks before Christmas, took the form of riots, accompanied by violence and efforts to storm the party headquarters.[60] The involvement of *agents provocateurs* in the damage was never ruled out.

The investigation of these cases depended on whether the statute of limitations applied to communist-era crimes. In 1991, the Constitutional Court dealt a serious blow to transitional justice through court proceedings when it rejected the law giving the Committee for the Research of Hitler's Crimes additional responsibilities to investigate communist crimes. The court argued that by defining Stalinist crimes too broadly, the law retroactively lifted the statute of limitations and contradicted Article 1 of the Constitution, which recognized Poland as a democratic state under the rule of law. After the ruling, the courts were confused about which communist crimes the statute of limitation applied to, the more so since the statute did not apply to crimes perpetrated by Nazis against Poles. Some judges argued that the statute had lapsed for most communist-era cases except those involving murder and crimes against humanity, while other judges claimed that the statute applied to all cases which could not be fairly tried before the end of the communist regime.[61] This later position was reflected in the amendments to Article 108.2 of the Penal Code the UW proposed in 1991. The changes read that "the statute of limitations for deliberate crimes against life, health, freedom or the administration of justice, which are punishable by the deprivation of liberty for a period of more than three years and were committed by public officials from 1 January 1944 to 31 December 1989 during or in connection with those official duties, begins to run as of 1 January 1990." The SLD majority rejected the changes, proposing instead that trials be carried out under the guidelines of international law, which applied the statute to crimes other than murder, war crimes and crimes against humanity. Ultimately, the Sejm approved the changes on tolling the statute as part of a larger package of reforms to the Penal Code. As a result, the statute of limitations was extended for some important cases from the martial law era, including the case of the shootings at Wujek in 1981. Neither the Ministry of Justice nor the Committee for the Research of Hitler's Crimes collected data on the number of trials involving communist state officials, but Calhoun identified at least 30 trials stemming from both the Stalinist and martial law eras, and launched before 2001.[62]

Important moral triumphs for the anticommunist camp occurred in 1998. On 16 April, the Senate declared the Soviet-occupied Poland a non-democratic, totalitarian state, whose political structures violated the 1935 constitution, and invalidated the 1952 communist constitution. Two months later, on 18 June, parliament condemned the "communist dictatorship imposed in Poland with force and against the will of the nation by the Soviet Union and Joseph Stalin," and blamed the PZPR for the "crimes and offences" of a regime which "protected foreign interests" and was maintained "by force, lies and the threat of Soviet intervention."[63] Notwithstanding these decisions, hailed as a long overdue moral condemnation of the communist regime, the individual prosecution of communist officials who ordered the atrocities, and secret political police agents who executed them, proved to be difficult. Most trials were based on circumstantial evidence, as the evidential material was often destroyed after the crime was committed. When witnesses were incapable of identifying the guilty, the defendants denied the accusations.

Prosecuting the abuses of the Stalinist period

In 1991, parliament enabled two committees to investigate Stalinist-era crimes. While their responsibilities overlapped, the committees complemented rather than competed with one another. In April, the house gave the Committee for the Research of Hitler's Crimes the task to investigate communist crimes. The law aimed to facilitate criminal trials of individuals responsible for human rights abuses during the late 1940s and early 1950s by creating an investigative group responsible for examining the cases and by abolishing the statute of limitations for these crimes. The committee made little progress in studying those crimes and preparing cases for prosecution. By August 1992, it investigated 293 crimes but investigations led to no arrest. Some of the accused were already dead, old or gravely ill and unable to travel, and the evidence linking them to the atrocities was patchy, inconclusive or locked in unavailable archives. Many documents had been destroyed, making it difficult for the courts to have a legal basis for acting. Archival documents were difficult to verify against and complement with information obtained from other sources, and oral testimonies were unreliable, as events happened five decades earlier, people had partial recollections, and memories were subjective.[64]

Somewhat more successful was the Coordinating Committee for the Study of Crimes against the Polish Nation, which from 1991 to 1995 conducted over 500 inquiries and passed 95 cases to the State Attorneys' Office, which issued 20 indictments. Only the case of former head of the Investigations Department of the Ministry of Public Security, Adam Humer, led to a public trial. The hearings, seen as a trial of the entire Stalinist system in Poland, lasted five years. On 6 September 1993, just two weeks before the general elections, the trial of Humer and 15 of his associates began, and quickly became a reference point in the electoral campaign. While the SLD defended the old regime and claimed that the crimes of the Polish communists represented a far lesser evil than Nazism, their political rivals insisted to expose publicly the communist atrocities. Humer was charged with murdering an opposition activist, beating and torturing political prisoners (including women) from 1946 to 1952 in Soviet-occupied Poland, and ordering the police not to interfere in the Kielce murder of Jews on 4 July 1946. His conduct during the trial was ostentatiously unrepentant. On 7 March 1996, the Warsaw Court found Humer guilty of nine of the 12 charges of torture, and sentenced him to nine years in prison. Ten of his subordinates received sentences of three to eight years. The judge stated that "the case captured a history that was an open wound in the hearts of many Polish families. It exposed unprecedented acts of terror and lawlessness."[65] Because of Humer's health problems, in mid-1998 his sentence was reduced to seven years to be spent at home, a decision many Poles contested on grounds that the Stalinist regime rested on terror and thus no leniency should be shown to its executants. Prosecutor Lucjan Nowakowski and former head of the Coordinating Committee Witold Kulesza continued to examine new materials concerning the Kielce pogrom, but no other cases were brought to trial since then.

By 1993, former victims of communism became increasingly dissatisfied with Poland's lack of progress in reconsidering its communist past. *Gazeta Wyborcza* published an open letter of Home Army veterans, who had been heavily persecuted immediately after World War II, expressing disappointment that Stalinist criminals responsible for sending to death Home Army patriots had not been punished. The letter was criticized by intellectuals like Michnik, who stressed that Polish Stalinism was milder than elsewhere and communists helped to make the country "the most comfortable barrack in the block," dismantle Stalinism and pave the way for democracy. Scolding those who assumed that "People's Poland should be treated as a form of Soviet occupation, and the PZPR as an organization of traitors and collaborators with a foreign power,"[66] Michnik called for national reconciliation and amnesty for former communists. But following the SLD's electoral victory in 1993, Michnik became increasingly isolated as many Poles contended that maintaining normal relations with the SLD paved the communists' return to power by blurring the distinction between good and evil. Minister of Justice Wlodzimierz Cimoszewicz deplored the lack of political will to prosecute the crimes of the past, and spoke of a pseudo-Christian tendency to absolve all sins in a universal forgiveness. Supreme Court president Adam Strzembosz suggested that the entire pre-1956 PZPR leadership should be treated as a criminal organization, but supported a blanket amnesty law, not applicable to murders and crimes against humanity.

In August 1995, the 80-year-old judge Maria Gurowska stood accused that in 1952 she sentenced to death General August Emil Fieldorf (alias Nil), the Home Army's chief of diversionary activities, following a show-trial. Gurowska rejected the charge, insisting that she had acted in accordance with her conscience. Fieldorf was unable to change, and thus had to be "eliminated from society." Gurowska died before her case came to court, but Fieldorf's death was not forgotten. In October 1998, Poland summoned the 79-years-old Stalinist-era prosecutor Helena Wolinska to answer charges that she fabricated evidence, failed to follow arrest rules, and kept Fieldorf in jail without charge for more than 14 days. Arrested in 1951 and executed on 24 February 1953, Fieldorf was purged by communist authorities at Moscow's urging because the Home Army fostered a spirit of independence among Poles resentful of Soviet domination. In 1989, the Prosecutor General cleared Fieldorf of all charges. Wolinska was accused of fabricating evidence and arresting hundreds of opponents of the Polish Stalinist regime, including dissident Wladislaw Bartoszewski, who spent 18 months in prison without charge, awaiting trial in 1946–1948. Wolinska took refuge in England after losing her job in 1956, when a milder leadership denounced the excesses of early communism. As Wolinska failed to answer the charges, in 1998 the Warsaw District Army Court issued a one-month arrest warrant, but she was never extradited to Poland, where she claimed her case would not be tried justly.[67]

Prosecuting the authors of the martial law

For Solidarity, the most important issue was to settle accounts with the martial law regime, a task made possible only after Jaruzelski renounced the presidency. On 1 February 1992, parliament created a Parliamentary Commission on Constitutional Responsibility to determine whether the State Tribunal should judge Jaruzelski for proclaiming the martial law, Military Council of National Salvation members for implementing it, and State Council members for endorsing it. The commission was interested not to discuss concrete cases of extra-judicial killings, disappearances or torture, but to establish if the introduction of the martial law was justified. The parliamentary debates preceding the vote revealed two opposing views on Polish late communism. On the one hand, Jaruzelski's defenders argued that the declaration of the martial law spared many Polish lives by preventing a Soviet occupation. Stefan Niesiolowski distinguished between the dark period of Stalinism, when hundreds of victims suffered a cruel fate, and the "mild" martial law regime, when limited numbers of people were imprisoned or lost their lives. On the other hand, Jaruzelski's critics saw the martial law as an unpardonable "crime against the Polish people."[68] These arguments spilled over in the work of the committee, whose second meeting was preceded by a press conference in which member Jaroslaw Kaczynski anticipated the outcome of the inquiry by declaring that "General Jaruzelski and his comrades are guilty of betraying the nation and thus should be prosecuted."[69] That position was not shared by chairman Edward Rzepka, who accused defendants of the lesser crime of violating Article 246 of the Penal Code which said that public functionaries who used illegal means to promote their material and personal interests should receive up to ten-year prison terms. Jaruzelski rightly rejected the charge of self-enrichment through martial law. In reply, the committee charged the defendants with violating Article 123 of the Penal Code, which prescribed the death punishment for treason.

The treason charge touched on sovereignty, the issue every Pole recognizes as central to the country's history. Was the law proclaimed to protect Poles against a Soviet, East German or Czechoslovak invasion or to protect the interests of international communism? Did it amount to national defense or national treason? Jaruzelski strongly suggested the first possibility, insisting that at the time he genuinely believed that the martial law could forestall the imminent foreign invasion and avoid chaos and economic collapse. According to him, the country had plunged into anarchy, the economy disintegrated, the delivery of coal and food before the winter months was disrupted, thus threatening the people's survival, and the Solidarity's increased radicalism and mounting aggression against the police and secret police pushed Poland on the edge of civil war. Martial law was the lesser evil, and a remarkably mild operation, given its scale. To add insult to injury, Jaruzelsky deplored the fact that party reformists like him, committed to Gorbachev's perestroika, were humiliated not thanked. But his position took for granted that an invasion was imminent, that, if unavoidable, it would have been a greater disaster, that martial law was devoid of repressive intentions, and that he wanted to usher in democratization, not effect limited changes to keep the system alive. Mieczyslaw Rakowski, Jaruzelski's friend and the last PZPR general secretary, believed that "Jaruzelski would have called martial law, Soviet threat or no."[70] The opposing experts argued that the PCPR leadership explicitly asked the Soviet military and party leaders not to send troops to Poland, and thus the latter fully knew that no Polish leader endorsed plans for intervention. Brezhnev's interventionist impulses were further tempered by the active Polish resistance to outside intervention, and the problems the Soviet campaign in Afghanistan was then facing. Of these two opposing views, Jaruzelski's proved the most popular. Some 71 percent of Poles believed martial law had been justified.[71]

After the 1993 elections, the SLD parliamentary majority reshuffled the commission, making sure a majority of its members represented that party. In December 1994, the opposition asked the house to condemn the martial law as unconstitutional, even by communist standards, but the leftist majority toned the proposal down to a tribute to the victims of the struggle for freedom, a reformulation condemned by the opposition as a moral crime against the nation. After four years of activity, in 1996, the commission ended its investigation and recommended that parliament drop the case against Jaruzelski and his collaborators, without presenting a convincing case for either decision. The vote was split, five out of 18 members announcing their intention to ask parliament to call for court proceedings be launched against the authors of the martial law. Jaruzelski also believed that only a court decision could clear his name.[72]

Jaruzelski and his supporters claimed that the martial law was mild, and refused to admit that political killings did occur in the 1980s. In August 1989, the Sejm set up a commission headed by Jan Rokita to investigate allegations that the SB was involved in political murders after the martial law was proclaimed. The so-called Rokita commission submitted its final report to parliament just before the 1991 general elections. According to the report, which was never released to the larger public, the commission investigated 122 suspicious deaths in the custody of the SB, recommending in 88 cases that prosecutors launch criminal proceedings against Ministry of Internal Affairs officials and prosecutors who tried to cover up the cause of death. The commission named 100 secret officers and 70 prosecutors unsuitable for further employment in the state organs, and concluded that under communism secret agents acted with almost total impunity because they enjoyed the protection of the PZPR and the judiciary. The ministry often issued express instructions to the prosecutors on how to conduct investigations and sometimes carried out investigations itself. The judiciary cooperated extensively and systematically with the ministry: prosecutors did not request documents from the SB, and the courts routinely dropped charges against SB officers violating the law.[73] Few of the cases mentioned in the Rokita report reached the courts. Characteristic features were the long duration of all inquiries and the extraordinary slowness of the court trials. Of those which did reach the courts in the early 1990s, some of the most important are mentioned below.

On 24 July 1990, an inquiry into the death of Father Jerzy Popieluszko began. The October 1984 brutal killing of the well-known Roman Catholic priest, the Solidarity chaplain, was investigated by the courts after his funeral attracted close to one million mourners. Such a reaction could not be ignored, as might have happened in the earlier days of Solidarity. To maintain order and incur favor with foreign governments, Jaruzelski allowed a trial. Four SB agents received prison terms of between 14 and 25 years, which were later drastically reduced for undisclosed reasons. The communist prosecutor asked for the death penalty for the perpetrators, but also condemned the priest for defying the communist authorities, and allowed the court to become a forum for open attacks on the church. The trial manipulated the public into believing that the murder was an isolated case and all those guilty were punished. In 1990, the Ministry of Justice announced that new evidence confirmed suspicions that two high-ranking officials of the Ministry of Internal Affairs had abetted the crime and supervised its execution. The two were acquitted in mid 1994, but two years later the verdict was quashed by the Court of Appeal. Eventually more charges were added and a new trial was to begin in 1998, but the case was returned for further investigation. The Supreme Court ruled that the Ministry of Internal Affairs leadership had known about and approved of their subordinates' criminal actions. No one from the then leadership was charged in this case.[74]

In 1993, Kiszczak was accused of causing the deaths of nine miners and wounding 25 others in a clash with special anti-riot police at Wujek in 1981. The secret forces were authorized to use live ammunition without strict instructions about when this would be justified. Evidence was destroyed, witnesses were convicted on fabricated evidence or forced into giving false statements. While traveling to the court, Kiszczak had a heart attack and could not cooperate with the investigating magistrates. The courts also had to reckon with the fact that the legal basis of prosecution was the communist law, which condemned the opposition and defended the secret police. In May 1996, Michnik spoke at the trial as a witness for the defense, testifying that Kiszczak had always maintained that the Wujek killings disregarded his orders. Three months later, Kiszczak was acquitted of all charges, but the case was reopened after this verdict was quashed by the Court of Appeals. A protracted trial of 22 other men accused in the killings started in late 1992 and ended in November 1997 with the acquittal of all defendants.

The Warsaw Court indicted three militia men for the alleged beating and death of Grzegorz Przemyk, the teenaged son of the opposition poet Barbara Sadowska, in May 1983. In April 1997, the trial ended as inconclusive. While the judge ruled that there was no doubt that Przemyk's death was caused by the militiamen, there was insufficient evidence to identify the culprits. An accused was acquitted, another one was sentenced to four years in prison for instigating the beating, and the director of the Militia Investigation Bureau received a suspended sentence of one and a half years for trying to cover up the murder. Kiszczak and the Politburo members who orchestrated the murder and cover-up were not on trial, although their involvement was well-documented. In May 1998, the Court of Appeal acquitted the director, quashed the acquittal of a militiaman, and prohibited the other from working in the police for five years, in addition to his four-year prison sentence. The courts also heard arguments against three commanding militia officers for shootings that occurred during the suppression of a 31 August 1982 peaceful demonstration in Lublin, which resulted in killing three people and wounding more than a dozen. The trial resulted in the acquittal of all three militiamen. The Court of Appeal ordered a retrial, but in 1998 the lower court made a controversial legal decision to stay the charges based on past amnesties.[75]

Conclusion

The only country to give lustration a second chance, Poland moved from mild to radical lustration within a decade. After the Constitutional Court killed the 2006 law before that law had a chance to produce concrete results, Poland's lustration record was restricted to the 1997 law, which was overall milder than its Czech counterpart. Of the roughly 23,000 people who submitted lustration statements, only several dozens of officials who denied their previous ties to the SB were found to be lustration liars, and even fewer gave up their public posts as a result. The Lustration Court was extremely slow to verify the accuracy of lustration statements, and the 2001 legislative amendments made it more difficult to weed out secret agents from among post-communist politicians. The country has scored rather modestly in two other transitional justice areas: file access and court proceedings. Only Poles who were wronged by the communist regime have access to their own files, and only a fraction of the extant secret archive (which itself is but a fraction of the original SB archive) is opened to the public. As time passes and the perpetrators of communist-era crimes die or become ill, it is even more improbable that court proceedings would succeed in prosecuting such crimes.

Notes

1 A. Dudek and A. Paczkowski, 'Poland', in K. Persak and L. Kaminski (eds) *A Handbook of the Communist Security Apparatus in East Central Europe, 1944–1989*, Warsaw: Institute of National Remembrance, 2005, p. 228.
2 Ibid., p. 244.
3 Ibid., pp. 238–244.
4 Ibid., pp. 254–255.
5 Ibid., pp. 258–259.
6 Ibid., pp. 272–274. NKVD data suggest that estimated number of Poles deported in 1939 and 1940 reached only half a million. I thank Dariusz Stola for this information.
7 M. Los and A. Zybertowicz, *Privatizing the Police-State. The Case of Poland*, London: Palgrave Macmillan, 2000, and M. Los, 'Reshaping of Elites and the Privatization of Security: The Case of Poland', *Journal of Power Institutions in Post-Soviet Societies*, 2005, vol. 2. Online. Available HTTP: http://www.pipss.org/document351.html (accessed 28 December 2007).
8 J. Freeman, 'Security Services Still Distrusted', *Transition*, 21 March 1997, 52.
9 N. Calhoun, *Dilemmas of Justice in Eastern Europe's Democratic Transitions*, New York: Palgrave Macmillan, 2004, p. 105.
10 Ibid.
11 For the 2002 reforms, see D. M. Dastych, 'No 'Zero Option' But a Shake Up'. Online. Available HTTP: http://www.fas.org/irp/world/poland/dastych.html (accessed 2 January 2008).
12 In January 1990, the Polish communists regrouped under the banner of the Social Democracy of Republic of Poland (SdPR). The SdPR and its allies participated in the 1993 elections as the SLD.
13 A. Szostkiewicz, 'The Time for De-communization Has Past', *The Warsaw Voice*, 28 June 1998, and A. Walicki, 'Transitional Justice and the Political Struggles of Post-Communist Poland', in J. A. McAdams (ed.) *Transitional Justice and the Rule of Law in New Democracies*, South Bend: University of Notre Dame, 1997, pp. 193–196. Mazowiecki's speech appeared in *Sprawozdanie stenograficzne Sejmu PRL*, 24 August 1989, pp. 84–86. Three recent publications worth noting are P. Grzelak, *Wojna o lustracje*, Warsaw: Trio, 2005, P. Spiewak, *Pamic po komunizmie*, Gdans: Slowo/Obraz/Terytoria, 2005, and A. Wolek, 'Lustracja jako walka o reguly polityki I proba wzmacniania legitymizacji nowych demokracji', *Studia Polityczne*, 2004, vol. 15, 147–173.

14 A. Szczerbiak, 'Dealing with the Communist Past or the Politics of the Present? Lustration in Post-Communist Poland', *Europe-Asia Studies*, 2002, vol. 54, 559–560.
15 When confronted with one of his victims, an elderly woman, Adam Humer, an SB officer accused of carrying out brutal torture, replied: "Shut up, you old bitch!" The case is detailed below.
16 Walicki, 'Transitional Justice', p. 190.
17 Of the total 3,278 prosecutors, 311 were dismissed. Other 48 dismissal recommendations were overturned by an appeals commission. See Sprawozdanie stenograficzne Sejmu RP, 4 February 1994, pp. 24–25, and Sprawozdanie stenograficzne Sejmu PRL, 29 September 1989, pp. 84–87, 13 October 1989, pp. 89–93, and 30 December 1989, pp. 134–143.
18 A. Sabbat-Swidlicka, 'Poland: A Year of Three Governments', *RRF/RL Research Report*, 1993, vol. 2, p. 103, L. Vinton, 'Poland's Government Crisis: An End in Sight?', *RFE/RL Research Report*, 1992, vol.1, 16–20, and W. Osiatynski, 'Agent Walesa?', *East European Constitutional Review*, 1992, vol. 1, 28–30.
19 Walicki, 'Transitional Justice', p. 197.
20 A second list of 37 names was circulated to a narrower circle of top politicians, including President Walesa.
21 Only four of those Macierewicz named had not been collaborators.
22 A. Michnik, J. Tischner and J. Zakowski, *Miedzy panem a plebanem*, Cracow: Znak, 1995, p. 588.
23 For his unwise disclosure of the list, Macierewicz faced a trial behind closed doors, which was discontinued when parliament refused to indict him.
24 Los and Zybertowicz, *Privatizing the Police-State*, p. 147.
25 Quoted in Los, 'Reshaping of Elites'. Also J. Karpinski, 'Polish Security Services and the Oleksy Case', *Transition*, 1 November 1996, 9–13, and K. Karpinski, 'The Mystery of "O" ', *Transition*, 14 June 1996, 3–4.
26 'Poland's Speaker Offers to Resign His Post', *New York Times*, 30 December 2004. Online. Available HTTP: http://www.nytimes.com/2004/12/30/international/europe/30poland.html (accessed 28 January 2008).
27 N. Calhoun, 'The Ideological Dilemma of Lustration in Poland', *East European Politics and Societies*, 2002, vol. 16, 512.
28 Walicki, 'Transitional Justice', p. 200.
29 Szczerbiak, 'Dealing with the Communist Past', pp. 562–564.
30 'Polish Parliament Forms Commissions', *RFE/RL Newsline*, 25 October 2001. Online. Available HTTP: http://www.rferl.org/newsline/2001/10/251001.asp (accessed 28 January 2008).
31 'Polish President Signs Amended Lustration Law', *RFE/RL Newsline*, 16 October 2002. Online. Available HTTP: http://www.rferl.org/newsline/2002/10/161002.asp (accessed 28 January 2008).
32 'Polish Deputy Minister Resigns before Lustration Verdict', *RFE/RL Newsline*, 8 June 1999. Online. Available HTTP: http://www.rferl.org/newsline/1999/07/080799.asp (accessed 28 January 2008).
33 'Poland', *East European Constitutional Review*, 1997, vol. 6, p. 22.
34 L. Palata, 'Split Decision', *Transitions Online*, 14 August 2000. Online. Available HTTP http://www.tol.cz (accessed 5 June 2006). During the same electoral campaign, Wieslaw Walendziak, head of the election team of Solidarity leader Marian Krzaklewski, sued for libel his counterpart from incumbent President Kwasniewski's election team, Ryszard Kalisz, for suggesting that Walendziak may have pressured the UOP to provide the Lustration Court with documents alleging that Kwasniewski was a secret agent.
35 'Poland's Presidential Hopeful Admits Collaboration with Communist Secret Services', *RFE/RL Newsline*, 18 July 2000. Online. Available HTTP: http://www.rferl.org/newsline/2000/07/180700.asp (accessed 28 January 2008), 'Polish Secret Services

Blamed for Infringements over President's Lustration', *RFE/RL Newsline*, 1 August 2000. Online. Available HTTP: http://www.rferl.org/newsline/2000/08/010800.asp (accessed 28 January 2008), and 'Polish President Cleared of Secret Police Links', CNN, 10 August 2000. Online. Available HTTP: http://archives.cnn.com/2000/WORLD/europe/08/10/poland.president/ (accessed 28 January 2008).

36 In 1993, in the book *Lewy Czerwcowy* Kaczynski accused Walesa's presidential aid Mieczyslaw Wachowski of collaboration. Walesa asked the Minister of Interior to release his secret file, but the minister refused, on grounds that the president had no legal authority to order the release of secret documents. A. Sabbat-Swidlicka, 'Crisis in the Polish Justice Ministry', *RFE/RL Research Report*, 1993, vol. 2, p. 14.

37 Palata, 'Split Decision'.

38 The Lustration Court ruled that Jurczyk lied in his declaration by not disclosing that he worked for the SB in 1977–1979 out of fear for his life. The ruling cost Jurczyk, the leader of Solidarity protests in Szczecin in August 1980, his seat in the Senate. Supreme Court judge Piotr Hofmanski argued that the lower court overlooked evidence showing that the information Jurczyk provided to the SB "had no effect." Jurczyk always insisted that the SB deemed the information he supplied "operationally useless." The verdict did not convince Solidarity founder Andrzej Gwiazda, who claimed that Jurczyk was not a regular informer, but an agent of influence who could "render greater services by speaking on some matter than by reporting that someone was about to distribute leaflets." See 'Former Solidarity Leader Cleared of Violating Polish Lustration Law', *RFE/RL Newsline*, 3 October 2002. Online. Available HTTP: http://www.rferl.org/newsline/2002/10/031002.asp (accessed 28 January 2008). Jurczyk convinced communist authorities to endorse the strikers' demands on 30 August 1980, one day before Walesa did so in Gdansk. Jurczyk was arrested from 1981 to 1984. In 1980, he unsuccessfully challenged Walesa for the Solidarity leadership, and then criticized Solidarity leaders for violating the union's statutes when entering the Roundtable talks. After giving up his seat in the Senate, he founded the League of Families, which later became the ultra-Catholic League of Polish Families.

39 'Polish Deputy Premier Resigns over Lustration', *RFE/RL Newsline*, 3 September 1999. Online. Available HTTP: http://www.rferl.org/newsline/1999/09/030999.asp (accessed 28 January 2008), and 'Poland. Dirty Hands', *Transitions Online*, 6 September 1999. Online. Available HTTP http://www.tol.cz/look/TOLrus/article.tpl?IdLanguage=1&IdPublication=4&NrIssue=2&NrSection=7&NrArticle=8363 (accessed 5 June 2006).

40 'SLD Parliamentary Caucus Leader Cleared of Lustration Lie', *RFE/RL Newsline*, 31 July 2002. Online. Available HTTP: http://www.rferl.org/newsline/2002/07/310702.asp (accessed 28 January 2008).

41 The opposition asked for Wiatr's removal, as to permit "a person who quite recently served the secret services that fought against institutions of the Free World" to oversee Poland's European integration "discredits the idea of integration and affects Poland's international image," but Miller said that Polish lustration was not high on the European Union agenda. 'Poland's EU Campaign Chief Admits Spying for Communist Secret Services', *RFE/RL Newsline*, 30 August 2002. Online. Available HTTP: http://www.rferl.org/newsline/2002/08/300802.asp (accessed 28 January 2008).

42 'Ustawa z dnia 18 października 2006 r. o ujawnianiu informacji o dokumentach organów bezpieczeństwa państwa z lat 1944–1990 oraz treści tych dokumentów'. Online. Available HTTP http://www.abc.com.pl/serwis/du/2006/1592.htm (accessed 27 March 2007).

43 V. Mite, 'Poland: Tough Lustration Law Divides Society', *RFE/RL Reports*, 23 March 2007. Online. Available HTTP: http://www.rferl.org/featuresarticle/2007/03/38d9250c4dd3–49fc-8e44-d2f21f83a190.html (accessed 28 January 2008), and 'Former Polish PM Refuses to Sign Lustration Document, *RFE/RL Newsline*, 26 April 2007. Online. Available HTTP: http://www.rferl.org/newsline/2007/04/260407.asp (accessed 28 January 2008).

44 Dudek and Paczkowski, 'Poland', pp. 246–255.
45 Giovanni Cubeddu, 'From a Distant Country, to spy close up', *30 Days in the Church and the World*, 2005, vol. 8. Online. Available HTTP: http://www.30giorni.it/us/articolo.asp?id=9211 (accessed 28 December 2007).
46 J. Luxmoore, 'Poland Fears Its Judas Files', *The Tablet*, 7 August 1999. Online. Available HTTP: http://www.thetablet.co.uk (accessed 3 June 2005).
47 J. Karpinski, 'Politicians and the Past', *Uncaptive Minds*, 1992, vol. 5, pp. 99–106.
48 In 1993, Minister of Interior Jerzy Kaminski estimated that half of all SB operational materials and 50 to 60 per cent of its informer files were missing, and announced that in some districts officers destroyed even more documents. According to him, 90 per cent of the SB documents in Gdansk, the birthplace of the Solidarity movement, had been lost. These figures were never confirmed from independent sources.
49 Sprawozdanie stenograficzne Sejmu RP, 17 May 1993, p. 137, and Los and Zybertowicz, *Privatizing the Police State*, Chapter 8.
50 After reading his friends' files, Michnik, the intellectual who has led the fight against lustration, emerged shocked at how many of his colleagues had been SB informers. *Rzeczpospolita*, 21 January 1992.
51 The Ministry of Interior began to declassify files on 1 January 1997, with additional files thirty years past being made available to the public, the courts and the prosecutors' offices each year on 1 January. Files documenting the activity of the informers were declassified only if helpful in special murder investigations. M. Ellis, 'Purging the Past: The Current State of Lustration Laws in the Former Communist Block', *Law and Contemporary Problems*, 1996, vol. 59, pp. 181–196.
52 'Communist Secret Files to be Opened with Caution', *RFE/RL Report*, 13 June 2000. Online. Available HTTP: http://www.ukrweekly.com/Archive/2000/300006.shtml (accessed 28 January 2008). For Kieres's statements, see also 'Jan Ordynski's conversation with professor Leon Kieres, the chairman of the Institute of National Remembrance. Honor Means Facing the Truth', *Rzeczpospolita*, 2 September 2002.
53 P. Gentle, 'Letter from Poland', Radio Polonia, 8 February 2005.
54 Associated Press, 13 February 2005. For a while the list was available online at http://lista.atspace.org.
55 'Poland in Uproar over Leak of Spy Files', *Guardian*, 5 February 2005. Online. Available HTTP: http://www.guardian.co.uk/international/story/0,3604,1406281,00.html (accessed 28 January 2008), and D. Dastych, 'Better Late than Never: Retarded De-communization in Poland', *Gazette*, 9 January 2007. Online. Available HTTP: http://www.axisglobe.com/article.asp?article=1192 (accessed 28 January 2008).
56 Wildstein unmasked Leslaw Maleszka as an SB informer. A journalist with Gazeta Wyborcza, the most important anti-lustration daily, Makeszka reported on the opposition Student Solidarity Committee he co-founded in 1977 with Wildstein. In 1980, Wildstein emigrated to France, where he worked as a journalist for the Polish monthly Kontakt and Radio Free Europe.
57 Niezabitowska's undisclosed past came up when another member of Solidarity Weekly, Krzysztof Wyszkowski, examined his own file and learned that was spied by a secret collaborator code named Nowak. Researchers at the Institute of National Remembrance determined that Nowak was Niezabitowska, and Wyszkowski gave that information to the press. A. Purvis, 'The Reckoning. How Accusations of Communist-Era Collaboration Are Shaking up Central Europe', *Time Europe*, 4 April 2005.
58 'Poland', *East European Constitutional Review*, 1998, vol. 7, 25–26, and 1999, vol. 8, 26–27. Online. Available HTTP: http://www.law.nyu.edu/eecr (accessed 28 December 2007). Also J. Luxmoore, 'Poland Fears Its Judas Files'.
59 Walicki, 'Transitional Justice', p. 223.

60 J. B. de Weydenthal, 'Inquiry into the Murder of Father Popieluszko Reopened', *Report on Eastern Europe*, 17 August 1990, pp. 12–15, and N. Ascherson, *The Polish August*, Harmondsworth: Penguin, 1981, p. 101.
61 Los and Zybertowicz, *Privatizing the Police State*, pp. 190–191.
62 Calhoun, *Dilemmas of Justice*, pp. 179–180.
63 'Polish Parliament Condemns Communist Rule', *RFE/RL Newsline*, 11 June 1998. Online. Available HTTP: http://www.rferl.org/newsline/1998/06/4-SEE/see-110698.asp (accessed 28 January 2008).
64 Calhoun, *Dilemmas of Justice*, pp. 106–107.
65 'Warsaw Court Sentences Stalinist-Era Torturers', *RFE/RL Daily Digest*, 11 March 1996. Online. Available HTTP: http://www.rferl.org/features/1996/03/f.ru.96031317083328.asp (accessed 28 January 2008).
66 A. Michnik, 'Editorial', *Gazeta Wyborcza*, 25–26 September 1993, p. 1.
67 'The Three Lives of Helena Brus', *Sunday Telegraph*, 6 December 1998. Online. Available HTTP: http://www.anneapplebaum.com/communism/1998/12_06_tel_brus.html (accessed 28 January 2008).
68 For more details on the parliamentary debates preceding the vote, see Walicki, 'Transitional Justice', pp. 206–207, and T. Rosenberg, *The Haunted Land: Facing Europe's Ghosts after Communism*, New York: Vintage Books, 1995, pp. 125–258.
69 Walicki, 'Transitional Justice', p. 223.
70 Rosenberg, *The Haunted Land*, p. 217.
71 Ibid, p. 242.
72 Ibid., pp. 253–258.
73 'Sprawozdanie Komisji Nadzwyczajnej do Zbadania Dzialalnosci MSW z dzialalnosci w okresie X Kadencji Sejmu RP (1989–1991)', *Druk*, 25 September 1991, no. 1104.
74 Weydenthal, 'Inquiry into the Murder', pp. 12–15, A. Sabbat-Swidlicka, 'Former Security Officials Arrested', *Report on Eastern Europe*, 26 October 1990, pp. 18–21, Los and Zybertowicz, *Privatizing the Police-State*, p. 71.
75 Los and Zybertowicz, *Privatizing the Police-State*, pp. 63–64, 67–69.

5 Hungary

Lavinia Stan

There is a widespread belief in Hungary that the best revenge the new democracy could take for the decades of communist rule it experienced at the hands of an unscrupulous and rapacious nomenklatura is to live well and to prosper.[1] Economic redress for political injustice has been the Hungarian answer to de-communization and transitional justice, the two intertwined processes that have gained prominence throughout the post-communist Eastern European bloc. While its neighbors have struggled to deal with their dictatorial experience by reexamining their recent history, adopting lustration, bringing communist officials and secret agents to court, and opening the secret archives, Hungarians have embraced the position that "the best way to deal with the past is to do better now."[2] What exactly "doing better" means has never been spelled out, perhaps because ordinary citizens have generally been disinterested in the subject, the political class has been embroiled in its daily struggle for the people's minds and votes, and all Hungarians have taken pride in their exceptionally mild communist regime. In this general climate of apathy for the process of coming to terms with the past, the question we should raise is not "why Hungary failed to take a firmer stand toward its recent past?" but rather "why did it pursue limited lustration, file access and court proceedings at all?" Why did it stop short of embracing the Spanish model of "forgiving and forgetting," when other European post-communist countries were inclined to "prosecute and punish" former communist officials and secret agents? The answer lies partly with the nature of Hungary's communist regime, partly with its type of transition and exit from communism, and partly with its continuing post-communist struggle for power.

Mild, dare we name it "goulash," transitional justice was called for by the mild "goulash communism" of the 1960s and the 1970s. Hungary was one of the most progressive communist countries in Eastern Europe, allowing multi-candidate elections to be organized in 1985, tolerating political parties other than the ruling Socialist Workers' Party, and permitting opposition associations to form in the late 1980s. In contrast to neighboring Romania, Poland, Czechoslovakia or East Germany, Hungary's road to socialism cut across the happy hills of state–society cooperation and accord more than the valley of sorrows harboring outright repression and the leader's cult of personality. True, the communist rule started in Hungary the same way it started throughout Eastern Europe, with massive arbitrary arrests, show-trials of predetermined outcome, prison and labor camps, a ruthless secret political police orchestrated by NKVD agents, and "liberating" Soviet troops. But the 1956 Hungarian Revolution showed the population's impatience with communist intimidation tactics, and the citizens' willingness to take to the streets and openly challenge a regime delivering few political and economic benefits. Thus, instead of working against the people, the Hungarian communist leadership was forced to work with them and transform communism into a local-grown, liberalizing variant. Although the revolution was crushed, it helped Janos Kadar to create the soft "Kadarist" dictatorship. By 1989 the abuses of early communism were a distant memory for much of the population, which was therefore little inclined to seek reparations from a reformed communist leadership it had cooperated with so well.[3]

Its non-violent exit from dictatorship further prepared the country for mild, incremental de-communization. Whereas the regimes of Romania and East Germany collapsed quickly without talks between the hard-line communist leaders and the disorganized opposition representatives, the Hungarian roundtable talks took several months of negotiations, even longer than in the Czechoslovak and Polish cases. On 13 June 1989 the ruling party invited the political opposition and "third party" organizations traditionally associated with the communist authorities (mainly trade organizations) to formal negotiations in view of effecting a peaceful transition of political power. Deliberations took place at three different levels concomitantly. There were plenary sessions opened to the media, political negotiations between the three groups, and closed expert debates on matters of detail. Decisions were made by consensus among the delegations. The end-product of all those lengthy negotiations consisted of constitutional amendments ratified on 18 October by the communist-dominated parliament, whose members had been elected in the 1985 multi-candidate elections. Although the legislature was regarded as largely unrepresentative and negotiations were pursued in the absence of concerted efforts to promote meaningful public participation, there was a strong desire on the part of all bargaining parties to proceed in a constitutional manner.

Hungary's negotiated transfer of political power meant that perpetrators of communist crimes have remained very much part of the society undergoing the democratic transition, and have belonged to the political elite responsible for the move away from communism. As in Poland, "the loyalty of the Communist Party activists (however renamed or reformed) to the negotiated rules was a central factor in the peaceful and eventually successful transition."[4] The weak lustration Hungary adopted in the early 1990s reflected the former communists' influence over the legislative process, and the opposition's tacit recognition of the communist-era institutional and legal systems. That recognition, and its implied continuity between the communist and post-communist Hungarian states, seriously influenced the Constitutional Court decisions regarding the scope of lustration and prevented the adoption of a radical vetting similar to the one adopted in Czechoslovakia.

Last but not least, the Hungarian mild transitional justice has been the result of its post-communist struggle for power. Three arguments are worth mentioning here.

First, in other Eastern European countries, demands for retribution were voiced by groups wronged under communism, including former political prisoners, anti-communist dissidents, owners of property abusively confiscated, among others. In Hungary the peculiarities of post-communism led to an unlikely alliance between the former communists and the former hard-core anticommunist dissidents. By 1994 the Socialists had already won the support of the smaller Alliance of Free Democrats (*Szabad Demokratak Szovetsege*), which preferred to join forces with their former abusers than to lend support to the nationalist camp. Such a political choice discouraged an important group of former victims from seeking retribution and redress. Second, radical transitional justice has been unpalatable to the liberal camp, both because it would have exposed the numerous former spies drawn from among its own ranks and because it would have resembled an act of revenge taken on the exponents of "communism with a human face." Third, Hungarian parties have attempted "to restructure the scope of the original lustration laws to strengthen their political power vis-à-vis other political parties. As the intensity of the political competition between parties increases, one would expect to see commensurate changes proposed to the scope of the lustration legislation." The scope would be expanded "to permit more intensive use against political rivals." Horne and Levy further noted that, "as socialist parties have increased their political power, center and right wing political parties have attempted to increase the scope of the laws so as to counter the growing political competition posed by those political candidates."[5] Successive governments have used transitional justice as a bargaining chip, but their choice was always for variants of limited de-communization that would affect them minimally in the event of an electoral defeat.

The communist political police

In November 1945, the Independent Smallholder Party formed a coalition government after winning 57 percent of the vote in free elections. Although the Hungarian Communist Party (*Magyar Kommunista Partja*) garnered barely 17 percent of the vote, Matyas Rakosi was named deputy premier and other communists received key cabinet positions with the assistance of the occupying Soviet troops. During the war, Rakosi had led the Moscow-based Hungarian communists, who returned to Budapest after the Soviet Army invaded Hungary in September 1944. Their close ties to Moscow allowed Rakosi's Muscovites to take the lead of the country's communist movement, a position which the home-based cell of Laszlo Rajk also aspired to. To help communists assert control, the Red Army set up the *Allam-vedelmi Osztaly* (AVO) as the Hungarian secret police charged with suppressing and eliminating anticommunist opposition groups. Initially the AVO was headed by Gabor Peter, an NKVD (People's Commission for Internal Affairs) agent who used purges to weaken the Smallholders' social basis.[6] The secret police arrested outspoken anticommunist critics, accusing them of fascist sympathies and wartime collaboration with parties supportive of Nazi Germany. Many of the 40,000 individuals who stood accused by 1948 had indeed been sympathizers of the fascist Arrow Cross movement, and supporters of Hungary's alignment with Nazi

Germany.[7] The purge also extended to thousands of loyal communists, who were jailed, tortured, killed, and subjected to show-trials.

In the 1949 elections the communists, by then reorganized as the Hungarian Workers' Party (*Magyar Dolgozok Part*), ran unopposed. The new government appointed by President Rakosi continued to use show-trials to consolidate its position. In the process, Interior Minister Laszlo Rajk was sentenced to death, together with his entire extended family, after a mock trial condoned by Moscow. Throughout the 1950s, all those who headed the Interior Ministry and the AVO lost their positions in power struggles taking place within the party, or between the party leadership and the intelligence services. Rajk's successor, Janos Kadar, fell from grace in 1951, when he was arrested, tortured, and stripped of all his privileges. He was rehabilitated five years later to play a dominant role in the aftermath of the Hungarian Revolution. In 1952 Sandor Zold, Kadar's unfortunate successor, killed his wife, children, mother-in-law, and himself just before he was about to be purged. The following year Stalin denounced the AVO head Gabor Peter as a Western intelligence agent. After his arrest, Peter "confessed" to having collaborated with British and "Zionist" intelligence services to avoid receiving the death penalty. Six years later, he was released from prison by Premier Janos Kadar, who gave him a low-ranking government position until his retirement. After Khruschev's denunciation of Stalinist purges, Hungarian authorities admitted that the case against Rajk had been fabricated.[8]

The consolidation of communist power in Hungary followed patterns established elsewhere in Eastern Europe and were reminiscent of campaigns conducted earlier in the Soviet Union. As part of the forced collectivization of agriculture program farmers were compelled to join the collectives, surrender their land and working tools for free, and make deliveries to the government at prices below the costs of production. Nationalization of banking, trade and industry was completed by late 1949, and central planning was introduced in all economic areas. Landowners were expropriated and driven into exile, while their land was divided into tiny plots allotted to the poorest peasants. In what Rakosi referred to as the "salami tactics" political parties that could serve as an alternative or opposition to the communists were gradually marginalized, co-opted or banned. Non-communist politicians were discredited as "antidemocratic," removed from the government or jailed on trumped up charges. Trade unions lost their independence, while religious groups were robbed of much of their property. Protestant churches skillfully avoided further persecution by reaching a compromise with the communist authorities, but the Roman Catholic Church stubbornly resisted, prompting the government to retaliate by disbanding its orders and secularizing its schools. After 1989, demands for retribution and reparations were voiced primarily by members of the social categories wronged during these early campaigns.

Though the secret police was initially part of the regular police, by 1950 it was subordinated directly to the Council of Ministers and had divisions at the district, town, county, and national levels. In 1953 the AVO's independence ceased when different Interior Ministry divisions took over its tasks and operations. The AVO's final organizational structure came into being a decade later, when Department

III was organized within the Interior Ministry. Its five divisions were Main Division III/I (foreign intelligence), Main Division III/II (counter-intelligence), Main Division III/III (counter inside reaction service, equivalent to domestic repression), Main Division III/IV (military intelligence and counterintelligence), and Main Division III/V (providing technical supply for all other divisions). The state security service, later known as the AVH (*Allamvedelmi Hatosag*), also included the border guards. The Military Political Department of the Defense Ministry was set up in March 1945 with Soviet permission and support to reflect Kremlin's interests. This overall intelligence structure was maintained, with some minor changes, until the collapse of the communist regime.

In the organization of these structures political reliability took precedence over training, professionalism or personal skills, and thus mostly unprofessional, undereducated, and brutish careerists occupied the higher positions. Operating without civil and parliamentary control, the AVO generated public fear by using forced interrogation, torture, and arbitrary arrests to make innocent prisoners plead guilty. It ran cruel and crude labor and prison camps for political prisoners. Before 1953 ex-communist party members were treated more harshly than other political prisoners, but after 1953 they were a virtual aristocracy in political prisons. Prosecutors and courts were asked to cooperate closely with the security services to maintain an appearance of legality and secure the conviction of selected individuals. The AVO assisted the Soviet security services, which in turn helped its efforts to imprison the Roman Catholic Primate Jozsef Cardinal Mindszenty in 1948, and bring Interior Minister Rajk to trial for Titoism the following year. Security services thus operated as a political police defending the communist regime and leaders more than the national interest, which was reflective of the regime's desires and priorities. Thus, with respect to the relationship between secret services and the party-state, Hungary replicated the model characteristic of the communist block. The party was the brain, deciding the main goals, setting the agenda and controlling the mix of carrots and sticks offered as punishment for opposition and criticism or reward for compliance and loyalty. In turn, secret services were the muscle that transposed the party's wishes into reality.

After Stalin's death, the new Soviet leadership summoned Hungarian party leaders to Moscow, and harshly criticized them for the country's dismal economic record and use of terror. Rakosi remained party head, but Nagy became premier and quickly won the support of the party membership and intelligentsia for his sweeping reforms. He ended the purges, freed up the political prisoners, and closed notorious labor camps. He allowed peasants to leave collective farms, canceled compulsory production quotas in agriculture, granted subsidies to private producers, and increased investments in the production of consumer goods. However, Nagy failed to fundamentally alter the structure of the communist economy, an oversight that led to production levels below those registered in 1953. Following that announcement, Rakosi seized the moment to disrupt reforms, attack Nagy as a right-wing deviationist, and force his resignation from government and ban from the party in April 1956. Some of Nagy's economic reforms were reversed, but the purges did not resume, although Rakosi had to contend with many outspoken critics within the party, including purge victims rehabilitated and readmitted into the party at Moscow's prompting.

During that summer Rakosi's position eroded to the point that it became untenable. The general population and the reformist-minded party members deplored the reversal of economic policy and the lack of any concrete (and realistic) plan for economic revival, and became increasingly frustrated with the faltering living standards. The police and intelligence services became disgruntled when an investigation into earlier purges cleared Rakosi of wrongdoing while blaming them alone for purging innocent victims through abuse of power. Students, writers, and intelligentsia criticized the Central Committee's decision to dissolve the Petofi Circle, which had served as a debate forum, and to expel intellectuals from the party. The press printed official attacks against Rakosi, who in mid-July resigned the position of First Secretary in favor of his deputy, Erno Gero. Intended to help the party-state to acquire a new lease on life, the move turned into a political fiasco. Gero's close proximity to Rakosi reflected poorly on his popularity, and therefore the change of guard was unable to stop public discontent and avert the Hungarian Revolution.

The ruthlessness of the secret political police became apparent on 23 October 1956, when students took to the streets of Budapest in anti-governmental protests. Clashes with the AVH agents resulted in several protesters being killed and wounded that evening. In retaliation, protesters took control of key institutions and important territories sometimes resorting to violence. The nationalist group of Jozsef Dudas executed pro-Soviet communists, and known or suspected AVH agents and informers were caught up in the uprising. On 29 October Dudas's commandos stormed the AVH headquarters and massacred the agents inside. The crowd lynched more AVH members when wage ledgers were found attesting to the fact that agents received salaries 10 times higher than ordinary wages. Ironically, the AVH was housed in a building that once belonged to the Arrow Cross Party, the inter-war fascist formation that ruled the country from October 1944 to January 1945 and was responsible for sending some 80,000 Jews on a death march to the Austrian border.[9] As the situation rapidly deteriorated the Hungarian party leadership asked Moscow for help. Protests continued while Kremlin pondered whether Soviet troops should pull out of Hungary or quell the revolution. Meanwhile, Nagy, whom the Central Committee had appointed as premier, announced plans to negotiate the withdrawal of Soviet troops, disband the AVH, dismantle the one-party system, and allow Hungary to return to its pre-communist political system. The announcement prompted Moscow to dispatch future KGB head and Soviet Premier Yuri Andropov to Budapest. On 1 November Nagy woke to the news that Soviet tanks had entered Hungary, but Andropov assured him that they only sought to protect the withdrawing Soviet troops. That day, Nagy declared Hungary's unilateral withdrawal from the Warsaw Pact and announced its intention to join the United Nations. The revolution ended two days later, when Soviet troops began their assault on Budapest. Nagy was arrested, spirited to Moscow via Bucharest, tried, found guilty, and executed in June 1958.

The 1956 uprising significantly impacted state–society relations in communist Hungary. The revolt resulted in 2,500 people being killed, and around 200,000

Hungarians leaving the country for Western Europe and North America. Between 1957 and 1962, some 22,000 people were sentenced in courts, among them 250 to 350 to death.[10] Despite Andropov's promises, Soviet troops were not withdrawn, massive arrests were operated, and Kadar established a tight control over the party-state.[11] The fate of the security services remained unclear. Kadar criticized the AVH's methods, but not the thrust of the security work or its ideological foundations, which were left untouched. Many Hungarians sincerely and naively believed that the domestic intelligence service was never resurrected after Nagy's promise to disband the AVH. While some took pride in living in the only communist country without secret political police forces, others cautiously suspected that Kadar reorganized the AVH within the regular police force. Because the uprising took the state security services by surprise, and attested to their failure to predict popular support for student demonstrations, communist authorities in Budapest accepted the KGB to operate directly on Hungarian soil. The AVH continued to recruit ordinary Hungarians as informers and conduct comprehensive surveillance operations, even after the regime adopted the liberalized "goulash communism" and the ruling party membership swelled.[12] Until 1989 the AVH operated under the direct control of the party-state, the leadership of a Deputy Interior Minister, and the confines of a myriad of secret internal orders and directives.

Those convinced that, compared to its Eastern European counterparts, the mild "goulash communism" of the 1960s and the 1970s required a smaller state security force and elicited lower levels of daily secret surveillance of individuals and groups voicing opposition to the communist regime, ideology, and leaders were disappointed to find out that the AVH kept tabs on opposition leaders for the benefit of the Workers' Party even after 23 October 1989, the day marking the official proclamation of the post-communist Republic of Hungary. The AVH reportedly identified 2,029 new surveillance targets (victims) in the first six months of 1989 alone, and there are reasons to believe that rate was not significantly lower than that registered throughout the decade.[13] During the June–September roundtable talks organized that year, the ruling party received regular information reports on the opposition's activities, thus having the upper hand in a negotiation it already initiated and shaped to its liking. While publicly committed to peaceful democratization and increased power sharing with the opposition, top governmental officials like President Matyas Szuros, Premier Miklos Nemeth, Minister of State Imre Pozsgay, Exterior Minister Gyula Horn, and Deputy Premier Peter Medgyessy continued to receive secret intelligence reports.

Following the roundtable talks, the constitution was amended in October 1989 to allow for a multiparty system, and free elections were organized in 1990. Soviet troops were gradually withdrawn by mid-1991, thereby ending some 47 years of military occupation. Secret services were also reorganized, but not before facing the most severe scandal in their history, the so-called Dunagate. On 5 January 1990 the Alliance of Free Democrats and the Alliance of Young Democrats produced operative information reports proving that secret services had collected information on the opposition in spite of the new constitutional changes endorsing a multiparty system. While their master, the Workers' Party, formally agreed to democratic changes, secret services continued their usual operative activities, identifying individuals and groups perceived as the "hostile opposition," and serving up information to the communist leadership. Security services had remained behind the times, as the transformation they envisaged was largely superficial, leaving their core secret operative activities unaffected. The opposition called on the government to distance itself from the unlawful activity of secret services, and to dismiss those responsible for gathering the information. Following lengthy investigations into the Dunagate scandal, on 21 January 1991 the Main Division III/III was disbanded without a legal successor. For many Hungarians, the move aimed to shrewdly preserve the bulk of the communist secret services at the expense of one of its divisions, treated as the main scapegoat. Division III/III remained the only intelligence service declared unconstitutional.[14]

The scandal brought about a limited reorganization of security services, after several similar proposals were rejected both during and immediately after the roundtable talks. On 6 September 1989 the negotiating subcommittee charged with finding methods to avoid violence and guarantee a peaceful regime change interviewed Deputy Interior Minister Ferencz Pallagi about the status of the security services. Pallagi blatantly lied, claiming that since December 1989 secret services had reported to the government not the ruling party, and that all security-related tasks were performed by the regular police not an independent secret service. Paradoxically, the subcommittee failed to question Pallagi in detail, and showed interest in recovering the confiscated samizdat literature and dismantling the Workers' Guard, the ruling party's armed unit. Following opposition leader Ferencz Koszeg, these two topics were launched as top negotiation priorities in an effort to divert attention from the more critical issue of state security services. A week later opposition leader Peter Tolgyessy demanded the creation of a self-standing security service without knowing that secret services were already operating outside of the regular police. The ruling party rejected the proposal. With this, the fate of the security services remained undecided and outside the purview of the new constitution.

The legislation governing the activity of the post-communist security services included Act X of 1990, which terminated the state security tasks of the Interior Ministry, laid down the procedure for authorizing special clandestine methods, and served as basis for Governmental Decree 26/1990 and Act CXXV of 1995, which provided a new legal framework for national security. Security tasks were bestowed on two newly-created civilian structures: the National Security Office (*Nemzetbiztonsagi Hivatal* or NBH), responsible for gathering and processing both domestic and foreign intelligence information, and the National Security Services (*Nemzetbiztonsagi Szakszolgalat* or NBSzSz), responsible for protecting the national interest within the country's borders and providing protection for Hungarian government officials and diplomats both inside the country and abroad. The NBH has fulfilled national security tasks and has operated under governmental direction and parliamentary supervision, with a nationwide scope of authority and a budget of its own. In addition to civilian structures, Hungary maintains military intelligence forces, including the Military Security

Office (*Katonai Biztonsagi Hivatal* or KBH) and the Military Detection Agency (*Katonai Felderito Hivatal* or KFH).

The Hungarian model: lustration without the lustrati

As a result of the 1990 general elections, political power reverted to a loose coalition of opposition parties, which together controlled a comfortable majority of 230 seats (out of the total 386) in the unicameral legislature. The Hungarian Democratic Forum (*Magyar Demokrata Forum*), the Independent Smallholders' Party (*Fuggetlen Kisgazda Part*) and the Christian Democratic People's Party (*Keresztenydemokrata Neppart*) formed the government under the leadership of Premier Jozsef Antall. While committed to sidelining the communists, the ruling partners were unable to bridge their differences, and pursue lustration concomitantly with designing strategies to move the country away from communism and closer to democracy and free market economy. Political instability and the nomination of a new government headed by premier Peter Boross, after Antall's untimely death, postponed the adoption of a screening law until the weeks leading to the 1994 elections, by which time a number of drafts were discussed and rejected. As serious procrastination threatened to block de-communization altogether, deputies of the ruling coalition introduced the legislative proposal in the house before fine-tuning its details. This oversight came to haunt them later, when the screening law was seriously challenged by the Constitutional Court. Because of its delayed adoption, in which premier Antall was believed to have played a key role, the bill did not apply to members of the first democratically-elected parliament.

The Lustration Act was preceded by another legislative proposal never seriously debated in parliament. On 3 September 1990 deputies Gabor Demszky and Peter Hack, representing the opposition Alliance of Free Democrats, called for the opening of all secret police files and the drafting of a list of all secret officers and informers who worked for Division III/III. The list was to be deposited with the President of Hungary, the Prime Minister, and the legislative national security committee. Public office holders whose name appeared on the list could resign within 60 days, in which case their tainted past remained secret. The identity and past involvement with communist secret services of those who refused to give up their office were to be made public. The proposal failed to gain support, because rumor had it that the ruling coalition planned to employ the files to compromise their political rivals. According to unconfirmed reports, while in office Prime Minister Antall handed out to his opponents within the governmental coalition and his own party sealed envelopes allegedly containing incriminating data about their ties to the communist secret political police. A victim of that process was chauvinist politician Istvan Csurka, then a member of the Hungarian Democratic Forum. After some hesitation, Csurka ultimately admitted to have signed a collaboration pledge under the code name "Rasputin," but claimed that he never provided any information reports.[15]

The Law on the Background Checks of Individuals Holding Certain Important Positions (Act XXIII of 8 March 1994 or the Lustration Act) subjected some

12,000 current officials to a screening process by at least two three-judge panels, which had to examine the archives of the domestic secret service departments and to complete their work between 1 July 1994 and 30 June 2000.[16] The panels examined whether selected public office holders had collaborated with the communist domestic state security, supplied secret reports as informers, received secret information reports, or belonged to the fascist Arrow Cross Party. Collaboration with the communist secret services was established if a pledge to collaborate was found together with proof that the person was remunerated for his or her services. Those screened were not required to give depositions concerning their past before the lustration panel. Vetted officials included only those who had taken an oath before parliament or the President of the Republic: the President, ministers, deputies, judges, journalists working for public mass-media outlets, and leaders and managers of state universities and public companies. If collaboration was determined, the information was made public only if the persons refused to resign from their post. Those persons could keep the job even if such information was publicized. Thus, the law lustrated only a tiny fraction of public officials who wanted to continue to keep secret their tainted past. In practice, no Hungarian public official unmasked as a former collaborator chose to step down, either before or after sensitive information was made public.

The Hungarian Lustration Act represented a milder solution compared to similar proposals adopted in neighboring countries, as it neither declared incompatible the holding of present public office with past collaboration with the secret police, nor proposed to unveil the entire communist surveillance system. It promoted limited transparency rather than punishment. Complete transparency, the kind that permitted the public to find out the tainted past of post-communist political luminaries, came only when public officers rejected the resignation offer. Hungary's toothless lustration was the result of its liberalized communist past, negotiated transition, and post-communist reality. Following historian Laszlo Varga, soft lustration was "a direct continuation of the 'soft' dictatorship, or Goulash Communism, of the previous era in that those who held high positions in the old regime were permitted to remain in leading posts under the new dispensation."[17] Lustration was not discussed during the roundtable talks, but there was a strong desire on negotiating partners to maintain the credibility of the talks by not attacking the credibility of the players. Afterwards, lustration was reluctantly pursued in a general climate of public disinterest in such matters, and a wide-spread belief that the best revenge was to live well, not to ban communist officials from playing a role in post-communist politics.[18] Proponents of lustration stressed that public office holders with a tainted past were susceptible to blackmail.[19] Their critics mocked the threat of blackmail as unreal, although former secret officers have often come forward to disclose information about post-communist politicians who used to work for them as secret informers.

The change in government brought about by the 1994 elections raised a number of important challenges to the lustration process. Dissatisfied with the poor performance of the center-right government, Hungarians brought the former communists back in government. The Socialist Party and the Alliance of Free Democrats, which together controlled 278 seats in Parliament, nominated Socialist Gyula Horn as premier. The ruling coalition represented an uneasy partnership between the former communists and the former hard-core anticommunist dissidents, one time arch-enemies united in their efforts to contain the political right. The new rulers asked the Constitutional Court to review the constitutionality of the Lustration Act. On 24 December 1994 the court passed Decision 60, which deemed the law partly unconstitutional and offered July 1996 as deadline for its implementation. The court criticized the act on several grounds. First, it declared that one of the main functions of lustration – to protect democratic transition against those with a compromised past – was no longer relevant. The Hungarian transition had occurred five years earlier, and thus its protection could not serve as a rationale for lustration. Second, the court explained the need to balance the right of personal data protection (provided by Article 59 of the constitution) with the right to acquire and disseminate information of public interest (protected by Article 61 of the constitution). It held that public persons do have a smaller sphere of privacy than private persons, and thus it would be just to come down in favor of the principle of freedom of expression/acquisition of information.[20] Third, the court declared unconstitutional and discriminatory the fact that the act allowed for the verification of members of the public print media, but not members of the electronic media.[21]

In response to the court's recommendations, in July 1996 the Socialist-dominated parliament set up the Historical Office and amended the Lustration Act to significantly narrow the scope of mandatory lustration and end its application in year 2000. After screening committees examined the records of some 600 officials, in April 1997 they announced that several deputies were suspected of having worked as secret agents.[22] During the ensuing public scandal, premier Horn admitted the screening process revealed his own prior activity as a communist-era spy, both on account of his service in the militia assembled to help crush the 1956 revolution and because later he received secret information as Exterior Minister. Ignoring the public outcry, Horn declined to resign and said he regarded the matter as closed. His revelations and his refusal to repent for his past mistakes cost Horn and his Socialists valuable electoral support.[23] The following year, general elections brought the opposition Fidesz (renamed Fidesz – Hungarian Civic Party), the Hungarian Democratic Forum and the Smallholders' Party back to power. Act XC of 2000 extended the scope of mandatory screening to journalists working for electronic and printed media and leaders of political parties receiving national budget shares. The new legislation opened the possibility for voluntary lustration for attorneys, notaries, religious leaders and mass-media journalists and reporters not subject to mandatory screening. Mandatory screening was extended until 2004 and the pool of people to be screened was enlarged from 900 to some 17,000, but the purview of lustration remained limited to involvement with the domestic intelligence branch.[24]

After the 2002 elections, the Socialist Party and the Alliance of Free Democrats again formed the cabinet with a narrow parliamentary majority. Soon after taking office, Socialist premier Peter Medgyessy was denounced by the leading conservative daily *Magyar Nemzet* as a communist-era spy. According to documents – some of questionable authenticity – the daily published on 18 June, the premier worked between 1961 and 1982 as the counter-intelligence secret agent code-numbered D-209. At first, Medgyessy denied all accusations, insisting that he already had been subject to lustration and cleared of past collaboration, but after more details about his past emerged he defended himself by saying he was an "honest, law-abiding and patriotic citizen" who had only served his country as Deputy Interior Minister and member of the Finance Ministry's counter-intelligence service. As he said, "for five years [1977–1982] I helped ensure that foreign informers did not get a hold of Hungarian secrets so as to prevent Hungary from being admitted to the International Monetary Fund." He further suggested that Hungarians should thank him for securing the country's accession to that international structure in 1982 despite opposition from Moscow and the KGB, and that further disclosure of his past would violate the data-protection and national-security legislation. His case officer, lieutenant-colonel Lajos Toth, publicly contradicted Medgyessy, saying the premier's counter-intelligence activities were directed against the West, not against the Soviet Union.[25]

Both the opposition and the government demanded details on the premier's past. The opposition asked the Alliance of Free Democrats to support a no-confidence vote against Medgyessy. After some initial hesitation, the junior governing partner decided to support the premier and thus avoid the fall of the entire cabinet. The opposition had to give up on the no-confidence motion, although a public poll revealed that 66 percent of respondents believed the premier should step down.[26] The same poll showed that only 15 percent of the respondents were "very interested" in finding out which politicians collaborated with the communist secret police, 49 percent was "not at all interested," and twice as many thought that the scandal hurt the opposition more than the government.[27] The scandal revealed some important weaknesses of the Lustration Act, and resulted in a mushrooming of legislative amendments. Medgyessy was able to pass the screening process originally because his primary ties were to the counter-intelligence division. The Lustration Act called only for screening past involvement with Division III/III (domestic repression), not with other state security branches, although in reality documents and information moved freely between branches. None of the changes proposed to address this legislative loophole gained parliamentary support, in part because ambiguity provided opportunities for political blackmail.[28]

On 24 June the government and the opposition proposed competing amendments to Act X of 1990 on secret services. The act allowed the disclosure of the identity of domestic informers only in the exceptional case of "public figures." The opposition's more radical proposal stipulated that former communist spies could not occupy post-communist public office because of a "conflict of interest." The bill asked for the public release of the names of all members of the Politburo and Central Committee of the Workers' Party, full-time party secretaries, and secret intelligence agents working for Division III/III. These individuals were barred from occupying high ranking state positions such as those of parliamentary deputies, deputy ministers and ministers, President of the republic, Prosecutor-General, Supreme Court president or National Bank governor.[29] The house rejected the proposal. The government's more modest proposal asked for the release of names of full-time former Division III/III spies, if they were public figures or sought public office, and set up the Security Services Historical Archive to make available documents produced by Division III/III, but not files of Divisions III/I and III/II, classified as state secrets for reasons of national security. The opposition criticized the proposal for "authorizing merciless action against those on the lower echelons of the party-state pyramid, while exempting actual regime operators."[30] Presenting it to parliament, Justice Minister Peter Barandy said the bill promoted transparency in public life and settled disputes on the communist past. As such, the rights of persons figuring in secret documents were outweighed by the need for transparency and the demands of national security. The government further limited the categories of screened public officials, and set up lustration committees consisting of 12 judges appointed by parliament to four-year terms.[31] On 10 December 2002 the house adopted the amendments with 173 votes in favor, 168 votes against and 3 abstentions. As a result, lustration was restricted to the President, ministers and deputy ministers, leaders of the Constitutional Court, the Supreme Court, the Prosecutor General's Office, the State Audit Office, the Ombudsman, the Central Bank, the county council presidents, and mayors of towns with more than 10,000 residents. Vetting did not affect church leaders, journalists working for private news agencies or members of trustee boards founded by parliament or government.[32] At the same time, the Historical Office was replaced with the Security Historical Archive.[33]

Medgyessy was not the only top official to confess to his tainted past. The head of the Hungarian Police, Major General Laszlo Salgo, had to admit he reported the activities of fellow citizens. He did not resign his position. Soon afterwards, a well-known ex-communist journalist casually mentioned that he knew the father of deputy Zoltan Pokorni was a former spy. For Pokorni, who immediately resigned his position as Fidesz chairman, it was a tragedy to uncover the past, to understand why his parents split in the early 1970s after his mother discovered that her husband had been involved with the secret police since 1956. Pokorni's father was a political prisoner between 1953 and 1956, and he could only survive by reporting.[34] In response to these two cases, on 9 July 2002 parliament set up two parallel investigative committees. The first committee was formed at the request of the opposition to investigate Medgyessy's career as a secret agent, and establish whether he had worked for Divisions III/III (domestic repression) or III/II (counter-intelligence). Chaired by Hungarian Democratic Forum deputy Laszlo Balogh, the committee wrapped up its activity on 15 August in the midst of a fierce public debate, without producing a final report or uncovering anything substantive. Committee members representing the government and the opposition blamed each other for the failure. Government representatives insisted that Medgyessy's counter-intelligence activity served the national interest and he was not morally responsible for communist wrongdoings. By contrast, opposition representatives concluded that Medgyessy had been involved in activities typical of an oppressive regime, was vulnerable to blackmail, and posed a threat to national security. On 20 August the Socialist committee members presented parliament with a report claiming that Medgyessy did not violate past or present legal regulations. Their colleagues representing the opposition never drafted a final conclusion. Apparently the premier even benefited from the procedure, with his support in opinion polls increasing.

The other committee was set up at the government's request to look into the past of all post-communist government officials. Chaired by Free Democrat deputy Imre Mecs, who spent two years on death row after 1956, the committee explored the past of some 200 senior top public officials by relying on information provided by the National Security and the Historical Offices. Unsurprisingly, the information it unearthed tended to be detrimental to the opposition. On 31 July the committee announced that five unnamed ministers of the previous cabinet were communist spies, and revealed that a former minister signed a cooperation pledge and three others filed information reports. A week later opposition members walked out of the commission, accusing the Socialists of using it to divert attention from Medgyessy's past.[35] Soon afterwards, Mecs announced that 10 former ministers had collaborated with the AVH: five served in the 1990–4 cabinet of Jozsef Antall, two in Gyula Horn's cabinet of 1994–8, and four in Viktor Orban's cabinet of 1998–2002. This time, Mecs pledged to release the names of those individuals.[36] The ombudsman Attila Peterfalvi recommended against such a move and criticized the committee on grounds that its activity infringed the data protection law and violated the prohibition of ex post facto legislation. President Ferenc Madl – a member of the first post-communist cabinet – also questioned the committee's constitutionality and refused to undergo screening, a position from which he later withdrew. Article 21 of the constitution allows parliament to establish investigative committees, while Act LXIII of 1992 on date protection permits the disclosure of the names and position of all government officials whose name and rank do not constitute a state secret.

Dissatisfied with the slow pace of lustration, on 24 August *Magyar Hirlap* published, without the consent of those named, the names of post-communist public officials allegedly with ties to the communist secret services. The list included members of the Orban cabinet (State Secretary Laszlo Bogar, PHARE Funds Minister Imre Boros, Finance Minister Zsigmond Jarai, Foreign Affairs Minister Janos Martonyi, and Transport Minister Laszlo Nogradi), members of the Antall cabinet (International Economic Trade Relations Minister Bela Kadar, Finance Minister Ferenc Rabar, Defense Deputy Minister Erno Raffai, and Agriculture Deputy Minister Laszlo Sarossy), Trade Minister Szabolcs Fazakas of the Horn cabinet, and premier Peter Medgyessy (a former Finance Minister from 1996 to 1998). Those named either denied the revelations or claimed they collaborated under duress. The following week, Mecs released a list of tainted politicians that included all names *Magyar Hirlap* identified but Jarai. As a result of his identification as Comrade D-8 of Division III/II, Boros was expelled from the Hungarian Democratic Forum, but continued to serve as an independent deputy. The final report the Mecs committee submitted to parliament included no names.[37]

On 25 September 2003 the press identified the public radio head Katalin Kondor as a counter-intelligence agent working from 1974 to 1983. Kondor denied the allegations, and opposition Fidesz leader Annamaria Szalai accused the ruling

Socialists of resorting to trumped-up charges to smear the public radio for its refusal to become a left-wing mouth-piece. Similar to Medgyessy, Kondor was unaffected by the lustration law, which applied only to domestic security agents. Days later Levente Sipos, chairman of the three-member commission supervising the transfer of secret archives from the National Security Office to the Historical Archive, confirmed that Kondor appeared as an unpaid secret agent in documents transferred on 7 October, but admitted that her recruitment file was still missing.[38] After reading her secret file, Kondor announced that she never contacted Division III/II, the secret documents described an attempt at recruiting her, and they included no information reports filed by her. On 27 October *Nepszava* reported that a secret agent who knew Kondor in the 1970s described her as a "highly qualified and disciplined agent working to high professional standards." The agent claimed to have met Kondor in a "conspiracy flat," and argued that Kondor helped to blow the cover of an industrial spy who wanted to sell documents from strategically important institutions to foreign spies. Government representatives asked for Kondor to be screened officially due to the fact that she helped to form public opinion in her position as head of a state-run media outlet.[39]

In February 2005 another scandal erupted in Budapest when the Political Culture Institute released a list of 19 post-communist politicians who allegedly collaborated with the communist secret services. The list, largely old news, named people who admitted to having collaborated and individuals declared as former collaborators by a screening court. The Institute announced it will continue to release new names from the list of 97 agents it uncovered through scientific research, because it wanted to "pressure politicians to keep their promises to disclose all former communist agents." Among those named were former Socialist premier Peter Medgyessy, Central Bank governor Zsigmond Jarai, and the parents of writers Peter Esterhazy and Zoltan Pokorni, who is also a former Fidesz chairman. Also named was Istvan Csurka, leader of the xenophobic Justice and Life Party (MIEP), represented in parliament from 1998 to 2002.[40]

Secret file access

Act XXIII of 1994 on the Screening of Holders of Some Important Positions, Holders of Positions of Public Trust and Opinion-Leading Public Figures and on the History Office granted access to the secret political police archive. Promoted by the Socialist government, the act provided for extremely limited access to few files. One could only request to read his own secret file, from which the names of informers and third parties had been blackened. To protect personal data, sensitive information was erased from documents supplied to ordinary citizens and researchers. Curiously, even the act of having been recruited as an informer was classified as sensitive information, in a move which rendered the entire file access effort pointless. The fact that someone had acted as a secret informer for the communist political police was a piece of personal data that needed to be strictly protected, unless that person was a "public figure." Secret informers were denied access to the reports they had submitted to the state security.

A newly-created History Office became the custodian of the secret archive, and had to receive from post-communist information services the archive generated by all branches of Division III. Important archival materials remained classified. They included files needed for the uninterrupted functioning of the intelligence services, and files containing both the vital data that could lawfully be handled by the security services and the data that could be disclosed, if the separation of these data proved technically impossible. It was up to the intelligence services alone to determine which files could be transferred to the History Office, as the legislation did not provide for any review procedure in this case. Most pre-1980 secret files were declassified, but the History Office received only 5 percent of the files produced by the military and counter-intelligence services. Although the file transfer had to occur within 60 days, it was completed only in 2000. The following year, the office asked parliament to recognize it as an archive mandated to distinguish clearly between victims and spies in order to grant them different levels of access to their own files, and to release more secret archival materials to researchers. Those requests were granted in 2003.

Act III of 14 January 2003 on the Disclosure of the Secret Service Activities of the Communist Regime and on the Establishment of the State Security Historical Archive turned the Historical Office into a Historical Archive responsible for both communist secret files and documents produced as part of the lustration process.[41] The activity of the Historical Archive was supervised by the Speaker of parliament, who appointed and dismissed the archive chair. Victims of communism were granted access to all secret files. To gain information about the communist repression mechanisms and clearly distinguish between communist and post-communist information services, researchers were granted broader access to secret files and the mass-media could widely publicize the role of the communist secret services. Any person could read or publish data needed to identify a "public figure" as a secret full-time agent or part-time informer. If the identified persons refused to recognize themselves as public figures, the courts could be asked to identify the person as a public figure. File access was allowed to the extent it did not endanger national security interests. To this end, data that remained classified included the names of post-communist secret agents, the names of agents whose public identification would lead to their deportation from a foreign country, prohibition to enter another country, criminal prosecution or a threat to their and their relatives' lives, safety and freedom. After the Medgyessy scandal, Act III was amended to allow for greater file access. As a result, victims could access the records of those who spied on them, provided those records are over 30 years old. Some documents remain classified for longer periods of time in the interest of privacy: state secrets, official secrets, and confidential business data.[42]

Given the way the legislation was formulated, file access depended heavily on the willingness of the post-communist information services to relinquish the communist-era secret files. By 2000 the services announced that they had declassified 1,788 archival "items." According to their own declarations, three-quarters of those items were victims' files, while the remainder represented "object files" (reporting on Hungarian émigré organizations), "B" (personal) and "M" (job) agent files from the 1950s. After another periodical file revision, in late 2002 the Service transferred one million secret pages, including 650,000 pages of intelligence reports and briefs from 1957 to 1975 (recorded on 210 microfilms); 4,000 pages of assessments produced in 1975 (1,611 files in total); seven files produced from decrypted materials (stored on microfilms or paper); 50,000 pages of encrypted materials produced by foreign ministries, embassies and international organizations (around 60,000 page-long micro-fiches pages and 17 film rolls); 10,000 pages produced before 1970; and 98 search files compiled on individuals and organizations before 1970 (in total 112 volumes of 8,000 pages). The service claimed it handed over a total of 400 linear meters of secret documents. As of 2000, the Historical Archive housed some 70,000 investigation files, 15,000 operative files, 5,600 recruitment files, 8,000 work files, and almost 4,000 "building" files (covering life in economic units), reports, studies, lists, and manuals. Hungarians have been slow to ask for access to files. During the 1997–2000 period, only 5,000 persons requested to read their files. In almost half of all those cases, no secret file was found.[43]

Extant files represent only a fraction of the original archive. Communist secret services regularly destroyed materials deemed unimportant, and carried out document destruction campaigns in 1956, the early 1970s and late 1989. There are no reliable estimates of the number of documents destroyed in regular and irregular file selections. Varga claimed that 70 percent of secret files were lost in 1989 and 1990, when, "as part of the last throes of the communist regime, a frenzied wave of shredding swept through the secret services."[44] Rainer argued that "the destruction of documents took place at a panic-stricken speed" and affected the observer files still in use and some archived material. As a result, "most of the pre-1956 operative files have vanished and so have the ones for immediately before 1989." About 100,000 of the 110,000 agent-recruitment files were also lost.[45] As no independent investigation was ever carried out to estimate the number of extant files, conspiracy theories abound. Some say the secret archive was moved to Moscow, others believe it remained in Hungary at the disposal of security services eager to determine the course of the new democracy, and still others argue that most files were destroyed.[46] In September 2002 the Historical Office admitted that 54 of its original secret files had been replaced with photocopies. Some of the missing documents concerned Gabor Szalay of the ruling Free Democrats, who admitted his collaboration with Division III/II (counter-intelligence) from 1978 to 1988. During investigations, the legislative security committee interviewed the head of the Interior Ministry records office, the head of the Historical Office, and Gabor Kuncze, Interior Minister in 1995 when the original documents went missing.[47]

Szalay's file was not the first to be altered. During the 1989 roundtable talks the secret political police made considerable efforts to conceal its surveillance operations directed against the anticommunist opposition. In July 1989 the Interior Ministry selected the files that needed to be closed and archived because surveillance of those targets had been terminated. In the process, observers alleged, the secret services covered not only their domestic activities, but also their counter-intelligence and military intelligence operations. In October that year, Division

III/III reviewed its operative records with an eye to destroying the files incompatible with the changed legal situation, which allowed opposition activity. On 18
December Pallagi authorized the destruction of files still used by agents on a daily
basis, some archived files detailing the activity of victims, agents, informers, and
collaborators. Files detailing ongoing operations were altered to remove all signs
of surveillance of crimes against the state which ceased to exist. The order asked
for the destruction of archived files detailing the surveillance of schools, opposition parties, religious groups, and the production and distribution of samizdat
literature. Among the "network" files slated for destruction were selected files of
retired recruiting agents (*beszervezesi dosszie* or *'B' dosszie*), files detailing confidential investigation methods, combinations or security games, files of recruitment agents who were also Workers' Party members, and files of retired network
members (*kizart halozatok*). Only the personal information cards of active agents
were preserved. Work files (*munka dosszie* or *'M' dosszie*) containing information
reports received from network persons were cleansed. Disregarding the services'
own internal rules of data organization, Pallagi asked for the removal of memos
reporting file destruction. The opposition leaders were told of this file destruction
campaign only after it was completed.

The autumn of 2004 turned up more former spies among elected officials, while
various lists of agents emerged on the internet and in the press. This prompted
new interest in parliamentary circles to amend the legislation exposing communist secret agents. Completely unexpected, Socialist premier Ferencz Gyurcsany
took the lead in advocating full disclosure of all secret agents. His vague initial
policy proposal met the liking of all political parties represented in parliament, but
the more concrete the proposal became, the more rapidly it fell short of consensus. Ultimately, the Constitutional Court rejected the legislative changes adopted
in 2005. That year the opposition Fidesz called for opening all communist secret
archives, including the files still housed with various ministries, estimated to total
around one linear kilometer. The party further asked for the public disclosure
of the communist past of post-communist politicians, and the marginalization of
tainted public figures who "pursued state security activities against Hungarian
citizens, not upon coercion but on their free will." The resolution called for sanctions for those who tampered with the secret archives, a clearer definition of the
"public figure" term, and an investigation of the involvement in human rights
violations of former communist party officials.[48] The proposal received a cold
shoulder in parliament.

Court proceedings

In Hungary economic injustices inflicted under communism were redressed
through the compensation law of 1991, but little was done about the political
crimes committed by communist officials. In many cases the relatives of those
executed, tortured, and harassed during the communist period still wait for the
names of those responsible to be revealed. While some offences committed by
communist officials and secret agents were legal under the communist law, many

other offences amounted to crimes even by those standards but the political circumstances of the time impeded victims from asking for an investigation or trial.
For example, contrary to communist legislation minors were executed for their
involvement in the 1956 revolution and other adult protesters were tortured during
interrogation and died as a result of their beatings. Kadar's regime ended these
practices only as a result of international pressure. As Pataki noted, individual officials whose identity remained unknown were responsible for ordering the shooting into defenseless crowds in Mosonmagyarovar, Salgotarjan and other towns
during and after the 1956 revolution.[49] Because the period with the gravest crimes
accompanied the 1956 uprising and the limitation periods for these crimes had run
out, criminal suits against human rights violators could not be brought easily.

Hungary was first among Eastern European countries to adopt the legislative
framework needed for the criminal prosecution of communist officials. The law
on the prosecutability of communist crimes was introduced in parliament by
the Hungarian Democratic Forum deputies Zsolt Zetenyi and Peter Takacs and
approved in December 1991 by a large majority, despite warnings that such a
measure might be impractical for legal, political and moral reasons. The bill called
for the suspension of the statute of limitations for cases of treason, premeditated
murder and aggravated assault leading to death in those cases where, for political
reasons, prosecutions had not been previously possible. The law covered crimes
committed during a period of time which started with 21 December 1944, the day
when the first Hungarian Parliament convened in Debrecen following the era of
Admiral Miklos von Horthy, and ended with 2 May 1990, the day when the first
freely elected post-communist parliament met. Its primary aim was "not to punish
the criminals, but to unmask them," as its jurisdiction was rather limited.[50] The
law only covered acts that were crimes at the time when they were committed,
targeted only those cases where there had been no trial due to political reasons,
and provided for lighter sentences than normal, where applicable.

Court trials were not directed against ordinary communist party members, but
against those involved in torturing or killing innocent individuals. Yet, the president refused to sign the law and instead he sent it to the Constitutional Court,
which unanimously overturned the bill as lifting the statute of limitations and
failing to define treason. The court justified its decision by adherence to the rule
of law principles, and argued that "legal certainty, based on objective and formal
principles, takes precedence over justice which is partial and subjective at all
times."[51] Stressing strict adherence to the rule of law, the court refused to let the
political change lead to a devaluation of the fallen regime's legislation. Instead the
court identified the security of law, understood as "the protection of rights previously conferred, non-interference with the creation or termination of legal relations, and limiting the ability to modify existing legal relations to constitutionally
mandated provisions," as the highest principle. In emphasizing procedural over
substantive justice, the court forced parliament to reconcile the quest for a just
outcome with the requirement of formal legality.[52] As Teitel noted, the decision
further ignored international legislation with respect to crimes against humanity.
"Protection of the rule of law also implies adherence to fundamental international

law norms such as the principle of the imprescriptibility of crimes against human-ity. The failure to refer to any national or international precedents on this question is a glaring omission in the Hungarian constitutional court's opinion."[53]

In February 1993 parliament amended the 1973 Criminal Code to allow the prosecution of communist-era crimes for which the limitation period had run its course, and passed an "authoritative resolution" reading that the statutes of limi-tations should not apply to the 1944–1989 period. After the Constitutional Court rejected both decisions, parliament adopted the Law on Procedures Concerning Certain Crimes Committed during the 1956 Revolution based on international instruments such as the Geneva Convention Relative to the Treatment of Civilians in the Time of War and Relative to the Treatment of Prisoners of War of 1949 and the New York Convention on the Non-Applicability of Statutory Limitations to War Crimes and Crimes against Humanity of 1968. The law interpreted the 1956 events as war crimes and crimes against humanity. For these types of crimes the statutes of limitations were excluded by the Geneva and New York Conventions, which Hungary had ratified. The Constitutional Court again struck down some parts of the law, but upheld its main provisions grounded in these international norms. According to the court, "the legal system of Hungary shall respect the universally accepted rules of international law, and shall ensure, furthermore, the accord between the obligations assumed under international and domestic law." The law, ensuring the enforcement of "universally accepted rules of international law," entered into force in October 1993.[54]

While the law was procedurally acceptable, many wondered whether communist-era crimes could really qualify as crimes against humanity under a regime where political killings were usually masked as suicides. Unlimited privileges for the nomenklatura and a broad array of controls over society exercised through legal measures, a lack of human rights and due process, the absence of individual rem-edies, censorship, controlled mobility inside the country and abroad, a selective system of benefits to promote loyalty to the system and to create an atmosphere of constant fear – those were the main crimes of the communists during the last two decades of its existence. In that environment, homicide acts, disappearances, torture, though occurred, were not mass-scale, but rather isolated cases.

For Sadursky, the Constitutional Court's intervention in the "parliamentary action aimed at bringing the perpetrators of some of the crimes to justice can be seen as an arrogation of the power, by the Court, to dictate the terms of the transition, under the guise of a self-righteous legalism and commitment to the rule of law. For this reason perhaps, the decision was so broadly applauded by the Western observers and commentators: they could identify with the Court speaking the idiom of lib-eral constitutionalism and the 'civilized' rule of law, as opposed to the apparently revengeful and populist parliament." At the same time he warned that "there is noth-ing canonical about this particular interpretation of the rule of law" because "by denying Parliament the authority to define the parameters of transition – the propor-tions of continuity and discontinuity with the old legal system – the Court opted for a highly arbitrary interpretation of the rule of law to prevail over politically defined understanding of the mix of continuity and discontinuity."[55] Teitel also observed that the court decision on the statute of limitation amounted to a "brilliant power grab," which only apparently "represented a victory for the rule of law."[56]

On 30 October 1993 Parliament passed unanimously a version of the law revised in light of the Constitutional Court's recommendations. The new legal framework defined by Act XC allowed the Ministry of Justice to investigate fifty episodes of mass shootings that occurred from 23 October to 28 December 1956, during the revolution. In several cases, once investigations were concluded the Prosecutor General promptly brought charges, and court proceedings were launched by the Budapest City Court, the only court allowed to hear those cases. The first trial started in mid-1994. Six months later the court reached an impasse, when two of its chambers adopted two different conclusions, each appealed to the Supreme Court. One chamber ruled that the government forces' shooting into unarmed demonstrators in December 1956 in the town of Salgotarjan were not war crimes, but could count as crimes against humanity. The shootings were deemed to be "prohibited acts in the case of armed conflict not of an international character." Two of the 12 defendants were found guilty, and were each sentenced to five years in prison. In a similar case related to the same incident, another chamber of the Budapest City Court ruled that the acts were to be judged by domestic, not international, norms. As it decided that the statute of limitations applied to the case, the chamber set it aside. Instead of ruling on the two cases before it, the Supreme Court unexpectedly petitioned the Constitutional Court for an interpretation of Act XC of 1993. The petition claimed that the law was unconstitutional because it failed to specify both the procedures under which cases could be brought before the ordinary courts in Hungary and the criminal procedure applicable to those cases. The Constitutional Court sided with the Supreme Court and asked parliament to amend the law before the ordinary courts could hold more trials.[57]

Conclusion

Mild lustration not leading to loss of public office, delayed and limited access to the secret archives, and very few court cases bringing to justice communist officials and secret agents responsible for human rights violations – these are the results of the Hungarian transitional justice process. Weak political will and public apathy prompted Hungary to shy away from comprehensive lustration, full opening of secret files and vigorous prosecution of communist officials and spies, and instead embrace softer methods of atonement and retribution. Act XXXVI of 1989 overturned the court judgments handed down in connection to the 1956 revolution, Act XXVI of 1990 annulled politically-motivated court verdicts and condemnations handed down from 1945 to 1963, while Governmental Decree 93 of 1990 redressed some injustices resulted from the communist labor law. This legislative framework, however, brought vindication only to those whose conviction was somehow related to the 1956 events and specifically included the words "revolution" or "political." Echoing general public sentiment, philosopher Gaspar Miklos Tamas, a former opposition activist, said he would send the secret archive to the bottom of the Danube river, signaling thus his personal preference for the Spanish solution of "forgiving and forgetting." The patchy archival material that has survived the extensive destruction sweep of the 1989–1990 might just allow Hungarians no alternative to forget about ever piecing together the puzzle of the activity of the communist-era secret information services. Tamas's radical position would allow Hungary to contemplate its future by forgetting its past, but would also leave important moral questions unanswered. Luckily, his advice was not heeded by the Historical Archive, whose secrets are yet to be uncovered.

Notes

1 An earlier version of this chapter was published as L. Stan, 'Goulash Justice for Goulash Communism? Explaining Transitional Justice in Hungary', *Studia Politica: The Romanian Political Science Review* 2007, vol. 7, 269–292. It is used here with permission.
2 G. Halmai and K. Lane Scheppele, 'Living Well Is the Best Revenge: the Hungarian Approach to Judging the Past', in J. A. McAdam (ed.) *Transitional Justice and the Rule of Law*, Notre Dame: University of Notre Dame Press, 1997, pp. 155–184.
3 H. Nyyssonen, 'Salami Reconstructed. 'Goulash Communism' and Political Culture in Hungary', *Cahiers du Monde Russe* 2006, vol. 47, 167.
4 W. Sadurski, "De-communization', 'Lustration' and Constitutional Continuity: Dilemmas of Transitional Justice in Central Europe', *EUI Working Paper LAW* 15, 2005, 24. Online. Available HTTP: http://cadmus.eui.eu/dspace/bitstream/1814/1869/2/law03–15.pdf (accessed 4 January 2008), and J. M. Rainer, 'Opening the Archives of the Communist Secret Police – the Experience of Hungary', paper presented at the Congress of Historical Sciences, Oslo, Norway, 6–13 August 2000. Online. Available HTTP http://www.rev.hu/archivum/rmj_oslo_00_eng_long.html (accessed 6 December 2006).
5 C. M. Horne and M. Levy, 'Does Lustration Promote Trustworthy Governance? An Exploration of the Experience of Central and Eastern Europe', October 2002. Online. Available HTTP http://www.colbud.hu/honesty-trust/horne/pub01.html, pp. 24–25 (accessed 7 June 2006).
6 When in May 1947 Premier Ferenc Nagy went on holiday in Switzerland, he was sent word he will be arrested upon his return to Budapest.
7 L. Karsai, 'Crime and Punishment: People's Courts, Revolutionary Legality, and the Hungarian Holocaust', *East Central Europe* 2004, vol. 4. Online. Available HTTP http://sipa.columbia.edu/regional/ece (accessed on 12 June 2006).
8 P. Kenez, *Hungary from the Nazis to the Soviets. The Establishment of the Communist Regime in Hungary, 1944–1948*, New York: Cambridge University Press, 2006, and M. G. Roskin, *The Rebirth of East Europe*, Upper Saddle River, NJ: Prentice-Hall, 2002, 4th edition, pp. 72–73.
9 After 1989, the building became a museum commemorating the victims of both the fascist and communist regimes.
10 In June 1988 the Committee for Historical Justice (*Tortenelmi Igazsagtetel Bizottsaga*) was founded illegally. Its founding platform insisted on "the full moral, political and juridical rehabilitation of victims, both alive and dead, from the retribution which followed the [1956] revolution." The committee demanded "reliable history-writing on the post-1956 period, publication of documents about 1956, and a national memorial, as well as the reburial of those executed." Nyyssonen, 'Salami Reconstructed', p. 168.

11 By 1963, all political prisoners arrested in conjunction with the 1956 revolution were released. The number of party members in parliament was the lowest in 1953 (69.9 per cent), and the highest in 1958 (81.6 per cent). Nyyssonen, 'Salami Reconstructed', p. 150.

12 In 1985 the Hungarian Socialist Workers' Party membership reached some 871,000 in a total population of about 10.5 million.

13 R. Uitz, 'Missed Opportunities for Coming to Terms with the Communist Past: The Hungarian Saga of Lustration and Access to Secret Service Files', paper presented at the American Association for the Advancement of Slavic Studies conference, Salt Lake City, 3–6 November 2005, p. 16.

14 P. N. Nagy, 'A vad titka', *Nepszabadsag*, 19 June 2002, quoted in C. Kiss, 'The Misuses of Manipulation: The Failure of Transitional Justice in Post-Communist Hungary', *Europe-Asia Studies* 2006, vol. 58, 928.

15 I thank Peter Hack for this information. Details are reported by Kiss, 'The Misuses of Manipulation', p. 930.

16 'Hungary: Law on the Background Checks to be Conducted on Individuals Holding Certain Important Positions. Law no. 23, 8 May 1994', in N. Kritz (ed.) *Transitional Justice: How New Democracies Reckon with Their Authoritarian Past*, Washington, DC: US Institute for Peace, vol. 3, 1995, pp. 418–425.

17 P. Gerson, 'Dunagate's Waters Run Deep', *The Budapest Sun*, 9 March 2000.

18 As argued by Halmai and Scheppele in their suggestively-titled chapter, 'Living Well Is the Best Revenge'.

19 E. Oltay, 'Hungary's Screening Law', in Kritz (ed.) *Transitional Justice*, vol. 2, p. 667.

20 Sadurski, "Decommunization', 'Lustration' and Constitutional Continuity', p. 24.

21 A. Hussain, 'Civil and Political Rights, Including the Question of Freedom of Expression. Report of the Special Rapporteur on the protection and promotion of the right to freedom of opinion and expression', United Nations Economic and Social Council, Commission on Human Rights, 29 January 1999. Online. Available HTTP http://www.unhchr.ch/Huridocda/Huridoca.nsf/0/16583a84ba1b3ae5802568bd004e80f7?Opendocument (accessed on 4 January 2008).

22 Kritz (ed.) *Transitional Justice*, vol. 2, p. 184.

23 T. Garton Ash, *History of the Present: Essays, Sketches and Dispatches from Europe in the 1990s*, London: Vintage, 2001, p. 305.

24 E. Barrett, P. Hack, and A. Munkacsi, 'Lustration in Hungary: An Evaluation of the Law, Its Implementation and Its Impact', paper presented at the American Association for the Advancement of Slavic Studies conference, Boston, 4–7 December 2004. The paper is an abridged version of an earlier draft prepared for the Institute of Criminal and Transitional Justice, New York. Also Kiss, 'The Misuses of Manipulation', p. 933.

25 'Pro-Fidesz Daily Says Hungarian Premier Was Secret Police Agent', *RFE/RL Newsline*, 18 June 2002. Online. Available HTTP: http://www.rferl.org/newsline/2002/06/180602.asp (accessed 28 January 2008), 'Hungarian Premier Admits to Communist Secret Service Past', *RFE/RL Newsline*, 19 June 2002. Online. Available HTTP: http://www.rferl.org/newsline/2002/06/190602.asp (accessed 28 January 2008), and 'Hungarian President Vows Not to Intervene in Medgyessy Affair', *RFE/RL Newsline*, 2 July 2002. Online. Available HTTP: http://www.rferl.org/newsline/2002/07/020702.asp (accessed 28 January 2008).

26 'Hungarian Premier Apologizes to Electorate', *RFE/RL Newsline*, 24 June 2002. Online. Available HTTP: http://www.rferl.org/newsline/2002/06/240602.asp (accessed 28 January 2008).

27 Kiss, 'The Misuses of Manipulation', p. 935.

28 'Hungary', *East European Constitutional Review* 2002, Vol. 11, pp. 24–25.

29 'Hungarian Premier Pledges to Expose Informers', *RFE/RL Newsline*, 20 June 2002. Online. Available HTTP: http://www.rferl.org/newsline/2002/06/200602.asp

(accessed 28 January 2008), and 'Hungarian Government Publicizes Proposed Amendments to Law on Former Agents, *RFE/RL Newsline*, 24 June 2002. Online. Available HTTP: http://www.rferl.org/newsline/2002/06/240602.asp (accessed 28 January 2008), 'But Opposition Will Submit Own Amendments', *RFE/RL Newsline*, 24 June 2002. Online. Available HTTP: http://www.rferl.org/newsline/2002/06/240602.asp (accessed 28 January 2008).

30 'Hungarian Socialists Insist on Amending Vetting Bill', *RFE/RL Newsline*, 10 September 2006. Online. Available HTTP: http://www.rferl.org/newsline/2006/09/110906.asp (accessed 28 January 2008).

31 'Hungarian Opposition Criticizes Vetting Bills', *RFE/RL Newsline*, 12 September 2006. Online. Available HTTP: http://www.rferl.org/newsline/2006/09/120906.asp (accessed 28 January 2008), and 'Hungarian Coalition Parties Propose Reducing Scope of Vetting Process', *RFE/RL Newsline*, 26 September 2006. Online. Available HTTP: http://www.rferl.org/newsline/2006/09/260906.asp (accessed 28 January 2008).

32 Parliament rejected a proposal of the radical populist Hungarian Justice and Life Party, whereby church leaders could have been screened if 20 percent of all active priests had voted in favor of such action. Kritz (ed.) *Transitional Justice*, vol. 2, p. 665.

33 'Hungarian Parliamentary Committees Approve Vetting Bills', *RFE/RL Newsline*, 11 July 2002. Online. Available HTTP: http://www.hri.org/cgi-bin/brief?/news/balkans/rferl/2002/02-07-11.rferl.html (accessed 28 January 2008), and 'Hungarian Parliament Weakens Secret-Agent Bill', *RFE/RL Newsline*, 11 December 2002. Online. Available HTTP: http://www.hri.org/news/balkans/rferl/2002/02-12-11.rferl.html (accessed 28 January 2008).

34 'Collaboration Issue Backfires on Hungarian Opposition Leader', *RFE/RL Newsline*, 8 July 2002, 'Who Says He Needs Time to Deal with Revelation', *RFE/RL Newsline*, 8 July 2002, and 'And Prime Minister Condemns 'Collaboration' Tack in Politics', *RFE/RL Newsline*, 8 July 2002. Online. Available HTTP: http://www.rferl.org/newsline/2002/07/080702.asp (accessed 28 January 2008).

35 'Hungarian Parliament Sets Up Two Investigative Commissions', *RFE/RL Newsline*, 10 July 2002. Online. Available HTTP: http://www.rferl.org/newsline/2002/07/100702.asp (accessed 28 January 2008), 'Hungarian Former Prime Minister Invites Media to Committee Hearings', *RFE/RL Newsline*, 31 July 2002. Online. Available HTTP: http://www.rferl.org/newsline/2002/07/310702.asp (accessed 28 January 2008), 'Hungary's Fidesz-Era Ministers Deny Links with Communist-Era Secret Services, *RFE/RL Newsline*, 1 August 2002. Online. Available HTTP: http://www.rferl.org/newsline/2002/08/010802.asp (accessed 28 January 2008), 'As Medgyessy Commission Members Leak Intended Questions to Media', *RFE/RL Newsline*, 1 August 2002. Online. Available HTTP: http://www.rferl.org/newsline/2002/08/010802.asp (accessed 28 January 2008), 'Hungarian Opposition Walks Out of Commission Hearings', *RFE/RL Newsline*, 6 August 2002. Online. Available HTTP: http://www.rferl.org/newsline/2002/08/060802.asp (accessed 28 January 2008), and 'Hungary', *East European Constitutional Review* 11, 2002.

36 'Hungarian "Medgyessy Commission" Chairman Says Bullet Is "A Message"', *RFE/RL Newsline*, 8 August 2002. Online. Available HTTP: http://www.rferl.org/newsline/2002/08/080802.asp (accessed 28 January 2008), 'Hungarian National Bank Governor Slams Mecs Commission', *RFE/RL Newsline*, 15 August 2002. Online. Available HTTP: http://www.rferl.org/newsline/2002/08/150802.asp (accessed 28 January 2008), and 'Vetting Denied to Medgyessy Commission Experts', *RFE/RL Newsline*, 15 August 2002. Online. Available HTTP: http://www.rferl.org/newsline/2002/08/150802.asp (accessed 28 January 2008). Two individuals served in more than one cabinet.

37 On 23 September 2003, the Constitutional Court deemed both committees as unconstitutional. 'Another Former Hungarian Minister Admits Collaborating with Communist Secret Services', *RFE/RL Newsline*, 19 August 2002. Online. Available HTTP:

http://www.rferl.org/newsline/2002/08/190802.asp (accessed 28 January 2008), 'Hungarian Police Investigate Whether Newspaper Violated State-Secrecy Laws', *RFE/RL Newsline*, 23 August 2002. Online. Available HTTP: http://www.rferl.org/ newsline/2002/08/230802.asp (accessed 28 January 2008), and 'Former Hungarian Ministers React to 'Magyar Hirlap' Revelations', *RFE/RL Newsline*, 27 August 2002. Online. Available HTTP: http://www.rferl.org/newsline/2002/08/270802.asp (accessed 28 January 2008).

38 'Hungarian Radio Chairwoman Vows to Sue Over Reports of Spying', *RFE/RL Newsline*, 26 September 2003. Online. Available HTTP: http://www.rferl.org/ newsline/2003/09/260903.asp (accessed 28 January 2008), 'Hungarian Radio Chair-woman Listed as "Unpaid Agent"', *RFE/RL Newsline*, 8 October 2003. Online. Available HTTP: http://www.rferl.org/newsline/2003/10/081003.asp (accessed 28 January 2008), 'Hungarian Radio Chairwoman Was "Secret" Agent, Not 2Social"', *RFE/RL Newsline*, 9 October 2003. Online. Available HTTP: http://www.rferl.org/ newsline/2003/10/091003.asp (accessed 28 January 2008), and 'Hundreds Demon-strate in Support of Hungarian Radio Chairwoman', *RFE/RL Newsline*, 14 October 2003. Online. Available HTTP: http://www.rferl.org/newsline/2003/10/141003.asp (accessed 28 January 2008).

39 'Hungarian Radio Chairwoman Denies Counterespionage Links', *RFE/RL Newsline*, 15 October 2003. Online. Available HTTP: http://www.rferl.org/newsline/2003/10/151003. asp (accessed 28 January 2008), and 'Hungarian Radio Chairwoman's Communist-Era Operator Steps Out of Shadow', *RFE/RL Newsline*, 27 October 2003. Online. Avail-able HTTP: http://www.rferl.org/newsline/2003/10/271003.asp (accessed 28 January 2008).

40 'Nume celebre pe lista colaboratorilor serviciilor secrete comuniste ungare', *Cotidi-anul*, 12 February 2005.

41 Act III of 2003. Online. Available HTTP http://www.th.hu/html/en/acts/ABTL_4_2003_ evi_III_tv_e.pdf. (accessed on 14 July 2007).

42 'Hungary to Open Spy Files', *Deutsche Welle*, 9 December 2004. Online. Available HTTP: http://www.dw-world.de/dw/article/0,1564,1423227,00.html (accessed 28 Jan-uary 2008).

43 J. M. Rainer, 'Opening the Archive of the Communist Secret Police – The Experience of Hungary'.

44 Gerson, 'Dunagate's Waves'.

45 Rainer, 'Opening the Archives'.

46 According to Rainer, during the Dunagate scandal "the 'observer files' still in use were destroyed (these have been kept on members of the opposition) and the closed files were not spared either. Most of the pre-1956 operative files have vanished and so have the ones for immediately before 1989 (the destruction was begun at the two ends, with 1945 and 1989). About 100,000 of the 110,000 agent-recruitment files fell victim." The data seems exaggerated. See Rainer, 'Opening the Archives'.

47 'Hearing on Missing File Delayed in Hungary', *RFE/RL Newsline*, 24 September 2002, and 'As Poll Reiterates that Public Doesn't Care', *RFE/RL Newsline*, 24 September 2002. Online. Available HTTP: http://www.rferl.org/newsline/2002/09/240902.asp (accessed 28 January 2008).

48 *The Position of Fidesz – Hungarian Civic Union on the Opening of Former State Secu-rity Files*, 17 March 2005.

49 J. Pataki, 'Dealing with Hungarian Communists' Crimes', *RFE/RL Research Report*, 28 February 1992, p. 21.

50 Ibid, pp. 21–22.

51 'Hungary: Constitutional Court Decision on the Statute of Limitations, No. 2086/ A/1991/14, 5 March 1992', in Kritz (ed.) *Transitional Justice*, vol. 3, pp. 629–640.

52 Wilke, 'Politics of Transitional Justice', p. 6.

53 S. J. Schulhofer, M. Rosendelf, R. Teitel and R. Errera, 'Dilemmas of Justice', in Kritz (ed.) *Transitional Justice*, vol. 1, p. 659.
54 K. Morvai, 'Retroactive Justice Based on International Law: A Recent Decision by the Hungarian Constitutional Court', *East European Constitutional Review*, vols. 3–4, 1993–1994, pp. 32–34.
55 Sadurski, "De-communization', 'Lustration' and Constitutional Continuity', pp. 42–43.
56 R. Teitel, 'Paradoxes in the Revolution of the Rule of Law', *Yale Journal of International Law* 1994, vol. 19, 244–245.
57 Halmai and Scheppele, 'Living Well Is the Best Revenge', pp. 166–171.

6   Romania

Lavinia Stan

Since 1989 a combination of factors concurred to delay and then block the Romanian process of coming to terms with the recent communist past. While calls for lustration accompanied the December 1989 regime change and featured prominently in the political program of the budding opposition, the country as a whole opted against banning former communist officials from post-communist politics. Legislation adopted in 1999 allowed citizens to view their secret files, and empowered a state Council for the Study of Securitate Archive (known as the CNSAS) to examine past involvement with the communist secret political police, the Securitate, of electoral candidates, governmental officials, and candidates to or holders of public posts. Unfortunately, months after its creation, the council became embroiled in a public scandal from which it never fully recovered. Today few Romanians trust the council, most of them believing that it has deliberately or unwittingly blocked an honest search of the communist past, and that its activity has been rendered meaningless by legislative loopholes and lack of political will. Because until 2006 it was denied direct access to the secret archive, the council allowed only a fraction of the petitioners to read their files, passed a number of incorrect verdicts the courts later overturned, and cleared thousands of candidates in the 2000 and 2004 elections without full verification. Progress in the area of trials prosecuting human rights abuses has been equally disappointing, with most cases relating to the 1989 bloody events, not the atrocities of early communist rule.

True, in 1999 Romania seemed committed to take unprecedented steps to deal with its past by bringing lustration to public attention, granting access to the secret archive, paving the way for the public identification of Securitate agents, and convicting top-ranking army generals for their involvement in the 1989 massacres. While there were hopes that these measures were part of a comprehensive effort to seek truth and justice, the country failed to sustain the progress, and all three transitional justice areas were left wanting. Public debate surrounding the Timisoara Declaration did not lead to lustration legislation in view of the 2000 elections, tainted electoral candidates continued their political careers with impunity, secret file access remained restricted, most communist officials and army, police, and intelligence officers were not prosecuted, and higher courts overturned some sentences condemning such individuals for their human rights trespasses.

The political class, drawn predominantly from the lower echelons of the communist elite, continued to block transitional justice. Until 1996, President Ion Iliescu and his Social Democrats, initially known as the National Salvation Front, opposed an examination of the communist human rights record on grounds that the country needed to address its socio-economic problems not to dwell on the past, and the Ceausescu family alone was responsible for past crimes more than the communist regime. After winning the popular vote with the promise to identify and prosecute communist torturers, President Emil Constantinescu and the Democratic Convention lacked the political will to support the call for lustration and file access of Christian Democrat senator Constantin ('Ticu') Dumitrescu. After 2000, President Iliescu and the Social Democrat government proved equally unwilling to open the Pandora's box of collaboration with the communist regime, for fear of losing popular support once their own involvement was made public. Following the 2004 elections, President Traian Basescu and the Liberal-dominated government have revived the process, but it is still too early to say whether their outspoken commitment to truth and justice at the level of the discourse will translate into legislation unblocking lustration, expanding access to secret files, and launching court trials against former communist torturers.

The ruthless Securitate

The Romanian communist secret political police was set up under the direction of NKVD agents soon after Soviet troops entered Bucharest on 30 August 1945. Three years later, the refashioned pre-communist Siguranta, augmented with Secret Intelligence Service agents and militia Patriotic Guard troops, was renamed the General Directorate of People's Security (*Directia Generala a Securitatii Poporului*, popularly known as the Securitate), a repression agency called upon to eradicate existing political institutions and social structures to consolidate communist power, and ensure compliance once change was effected. According to Decree 221 of 30 August 1948, the Securitate included 10 directorates on domestic intelligence, counter-sabotage, counter-espionage in prisons and the police, counter-espionage in the armed forces, penal investigation, protection of ministers, technology (telephone tapping and eavesdropping), cadres, political (responsible for Communist Party purity) and administration, and four auxiliary departments on mail interception, surveillance, eavesdropping, and cipher. In 1949 two other internal security bodies were established: the militia replaced the police, while the Securitate troops took over the duties of the gendarmerie. The 64,000-strong security troops maintained public order in major industrial centers and quelled resistance to the unpopular collectivization of agricultural land and nationalization of private homes. In 1951, the Securitate was restructured to include 12 directorates, one specifically designated for foreign intelligence, and additional auxiliary departments dedicated to archives and transport of secret documents.[1] Except for minor changes, the structure remained unchanged until 1989. The Securitate Bucharest headquarters oversaw the activity of offices at the county, town and commune level, ensuring comprehensive territorial coverage of all aspects of life. The Securitate was the only Eastern European repression structure to include an anti-KGB department, later called to counter other Soviet bloc operations against Romania and its leader (1978–1989), and the only one free of Soviet advisers (withdrawn in 1964). Nevertheless, the Securitate continued to collaborate with the Soviet KGB, whose intelligence objectives it endorsed.

Throughout its existence, the Securitate tried to win a degree of autonomy from the ruling Communist Party, whose repression instrument it remained. While the details on its specific operations and organizational structure remained secret, the political police never truly behaved like a "state within a state" for extended periods of time, but rather remained accountable to the top party leadership, which set its overall mission and specific goals, and provided it with the financial means to reach them.[2] A legal framework for the Securitate's activity was set up as early as 1949, when opposition to the regime and resistance to property expropriation were deemed criminal offenses punishable with terms of prison and hard labor. The following year, the death penalty was extended to treason, economic sabotage, crimes against national independence and sovereignty, negligence leading to public disaster, theft and destruction of military equipment, plotting against the state, and spying for and betraying state secrets to foreign services. What the legal framework did not allow, the political police assumed with impunity. Although no legislation authorized them, tens of thousands of house arrests were operated and thousands of private homes were nationalized in the early stages of communism.[3] The Securitate sought to defend the country against foreign intelligence penetration and engage in industrial and scientific espionage abroad, but the bulk of its daily activity was directed against the Romanian people. This is why it resembled a repressive political police more than a Western-style intelligence service compatible with democracy.

The terror characteristic of the 1945–1964 period, when massive arrests and internal deportations were operated with little regard to the law, political prisoners were tortured and exterminated, and anticommunist protests were crushed with brutality, gave way to fear and alienation after Nicolae Ceausescu became the leader of the party-state in the mid-1960s. In a shrewd calculation designed to win Western financial support for his megalomaniac projects, Ceausescu discontinued the politics of blind subservience to Moscow and direct confrontation with the West in favor of a highly secretive influence operation designed to show the West that his Romania was independent from all other communist countries, and as such worth supporting.[4] Ceausescu, who thought of himself as the nation's *Conducator* (Fuhrer) and the world's greatest statesman, believed that his Horizon secret program was a great achievement.[5] In line with this new strategy, a measure of "socialist legality" was introduced to give the courts more power and limit to 24 hours the time a citizen could be held without being charged. Ceausescu denied the existence of dissidence and opposition in the country. Instead of being imprisoned dissidents were placed under house arrest, instead of being convicted for their political opinions they were sentenced as petty criminals or confined to psychiatric hospitals, and instead of being killed they were encouraged to emigrate.[6]

When it came to domestic repression, the political police engaged in evidence-gathering through visual surveillance, wire-tapping, mail and phone call interception, interviews with co-workers, relatives and neighbors, direct threats and promises. The fear the Securitate inspired to ordinary citizens was more the result of the clever workings of the Disinformation department than of its visible presence on the street, in schools, workplaces or apartment blocks. The network of full-time agents with military rank varied over the years, according to the needs of the political police. In 1948 there were 3,549 Securitate agents in a population of about 17 million.[7] The Securitate employed 20,297 officers in April 1977 and 23,381 officers six years later, when the country's population reached 24 million.[8] Official estimates indicate that on 22 December 1989 the secret police employed only 13,275 officers and 984 civilian personnel, but the need to reduce its staff during the last five years of communist rule was never adequately explained, and thus has little credibility.[9] The network of informers was gradually enlarged from 42,187 in 1948 to 507,003 in 1989. The 1989 figure included 29,613 Nazi sympathizers, 10,367 members of the inter-war Peasant and Liberal Parties, and 2,753 former political prisoners. Demographically, 241,932 were sixty and older, 145,294 between forty and sixty, 81,572 between thirty and forty, and 17,995 under thirty years of age. The number of active informers also increased from 73,000 in 1968 to 144,289 in 1989. Following an undated socio-economic analysis of 3,007 new informers, 39 percent had university and 37 percent had high school education, 18 percent were engineers and researchers, 17 percent were professionals, 19 percent were public servants, and 32 percent army officers, workers or peasants.[10] Nine in 10 secret agents were party members, but party membership was not required of part-time informers. After 1968 agents were forbidden to recruit party members and public officials as informers without the consent of the county party leader. This measure was designed to further bring the political police under the party's control.

The Securitate took over the reports, information notes and denunciations gathered by the pre-communist Siguranta, and gradually produced new files reflecting its interests, needs, and outlook on life. The secret archive included nominal files on victims and informers as well as "case files" on issues like Religious Life, Political Parties, Collectivization or Armed [Anticommunist] Resistance in Mountainous Areas. Starting in 1971, paper files were also transferred on electronic support, after the Securitate acquired an IBM computer. Once archived, the files were stored in the central archive, where individual agents could access them on request with the help of a card system ordering nominal files alphabetically. Files were lost in the so-called Jarul operation (which led to the destruction of around 240,000 files of party members acting as informers in 1968–1974) and the December 1989 revolution (when 100,000 other files were destroyed or "misplaced" by case officers).[11] In the early 1990s, official estimates claimed that the extant Securitate archive totaled 35 linear kilometers of documents, of which 25 kilometers were victim files, four were informer files, and the remaining six were folders of information reports and denunciations attached to the victim files. Every meter of archive contained some 5,000 documents, and every file was on average 200 pages in length.[12]

Once the Ceausescu regime collapsed, the Securitate was declared officially dismantled, although the country's new leaders were careful to keep the secret agents and the secret archive close by. Months later, in 1990, as many as nine information services reemerged from the ashes of the communist secret police departments. Only two such information services, the Romanian Information Service and the External Information Service, were placed under parliamentary supervision, while the others were accountable to the executive (the Presidency, the Ministries of Defense, Internal Affairs and Justice or the Prime Minister's Office). All information services have had their share of public scandals, but the Romanian Information Service has remained the most controversial by far. In 1990, the service lost much of its credibility in an ill advised attempt to destroy secret documents by burying them in the Berevoiesti forest ravine eighty kilometers northwest of Bucharest. After being unearthed by local peasants, the documents were published by several Bucharest dailies, embarrassing the service as well as the government. The incident reopened the debate about the continuity between the old Securitate and the new service which, some claimed, had inherited the archive, personnel and methods of the domestic repression branch of the communist political police. During the 1990s, the service became embroiled in the wars dividing the heirs to the Communist Party, the Social Democrats, and the weak democratic opposition represented by the Liberals and the Christian Democrats, and managed to control parliament more than parliament was able to control it. After the Council for the Study of Securitate Archive was constituted in March 2000, the service became a public enemy for its refusal to surrender the secret archive to the Council, designated as its legal custodian, on grounds that the file disclosure would endanger its operations and reveal the identity of its agents. The political opposition and the civil society retorted that a service claiming to be akin to Western-style intelligence agencies should retire the agents and cease the operations of the old Securitate.

Lustration: the revolution's stillborn?

The first calls for lustration came on 11 March 1990 when the Timisoara Declaration was presented to the public.[13] The Declaration praised Timisoara as the birthplace of the revolution, criticized Bucharest's neglect of and disinterest toward the provinces, and denounced the Salvation Front's decision to register as a political party in order to compete in the first free elections of May 1990. Following the document, the authors, "direct participants in the 16–22 December 1989 events, feel compelled to explain to the entire nation why Timisoara's residents triggered the revolution, what was fought for, what so many of them gave their lives for, and why we are determined to continue [our] fight." The Declaration included 13 articles calling for political reform. It started off by noting that the revolution was in essence anti-communist, not merely anti-Ceausescu, and sought "the return to the true values of democracy and European civilization" (Articles 1–2). With the exception of the discredited Communist Party, all political parties should be allowed to compete in elections, the communist practice of *divide et impera* should be abandoned, and the right to political opinion should be respected (Article 5). The new leaders should refrain from manipulating the past in order to discredit "historical parties," since communist officials had betrayed the country by aligning themselves with Moscow, and a truthful account of the 1944–1950 period should be published (Article 6). Timisoara had protested against the entire communist system, not "to facilitate the political ascension of a group of anti-Ceausescu dissidents within the Communist Party" (Article 7).

Article 8 was the first Romanian text unequivocally calling for lustration. According to it, the electoral law should be changed to ban communist party leaders, state dignitaries, and secret political police officers from being included on party lists for the first three consecutive post-communist elections amounting to a total of 12 years, since "their presence in politics is the main source for the tension and suspicions that currently plague Romanian society. Until the political situation stabilizes and the nation is reconciled, it is absolutely necessary that they stay away from public life." The electoral law should also ban communist officials from running in presidential elections, because "the President of Romania should be a symbol of our break with communism. To have been a Communist Party member is not a fault in itself … [but] activists gave up their professions to serve the party and benefit from the material privileges it provided. An individual who made such a choice lacks the moral guarantees needed to be a President." In addition, presidential prerogatives should be reduced. The authors also took a stand against inflationary wage increases and in favor of private property, privatization, and administrative decentralization (Articles 9–12). They reminded once again that the revolution was accomplished by the people not the nomenklatura members, was a true revolution not a coup d'état, and was anti-communist not only anti-Ceausescu.[14]

The Timisoara Declaration must be understood in the political context of early Romanian post-communism. On Christmas Day 1989, Nicolae and Elena Ceausescu were executed after a show trial of predetermined outcome, and political power changed hands to a self-styled, unelected National Salvation Front that took over the Communist Party cell structure at all levels and controlled all three branches of government. The Front's leaders – Iliescu, Ceausescu's former collaborator who turned against his master after being marginalized from national politics, and Petre Roman, a Bucharest university professor and the son of communist underground leaders – symbolized the two distinct factions of the Front. On the one hand, there were the older second-echelon communist leaders who rejected Ceausescu's control of the Politburo more than the party's control over the country. On the other hand, there were the younger, better educated individuals who made enough compromises to pursue a successful career under communism but not too many to be allowed to join the higher echelons of communist political power. Tainted by different degrees of collaboration with the communist regime, the Front members soon faced opposition from the reorganized National Liberal Party and Christian Democrat Peasant Party, the "historical" formations that dominated Romanian inter-war politics. On 28 January, the Front announced plans to register as a political party, a move criticized by the opposition and the civil society, worried that its dominant position gave the Front an unfair advantage over all possible contenders. Written by a group of Timisoara writers, the Declaration reacted to the Front's and Iliescu's attempt to legitimize their hold of the country through unfair elections and to discredit their political adversaries.

The document received a cold shoulder from the political class, mainly because the Front (by then renamed the Party of Social Democracy) controlled a plurality of seats in Parliament, and resisted attempts to legislate lustration. Following the 1996 elections, Declaration author and Timisoara Society leader, psychologist George Serban, represented the Christian Democrats in the lower Chamber of Deputies. With renewed hope, Serban told the legislature that the revolution was "temporarily defeated by the counter-revolutionary conspiracy of some *ancien regime* members. The popular decision to topple not only the Ceausescu but also the entire communist regime provoked panic among leaders of the army, Securitate, Procuracy, militia and the [Communist] Party, and forced them to unite." As a result, "Ceausescu's accomplices slowly took control of politics and saved their skins. For seven years, this counter-revolution made an imprint on the Romanian transition," a process that ended with the 1996 change of government.[15] Unfortunately, Serban's optimism was short lived. While Article 8 had figured prominently in the electoral platform of the Democratic Convention, in March 1997 Christian Democrat President Emil Constantinescu told Timisoara residents that the Declaration and its lustration call had become "obsolete" once political power reverted from the Front to the Convention. The statement stirred condemnation from civil society groups, and effectively stopped lustration in its tracks, but later came back to haunt Constantinescu for alienating his only electoral basis.

Serban's death in 1998 prevented him from introducing a legislative proposal on temporarily limiting the access to state and civil offices of individuals who occupied positions in the communist state and party structures during the 6 March 1945–22 December 1989 period. The proposal drew heavily on Article 8 of the Declaration but went further by calling for the verification of the past of all Romanian citizens born before 15 December 1971. His proposal was not forgotten, and on 27 May 1999 some 33 Christian Democrat deputies introduced it in Parliament as "the George Serban bill."[16] The house gave its Legislative Council six weeks to make a pronouncement, and sent the proposal to two of its committees, not one, as it was customary, for approval. Soon after receiving it, the Legislative Council chairman, Social Democrat leader Valeriu Dorneanu, told journalists that the proposal will be rejected because

> ten years after the Revolution, it is socially and morally dated. Under [communism] successive generations of Romanians had no moral and political standards other than those provided by the state, the society and the law. They had no option, but it was not their fault. Following the draft, their main "sin" was the fact that they were born before 6 March 1945 [the day when the Communist Party formed the government for the first time]. Given life conditions under communism, it is hard to blame them for not being born dissidents or heroes, with no direction other than the official one.[17]

The Council took six months to formulate an official position on an initiative that it did not consider a priority, while the two committees never discussed the proposal. On 1 February 2001 the new Social Democrat parliamentary majority abandoned the initiative on grounds that it was never included on the house's agenda, as Article 60.5 of the 1991 Constitution stipulated. It is unclear whether the non-inclusion was an oversight of the Standing Committee or a cleverly designed strategy to undermine the proposal. At the time the initiative proposal was introduced, the Standing Committee was dominated by the Democratic Convention, where Serban's Christian Democrats had the upper hand.

Serban's legislative proposal was not even embraced by his fellow Christian Democrats, who were divided over lustration, with Serban and his followers supporting a separate law on lustration and another group arguing that lustration should inspire the electoral law. While "the George Serban bill" was introduced in the house, deputies Mihai Grigoriu and Mihai Gheorghiu asked for electoral law amendments banning former communist officials from running in the 2000 and 2004 elections. The comprehensive list of communist officials included heads of every Communist Party cell, managers, directors and administrators, state officials, and political police, army and police officers. The proposal was criticized by the Social Democrats, who saw it as a disguised attempt to block Iliescu's candidature in the 2000 presidential poll, following the Constitutional Court's refusal to ban Iliescu from seeking an unconstitutional second reelection.[18] Social Democrat leader Miron Mitrea confidently stated that promoting the Timisoara Declaration "nine years after the revolution only shows how scared of Iliescu the governing [Democratic Coalition] parties are, and how much they consider him a strong electoral competitor."[19]

While the Declaration never directly informed legislation, it was faithfully mentioned on each anniversary of the revolution, and hailed as a moral standard the country should aspire to. Unfortunately, the exercise was nothing more than lip service politicians paid in an effort to gain the votes of communist-era victims. In 2000, President Emil Constantinescu failed to visit Timisoara for the Declaration's tenth anniversary, sending instead a statement boasting that his entire activity "stood under the sign of the Declaration. During [the first] three years [of my presidential mandate], Communist Party and Securitate structures received serious blows, as confirmed by the renewed offensive of the old communist elite. To regain their lost positions, former activists and Securitate members tried to block the reform process by every means."[20] The statement was contradicted by civil society advocate Ana Blandiana, who argued that "if applied, Article 8 of the Timisoara Declaration would have drastically reduced the ranks of our political class."[21] After the Social Democrats won the general elections of that year, the Declaration was not mentioned again during parliamentary debates.

When Dorneanu criticized the "George Serban bill," he argued that before any Romanian citizens could be blamed for collaborating with the former authorities, the communist regime itself should be condemned. The condemnation of communist regimes constituted the heart of the resolution the European Popular Party, representing 65 center-right political formations from European member states, adopted at its 16th congress. On 10 July 2003, the Council of Europe Parliamentary Assembly registered Resolution no. 9875 on the need to condemn totalitarian communism internationally, which asked former communist countries to declassify all archival material and to set up national commissions to investigate communist-era human rights abuses, including summary executions, abusive searches of the homes of political dissidents, persecution of religious leaders and faithful, restrictions on association, information and movement, deportations of ethnic minorities, abusive confiscation of property, and the absolute control of the lives of the citizens by the secret political police. Despite criticism from the representatives of Eastern European candidate states, on 7 February 2004 a modified version of the resolution was adopted. It banned members of communist repression organs and individuals involved in crimes against humanity from occupying positions in the European Union structures.[22] The Romanian mass media praised the resolution as "Article 8 of Brussels," but Bucharest authorities ignored it. Liberal leader Radu F. Alexandru declared that "a Securitate officer must be excluded from state office, since no one can tell what he did for the political police," but Social Democrat senator Sergiu Nicolaescu believed that "we cannot do without Securitate officers, trained individuals, experts working for the Romanian Information Service ... As long as all state positions are occupied by former [communist] party activists, why should the Securitate officers be denied access?"[23]

During the 2004 electoral campaign, the country's failure to adopt lustration and renew its political class became a major concern for the voters, ever more dissatisfied with corrupt politicians. For many, lustration was an option because from 1989 to 2004 the two presidents, all seven premiers but Radu Vasile, and many ministers and deputy ministers, deputies, and senators were drawn from the communist state, party, and managerial leadership. Despite its declared commitment to effect democratization and raise living standards, the political class had problems adapting to the new democratic order, accepting the need for accountability, and setting aside its group interests to promote the common good. In the region, Romania has constantly ranked high in terms of corruption and bribery, and low in terms of living standards and foreign investment. Voicing public dissatisfaction, journalist Tudor Flueras lamented that "those who rise against former communists and Securitate agents are immediately labeled Talibans and extremists, are told that they should adapt, instead of continuing to live in the past, and are treated arrogantly by the former Communist Party secretaries and youth leaders, now prosperous businessmen and successful politicians ... [They] are now respected, genuine capitalists seeking entrance to the European Union" by means of "pull, theft and lies."[24]

In the absence of political will to endorse lustration, a grass-roots Coalition for a Clean Parliament announced plans to screen party lists for tainted individuals, identify them publicly and encourage voters not to support parties that nominated controversial candidates. Candidate biographies were compiled from press and governmental reports the Coalition obtained from courts and the police, but no state organs directly supported the initiative. Presidential candidate Traian Basescu referred to the long shadow of the communist past in a televised confrontation with Iliescu's successor, Social Democrat leader Adrian Nastase:

> what kind of curse [was put in effect] for the people to have to choose between two former communists? Between Adrian Nastase and Traian Basescu.

In fifteen years no other [politician] emerged ... untainted by communist
habits ... I sometimes look in the mirror asking myself, 'Do you, Basescu,
show respect for the Romanian people?' And I say 'Yes' ... Maybe it's time
for another type of candidate to come before the people. True, I did not make
a living by working for the [Communist] Party, but I was a member ... The
point is that we cannot share the mentality of the communist regime fifteen
years after its collapse. Every day you [Nastase] convince me that you are
incapable to understand that institutions should function by themselves.[25]

It was these candid remarks that convinced voters of Basescu's honesty and sin-
cerity with regard to his past tainted by collaboration with the Securitate while a
representative of the communist Romanian Navrom company in Antwerp. Taking
advantage of the political change brought about by the 2004 elections, when
Basescu helped his Justice and Truth Alliance to form the government, political
parties and civil society groups advanced several different lustration proposals
aimed at banning nomenclatura members or secret agents from post-communist politics. By the time this volume went to press in early 2008, amid public
apathy and civil society undecisiveness regarding the topic, the lower Chamber of
Deputies had either blocked or set aside all those proposals.

Access to Securitate files and identification of secret agents

Of the three transitional justice areas discussed here, file access is the one in which
Romania made the most consistent progress in terms of legislation adoption and
institutional organization, although it was only in late 1999 that Parliament passed
the Law on access to Securitate files (Law no. 187) that set up the Council for the
Study of Securitate Archives. The law allows Romanian citizens to read their own
file, obtain copies of file documents and statements detailing their collaboration
(or lack thereof) with the Securitate, and find out the names of those who contributed information to the files. The Council is an autonomous governmental agency
that identifies Securitate officers and informers, grants access to political police
files, and deposits and analyzes Securitate archives transferred from other institutions (including the Romanian Information Service, the External Information
Service, and the Ministries of Justice and Defense). Two different procedures are
observed for verifying the past of politicians, with candidates running in general
elections being automatically investigated by the Council, and candidates running
in local elections being verified at the request of the Election Bureau. In addition, any Romanian citizen and institution can ask the Council to verify elected
or appointed state officials at all levels, as well as leaders of officially-registered
religious groups, mass media, and private and public universities. Final verification results are published in *Monitorul Oficial*, not before the Council interviews
the candidate and allows him or her to challenge the verdict in the court.

From the beginning, the law was not intended to be a lustration tool, rather it
was hoped that politicians with a tainted past would step aside for fear of being
found guilty of collaboration with the communist political police. The council was

asked to identify publicly the political police informers and agents, with the mass media and the civil society explaining the incompatibility between state office in post-communist democracy and involvement with the repressive *ancient regime*, and applying pressure on tainted politicians to justify their past collaboration or to refrain from engaging in post-communist politics. But the numerous commissions and omissions of the legislative framework, the bitter divisions among and shifting political allegiances of council leaders, Romania's weak judiciary and traditional disregard for the law, and lack of political will of both government and opposition together rendered the council superfluous and its verdicts highly interpretable. Instead of becoming the solution to the "dealing with the past" problem, the council quickly transformed into one of its major problems.

Set up with considerable delay, the council had little time to formulate its first set of verdicts regarding the past of candidates in the 2000 general elections. To mitigate lack of time and personnel and meet high public expectation to quickly solve thousands of cases, the council reinterpreted, and in the process misinterpreted, the law. Instead of interviewing candidates before publicly identifying them as collaborators, the council published their names without directly confronting them, leaving verdicts open to appeal on technical grounds. Instead of verifying all candidates, it verified only those included on the lists of parties likely to gain parliamentary representation. Instead of using a plurality of archives to formulate its verdicts, the council used the Romanian Information Service documents exclusively, though the service housed only 60 percent of the Securitate archive and relevant archival material was housed with the Ministries of Defense and Justice and the Communist Party Archive. Instead of relying on a variety of information sources, the council used only archival material, overlooking victims' personal testimonies. Instead of examining the files directly by going to the shelves, it asked the service to search the archive's card system, ignoring the risks of the service misreporting its findings, the card system not reflecting the archive adequately, and the Securitate identification of informers being erroneous. Instead of admitting that verdicts were provisory and could be altered (even reversed) as new information becomes available, the council claimed they were final. Instead of arriving at its verdicts based on dispassionate analysis and interpretation of evidence at hand, council members allowed political and personal factors to dictate their position, and decided that a person was guilty of collaboration if a simple majority of council members said so. More recently, instead of releasing its verdicts before the 2004 local elections, the council made them public afterwards, making the exercise of unmasking spies redundant, since mandates of elected officials cannot be legally revoked. The way the council conducted verifications in 2000 and 2004 greatly compromised its public image, and ultimately rendered the entire identification effort meaningless.

To date, the council has maintained an unenviable record, acquired the reputation of an unreliable, inefficient and irresponsible institution, and has become the subject of numerous press scandals that tarnished its image. In its first 40 months of activity, the council identified fewer than 100 Securitate agents and informers (around 0.003 percent of the verified local and national post-communist political elite, far less than the 5–10 percent the Securitate information network accounted for in communist Romania's adult population), invited 29 Securitate officers to its headquarters, and interviewed 20. Around 12 of the political agents named were deceased and most others had occupied low-ranking positions within the Securitate apparatus, the council being unable to unmask individuals notorious for their ties to the secret police. During the same period, only around 67 percent of those who asked to read their files were allowed to do so, and the council was brought to court 38 times.[26] Council leaders were criticized for media over-exposure, hiring former Securitate officers as investigators, and firing the young historians who leaked that information to the press, failing to present annual reports to Parliament as the law required, refusing to share basic information with the press, and taking sides in the political debate that preceded national electoral polls.

From the beginning it became evident that there was ample room for the council to improve its activity. In 2000, it released the names of former informers turned post-communist politicians only for the press to demonstrate that those informers and politicians had the same name but different birthplaces. When deputy Laszlo Rakoczi criticized them for not interviewing him before publicly branding him a Securitate informer, council leaders directed the deputy to an interview one of them granted to an obscure journal, although by law the council was obliged to contact the deputy directly to arrange for an interview. Different standards seem to apply to different electoral candidates, depending on their political clout. Basescu publicly admitted that as a communist commercial ship commander he filed thousands of reports with the Securitate, but insisted that none of them offered damaging information on his peers. The council embraced that viewpoint, announcing that Basescu was "clean as a whistle," and that only the names of the informers whose activity infringed on fundamental human rights will be published in *Monitorul Oficial*. Apparently, Rakoczi's secret reports were equally innocuous, but this fact did not protect him from public condemnation. The council decided to clear Corneliu Vadim Tudor, leader of the nationalistic Greater Romania Party, of charges of collaboration with the Securitate, although Tudor's reporting of fellow writers is a matter of public knowledge, and parts of his multi-volume secret file have already been made public.

While these mistakes reflect the council's inner workings, it is also true that the council has faced tremendous opposition from the Romanian Information Service and segments of the political class tainted by past collaboration. While claiming to be a new information service distinct from the political police, the service has eluded parliamentary control and adamantly refused to turn the Securitate archive over to its legal custodian. Political parties failed to support the identification of the Securitate informers, while the judiciary – weak, corrupt and subject to political interference – refused to prosecute electoral candidates who gave false declarations regarding their (non) involvement with the Securitate. The Greater Romania Party refused to forward its electoral lists to the council, and announced it welcomed secret agents. In 1998 and 1999, instead of openly opposing the adoption of the law on access to Securitate files, the then ruling Christian Democrats, Liberals and Democrats did not attend the legislative meetings during which the law was to be discussed. Lack of quorum delayed the law's adoption, giving the council little time for verifications. The most bitter opposition came from the most powerful political formation, the Social Democrats, which both in opposition (1996–2000) and in government (2000–2004) deployed intimidation, coercion and backstabbing to undermine the council and render the Law 187/1999 superfluous.

As a result of President Basescu's personal intervention, in 2005 the Service agreed to transfer 12 linear kilometers of secret files not touching on issues of 'national security' from its militarized units to the Council for the Study of Securitate Archive. The delay with which the archive changed hands raised serious doubts about the documents' authenticity, with some local observers believing that the service altered, replaced and modified so many files that the archive protected by the council significantly differs from the archive as it was in December 1989. Such claims are difficult to disprove, since only the service really knows what the original secret archive consisted of. Since mid-2006, the council has unprecedented access to the majority of Securitate archives, including the extant files of prominent post-communist politicians.

Trials against communist officials

Eastern European demands for transitional justice through court procedures have clustered around major incidents of police brutality against protesting citizens, and as such it is important to break down the communist period according to levels of dissent and repression. Romania registered the highest such levels 1) during the first two decades of communist rule, 2) in years 1977 and 1985, and 3) during the ten-day-long 1989 revolution. In between these temporal markers we can mention the isolated cases of engineer Gheorghe Ursu, Radio Free Europe/Radio Liberty correspondents Monica Lovinescu and Emil Georgescu, writers Mircea Dinescu and Andrei Plesu, and a number of individuals caught while trying to cross the Western border to freedom. Repression methods ranged from harassment and smear campaigns to imprisonment and staged accidents all the way to murder. As we shall see, only a handful of these cases have been heard by the courts to date.[27]

During the early stages of communist rule, political repression was directed against a number of social groups, including leaders of non-communist political parties and pre-communist state dignitaries (Iuliu Maniu, Corneliu Coposu, Gheorghe Bratianu, Mihai Vulcanescu, Gheorghe Tatarascu and Ioan Mihalache), the religious believers (most notably Greek Catholics and neo-Protestants), the organizers of armed resistance, and the communist leaders who fell victim to intraparty power struggle (Lucretiu Patrascanu and Stefan Foris).[28] We lack a complete picture of repression under Gheorghe Gheorghiu-Dej's rule, mainly because the Securitate records are contradictory. We do know, however, that from 1949 to 1960, a total of 134,150 political trials took place involving at least 549,400 accused who spent lengthy prison terms after, and often before, being charged. From 1950 to 1958 75,809 individuals were arrested, of whom 73,636 were convicted, and 22,007 other people were sent to labor camps often without being charged or tried. During 1949–1958 some 60,000 individuals were placed under house arrest.[29] Resistance to collectivization resulted in some 80,000 peasants being arrested, 30,000 of them being tried in public. After the 1.5 million-strong Greek Catholic Church was dismantled in 1948, all its six bishops and some 600 of its 1,500 priests who refused to convert to Orthodoxy were imprisoned. None of the arrested bishops were ever brought to trial, and only three bishops survived their prison terms. In 1951 alone, 417,916 people were kept under surveillance, 5,401 of whom were arrested for "hostile activity."[30] Armed resistance centered on the Nucsoara group, which the Securitate troops apprehended in 1958.[31]

Stalinist repression in Romania went down in history for the so-called Pitesti re-education experiment, a unique program which used brutality and torture to turn prisoners into new men apt to form the bedrock of the new communist state. Between 1949 and 1952, young students jailed in the Pitesti prison for their political beliefs were terrorized and cruelly beaten, compelled to confess real and imaginary crimes against the state, brainwashed and re-educated to betray their friends and publicly abjure their family. At Christmas and Easter, Christian prisoners were ordered to participate in blasphemy-ridden rituals accompanied by Satanic exhortations and an obscene Imitatio Christi. The tortured were turned into torturers, ready to apply to others the coarse methods of extreme physical degradation, constant psychological pressure and personal alienation from the deepest emotional ties they themselves endured. This ingenious last step, meant to prove the prisoner's full transfiguration into the new man, ensured that the distrust would render cooperation in an uprising unlikely. According to former participants, at that stage the majority of the tortured looked for ways to kill themselves, a "luxury" the program organizers were careful to deny them.[32]

The two most serious instances of workers revolting against communist authorities occurred in 1977 and 1987, but were successfully contained to Valea Jiului and Brasov, respectively. In August 1977 miners denounced legislation ending their disability pensions and raising the retirement age from 50 to 65, and asked to talk to top party leaders. First top cabinet ministers and then Ceausescu himself negotiated with the miners, finally dispersing protesters with promises of better working conditions and no retaliatory measures. Some 4,000 miners were relocated to other mines and towns, most of Ceausescu's promises were not respected, and the party-controlled local media failed to report the incident. After the introduction of draconian measures designed to reduce food and energy consumption and sell stocks against the hard currency needed to repay the country's foreign debt, in November 1987 workers at the Red Flag machine building factory in Brasov, the country's second largest industrial hub, refused to start their morning shift, and took out to the street to reach the headquarters of the county party leadership in search for answers for being denied salary payment. As in Valea Jiului, the army and the Securitate operated arrests and then deported the leaders of the uprising to other regions.[33] Writer Paul Goma was the only Romanian intellectual to endorse the Charter 77, and to ask the communist regime to keep its promises to respect basic human rights like freedom of speech and mobility. After much harassment by the Securitate, Goma was imprisoned and then convinced to emigrate to France, where he has lived with his family ever since.

The Romanian revolution of December 1989 was the only Eastern European anticommunist uprising which, according to official estimates, resulted in the deaths of 1,104 persons and the wounding of 3,552. Of these, 162 died and 1,101 were wounded in the period between 17 December and noon on 22 December, when Ceausescu and his wife fled Bucharest on helicopter only to be apprehended hours latter some one hundred kilometers away. Almost half of the casualties occurred in Bucharest during confrontations between citizens, on the one hand, and army and Securitate troops, on the other.[34] The latest research suggests that the army was responsible for more deaths than the Securitate, but the chain of command and the individual responsibility of each army and Securitate general remain shrouded in mystery, as all generals claim to be innocent or simply to have followed the orders of their superiors. After years of work, a special parliamentary investigative committee issued a detailed report which ultimately failed to answer key questions related to the revolution.[35]

The remainder of this section presents the show trial of Nicolae and Elena Ceausescu, together with two other major cases brought before the courts. Several reasons might explain why in Romania transitional justice through court proceedings has unfolded at a slow pace. The restrictions imposed by the statute of limitations, the difficulty of piecing together evidence that communist authorities tried hard to erase, and the defendants' old age and health problems have contributed to the difficulty of mounting a convincing case against Stalinist officials and secret political police agents involved in the 1949–1964 repression campaign. Alexandru Draghici, Minister of Interior at the time, and Alexandru Nicolski, the NKVD Soviet agent who created the Securitate, peacefully died of old age in the early 1990s, before their case was presented to the courts and before they could be held accountable for their role in setting up the Romanian Gulag. As for cases of human rights infringement that took place from 1964 to 1989, their number was kept relatively low by prosecutors, judges and political leaders interested to cover up their own tainted past. The trial of the Ceausescus, carried out during highly volatile times without observing minimal rules of procedure, further eroded the Romanians' trust in the willingness of a weak, corrupt and self-interested judiciary to shed light on communist-era atrocities.

In a step unprecedented in the region Romania's very exit from communism coincided, and was brought about, by the trial and speedy execution of its communist leader, but that very trial seemingly blocked further attempts to honestly come to terms with the recent past. Indeed, as Michael Kraus rightly argued, transitional justice in Romania "initially focused on several high profile trials of former [communist] leaders, while ignoring the machinery that facilitated the system of terror."[36] Iliescu and Roman defended the haste with which the trial hearings and executions took place by claiming that due process could not have taken precedence over the bloody confrontations in the streets, the ever mounting number of civilian casualties, and the real possibility that the country might descend into chaos and civil war. While not downplaying the gravity of the December 1989 events, their critics have underscored the fact that the speedy trial allowed the new rulers to blame the leader, not the communist regime, without giving Ceausescu a real chance to elaborate on the role second-echelon apparatchiks like Iliescu and Roman's parents had played in the repression system. The trial allowed the revolutionary forces to terminate Ceausescu and thus completely shatter the hopes of his loyal army and secret service members that the tide could be reversed. However, its many flaws prevented the hearing to accomplish the very task for which it was organized: bestowing a measure of much-needed legitimacy on the new self-appointed government. Instead of bringing Romanians together, the trial deeply divided them, speeded up the formation of political opposition groups, exposed the new rulers to an unprecedented wave of criticism which culminated in the June 1990 University Square demonstrations, and even absolved Ceausescu of at least part of his guilt. It could be that the real looer of this whole affair was the dictator's wife, Elena Ceausescu. Despised for her pretense of scientific notoriety and vain intellectual ambitions, Elena occupied high-ranking positions in the party-state, but was involved in the 1989 massacres less directly and intimately than other communist officials who managed to avoid the death squad.[37] The trial raised several questions which have not been convincingly answered yet: Can transitional justice be carried out by unjust procedures and with disregard to due process? Can an injustice heal another injustice?

On 17 July 1999, the Supreme Court of Justice sentenced army Generals Victor Atanasie Stanculescu and Mihai Chitac for ordering troops to shoot during the 1989 anticommunist protest rallies. The two generals, who were among Ceausescu's most trusted aids, were sent to the southwestern town of Timisoara to quell the popular revolt that started the revolution. As a result of their orders, 72 unarmed civilians died and 253 others were wounded on 17 December 1989. Demonstrating political flair, Stanculescu and Chitac quickly sided with Iliescu and thus rescued their careers and possibly their lives. After 1989 both of them were close to the highest echelons of political power. For his contribution in organizing the Ceausescus' trial, execution and burial, Stanculescu was rewarded with positions of power and responsibility in the first post-communist cabinet, and protected from prosecution. In 1990, he was appointed Minister of Economy and then Minister of Defense, and later became a prosperous arms dealer and one of the country's richest business tycoons.[38] While holding the key position of Minister of Interior, Chitac led the repression of anti-Iliescu protesters in June 1990, coordinating the moves of the army units deployed in Bucharest downtown with the detachments of miners bused in the city from the Valea Jiului "to defend" Romania's budding democracy, but had to step back when his involvement became public. After taking two full years to hear the case, the Supreme Court handed down 15-year-long prison sentences to each general, stripped off their military rank and ordered them to pay $31,000 damages to the victim's descendants. The appeal was denied.

After the sentence became public, representatives of associations of revolutionaries killed in December 1989 confidently told journalists that "it's a beginning, but it is only the tip of the iceberg. Those who zealously carried out the two generals' orders continue to have important positions in the army. We know them, and we wait for them to be convicted, too. Justice must be done, regardless of politics, as truth has no political color." They criticized the slow pace of the hearings, and urged authorities to bring to justice other army, police and intelligence officers involved in the 1989 events.[39] While those who took to the streets to protest against Ceausescu's policies felt vindicated, the verdict was criticized by leftist politicians seeing it as politically motivated and dictated by the then ruling Democratic Convention. Roman and Iliescu accused the center-right government of "political cleansing," on grounds that the generals were carrying out orders they could not refuse to obey. Minister of Defense Victor Babiuc emphatically declared that the Court had sentenced the entire army, and threatened that the army would no longer defend the post-communist regime. For Babiuc, "the blind revenge that animated the sentence could divide the Romanian society and dissuade the army from defending the nation," while the verdict was unjust, since the generals did not personally kill anybody. He reminded that "throughout history, the army received orders from the political regime," and as such "neither the individual officers nor the army as an organization could be judged outside the political, social, military and judicial context of the time, which gives legitimacy to the actions of the army." Rather than being condemned, the army should be thanked for helping to overthrow the communist regime. Stanculescu also needed to be thanked, since "like it or not, he played a major role in convincing the army to side with the revolutionary forces."[40] Babiuc had been a colleague of both Stanculescu and Chitac in the Roman cabinet of 1990–1991.

Christian Democrat Minister of Interior Constantin Ionescu contradicted Babiuc, arguing that the sentence was directed not against the entire army, but only against its tainted elements. However, Ionescu's position soon changed, and in the wake of the court verdict he asked for blanket amnesty for all soldiers involved in the 1989 violence.[41] Other prominent politicians believed that the army should not be tainted and harassed by sentences handed down against officers who merely followed orders. Ionescu embraced that proposal, and in April 1998 announced plans to initiate a draft law for granting amnesty to army personnel for non-criminal actions. Christian Democrat leader Ion Diaconescu declared that "most wrongdoing was done during the 45 years of communist rule. The December 1989 deaths represent only one chapter," and as such Romania needed a "trial of communism." The Civic Alliance asked the President to block a proposal that would prevent undergoing trials to be finalized, while Iliescu branded the amnesty proposal an aberration, since it assumed that the army was guilty of wrongdoing during the revolution, and warned that trials in which "patriotic officers" stood accused would "weaken the country's defense capability." The leader of the leftist Alliance for Romania Party Teodor Melescanu also criticized "the idea of a general amnesty, since it finds the entire army culpable. First we should shed light on the actions of each individual officer, and then amnesty them."[42]

As though to prove his own guilt, immediately after the verdict was handed down Stanculescu fled Romania. After much hesitation, in mid-May 2000 the Romanian authorities asked Interpol for help to locate and apprehend the convicted general.

Claiming to have left for England for medical treatment, Stanculescu agreed to return to the country voluntarily.[43] Chitac was arrested and served part of his sentence in prison, while enjoying preferential treatment and a number of amenities denied to other convicts.[44] In a surprising move, on 22 March 2004 the Supreme Court decided to start a nouveau the hearings in the Stanculescu and Chitac case, making use of *recurs in anulare*, a highly-criticized judicial procedure which allows the Prosecutor General to overturn definitive court verdicts, on grounds that those who had masterminded the killings, the Ceausescu couple, were already dead. The Court argued that the generals "did not have the intention to kill. They acted according to the laws of those days. They did not give the orders from their own volition, but obeyed the Supreme Commander [Nicolae Ceausescu], who was also the Head of the Army."[45] The court decided to free the generals.

Another high-profile trial related to the only documented case of murder of a political prisoner in communist prisons under Ceausescu's rule. On 21 September 1985 the 59-years-old engineer Gheorghe Ursu entered the infamous arrest of the Bucharest Militia on Rahova street. For close to a year, Ursu had been closely watched by the Securitate for establishing and maintaining contact with Romanian emigrant writers and Radio Free Europe/Radio Liberty journalists. The case culminated with two female workmates denouncing Ursu for keeping a diary that included negative comments toward the party-state and Ceausescu. Instead of being prosecuted for his political activity, Ursu was charged with an invented illegal possession of hard currency, a crime at the time. Within two months of entering the prison, Ursu reportedly died of "natural causes," but after 1989 prison doctors admitted that the death was a homicide resulting from cruel beating. After years of procrastination, on 14 July 2003 the Bucharest Court of Appeals judge Viorel Podar ruled that former head of the Criminal Investigations Department of the Bucharest Militia Tudor Stanica and his deputy Mihail Creanga were guilty of ordering Ursu's killing, and sentenced each of them to 22 years prison-terms, 8 years suspension of civil rights, military downgrading, and payment of Lei 1 billion (around 35,000USD) to the three surviving members of the Ursu family. The prison sentence was halved by the amnesty presidential Decree 11/1998. The prosecution argued that the officers ordered prisoner Marian Clita to "exercise acts of violence" against Ursu, and forbade the guards on duty from intervening or offering Ursu any kind of medical help. In 2000, Clita was sentenced to 20 years in prison, but his prison sentence was halved by the same amnesty decree. During Clita's trial enough evidence surfaced to convince Ursu's son to sue the two officers.

An arrest warrant was issued for Stanica's and Creanga's immediate apprehension, which could not be carried out, since the arresting policemen had once been subordinates of the two retired colonels and each time they raided the homes of Creanga and Stanica the two mysteriously disappeared. The running officers appealed the verdict to the Supreme Court, as did Prosecutor General Tanase Joita, on grounds that it was too harsh, but on 10 October 2003 the Supreme Court upheld the verdict, and within a month Stanica and Creanga were arrested. While in prison Stanica obtained a copy of Ursu's (legally unavailable) Securitate file, which he studied to prepare another appeal alleging that Ursu had in fact been an informer for the political police, which eventually ordered him killed. Before 1989, Stanica was one of the most feared communist criminal investigators, nicknamed the "Beast of Rahova." Former prisoners reported that, while at Rahova under Stanica's rule, they were savagely beaten on the head, face and groin, were left hanging from large wall hooks for hours until their hands and feet went numb, were denied basic medical treatment, and women prisoners were obliged to perform oral sex with the guards. After 1989, Stanica became a successful businessman and the head of the doomed Credit Bank.[46] The upholding of the verdict was in large measure the result of pressure applied by a Finish member of the European Parliament Astrid Thor, who on 21 August 2003 urged European Union ambassadors to Bucharest to keep a close eye on the Ursu case, "a case of injustice in Romania" resulted from "years of delays and abuse of justice."[47]

These two trials were not the only ones pertaining to transitional justice in Romania, but they are among the few which were finalized. As early as 1990, Prosecutor General Gheorghe Robu started to prepare the case against those responsible for the killings in Timisoara, Cluj, Sibiu and Bucharest, but after joining the Roman cabinet as Ministers of Defense and Interior Stanculescu and Chitac effectively blocked the procedures. All blame for Timisoara killings fell on army General Ion Coman, sentenced on 9 December 1991 by the military courts and again on 6 June 1997 by the Supreme Court to a 15 years prison term. Similar sentences were handed down to the head of the Timisoara police Popescu and the head of the Timisoara county party organization Balan. The tremendous political storm that followed Stanculescu's and Chitac's sentencing intimidated the courts. Following the public campaign demanding an independent judiciary, a court found Major Vasile Gabor innocent only two months after the generals were sentenced. Gabor had been accused of shooting a student during the miners' riot of 1991, but those defending him claimed that the shooting was accidental.[48] Other army and Securitate generals involved in the 1989 violence were never convicted, and army General Stefan Guse, nicknamed the "Butcher of Timisoara," had a statue erected in Bucharest.[49] The first criminal charge against a communist official was filed on 2 September 1991, but during the past 17 years none of these hearings progressed significantly, a fact benefiting the communist officials who are increasingly less likely to stand trial as they become older and sicker.

Conclusion

Romania had more reasons than any other Eastern European state to deal with its dictatorial past promptly and decisively. The country experienced the strictest version of communism, first under the rule of Gheorghiu-Dej, an unrelenting Stalinist who destroyed the last vestiges of civil society, and then under the thumb of Ceausescu, who imposed his own version of personalized rule centered on himself and his family. Terror and repression took different forms under the two leaders, with the physical beatings of early communism making way to more sophisticated but equally cruel psychological harassment of late communism. Accountable only to the top party leadership, the Securitate instilled fear not only with the fist and club but also with the pen and word by conducting brutal interrogations, harassing writers, and keeping detailed records on citizens with the help of an army of informers.

The 45-year-long unchallenged control over the country of the Communist Party and its loyal Securitate forces was not the only factor calling for resolute and comprehensive transitional justice. Equally important was Romania's violent mode of exiting communism and the readiness of its new leaders – most of whom were unreformed second-echelon communist officials – to harass the budding political opposition and to use the army, the police and the intelligence services to retain control over the political process at any price. Indeed, the Romanian revolution that toppled Ceausescu spanned only 10 days, but claimed the lives of around a thousand, mostly young, people. The conflict between the army and the Securitate forces, between the units loyal to Ceausescu and those supporting the change, and between the population and the government ended abruptly when Nicolae and Elena Ceausescu were executed on Christmas day in 1989.[50] Less than six months later, the new rulers called on the Valea Jiului miners to brutally crack down on Bucharest student protesters.[51] As a result of this chain of violent events, the nascent Romanian opposition felt that no radical break with the past was possible without an honest reassessment of the crimes committed by the communist regime.

As in other countries of the region, transitional justice pitted the society against the state, that is, groups of former political prisoners, owners of confiscated property, and individuals who had been wronged, against *ancien regime* leaders, including the Ceausescu family, state and party leaders, and political police agents. In Romania a generational gap has been evident. Victims demanding retribution tend to be old enough either to remember pre-communist times or to have suffered as a result of the arrests of late 1940s and late 1950s. Immediately after December 1989, transitional justice calls centered on banning communist leaders from engaging in post-communist politics, identifying political police agents, condemning the communist regime for its human rights trespasses, returning confiscated property to its rightful owners, rehabilitating former political prisoners, and prosecuting nomenklatura members. Almost two decades later the country has made little progress in reevaluating its communist past, and transitional justice has been stalled in its tracks.

The reasons for Romania's handicap relate to both the communist and the post-communist context. Despite the many deprivations of the late 1980s, communism brought many Romanians material benefits, and allowed for unprecedented upward social mobility for disadvantaged groups that strived under a regime protecting and promoting their interests. Among Eastern European countries, Romania had the largest percentage of party members relative to the total population (3.8 million members in a total population of 23 million) and one of the highest percentages of informers (between 400,000 and a million). None of these groups demanded transitional justice, mainly because they had not been the victims. Conversely, the number of victims of the communist regime tended to be relatively small. Few Romanians dared to confront the system directly, and those who did found it difficult to find kindred spirits when they were presented as traitors of the country and collaborators of foreign spy agencies. By 1989, many former political prisoners had died or had been blackmailed to become Securitate inform-ers. Despite its bloody revolution, Romania experienced elite reproduction, not elite replacement, as key post-communist leaders were Ceausescu's former col-laborators, individuals eager to hide their past, recast themselves as supporters of democracy, and blame the dictator more than the communist system.

Notes

1 D. Deletant, 'Romania', in K. Persak and L. Kaminski (eds.) *A Handbook of the Com-munist Security Apparatus in East Central Europe. 1944–1989*, Warsaw: Institute of National Remembrance, 2005, pp. 288, 294–295.

2 During the 1980s Germans and Jews could emigrate if payments between $4,000 and $8,000 per head were delivered to the Securitate, which complemented its vast resources with proceedings derived from its virtual monopoly over import-export oper-ations. R. Ioanid, *The Ransom of the Jews: The Story of Extraordinary Secret Bargain between Romania and Israel*, Chicago: Ivan R. Dee, 2005.

3 Also L. Stan, 'The Roof over Our Head: Property Restitution in Romania', *Journal of Communist Studies and Transition Politics*, 2006, vol. 22, 1–17.

4 These projects included the Danube-Black Sea canal, the huge Slatina and Galati alu-minum plants, the village systematization program, and the monumental House of the People located in downtown Bucharest.

5 I. M. Pacepa, *The Red Horizons. Chronicles of a Communist Spy Chief*, Washington: Regnery Gateway, 1987.

6 *Forced Labor, Psychiatric Repression of Dissent, Persecution of Religious Believers, Ethnic Discrimination and Persecution, Law and the Suppression of Human Rights in Romania*, New York: Amnesty International USA, 1978, and D. Deletant, *Ceausescu and the Securitate: Coercion and Dissent in Romania, 1965–1989*, London: Hurst, 1995, pp. 93–99. Romanian courts ordered the commitment of many mentally healthy persons found guilty of political crimes to psychiatric institutions on the basis of false diagnosis.

7 Of these, 64 percent were workers, 4 percent peasants, 2 percent intellectuals and 28 percent clerks. Eight years later the Securitate personnel reached 72,697, includ-ing 7,865 officers, 5,306 sergeants, 1,565 civilians and 57,961 high school graduates drafted for military service.

8 F. Dobre, F. Banu, C. Duica, S. B. Moldovan and L. Taranu, *Trupele de Securitate (1949–1989)*, Bucharest: Nemira, 2004.

9 C. Troncota, 'Noua politica in domeniul institutiei securitatii regimului communist din Romania, 1965–1989', *Arhivele totalitarismului*, 2001, vols. 32–33, 122.

10 L. Stan, 'Moral Cleansing Romanian Style', *Problems of Post-Communism*, 2002, vol. 49, 55, and L. Stan, 'Inside the Securitate Archives', Washington, DC: Cold War History Project, Woodrow Wilson Center, 2005. Online. Available HTTP: http://www.wilsoncenter.org/index.cfm?topic_id=1409&fuseaction=topics.item&news_id=109979 (accessed 29 December 2007).

11 'Recursul la discurs', *22*, 1998, no. 45, 5–8, and L. Stan, 'Access to Securitate Files: The Trials and Tribulations of a Romanian Law', *Eastern European Politics and Society*, 2002, vol. 16, 55–90.

12 L. Stan, 'Spies, Files and Lies: Explaining the Failure of Access to Securitate Files', *Communist and Post-Communist Studies*, 2004, vol. 37, 422.

13 L. Stan, 'Lustration in Romania: The Story of a Failure', *Studia politica*, 2006, vol. 6, 135–156.
14 For another English translation of the Declaration, see 'The Timisoara Declaration', *Report on Eastern Europe*, 6 April 1990, 41–45.
15 'Sedinta solemna comuna a Camerei Deputatilor si Senatului of 22 December 1997', *Monitorul Oficial al Romaniei, partea a II-a*, 12 January 1998.
16 'Legea lustratiei uitata', *Ziua*, 3 March 2004.
17 'Norme ale umilirii', *Cotidianul*, 13 March 2004.
18 Article 81 of the 1991 Constitution limited the number of presidential mandates an individual can hold over a life time to a maximum of two. Iliescu was President from 1990 to 1992, 1992 to 1996 and 2000 to 2004. His 2000 candidacy was allowed on grounds that his first mandate was interim, not a full four-year mandate.
19 N. Vera and T. Georgescu, 'Punctul opt de la Timisoara in Legea Electorala', *Evenimentul Zilei*, 10 March 1999.
20 V. Bota, 'Securitatea, invingator absolut in alegeri', *Evenimentul Zilei*, 18 March 2000.
21 Ibid.
22 'Documentul APCE considera ca exista forte populiste care mizeaza pe formarea unui sentiment de nostalgie pentru fostele regimuri', *Cotidianul*, 12 August 2003.
23 T. Georgescu, 'Legea ii protejeaza pe ofiterii de Securitate', *Evenimentul Zilei*, 14 February 2001.
24 T. Flueras, 'Tovarasi domni', *Evenimentul Zilei*, 27 July 2004.
25 S. Fati, 'Ultimul meci prezidential', *Evenimentul Zilei*, 10 December 2004, and L. Stan, 'The Opposition Takes Charge: The Romanian General Elections of 2004', *Problems of Post-Communism*, 2005, vol. 52, 3–15. I thank Dr. Radu Rautu for drawing attention to these excerpts.
26 Stan, 'Spies, Files and Lies', pp. 341–342.
27 R. Ursachi, 'Is the Trial of Communism a Criminal Trial?', paper presented at the Society for Romanian Studies congress, Constanta, Romania, 25–28 June 2007, and R. Ursachi and R. Grosescu, 'Les processus pénaux et la gestion du passé dictatorial. Le cas de la Roumanie postcommuniste', unpublished paper, 2007.
28 Some of these victims wrote powerful testimonials of their prison experience: I. Diaconescu, *Temnita, destinul generatiei noastre*, Bucharest: Nemira, 2003, I. Diaconescu, *Dupa temnita*, Bucharest: Nemira, 2003, I. Ioanid, *Inchisoarea noastra cea de toate zilele*, Bucharest: Humanitas, 1999, L. Constante, *The Silent Escape. Three Thousand Days in Romanian Prisons*, Berkeley: University of California Press, 1995, N. Valery-Grossu, *Binecuvintata fii, inchisoare*, Bucharest: Univers, 2002, R. Ciuceanu, *Potcoava fara noroc*, Bucharest: Meridiane, 1994, R. Ciuceanu, *Pecetea diavolului*, Bucharest: Institutul National pentru Studiul Totalitarismului, 2002, N. Corbeanu, *Vara transfugului*, Bucharest: Humanitas, 2002, E. Patrascu Buse, *Lumea pierduta*, Bucharest: Humanitas, 2003, A. Georgescu, *In the Beginning Was the End*, Brasov: Aspera, 2004, C. C. Giurescu, *Five Years and Two Months in the Sighet Penitentiary (May 7, 1950-July 5, 1955)*, Boulder: East European Monographs, 1994, A. Samuelli, *Woman Behind Bars in Romania*, London: Frank Cass, 1997, C. Coposu, *Confessions*, Boulder: East European Monographs, 1998, I. Corpas, *Secvente din fostele inchisori politice*, Bucharest: Humanitas, 2003, V. Ierunca, *Fenomenul Pitesti*, Bucharest: Humanitas, 1990, and S. Tanase, *Anatomia mistificarii*, Bucharest: Humanitas, 2003.
29 Deletant, 'Romania', p. 317.
30 Ibid., p. 306.
31 A. Liiceanu, *Ranile memoriei. Nucsoara si rezistanta din munti*, Bucharest: Polirom, 2003, and A. Mungiu-Pippidi and G. Althabe, *Secera si buldozerul. Scornicesti si Nucsoara. Mecanisme de aservire a taranului roman*, Bucharest: Polirom, 2002.

32 Ierunca, *Fenomenul Pitesti*, D. Bacu, *Pitesti. Centru de reeducare studenteasca*, Hamilton: Cuvantul Romanesc, 1989, and E. Magierescu, *Moara Dracilor. Amintiri despre Pitesti*, Alba Iulia: no publisher, 1994.

33 M. Oprea and S. Olaru, *The Day We Won't Forget. 15 November 1987, Brasov*, Bucharest: Polirom, 2003.

34 P. Siani-Davies, *The Romanian Revolution of December 1989*, Ithaca: Cornell University Press, 2005, pp. 97–98.

35 S. Nicolaescu, *Revolutia, inceputul adevarului: un raport personal*, Bucharest: Editura Topaz, 1995, and S. Nicolaescu, *Cartea revolutiei romane din decembrie '89*, Bucharest: Editura Ion Cristoiu, 2000.

36 Popular wrath was directed not only against Ceausescu and his wife, but also against their children and blood relatives, as it was felt that the entire family greatly benefited from the despotic regime. In December 1989, their three children, Valentin, Zoe, and Nicu, were arrested, imprisoned in the Bucharest Militia headquarters, and charged with undermining the national economy by using their privileged position to exploit party assets. Afterwards, valuable possessions were confiscated from Valentin's home, and part of them entered the National Art Museum collection. In late 1990, the three were released, and in January 1996 charges against them were dropped. Half a year later, Nicu died of cirrhosis, thus ending a life of alcoholism and substance abuse. Zoe died of cancer in 2006. In 2003, the courts awarded Valentin and Zoe most of the valuables confiscated in 1989. Most of the Ceausescu extended family members have died or are very old. None of them holds public office. For a memoir written by a family member, see M. M. Ceausescu, *Nu regret, nu ma jelesc, nu strig*, Bucharest: Editura Meditatii, 2004.

37 D. Golebiewska, G. Brycki and W. Sochacki, 'A Mixed Bag of Communist Trials', *World Press Review* 1996, vol. 43. Online. Available HTTP: http://scilib.univ.kiev.ua/doc.php?5779544 (accessed 28 December 2007), D. Ionescu, 'Old Practices Persist in Romanian Justice', *Report on Eastern Europe*, 9 March 1990, 44–48, M. Shafir, 'The Isolation of Romania and the Fall of Nicolae Ceausescu', *Report on Eastern Europe*, 5 January 1990, 28–32, S. Roper, 'The Romanian Revolution from a Theoretical Viewpoint', *Communist and Post-Communist Studies*, 1994, vol. 27, 401–410, and J. Sislin, 'Revolution Betrayed? Romania and the National Salvation Front', *Studies in Comparative Communism*, 1991, vol. 29, 395–412.

38 As other key participants in the December 1989 revolution, Stanculescu published a self-exonerating volume of recollections. D. Sararu and V. Stanculescu, *Generalul Revolutiei cu piciorul in gips*, Bucharest: Rao, 2005.

39 C. Oprea, 'MApN refuza sa plateasca despagubiri in dosarul Timisoara 1989', *Evenimentul Zilei*, 18 July 1999.

40 Ibid.

41 'Ministrul de Interne nu este de acord cu Babiuc', *Evenimentul Zilei*, 21 July 1999.

42 Ibid. According to the constitution, draft laws adopted by Parliament must be promulgated by the President. The President can send a draft law to the house, but has to promulgate a law re-adopted by Parliament.

43 'Romanian 'Hot Line Affair' Probed by Prosecutor-General', *RFE/RL Newsline*, 28 March 2000. Online. Available HTTP: http://www.rferl.org/newsline/2000/03/280300.asp (accessed 28 January 2008). In 2003 his wife committed suicide, leaving behind a note saying she is disgusted by the people's ungratefulness toward her husband. She was cremated in Bucharest.

44 A. Anghelescu and A. Artene, 'Chitac facut scapat', *Ziua*, 17 February 2004. Chitac was also tried for his role in putting down the anti-Iliescu demonstrations of June 1990 in the Piata University of Bucharest, but the trial was delayed on technical grounds. He received a two-year prison sentence for ordering the extradition of journalist Doru Braia in 1990.

45 I. Stoica, 'Chitac si Stanculescu dibleaza puscaria', *Evenimentul Zilei*, 23 March 2004.
46 A. Artene, 'Dreptate pentru Ursu', *Ziua*, 15 July 2003, and C. Levant, 'Surse din Parchetul General dezvaluie: Informatii clasificate, pe mina tortionarilor lui Ursu', *Evenimentul Zilei*, 10 November 2003.
47 In mid-2004, former Romanian Information Service General Eugen Grigorescu received a two-year prison term for facilitating the disappearance of the diary that prompted the Securitate to arrest Ursu. Ursu's relatives complained of Grigorescu's suspended sentence, since without the threat of actually going to jail Grigorescu is unlikely to return the diary, which the family believed remains extant.
48 'Romania', *East European Constitutional Review*, 1999, vol. 8, 15–16.
49 'Sedinta solemna comuna a Camerei Deputatilor si Senatului din 22 December 1997'.
50 G. Galloway and B. Wylie, *Downfall: The Ceausescus and the Romanian Revolution*, London: Futura, 1991, N. Ratesh, *Romania: The Entangled Revolution*, New York: Praeger, 1991, J. Eyal, 'Why Romania Could not Avoid Bloodshed?', in G. Prins (ed.) *Spring in Winter: The 1989 Revolutions*, Manchester: University of Manchester Press, 1990, pp. 139–160, R. A. Hall, 'The Uses of Adversity: The Staged War Theory and the Romanian Revolution of December 1989', *East European Politics and Societies*, 1999, vol. 13, 501–542, and J. Levesque, *The Enigma of 1989: The USSR and the Liberation of Eastern Europe*, Berkeley: University of California Press, 1997. Also M. Castex, *Un mensonge gros comme le siecle: Roumanie, histoire d'une manipulation*, Paris: A Michel, 1990, R. Portocala, *Autopsie d'un coup d'état roumain: au pays du mensonge triumphant*, Paris:Calman-Levy, 1990, and V. Loupan, *La révolution n'a pas eu lieu ... Roumanie l'histoire d'un coup d'état*, Paris: R. Laffont, 1990. There is also an extensive Romanian language literature produced by almost all key players of the revolution.
51 T. Gallagher, *Romania after Ceausescu: The Politics of Intolerance*, Edinburgh: Edinburgh University Press, 1995, M. E. Fisher, 'The New Leaders and the Opposition', in D. Nelson (ed.) *Romania after Tyranny*, Boulder: Westview, 1992, pp. 45–65, K. Verdery and G. Kligman, 'Romania after Ceausescu: Post-Communist Communism?', in I. Banac (ed.) *Eastern Europe in Revolution*, Ithaca: Cornell University Press, 1992, pp. 117–147.

7 Bulgaria

Momchil Metodiev

Once Pope John Paul II passed away on 2 April 2005, the international mass media brought again in the public eye the 1981 failed attempt on the pope's life, as part of a concerted effort to reevaluate his life, work, and legacy. Thus, almost 25 years after the unsuccessful attempt on the pope's life, historians, journalists, and investigators turned their attention to Bulgaria and its communist secret intelligence services as they tried once again to identify the organization that masterminded the plot, to reconstruct the political context leading to the event, and to discern the reasons behind that terrorist act. Whereas in 1981 Bulgaria was part of the communist block, and its secret police explained accusations linking it to the attempt on the pope's life as nothing more than a CIA plot meant to discredit the communist camp, in 2005 the country was a NATO member and a European Union candidate. Whereas in 1981 the involvement of the Bulgarian secret services was seen as probable even in the absence of hard evidence, by 2005 most observers believed that the Bulgarian secret services had no part in the affair but expected authorities to fully support the renewed investigation and make public all relevant secret archive materials.

These were the expectations of uninformed observers. Informed observers, by contrast, knew that hopes for greater transparency and access to secret archives were premature. Foreign pressure intensified the long-lasting and generally fruitless public debate that has rocked Bulgarian domestic politics since 1989 relative to the methods, goals and archives of the former State Security. Once again, the Bulgarian mass media gave the floor to former secret officers, who explained that in the 1980s the country was a target of Cold War propaganda sponsored by Western governments and secret archives should remain closed to the general public to protect national security interests. But pressure from the general public and the press compelled authorities to declassify a small part of the archive: the correspondence between the Bulgarian State Security and the German Stasi. Ironically, those documents had been made public several years before by the German authorities (through the Gauck Institute, the custodian of the Stasi archive), and had already been published by at least two Bulgarian newspapers. As such, the Bulgarian authorities' pledge to fully cooperate with the renewed investigation into the attempt on the pope's life remained unfulfilled, as no significant new documents were released to the public.

This story might seem unimportant to Westerners unfamiliar with Bulgarian political reality, but it highlights developments in a country that experienced a relatively successful – albeit delayed – post-communist transition without fully coming to terms with its communist past. The history of the Bulgarian communist political police remains yet unwritten, the secret archives are still beyond the reach of the researchers and the general public, attempts to legislate lustration during the early stage of the transition process failed, and few communist leaders or secret agents were prosecuted for human rights trespasses. Instead of going to jail and answering for their human rights abuses, the former communist leaders and their close collaborators have joined the new political and economic elite.

Popular sentiment toward the communist period remains ambivalent. Old symbols have been incorporated into the local pop culture, imbued with nostalgia for the *ancien regime*. Well-known communist-era songs delight the Bulgarian youth, chocolate candy and toothpaste producers advertise the bland but inexpensive communist-era brands, while the most famous communist-era female singer graced the cover of the first issue of the Bulgarian edition of the *Playboy* magazine. The slow and painful recovery of the local economy, which only in mid-2004 matched the 1989 Gross Domestic Product level, explains this ambivalence. Transitional justice stagnated because the debate on the virtues and horrors of communism was dominated by individuals associated with the former regime. While after the collapse of communism secret agents hid from the public eye, by 1995 they had gained notoriety for writing personal memoirs and accounts of the State Security.[1] As secret archives remain out of reach for independent historians, these agents have been able to selectively choose which part of the historical truth becomes public.

Apart from this biased literature, critical examinations of the State Security remain scarce. The few studies written to date were authored by investigative journalists. From 1997 to 2002, when the Ministry of Interior archives were open to the public, Hristo Hristov obtained access to secret documents to investigate State Security operations against Bulgarian emigrants. The volume was the first to disclose top secret orders instructing an unnamed secret agent to murder Boris Arsov, a Bulgarian emigrant in Denmark. Hristov also mapped the Bulgarian prison camps of the 1950s, and investigated the assassination of dissident writer Georgi Markov.[2] In a documentary movie, Tatiana Vaksberg presented the Revival Process and the Politburo resolutions related to it, and shed new light on the structure and activity of the notorious Fourth Directorate (Scientific and Technical Intelligence).[3] Jovo Nikolov reviewed the history and organizational structure of the State Security.[4] Other authors have tried to understand the mass violence characteristic of early communism, the role of the people's court, and the communist religious policy.[5]

This chapter investigates the link between the pace of democratization and the process of uncovering the past, explaining how Bulgaria could finalize its political and economic transition to become a NATO member and a European Union candidate without knowing the truth about its recent dictatorial past. Were the Bulgarian Communist Party successors right when claiming that the opening of the State Security archives would open the Pandora's box and endanger national security? To explain Bulgarian transitional justice, the chapter first presents the history, structure, and activities of the State Security, relying on previously unpublished documents from the Bulgarian Communist Party archive, and then examines lustration, access to secret files, and trials against communist officials. Pointing to Bulgarian political developments, the chapter claims that the debate on de-communization is not over yet, as recent events have opened the possibility for partial lustration and a better understanding of the communist political police. Mild optimism is warranted by the opening of secret archives and the exclusion from key public posts of individuals with ties to the former regime and its political police.

The Bulgarian communist regime and its state security

In Bulgaria, the communist rule began in September 1944, when the Fatherland Front, a communist-dominated coalition of leftist parties, seized political power in a bloodless coup days after the Soviet Red Army crossed the border and marched into the capital Sofia without encountering local resistance. After consolidating its hold of the country, on 6 December 1947 the communist government adopted a new constitution, popularly bearing the name of the then party leader Georgi Dimitrov. The new basic law abolished the monarchy a year after King Simeon II went into exile, and proclaimed the People's Republic of Bulgaria, with the Communist Party as the leading governing force. The adoption of the constitution marked the establishment of the 'people's democracy'. After the Allies withdrew and Bulgaria was included in the Soviet sphere of influence following the 1947 Paris Treaty, the opposition leaders, initially allowed to retain theirs seats in parliament, received death sentences or prison terms in show trials orchestrated in 1947.

The opposition's elimination signaled the beginning of Stalinization with a number of show trials being organized against the 'national communists', local leaders likely to mount resistance, however feeble, to the prevailing Soviet line the country had opted for. The best known victim of those trials was the then Deputy Premier Traicho Kostov, also leader of the underground Bulgarian Communist Party during World War II. Kostov was executed in 1949 on charges of conspiring with the Yugoslav communists against the Soviets. At that time Georgi Dimitrov, the secretary-general of the Comintern's executive committee since 1935, was the uncontested leader of the Bulgarian communists. In 1944, Dimitrov returned from Moscow to Sofia to become the Bulgarian Communist Party leader, and Prime Minister two years later. After his death in 1949, the leadership of the party reverted to Dimitrov's brother-in-law Vulko Chervenkov, who, as Dimitrov, had spent the war years in Moscow. Chervenkov became Bulgaria's Stalin-type leader.

Following Stalin's death in 1953, Todor Zhivkov emerged as the Bulgarian communist leader, skillfully using the political changes affecting the Soviet Union to obtain support for his personal rule and to blame Chervenkov for Stalinist excesses. After succeeding Chervenko as party leader in April 1956, Zhivkov consolidated his power by using the State Security to apply soft pressure and to control the society covertly, instead of openly persecuting political rivals and opponents. Chervenkov was allowed to remain vice-premier until 1961, a fact attesting to Zhivkov's dislike of open conflict.[6] Zhivkov became Moscow's closest ally in Eastern Europe to the point that in 1963 and 1973 he proposed Bulgaria's incorporation into the Soviet Union as the 16th republic. Fortunately for Bulgaria, Kremlin turned a cold shoulder to both proposals, which were nevertheless seriously discussed at and dully recorded in the transcripts of the Politburo meetings of the time.[7] By relying on good personal relations with Soviet leaders to obtain trade concessions and lower oil prices, by frequently rotating party cadres, and by playing his protégés against each others, Zhivkov remained in office for some 30 years, longer than other Eastern European communist leaders.[8] To his long tenure undoubtedly contributed Bulgaria's slow economic progress up to the mid-1970s and Zhivkov's efforts to ameliorate the social status of the intelligentsia, and the use of the State Security to silence his critics. As a result, the Bulgarian dissident movement remained marginal before the mid 1980s, at a time when the Czechoslovak, Hungarian or Polish civil society managed to coalesce. Throughout his rule, Zhivkov was never seriously challenged by contenders inside or outside the party. An open anti-communist revolt was unthinkable in Bulgaria.

The Bulgarian communist political police

Ironically, the State Protection Law of 1924 set up the notorious Bulgarian State Security as an institution designed to fight, not serve, the communists. The State Security was created by a post-coup government interested to curb the influence of leftist parties. From 1941 to 1944, the State Security was a division of the Police Department empowered to counteract the communist threat. After the communist takeover, the Communist Party assumed full control of the political police and directed it against its enemies, including leaders of democratic parties and Western representatives in the transitional governing commission. The Law for the Establishment of the People's Court of 1944 allowed the State Security to find and arrest the so-called counter-revolutionary elements, thus turning it into the repressive arm of the communist regime.[9]

The State Security was created in 1947 as a distinct department of the Ministry of Interior. Eighteen years later, it became an independent institution directly accountable to the government and was renamed the KDS (*Komitet za Durzavna Sigurnost*). That independence lasted for only four years, but by the time it was reincorporated into the ministry in 1969, the later was named the Ministry of Interior and State Security to reflect the committee's importance. In fact, the Ministry of Interior was placed under the authority of the Committee for State Security, whose head became the new minister. Throughout the communist period, Soviet councilors worked in each KDS division as liaison officers advising and supervising Bulgarian special agents.[10]

In 1962, the Committee for State Security adopted the structure that remained relatively untouched until 1989. The First Directorate (Foreign Intelligence) worked closely with other communist intelligence services against "the United States of America, their closest allies Greece and Turkey, and the [countries of the] Mediterranean region,"[11] and tried to prevent Bulgarian emigrants from organizing resistance against the communist regime. Initially, the Second Directorate (Counter-intelligence) took charge of the whole spectrum of civil counter-intelligence operations, but later some of that work was transferred to other Directorates. The Third Directorate (Military Counter-intelligence), one of the most powerful and autonomous State Security structures, secured the loyalty of the army toward the regime,[12] while the Fourth Directorate (Scientific and Technical Intelligence) supplied technical assistance to other directorates.[13] This directorate's four divisions were: 1) control of correspondence, 2) microphone and telephone eavesdropping, 3) design, construction and manufacturing of technical equipment for the secret services, and 4) radio intelligence, radio counter-intelligence and radio links.[14]

The Fifth Directorate (Security and Body-Guarding) was the most publicly visible and synonymous to the perks enjoyed by the communist nomenklatura. By 1989, this directorate had become one of the largest because it guarded and protected the communist elite and provided communist leaders and their families with everything necessary for their everyday life both within the country and during their official and unofficial visits abroad. This directorate managed the special shops, laundries, protocol residences, exclusive resorts, hunting grounds and other facilities used by the nomenklatura members. Created in 1967 as a splinter department of the Second Directorate, the feared Sixth Directorate was responsible for "fighting ideological diversion, counter-revolutionary, nationalistic and other activities against the state."[15] As a political police structure, it spied on intellectuals, journalists and political dissidents. As a counter-intelligence department, it worked within the ruling party, monitored Zhivkov's potential rivals, and detected instances of corruption involving party officials. Because of its notoriety, after the collapse of the communist regime this directorate was singled out as a scapegoat blamed for the regime's mistakes and atrocities. Among auxiliary departments were Central Operations, Cryptography, and Archive.[16] While less important, these departments – especially the archive custodian – became key to the post-communist transitional justice process.

The work of the committee was regulated by unpublished Minister of Interior orders and government ordinances. The most important was the Decree on the State Security Activity of 1974, which remained classified until 1989, with only some excerpts being published in the *State Gazette*.[17] To reign in the committee, the Politburo adopted several decisions regulating its activity. Despite these attempts, the State Security functioned almost as a state within the state, restrained only by the personal loyalty of the Minister of Interior to the Communist Party Secretary General. Usually the Minister of Interior was a Politburo member, thus formally accountable to that body. After 1960 the Ministry of Interior was ruled by a College including the minister, his deputies and representatives of the Central Committee, which College members could present with disputed issues.

As long as the Ministry of Interior archives remain closed it is difficult to estimate the total number of State Security officers and informers. The *Main Guidelines for the Activity of the Ministry of Interior* of November 1962 revealed that at the time the Committee for State Security employed around 6,200 full-time officers. It is believed that the total number almost tripled by 1989, because some 8,000 to 14,000 political police officers (representing 50–70 percent of all State Security personnel) lost their positions from 1990 to 1992 when communist secret services were dismantled. Estimates of the number of secret informers are even less reliable, depending on the occasional revelations made by former spies. Following the former Sixth Department officer Boncho Assenov, the State Security recruited 250,000–300,000 secret informers from 1944 to 1989,[18] but Baev and Grozev claim that after the mid-1950s the State Security relied on 50,000 to 65,000 secret informers (that is, close to 1 percent of Bulgaria's total population).[19] Article 2.D of the Central Committee Resolution on Intensifying the Prevention of Criminal Activities of 14 January 1960 directed the Committee for State Security to recruit Communist Party members as secret informers "only in exceptional cases, and only after obtaining the permission of the First Secretary of the respective Bulgarian Communist Party District Committee."[20] In 1965 the ban on the recruitment of ordinary party members was lifted, while that on the recruitment of party leaders was upheld. Because of this limitation, enforced until 1989, the secret police might have aggressively recruited from among pre-communist political parties and ethnic minorities as a way to compensate the loss of informers from within the Communist Party.[21]

It is unclear how much of the secret archive remains intact. Following Nedelchev, only 450,000 of the total 1,500,000 files on communist-era victims of the State Security are extant, but neither figure can be corroborated from independent sources.[22] In 1990 Minister of Interior General Atanas Semerdziev ordered the destruction of 150,000 files, mostly of the Sixth Directorate, a document destruction that was later used as an argument against the public opening of the secret archive. Other campaigns, official and unofficial, publicly known or unknown, affected the most important files. Thus, the extant files detail the activity of unimportant informers who provided trivial information on their victims. In 2000 Semerdziev was sentenced to six years in prison for file destruction, but three years later the Court of Appeals returned the case to the lower courts for further investigation.

Notorious crimes of the political police

Mass murders, prison, and labor camps

Initially, the State Security had the task of eliminating the political enemies of the communist regime. Numerous atrocities were perpetrated in the vast network of prison and labor camps that operated from 1944 to 1965. Political violence was rampant in the early 1940s, when the Communist Party, with Moscow's help, organized a guerilla movement against the pro-German Bulgarian government backed by King Boris III. The violence continued after communists seized power. In the late 1940s, more than 20,000 people were executed in extra-judicial proceedings in one of the most extensive purges per capita conducted in any country of the region.[23] The Law on the Establishment of the People's Court of 1944 quickly became an instrument of political repression. After 1989, communists claimed that the People's Court resembled the Nuremberg court because it targeted Nazi collaborators. In fact, the Court, whose jury was selected by the Communist Party's regional structures, purged pre-communist elite members irrespective of their position toward Nazi Germany. From November 1944 to April 1945, the court sentenced 2,600 people to death and 8,000 other to prison.[24] Most of the verdicts were reversed on technical and procedural grounds from 1993 to 1998.[25]

Analysts have claimed that political violence came naturally in the first years after World War II because at the time the communist government had to establish control over the country, but this excuse cannot justify later waves of repression. After the Communist Party established its control, members of its former allies, the Fatherland Front, the Social Democrat Party and the Agricultural Party, became the communists' new victims and these parties' leaders received death sentences on charges of conspiring with Western governments against Bulgarian authorities. Among the victims were communist leaders who did not spend the war in the Soviet Union, who were found guilty of siding with Tito against Moscow. The purge continued up until 1954 and affected all branches of the party-state and even the repressive State Security, which lost its entire leadership.[26]

The regime's political rivals were sent to prison and labor camps. The first camp briefly operated in 1945 at the Sveti Vrach railway station near Sandansky town. Several other small camps were opened in the following four years. In 1949, the Council of Ministers earmarked the Belene Island camp on the Danube river to receive only political prisoners, making the camp synonymous to communist political repression. According to Hristov, the camp initially accommodated 4,500 prisoners, but by 1952 the number decreased to 2,323. After being closed down on 1 January 1953, the Belene Island camp reopened in autumn 1956, after events in Hungary convinced the Bulgarian communists of the need to quash any form of dissent. The camp closed definitely on 27 August 1959, when the Politburo ordered the release of 276 political prisoners. Some 166 "incorrigible recidivists" continued to serve their prison terms at the newly established Lovech camp, which functioned until 1962. According to evidence presented at the trial of the Lovech camp jailers, 147 of the 1,501 individuals imprisoned in that camp died because of inhuman conditions.[27]

Human rights violations

After assuming the leadership, Zhivkov saw no need to use mass violence against the enemies of the regime, and as a result he closed down all camps for political prisoners. Afterwards, the State Security sought to prevent dissident activities, and to silence the politically active Bulgarian emigrants. In an effort to control and influence the emigration, the State Security went beyond Bulgaria's borders, and in the process became famous for killing well-known Bulgarian intellectuals living in the West. The threat that the Bulgarian émigrés posed to the communist regime should not be exaggerated, as the diaspora lacked unity and was relatively small and poorly organized. A 1966 Ministry of Interior report listed 5,933 emigrants as 'traitors of the motherland' and 372 others as "non-returnees."[28] The figures were insignificant in comparison to Bulgaria's population of eight million.

Given the small number of Bulgarian emigrants, it is surprising to see that secret services handled with brutality even relatively minor figures of the emigration. One case involved defector Boris Arsov, who set up the Union of Bulgarian Revolutionary Committees as a small anti-communist unit in Denmark. The State Security first hired an agent to murder Arsov, but the operation failed, although the agent received detailed instructions on how to execute the murder. In 1974 Arsov was kidnapped and brought back to the country. While in Bulgaria, he refused to allow authorities to use him as a propaganda tool against the emigration, and as such he was sentenced to 15 years in prison. A week after his conviction, he was found hanging in his prison cell on three neckties, although all his belongings had been retained by prison officials at the time of his imprisonment.[29]

In 1977, the Politburo endorsed a Ministry of Interior resolution proposing measures to subdue the emigration. Alongside propaganda actions, the document listed methods designed to limit the emigrants' contacts with their motherland and relatives left behind. More importantly, the resolution envisioned the creation of a "permanently operative working group, comprised of officers of the First, Second and Sixth Directorates… . who should organize and coordinate overall the operative work of the State Security against the Bulgarian emigration."[30] The group was authorized "to propose the implementation of extraordinary measures imposed by changes in the operative situation."[31] The following year, the State Security implemented one such extraordinary measure, which brought it notoriety far beyond Bulgarian borders. The measure called for the murder of writer and journalist Georgi Markov, who died on 11 September 1978, after being shot with poisonous bullets fired off from the soon-to-become-famous "Bulgarian umbrella." At the time, Markov lived in London and, as a BBC World Service journalist, had acquired the well-deserved reputation of a popular critic of the Bulgarian communist regime. In 2005, Hristov identified Francesco Gullino, a Dane of Italian origin, as Markov's assassin. Bulgarian authorities arrested Gullino in 1970 for custom crimes, but the State Security recruited him under the codename Piccadilly and sent him back home.[32] The book disclosed a report detailing Piccadilly's meeting with his contact officer, Colonel Micho Genkovski, on 7 April 1990 in Budapest. At the meeting, Genkovski told Gullino that the Bulgarian intelligence services decided to sever ties to him.[33]

Two weeks before Markov's assassination, journalist Vladimir Kostov escaped a similar fate after a secret agent made an attempt on his life using the same method. In 1977 Kostov escaped to France, where he worked as an intelligence officer under the cover of being a correspondent for a Bulgarian newspaper. Because of that, in May 1978, Kostov was sentenced to death in absentia by a Bulgarian court for his outspoken criticism of the communist regime.[34] Because Markov and Kostov both worked for respectable Western media and their cases were widely reported internationally, Bulgaria became known as the communist country with one of the most brutal political police forces.

Oppression of ethnic minorities

In the mid-1980s, the State Security once again engaged in massive persecution of the Turkish minority, an activity more characteristic of the early days of communist rule. Apart from the emotional fear posed by Turkey, a neighboring country that had more population, territory, and resources, and the widespread belief among communist leaders that the minority represented Turkey's "fifth column" in Bulgaria, no secret documents were found to explain rationally the reasons behind the adoption of a policy which seriously damaged the reputation and legitimacy of the Bulgarian communist regime. The Revival Process of the late 1980s, in which Bulgarian authorities obliged ethnic Turks to take on Slavic names, became a major destabilizing factor for the communist regime once the international media revealed its gruesome details. After the Turkish minority organized both peaceful protests and violent action, the Bulgarian government expelled some Turkish nationals from the country. This well-documented ethnic cleansing attempt, which predated Milosevic's policies, occurred toward the end of communist rule, but those who carried on and masterminded the violence never answered for their crimes.

The Revival Process represented the climax of a long-term communist policy to oppress the Turkish minority, which entailed the so-called Bulgarization of the Turkish and Muslim minorities, and the suppression of their national customs, rituals and religious practices with the use of more violent methods. Those minorities were prime targets for the State Security. Indeed, while there were on average 3.6 secret informers for every 1,000 Bulgarian citizens, that ratio almost doubled when it came to the Turkish minority, reaching 6 informers for every 1,000 individuals. According to Vaksberg, roughly one tenth of all Turkish students enrolled in Bulgarian universities acted as secret informers.[35]

The communist regime was seeking to solve the so-called "problem of the Turkish minority." In November 1984, the Politburo asked the Ministry of Interior to take military action against that minority. The operation, carried out on Christmas Eve, resulted in the military occupation of the southern Kardzali district, the hub of the Turkish minority in Bulgaria. The operation, executed expeditiously with army support, was met with resistance by the Turkish minority. In the aftermath, the Belene Island camp was reopened to receive the leaders of the Turkish minority who resisted the Revival Process. In the process, the camp became an "incubator of secret informers" at the order of Deputy Minister of Interior Grigor Shopov. Using international pressure as an excuse, on 31 March 1989 Zhivkov ordered the Minister of Interior to deport some 100,000–150,000 Turks from Bulgaria. In total, close to 200,000 Turks were forced to "emigrate" to Turkey, a move placing great strain on the relations between the two countries.[36]

The Revival Process ended when the communist regime collapsed. In December 1989, the newly elected leadership of the Bulgarian Communist Party allowed Turks to revert to their Turkish names and discontinued the discriminatory policies oppressing that ethnic group. To better defend their collective rights, the Bulgarian Turks organized politically as the Movement for Rights and Freedoms, which became an active and influential player in the country's democratization process. Also in response to the repression of the Turkish minority the first Bulgarian anti-communist dissident and human rights groups emerged. Later these groups became part of the anti-communist Union of Democratic Forces.

Export of communism

As a communist country, Bulgaria actively supported Soviet efforts to export communism to other regions of the world. As part of the effort, the Bulgarian government supplied armament and money to the guerilla groups and communist parties of Latin America, Africa, and the Middle East. Since the government did not distinguish between terrorist groups and freedom fighters, some archival evidence shows tacit or active support to some of the most notorious terrorists of all times. For example, the Ministry of Interior archive revealed that in the early 1980s Carlos the Jackal and his aides spent time in Bulgaria.[37]

More importantly, the State Security took part in activities which fell outside the scope of Bulgarian legislation and international law. Many communist-era economic crimes were carried out by the Fourth Directorate of the State Security and coordinated by the party-state leadership, which was eager to obtain much-needed hard currency through any means. After 1989, these criminal activities attracted much public attention because the first generation of post-communist business tycoons included many individuals with ties to the State Security. Details on these secret financial operations were offered in a special report prepared for the Minister of Interior in 1991, and partially published by the press a decade later.[38] The report concluded that "the secret transit trade was official state policy conducted by Bulgarian companies under the cover of foreign nationals. Because such trade usually involved goods placed under special international control, suppliers lacked official import permit for such goods. Besides gold, hard currency, electronics, cigarettes, liquors and others, this secret trade involved armament and ammunition, re-export and export of medicines controlled by the International Health Organization.[39]

The Council of Ministers Resolution 148 of 31 July 1978 allowed the state-owned trade monopoly Kintex to conduct secret trade operations, and asked the Second Directorate (Counter-intelligence) to facilitate these commercial activities. More specifically, secret officers had to prevent information leaks, block possible interference from foreign secret services, and prevent the conclusion of deals detrimental to the Bulgarian state. The total volume of the secret trade remains unknown. Those contraband channels were likely privatized in the early stage of post-communism by the State Security agents who maintained them, and who thus became the new Bulgarian business tycoons.[40]

Transitional justice in Bulgaria

Despite economic difficulties, the change of guard in Moscow and the rising opposition at home, Zhivkov continued to be sure of his hold over the country. When he met the United States Undersecretary of State John Whitehead in 1987, Zhivkov confidently stated, "I am the doyen among the first and general secretaries of the communist parties of socialist countries. I dare say that I am the vice-doyen head of state in the world. It is only the Japanese emperor that has had a lengthier term of office."[41] Such confidence did not help Zhivkov to politically outlive Mikhail Gorbachev, the last Soviet leader. Pressure from Moscow, the emergence of a new generation of Bulgarian Communist Party leaders, the collapse of other Eastern European communist regimes and the rise of a dissident movement in Bulgaria led to the end of Zhivkov's rule. Responding to popular calls for reforms, on 10 November 1989 the Central Committee replaced Zhivkov with his Minister of Foreign Affairs Petur Mladenov, allowing the Communist Party to have the upper hand in the political transition. Behind the scenes, the new strong man was Andrey Lukanov, whose strong family and political ties to Kremlin promoted him as Moscow's new protégé.

During the first two years of transition, the Communist Party gradually gave up political control in exchange for greater economic control. Political unrest and the emergence of the anticommunist Union of Democratic Forces led to the Round-table talks. Under pressure from the opposition, the constitution was amended in early 1990. Article 1, guaranteeing a "leading role in the society" for the Communist Party, was removed, and the name of the state was changed to the Republic of Bulgaria. The newly created position of President of the Republic, indirectly elected by legislators, was assumed by Petur Mladenov. The Communist Party, by then renamed the Socialist Party, won the first free general elections of June 1990 and nominated Lukanov as premier. Within months his government collapsed under a wave of anti-governmental demonstrations. On 1 August 1990 the Grand National Assembly elected Zheliu Zhelev, opposition leader and a communist-era dissident, as President. Zhelev also won the first direct presidential poll of January 1992.

After winning the 1991 poll, the Union of Democratic Forces nominated Philip Dimitrov as prime minister. Ironically, the consolidation of the budding Bulgarian democracy was threatened by the personal animosity between President Zhelev and Premier Dimitrov, both representing the same political formation. Following presidential criticism of Dimitrov and a scandal allegedly orchestrated by the Intelligence Chief, the government collapsed in 1992, being replaced by a technocratic cabinet supported by the Movement for Rights and Freedoms and the Socialist Party. That was post-communist Bulgaria's weakest government, but it allowed the Socialists to rehabilitate themselves. In 1994 Socialist leader Zhan Videnov assumed the premiership, only to lose it because of his government's inability to control economic decline and hyperinflation. In 1997, Petur Stoyanov became the President with support from the Union of Democratic Forces. Half a year later the Union won the general elections. Ivan Kostov's cabinet launched market reforms and thus opened the door to negotiations for NATO and European Union membership. After serving a full mandate, Kostov was succeeded by King Simeon II, who had returned to Bulgaria before the June 2001 poll to form the National Movement Simeon II. The Socialist Party won the 2005 general poll by a slim plurality, forming a coalition government with the National Movement Simeon II and the Movement for Rights and Freedoms. Socialist leader Georgi Parvanov secured the presidency in 2001 and 2006.

Trials against former communist officials

The political context some times facilitated, other times hindered the Bulgarian transitional justice process. Certainly, the most vehement debates revolved around the direction and speed of economic reforms and the country's foreign policy orientation, traditionally colored by pro-Russian attitudes. In 1990 and 1991, when former communists dominated the country, transitional justice was presented as an impediment to, more than a pre-requisite for, successful democratization. Construed as a new form of discrimination, transitional justice was portrayed as a dangerous idea, which can only waste public energy, intensify social cleavages or even lead to civil war. As such, transitional justice was quickly discredited as a subject of intellectual debate. Opportunities for the legal prosecution of former communist officials were quickly exhausted. Under public pressure, a number of communist leaders were placed under investigation. In most instances, these lawsuits reflected the heightened political tensions dividing the country more than a public expectation for revenge and retribution. Because charges of lesser importance were laid, the trials could not convince the public that former rulers were guilty of anything.

Bulgarians were appalled by the enormous privileges the communist nomenklatura once enjoyed. That was probably the reason why prosecutors concentrated their efforts on collecting evidence for those types of crimes, if crimes they were. Public attention turned to the so-called Case No. 1, the lawsuit filed in 1990 against the former party-state leader Todor Zhivkov and his right hand man, Milko Balev. Unable to account for the money they regularly withdrew from state coffers or the illegal distribution, at Zhivkov's personal order, of luxury cars and apartments, the two were accused of misusing state funds. Zhivkov was also accused of illegally spending from 1985 to 1989 one million Levs of taxpayers' money to subsidize the luxurious lifestyle of his family members, including his son Vladimir Zhivkov and grandson Todor Slavkov. Balev was also charged with illegally receiving 39,000 Levs to publish Zhivkov's writings. Proceedings dragged for so long that the public eventually lost interest in the trial. In 1992, Zhivkov was sentenced to seven and Balev to two years prison terms. Because of health problems, Zhivkov was allowed to serve his term under house arrest. In 1995 the Court of Appeals ruled that the trial should have never been launched, because Zhivkov enjoyed immunity as head of state.[42] Zhivkov died in 1998, aged 87. Milko Balev died in 2002, aged 82.

One of the rare cases resulting in the conviction of former communist party officials was launched in 1993 against the communist premier Georgi Atanassov and the Minister of Economy and State Planning Stoyan Ovcharov. Found guilty of unlawfully granting 210,000 Levs to nomenklatura members wishing to build new apartments, the two were sentenced to 10 and 9 year prison terms, respectively.

In 1994, President Zhelev pardoned Atanassov because of his failing health condition, but Ovcharov remained in prison.[43] Launched in 1993, the "Chernobyl Case" prosecuted the two top state officials who failed to take necessary prevention measures and warn the public of the risk of contamination when the radiation cloud reached Bulgaria after the explosion at the Soviet nuclear plant. The courts heard evidence proving that Deputy Prime Minister Grigor Stoychkov and Chief Health Care Inspector Lubomir Shindarov jeopardized the health of the public by not observing regulations for radiation protection. The court sentenced Stoychkov to two years in prison and Shindarov to two years probation term. Stoychkov served his full sentence.[44]

By the time the prosecution gathered evidence for the more complicated Trial of the Camps, Bulgarians had lost interest, the more so since they were unable to follow each step of the legal proceedings. The truth about the communist prison and labor camps was revealed immediately after 1989, but observers claim that the Union of Democratic Forces' references to the subject in the 1990 electoral campaign were counterproductive, as many Bulgarians, especially former Communist Party members, were afraid of possible retaliation. The Military Prosecution launched investigations into the case as early as March 1990, but evidence was gathered only with respect to the Lovech and Skravena camps, because the extant archive provided documents dealing only with those two camps. Public demand for justice forced parliament to lift the statute of limitations for post-1960 crimes involving the murder of two or more people, but the measure did not cover the murders that took place in camps in the 1950s. Prosecutors charged five people for 14 camp murders. The top official accused was the former Deputy Minister of Interior Mircho Spassov, a key figure in the camp system and a leader of communist repression. Spassov died a month before the trial begun in June 1993, well before a sentence could be handed down. For various reasons, the case was set aside until 2002, when the Supreme Court closed it on grounds of expired prescription. Thus, the accused spent just three months in prison during investigations. The only punishment Spassov ever received was handed down by the Socialist Party, which publicly took a stance against his crimes and expelled him in 1990. That year, President Mladenov revoked Spassov's army general rank.[45]

Other trials prosecuting the crimes of the State Security had the same fate, although a few involved other countries and legal systems. Under British pressure, Bulgarian authorities launched investigations into Markov's murder in the early 1990s. The case was a test for Bulgarian efforts to come to terms with the communist past. Investigations revealed that the former communist Deputy Minister of Interior Stoyan Savov and former Intelligence Directorate Vladimir Todorov had destroyed Markov's file. As the prosecution started to look closer into the deputy ministers' involvement in the case, Savov took his own life days before trial hearings began. Todorov received a ten-month prison sentence for his part in file destruction. To date, the case remains unsolved, although Markov's relatives have struggled hard to learn the truth. Another investigation the courts never heard was Case No. 3, initiated by the Prosecutor General in 1992. Some 22 top communist officials, including party leader Alexander Lilov and former premier

Andrey Lukanov, were accused of secretly supplying armament to communist and guerrilla movements abroad. Lukanov spent several months in prison during investigations, but prosecutors ultimately decided not to file a lawsuit because of lack of evidence. After the case was set aside in 1997, the European Court of Human Rights fined Bulgaria for Lukanov's imprisonment.

A hotly debated topic was the Revival Process, the last instance of mass atrocities conducted by the communist regime and one of the few cases in which the names of those who masterminded and executed the human rights abuses were known publicly. This public knowledge did not help the prosecutors. Investigations started in 1991, when the Army Prosecutor General charged the top communist officials like Zhivkov, Minister of Interior Stoyanov, Prime Minister Atanassov, Minister of Foreign Affairs Mladenov and Deputy Prime Minister Pencho Kubadinski for planning the Revival Process. In 1993 and 1997 the prosecution prepared lawsuits against Zhivkov, Atanassov and Stoyanov but the court sent the case back for further investigation on the pretext that prosecutors had failed to interview all ethnic Turks who suffered in the Revival Process. Obviously, such comprehensive evidence gathering was beyond the prosecution's capabilities, as most victims moved to Turkey after the 1989 deportation.[46] In April 2005, the European Court of Human Rights turned down the request of some 100 Bulgarian Turks to file a lawsuit against Bulgaria on grounds that in the 1980s the country was not a signatory to the European Convention on Human Rights. As in most other cases of court proceedings against communist perpetrators, history, not courts, must identify the guilty ones.[47]

This is the almost complete list of trials against Bulgarian communist officials, if we add the trial of prison guards Tsvyatko Gazdov and Nikolay Goranov. The trials did not fulfill expectations for expediency and did not result in the conviction of the accused, who had also used the mechanisms of the totalitarian state for personal gain. The trials were unsuccessful because public expectations were tainted by calls for revenge and the judiciary was interested to gain independence from the public and the executive more than to find the truth about the communist dictatorship. Except for investigative journalists, most Bulgarians have lost interest in the trials, even in those related to the prison camps and the Revival Process, which can help the most their understanding of communist repression. The cases' failure resulted in public cynicism toward the government, the political elite, and the judiciary's capacity to sort the good from the bad.

Lustration

In Bulgaria, lustration has sought to ban Communist Party leaders and State Security officers from high state positions. As in the case of trials against communist decision makers and access to secret archives, the adoption of lustration legislation was strongly influenced by political developments. In 1990, the local press mentioned lustration only in relation to other Eastern European countries, thus diminishing the initial impetus to screen tainted politicians. The term lustration was first employed in 1991–1992 by the Union of Democratic Forces government, inspiring mixed feelings to the general public. Calls for lustration were raised mostly by the civil society, but the process was quickly discredited by the then opposition Socialist Party as a process prone to political 'witch-hunt'. By the late 90s, the term was seen as politically incorrect, and thus it was only infrequently used.

In 1992, lustration was legislated as changes to the Law on Banks and Credit Activity, and as the Law for Temporary Introduction of Some Additional Requirements for the Members of the Executive Bodies of Scientific Organizations and the Higher Certifying Commission (the so-called "Panev bill"), abolished in 1995.[48] The first bill banned Communist Party leaders at all levels and State Security agents and collaborators from management positions in the banking system. The second bill banned from the leadership positions of universities, research institutes and the Science Academy down to the level of head of the human resources department former nomenklatura members, State Security officers and collaborators, individuals who planned and executed the Revival Process, and people who taught ideologically-related disciplines in schools.[49] These provisions affected intellectuals, professors and public figures, who organized a bitter campaign against the law in particular and lustration in general. The bills were abolished in 1997 and 1995.

In 1992, the Union of Democratic Forces cabinet drafted the Law on De-communization, which banned selected categories of communist decision-makers from assuming leadership positions in the executive, public companies, mass media, and other organizations. The proposal pitted Premier Dimitrov against President Zhelev, who opposed the law on grounds that "national reconciliation and successful economic reform represent true de-communization."[50] The government's collapse at the end of that year thwarted attempts to implement lustration through de-communization, the more so since the project gained little public support. Despite its failure to enact lustration legislation, the Union of Democratic Forces government made significant strides to effect broader justice by returning to initial owners the agricultural land, factories and dwellings abusively confiscated by the communist regime. Although a long and painful process, property restitution enjoyed public support, and ultimately contributed to the establishment of a local middle class.

After it returned to government in 1997, the Union of Democratic Forces tried again to legislate lustration. This time, lustration was tied to the work of a special commission authorized to disclose the identity of State Security agents. Article 26 of the Law on Public Radio and Television of 1998 read that former secret agents and collaborators could not sit on the newly created Media Regulatory Council. Candidates for those positions had to give signed declarations stating that they had never worked for the State Security.[51] In 2002, the council removed one of its members when the commission identified him as a former spy. Similar conditions applied to national and local government members after the Law on the Election of Members of Parliament, Mayors and Municipal Councilors was amended in 2001.[52] The commission verified candidates for those positions, and the regional election committees released the verification results. The provisions were mere recommendations. Political parties were not obliged to exclude former State Security agents from electoral lists. Although applied only to the 2001 general poll, the law led to bitter public scandals in which the integrity of Bulgarian luminaries (well-known actors, film directors and journalists), who launched their careers under communism, came under attack.

State security after State Security: the criminalization of the Bulgarian transition

Exactly what happened to the State Security after the collapse of communism has remained a mystery and the inspiration for numerous conspiracy theories. The possibility that the political police continued its existence after the State Security was officially closed down became a common explanation for the troubles facing transitional Bulgaria. The Sixth Directorate closed its doors in January 1990. By the end of the year other directorates were dismantled, and some 6,000 to 7,000 secret officers were laid off.[53] That was the moment when the Bulgarian post-communist transition began to be criminalized.[54] Readers could dismiss this statement as a gross exaggeration, but the State Security did 'privatize' itself after its officers launched private businesses and secured well-paid management positions in private firms set up by former communist apparatchiks. Relying on the agents' network of contacts and specialized knowledge, these firms established close ties to the emerging organized criminal groups and the budding local mafia.

At the onset of transition, new and surprisingly wealthy private firms like Multi-grup and TS Bank established powerful intelligence and information units. It was rumored that in 1993 the Multigrup president Ilya Pavlov paid USD 200,000 to acquire special equipment for his company's intelligence unit.[55] Many explained the Multigrup's emergence as a key player in the Bulgarian economy by the family ties linking Pavlov to the chief of the Fifth Directorate, but the information cannot be verified. We do know that in the mid-1990s Multigrup enjoyed significant economic and political clout, and Pavlov figured among Eastern Europe's wealthiest individuals. By the end of the decade, Pavlov had lost some of his influence. In 2003, he was killed in front of his company's headquarters in Sofia in a mafia-style shooting spree. The killers' identity and the reasons for his murder remain unknown. Bulgarians have lost interest in his empire, which recently shrank significantly.

Another reason for speedy enrichment in the first stages of post-communist transformation lay in the close-to-public privatization of the foreign companies the State Security had established and operated in communist times in an effort to counteract the sanctions imposed by Western governments. When post-communist authorities closed them down, these operations were in fact privatized and sold to the officers who once staffed them, the only ones acquainted with their activity. After 1990, the contraband channels created and operated by the State Security were abandoned to criminal groups which transformed them into key links in the Balkan trans-border criminal activities. Their importance augmented when Yugoslavia was placed under international embargo during the armed conflict in Bosnia, and these contraband channels no longer had to compete with official trade partnerships. Observers claim that at least some of these channels continue to exist today.

Equally important are the efforts to reform intelligence services. The first step was to de-politicize such structures and disassociate them from their communist predecessors. In 1991, the government banned secret officers from joining political parties. The step limited the Communist Party's influence on intelligence agencies, but its long-term significance was limited, as former and active intelligence officers could still informally promote party interests. These informal ties led to the re-politicization of intelligence services by the mid-1990s. The State Security's successors had privileged access to secret archives containing sensitive information on the new political elite that could be used to settle political scores. As a result, parties wooed intelligence services, which in turn sought the parties' protection, dragging Bulgarian politics into a "war by discrediting facts" taking the form of leaks of damaging information or spreading of rumors about political opponents. The leaks and rumors questioned the integrity of public figures by suggesting that secret informers turned politicians served their group interests more than they served the country's interests. Unproven accusations claimed that some politicians maintained contacts with foreign espionage agencies or organized crime groups.[56] In the absence of public access to secret archives, this disinformation campaign discredited the political elite as a whole. At first they gave credence to the rumors, but then Bulgarians gradually lost interest in the politicians' past, growing aloof to charges mixing fact and fiction. Public disinterest and lack of moral authority explain the failure of transitional justice in Bulgaria.

Intelligence services have continued to interfere in the political process, as showed by the notorious "That List" of Bulgarian secret spies allegedly delivered in 1991 to the Turkish embassy in Sofia by Bulgarian authorities. The list's authenticity remains doubtful, and many believe that the Secret Security prepared the list to trick Turkish intelligence agencies.[57] Another notorious case, the "Macedonian Affair," led to the collapse of the first Union of Democratic Forces government in 1992. The scandal erupted when the Bulgarian intelligence services chief Brigo Asparoukhov publicly accused one of Prime Minister's advisers of secretly negotiating, with the premier's knowledge, an armament sale to embargoed Macedonia.[58] Asparoukhov's reputation was further tainted when it became known that, as head of intelligence services, he destroyed the secret file of a business tycoon who was also one of his best friends.[59] In 2003, Asparoukhov, by then a Socialist deputy, was invited to become the Premier's security adviser. Public outcry and pressure from NATO partners prevented Asparoukhov from assuming the position.[60]

The struggle between government and opposition escalated in the 1990s with accusations of illegal eavesdropping on politicians and political parties bringing the State Security again in the public eye and raising suspicions that intelligence services continued to violate human rights even after the collapse of the communist regime. Since 1989, a number of politicians and political parties have claimed that their homes or headquarters were bugged. No devices were ever discovered, but reports were given credence, as it was widely believed that the State Security had bugged many buildings in Sofia. The end result was that the secret services' credibility was under serious attack. For some, the very fact that so many cases were reported, even in the absence of concrete proof, meant that secret services were tempted to serve the ruling party and to discredit the political opposition.[61]

The opening of the secret archives

It was in the context of criminalized transition that the debate on opening the State Security archives was held. The debate went through several stages reflecting the political situation. It is not difficult to guess that the Communist Party and its successor, the Socialist Party, fiercely opposed the opening of the archives. When in government, anti-communist parties vowed to declassify the archives without ever fulfilling their promise. Although the issue became part of each post-communist electoral campaign, the archives were partially opened to the public only from 1997 to 2001.

The topic provoked a heated debate in the 1990 electoral campaign. One of the first decisions of the Socialist-dominated parliament was to create the Special Parliamentary Commission on State Security Archives, chaired by Socialist Georgi Tambuev. The commission was unable to survive the public scandal which followed the publication of a list of deputies with alleged ties to the State Security. The little known newspaper responsible for the publication claimed that the list had been prepared by the parliamentary commission, a contention the commission bitterly denounced, without being able to prevent the scandal from ruining its reputation and credibility. In April 1991, parliament dissolved the commission and passed a resolution forbidding the publication of any information on former State Security collaborators.[62]

In October 1994 the Union of Democratic Forces parliamentary majority decided that documents containing information on the activities, methods, and agents of the State Security could be made public because they were not classified.[63] The resolution was never implemented, and never abolished. The first serious attempt to open the archives, made by the second Union of Democratic Forces cabinet, enjoyed wide public support.[64] In July 1997 parliament adopted the Law on Access to the State Security Archives, which laid down the procedure Bulgarians once prosecuted by the State Security had to observe in order to access their own files.[65] A commission headed by the Minister of Interior was created to unmask the State Security informers from among post-communist politicians. The commission's authority was seriously limited by the Constitutional Court ruling of 22 September 1997, which forbade it to publicly release the names of tainted persons for whom the secret archive contained a name card, but no file. In fact, those were the people whose records were destroyed at the orders of Atanas Semerdziev, and for whom there was no other proof of secret collaboration besides the name card. In 1997, the Minister of Interior Bogomil Bonev told parliament the names of 14 former legislators who had collaborated with the State Security. In time, the procedure allowing the victims of the political police to read their files proved slow and inefficient.

To correct legal loopholes and make the procedure more efficient, in 2001 parliament created the Commission Determining Connections to the Former State Security under the chairmanship of Metody Andreev, a Union of Democratic Forces deputy. The opposition Socialist Party questioned the reliability of a commission chaired by a representative of the ruling party and made up of members appointed by parties represented in parliament. The commission worked from April 2001 to March 2002, prepared nine reports unmasking State Security officers and informers turned politicians, verified the past of members of all post-communist legislatures and governments, monitored 1,100 people and disclosed the names of 53 deputies with undisputed ties to the State Security. The commission was unable to disclose the names of 76 tainted individuals because of the limitations set down by the Constitutional Court. In view of the 2001 general poll, the commission verified 5,600 candidates, unmasked 155 of them as secret informers, reported that other 217 names could not be disclosed, and withheld the identity of 16 active spies at the request of the intelligence services.[66] In its final report, the commission claimed it has fulfilled its mandate of uncovering the politicians' ties to the State Security by verifying a total of 7,000 individuals, and naming 208 of the 517 former spies. The Movement for Rights and Freedoms and the Socialist Party were the most affected by the commission's revelations, but verifications generated fierce public scandals involving artists, movie makers and journalists, who became post-communist deputies after being active as secret informers.

In 2001, the National Movement Simeon II adopted an ambiguous position toward the opening of the secret archives. The party cleaned its electoral lists of individuals whom the Andreev Commission had unmasked as secret informers, but not of other people whose ambiguous past it was aware of. The party did not publicly support file access, a position prompted by the former king's desire to win the premiership on promises to unify the nation. Few were surprised when parliament closed down the Andreev Commission. The commission had generated many public scandals and it could produce even more controversy with new rounds of verifications among members of the judiciary and the dominant Orthodox Church. The commission was closed down by the Law on Classified Information of 24 April 2002, which replaced the Law on Access to State Security Archives.[67] The government insisted that the new law facilitated Bulgaria's NATO integration by regulating public servants' access to classified information, but the law also sealed the secret archives and was the first to establish a mechanism for lustrating secret collaborators. A newly created State Commission on Information Security issued clearance permits to public servants and army officers seeking to work with NATO classified information. Important state officials were denied clearance, and several ambassadors to NATO countries and army generals representing the Bulgarian General Staff to NATO were unable to assume their posts. The commission is not required to make its decisions public or to disclose the reasons for refusing to issue clearance.[68]

The June 2005 general elections intensified the debate on secret file access. To the surprise of many, the new government opened the secret archives, although the Bulgarian Socialist Party and the Movement for Rights and Freedoms had been affected the most by revelations that their members were former secret informers. The Movement proposed the Law on Access and Disclosure of Documents and Determining Connections of Bulgarian Citizens to the State Security and Army Intelligence Agencies. Adopted by parliament in December 2006, the law provided for the public identification of post-communist politicians who had acted as communist-era secret officers and informers.

A new nine-member commission was formed under the leadership of Socialist Party deputy Evtim Kostadinov. In April 2007 the commission published lists of former secret collaborators who occupied positions in the Presidential Office and the Parliament or who ran in the local elections of that year. More spectacularly, the commission identified President Purvanov as a former secret collaborator. Purvanov accepted the charge, but claimed that he had only edited a volume on Bulgarian emigrants of Macedonian origins.[69] To prove his point, Purvanov published his entire secret file on the presidential website. The scandal embroiled not only the President, but also the previous Andreev Commission, which knew of Purvanov's ties to the State Security, but failed to publicly identify him as a former spy. That commission unconvincingly claimed that it was prevented by the Constitutional Court to disclose Purvanov's past, although Purvanov had an entire file extant, not just a name card, and as such his identity as a spy should have been made public. Six months later, the new commission revealed that former Socialist Premier Zhan Videnov had allowed the State Security to use his apartment as a meeting place,[70] and 139 post-communist deputies – mostly Socialist Party and Movement for Rights and Freedoms representatives – had been secret collaborators. The commission also verifies ministers, ambassadors, and opinion-makers from among journalists and civil society representatives.

Conclusion

Two decades after the collapse of the communist regime, Bulgaria remains a laggard in terms of transitional justice, but the debate on the communist past is not over yet. There are prospects for positive future development with regard to lustration and access to secret archives. Court hearings revolving around communist crimes are no longer an option, as most communist decision makers have died. A new independent agency is mandated to allow Bulgarian citizens to gain access to their secret files, and a legal procedure for lustrating public officials tied to the State Security was recently elaborated as a result of pressure on authorities in Sofia to honor Bulgaria's obligations as a NATO and European Union member. True, most of those banned continued their public activity, but the procedure would likely remain in force in the near future. Still another positive sign is the existence of the new commission, which is expected to set up a unified State Security Archive, collecting documents kept thus far by various successors to the communist political police, and make it available to the public.

Several reasons explain why Bulgaria pursued limited transitional justice. First, the country missed the window of opportunity opened during the early stages of post-communist transition. The Communist Party successors, which dominated early transition, blocked the opening of the secret archives. Politicians did not heed public demands for revisiting the past and for learning the truth about the former regime. Former State Security agents, who controlled the communist state and its resources, joined the post-communist elite and influenced politics as advisors to the business tycoons, many of whom had accumulated their first million because of their ties to the State Security.

Second, in the early 1990s de-communization was viewed as a means for elite renewal. Once the connections between the post-communist and communist elites were revealed, the public lost confidence in the post-communist elite and in the possibility to ever bring communist officials to justice. As conspiracy theories honing the State Security's all-pervasive power gained ground, the public lost interest in what it saw as pointless debates. While secret archives remained closed, secret officers became the feared gatekeepers to information on State Security operations, a position allowing them to influence political debates and to feed information to the public only when it served their interests. Thus, the debate on the recent past was trapped in a vicious circle: some Bulgarians are interested in the secrets of the communist regime, but they strongly doubt the elite's willingness to uncover the truth.

In Bulgaria, the politics of memory has been determined by hidden agendas and political actions. While file opening should have preceded lustration, since unmasking tainted individuals must rely on an analysis of the archives, in Bulgaria the process was reversed. The archives were opened after a government-appointed commission carried out partial lustration without disclosing the reasons behind its decisions. The Bulgarian lustration could become a slow, ad-hoc process lacking transparency. If Bulgaria follows in the footsteps of post-World War II Germany, a generational change will be needed for members of the public to face the totalitarian past unburdened by their personal involvement in the regime. De-politicizing the role of the Bulgarian State Security and regaining the public's interest in the subject could re-launch transitional justice in the country and reveal the roots of the post-communist political and economic elite.

Notes

1 The books written by former secret agents cover almost all aspects of State Security activity. The activity of the First Department was presented by its former section chief, D. Stankov, *Sled dalgi godini mulchanie. 42 godini v bulgarskoto razuznavane*, Sofia: Hristo Botev, 2001. The activity of the Fourth Department was revealed by former officer A. Bekiarov, *Chetvurt Vek v UBO*, Sofia: Letopisi, 1990. The Sixth Department was immortalized by its last two leaders: A. Mousakov, *Shesto*, Sofia: Reporter, 1991, and D. Ivanov, *Shesti Otdel*, Sofia: Trud, 2004. Two other Sixth Department officers wrote memoirs: C. Tepeshanov, *Otrovata*, Sofia: Meridian Press, 1993, and B. Assenov, *Ot Shesto – za Shesto*, Sofia: Polygraf, 1994.

2 H. Hristov, *Durzavna Sigurnost sreshtu Bulgarskata emigrazia*, Sofia: Ivan Vazov, 2000, H. Hristov, *Sekretnoto delo za lagerite*, Sofia: Ivan Vazov, 1999, H. Hristov, *Ubiite "Skitnik". Bulgarskata I britanskata durzavna politika po sluchaia Georgi Markov*, Sofia: Ciela, 2005, and H. Hristov, 'Prestupleniata po vreme na komunisticheskija rezhim i opitite za tiahnoto razsledvane sled 10 Noemvri 1989', paper

presented at the International Trial of Communism conference, Koprivshtitza, Bulgaria, 24–26 September 2004. Online. Available HTTP http://www.geocities.com/decommunization/Articles/Hristov4.htm (accessed 29 January 2008).

3 T. Vaksberg, *Tehnologia na zloto*, documentary movie, Bulgarian national TV, 2001, T. Vaksberg, 'Tehnologia na zloto', *Sega Daily* (5–7 February 2001), and T. Vaksberg, 'Ne brumbar, a kosher zentrali', *Capital Weekly*, 2000, No. 33.

4 J. Nikolov, 'Durzavna Sigurnost – maikata na bulgaskite spezsluzbi', *Capital Weekly*, 2001, No. 1, and P. Meshkova and D. Sharlanov, *Bulgarskata gilotina. Tainite mehanismi na Narodnia sad*, Sofia: Democracy Agency, 1994.

5 Meshkova and Sharlanov, *Bulgarskata gilotina*, D. Kalkandzieva, *Bulgarskata Pravoslavna Zurkva I Durzavata 1944–1953*, Sofia: Albatros, 1997, and S. Chureshki, *Pravoslavieto I Komunizmut v Bulgaria, 1944–1960*, Sofia: Prosveta, 2004.

6 Chervenkov was expelled from the Communist Party in 1962, and rehabilitated seven years later. He died peacefully in 1980 in Sofia.

7 Hristov, 'Prestupleniata po vreme'.

8 *The Stenographic Notes of the Talks between Comrade Todor Zhivkov and Comrade Leonid Brezhnev at the Voden Residence, 20 September 1973*, Bulgarian Communist Party Archive, Fond 378-B, File 360.

9 Nikolov, 'Durzavna Sigurnost'.

10 Ibid.

11 Bulgarian Communist Party Central Committee Secretariat Protocol B 8, *Guidelines for the Work and Activity of the Intelligence Department in the Committee for State Security (9 July 1963)*, Bulgarian Communist Party Archive, Fond 1B, Record 64, file 313.

12 Bulgarian Communist Party Central Committee Secretariat Resolution no. 6, *Guidelines for the Work and Activity of the Military Counter-intelligence in the Ministry of Interior (18 June 1963)*, Bulgarian Communist Party Archive, Fond 1B, Record 64, File 311.

13 Vaksberg, 'Ne brumbar, a kosher zentrali'.

14 *The Main Guidelines for the Work and Activities of the Ministry of Interior (November 1962)*, Bulgarian Communist Party Archive, Fond 1B, Record 64, file 302.

15 *Bulgarian Communist Party Central Committee Resolution on the Creation of the Sixth Department in the Committee for State Security (November 1967)*, Bulgarian Communist Party Archive, Fond 1 B, Record 64, File 368.

16 *Guidelines for the Work and Activity of the Ministry of Interior (November 1962)*, Bulgarian Communist Party Archive, Fond 1B, Record 64, file 302.

17 'Decree no. 1670 for State Security', *State Gazette*, No. 65, 20 August 1974; and Bulgarian Communist Party Central Committee Politburo Resolution B 4, *Main Guidelines for Decree for the State Security (3 April 1974)*, Bulgarian Communist Party Archive, Fond 1B, Record 64, File 438.

18 Assenov, *Ot Shesto – za Shesto*, p. 127. Bulgaria's population ranged from 7.7 to 8.9 million inhabitants from 1960 to 1989. See N. Genov and A. Krasteva, *Recent Social Trends in Bulgaria, 1960–1995*, Montreal: McGill-Queen's University Press, 2001, p. 38.

19 J. Baev and K. Grozev, *Bulgarian Intelligence & Security Services in the Cold War Years*. CD-ROM. Sofia: Cold War Research Group, 2005, p. 18.

20 *Bulgarian Communist Party Central Committee Resolution on Intensifying the Prevention of Criminal Activities, 14 January 1960*, Bulgarian Communist Party Archives, Fond 1B, Record 64, File 264.

21 Bulgarian Ministry of Interior, *Ordinance on the Recruitment and Utilization of State Security Secret Informers and Reliable Persons. 11 April 1989*. Online. Available at HTTP: http://www.geocities.com/decommunization/Communism/Bulgaria/Documents/MVR1989.htm (accessed on 10 March 2005).

22 M. Nedelchev, 'Disidentstvoto v Bulgaria v konteksta na obshtata antikomunisticheska saprotiva i na mnogoobraznite formi na nesaglasie s komunisticheskata sistema',

The Democratic Review, 2002, No. 49. Online. Available HTTP: http://dem-pr.hit. bg/2002_2/2002_2_10.html (accessed 31 January 2008).

23 L. Ognianov. *Durzavno-politicheskata sistema na Bulgaria 1944–1948*, Sofia: Bulgarian Academy of Sciences, 1993, p. 27.

24 Meshkova and Sharlanov, *Bulgarskata gilotina.*

25 Hristov, 'Prestupleniata po vreme'.

26 Ibid.

27 Hristov, *Sekretnoto delo za lagerite*, p. 36, and H. Hristov, 'The Bulgarian Gulag', *Vagabond*, no date. Online. Available HTTP: http://www.vagabond-bg.com/?page=business&sub=11&open_news=535 (accessed on 29 December 2007).

28 *Ministry of Interior Report of 1966*, Bulgarian Communist Party Archive, Fond 1B, Record 64, file 359.

29 Hristov, *Durzavna Sigurnost sreshtu Bulgarskata emigrazia.*

30 Bulgarian Communist Party Central Committee Politburo *Resolution No. 17 of 27 June 1977 On Improvement of the Work for Prevention and Neutralization of the Activities of the Bulgarian Enemy Emigration*, Bulgarian Communist Party Archive, Fond 1B, Record 64, file 504, p. 23.

31 Ibid, p. 24.

32 Hristov, *Ubiite "Skitnik"*, pp. 19–20.

33 Ibid, p. 17.

34 Ibid, pp. 401–402.

35 Vaksberg, 'Tehnologia na zloto'.

36 Idem. The investigation was published in *Sega* (5–7 February 2001).

37 Hristov, 'Prestupleniata po vreme'.

38 P. Kostov, 'Tainite na Durzavna sigurnost', *Sega*, 27 February – 7 March 2001. The articles quoted a May 1991 Report of the Ministry of Interior.

39 Ibid.

40 Ibid.

41 *Summary of the Talks between Todor Zhikov and John Whitehead, US Undersecretary of State, Sofia, 4 February 1987*, Bulgarian Communist Party Archive, Fond 1B, Record 60, File 392.

42 Hristov, 'Prestupleniata po vreme'.

43 *Bulgaria*, New York: Human Rights Watch, 1995. Online. Available HTTP: http:// www.hrw.org/reports/1995/WR95/HELSINKI-04.htm (accessed 29 December 2007).

44 'Soviet Disarray: Jail for 2 in Chenobyl Case', Reuters, 13 December 1991. Online. Available HTTP: http://query.nytimes.com/gst/fullpage.html?res=9D0CEFD91E3BF 930A25751C1A967958260 (accessed 29 December 2007).

45 Hristov, 'Prestupleniata po vreme'.

46 Ibid.

47 'Sudut v Strasbourg othvarli molbata na bulgaski turzi sreshtu Bulgaria', *Mediapool* (28 April 2005). Online. Available HTTP: http://www.mediapool.bg/show/?storyid=104376 (accessed 29 January 2008).

48 'Law on Banks and Credit Activity of 18 March 1992', in N. Kritz (ed.) *Transitional Justice: How Emerging Democracies Reckon with Former Regimes*, Washington, DC: United States Institute of Peace Press, 1995, vol. 3, p. 293, and 'Constitutional Court Decision on the Law on Banks and Credit Activity No. 8 of 27 July 1992', in Kritz, *Transitional Justice*, vol. 3, pp. 294–295.

49 'Law for Temporary Introduction of Some Additional Requirements for the Members of the Executive Bodies of Scientific Organizations and the Higher Certifying Commission', *State Gazette*, 1992, No. 104, reprinted in Kritz, *Transitional Justice*, vol. 3, pp. 296–299.

50 Quoted in Hristov, 'Prestupleniata po vreme'.

51 'The Law on Radio and Television', *State Gazette*, 1998, No. 138.

52 Article 45 of 'The Law on the Election of Members of Parliament, Municipal Councilors and Mayors', *State Gazette*, 2001, No. 24.
53 'Interview with Dimitar Ludzev', *Trud*, 10 October 1995. Quoted in C. Hristov, *Sekretnite sluzbi I prehodat*, Sofia: Cilea, 2004, p. 40.
54 Hristov, *Sekretnite sluzbi*, p. 42.
55 S. Angelov, quoted in Ibidem, p. 45.
56 Ibidem, pp. 45–84.
57 G. Milkov, quoted in Ibidem, p. 81.
58 Ibidem, p. 82.
59 E. Encheva, 'Temida si razigrava konia s Brigo Asparoukhov', *Sega*, 10 July 2003. In 2000 prosecutors charged Asparoukhov with destruction of the file of a former State security informer. The court returned the case in 2001 because Aspraoukhov received parliamentary immunity.
60 K. Karadzov, 'Simeon se otkaza ot Brigadir na sluzbite', *Sega*, 16 October 2003.
61 Hristov, *Sekretnite sluzbi*, pp. 77–89.
62 M. Andreev, 'Dekomunizatiata v Bulgaria', March 2002. Online. Available HTTP http://www.geocities.com/decommunization/Decommunization2/Andreev.htm (accessed 29 January 2008).
63 'Resolution of the National Assembly regarding information for the organization, methods and means in the implementation of the specific tasks of the institutions of the State security as well as regarding information by agents, collected by those institutions', *State Gazette*, 1994, No. 86.
64 Alpha Research Agency, 'Representative Poll for Sofia, 18–20 July 1997', *Capital Weekly*, 1997, No. 30, and Alpha Research Agency, 'Representative Poll for Sofia, 2 September 1997', *Capital Weekly*, 1997, No. 45.
65 'The Law on Access to the Archives of the Former State Security and General Staff Intelligence Department', *State Gazette*, 1997, No. 63.
66 '16 superagenti sred bivshite deputati I ministry ostanaha skriti', *Sega*, 15 April 2005.
67 'The Law on Classified Information', *State Gazette*, 2002, No. 45.
68 E. Raykov, 'Tunkiat led po patia kam tainite na NATO', *Sega*, 14 June 2004.
69 Commission for Revelation of Documents and Determining Connections of Bulgarian Citizens to the State Security and the Army Intelligence Agencies, *Resolution no. 7*, 19 July 2007. Online. Available HTTP: http://www.comdos.bg/pub/7.pdf (accessed 3 February 2008).
70 Commission for Revelation of Documents and Determining Connections of Bulgarian Citizens to the State Security and the Army Intelligence Agencies, *Resolution no. 14*, 4 September 2007. Online. Available HTTP: http://www.comdos.bg/pub/14.pdf (accessed 3 February 2008).

8   Albania

Robert C. Austin and Jonathan Ellison

"De-communization has followed different paths ... only in the Czech Republic and Albania has it led to a large-scale replacement of public administration
officials."[1] We chose this quote to begin the discussion because it indicates just
how confused and confusing are the assessments of post-communist transitional
justice in Albania. This statement is odd because evidence seems to suggest the
opposite – there has been no serious or sustained attempt by Albania's leaders to
deal effectively with the communist past. Having experienced possibly the harshest
forms of communism in Europe, one would think that Albania had the most compelling reasons to undergo sustained transitional justice. One need not look much
past the biographies of Albania's transition leaders to confirm that Albania did little
vis-à-vis the past. What Albania offered is simply political vengeance that is in
keeping with its traditions. Albania's post-communist justice is about the selective
destruction of the past not an attempt to deal with it. In fact, like much of Albania's
attempts at serious transition, whether economic or political, the process of transitional justice was fraught with mistakes and was largely botched. From 1991 to
1997, when a few attempts were made, the process was disorganized, politicized
and unsuccessful. More importantly, the process also failed to become relevant to
the wider population who largely saw the whole business for what it was.

There were huge purges of the public administration in the aftermath of the victory of the anti-communist Democratic Party in March 1992 and there were again
huge purges of the public sector after the Socialist Party (former communists)
won elections in 1997. This cannot be considered lustration as it is entirely consistent with Albania's twentieth century political culture, which has always left
open the door to be a hero one day and a traitor the next. The process was heavily
influenced by political vengeance. At different times between 1991 and 1997, the
banner of lustration was held aloft by both left and right wing parties in order to
justify political purges carried out purely to weaken their opponents. This "out
with the old – in with the new" mentality had it roots in Albania in 1920 and it was
certainly intensified during the period of so-called class struggle under communist rule. What we have seen take place in Albania is primarily politically-inspired
vengeance rather than an attempt to deal with the past in a constructive and objective way. This has had disastrous implications for Albania's overall transition from
communism to democracy. As Kathleen Imholz noted, "No doubt, more Albanians

were tried and many more lost their jobs in the name of de-communization than in other countries. But the facts on the ground nevertheless diverge from the legend. Rather than being ways of punishing the crimes of the former regime, trials and dismissals were used to demobilize lawful opposition to the present regime [the then governing Democratic Party] or, quite simply, as a method to exact personal revenge."[2] At the grassroots level, de-communization never really made it into the public debate as, to some extent, forgive and forget attitudes prevailed in a country where economic problems were considered to be paramount. Remzi Lani, of the Albanian Media Institute, probably best summarized the Albanian experience when he said that there was "lots of blackmail, but no public debate."[3]

Before we tackle just why issues related to transitional justice, lustration and file access were often not addressed, let's try to divide Albania's transition into successive periods. We intend to look at four periods: the nature of the Albanian communist system, the pre-1991 roots of collapse, the era of revenge between 1991 and 1997 and finally, the period of Socialist Party rule between 1997 and 2005. More to the point, we can discern two stages in Albania – a politicized process that starts in 1991 and ends in 1997 and the complete abandonment of the process in 1997 with a large scale reversal of the major legislative changes that took place between 1991 and 1997. In essence, Albania was largely unsuccessful in implementing a serious program of transitional justice.

The historic context

Albania's political culture was extremely undeveloped with little experience with democracy. As well, there was no tradition of opposition or debate – the last serious debate in Albanian political life took place between June and December 1924 when then Prime Minister Fan Noli tried to establish a democratic government in Albania. Noli's government was toppled in December 1924 and between then and 1939 Albania was essentially an authoritarian and quasi-feudal state. The communist period (1944–1990) offered an extreme form of Stalinism. In fact, there was no legacy whatsoever of participation in political life. As to dissidents, elsewhere, especially in Poland or Czechoslovakia, dissidents were able to draw on support networks not just within the communist bloc but from the West as well. As a closed society, there were few avenues to influence Albanian society. Finally, the middle and wealthier class along with the Roman Catholic Church leadership in northern Albania was completely decimated after the Second World War. In power since 1944, the communist government had been extremely successful in thwarting opposition both from within its own ranks and outside. Albanian communism was extremely centralized and the communists dominated all aspects of life. Albania went further than any other communist state in the collectivization of farms. Moreover, in an effort to destroy competing centers of loyalty, in the 1960s Albania embarked on its own version of the Chinese Cultural Revolution. The Albanian variant witnessed the complete abolition of Albania's three religions (Roman Catholicism, Eastern Orthodoxy and Islam) and the subsequent declaration that Albania was the world's first atheist state.

The key instruments for retaining power were a vast secret police network, regular and brutal purges, a profound limitation of foreign contacts along with a system of prison camps and internal exile.[4] All segments of society, including the party hierarchy, were subject to periodic purges. The courts, under strict party control, meted out harsh sentences for any deviations. The population and the existing elite were extremely cowed. The state was not just perceived to be strong – it was strong, and it took very little for someone to end up in jail. That said, the prisons were not filled with potential opposition, but people who had merely complained about the quality of bread. Moreover, Human Rights Watch noted that one in four Albanians collaborated with the communist secret police.[5] Figures on jailed or internally exiled individuals range from lows of 12–15 thousand to highs of 50–60 thousand. Party membership reached a peak of 122,000, or roughly between 3 and 4 per cent of the total population. Of that membership, only some 1,200 people really mattered.

Created on 20 March 1943 as a secret political police, the Directorate of State Security (*Drejtorija e Sigurimit te Shtetit*), popularly known as the Sigurimi, was one of the most shadowy secret police organizations in Eastern Europe. As in Yugoslavia, the communist monopoly on power was assured almost at the moment of liberation. Josip Broz Tito and Enver Hoxha had dominated their national resistance movements against the Nazi or Italian invaders and, despite pressure from outside, they accepted power sharing for only very limited periods.[6] Hoxha even credited the Sigurimi for helping his group assert political control over other resistance groups in Albania. The Sigurimi was part of the Ministry of Internal Affairs, which also exercised authority over the judiciary and law implementation and enforcement. The political police employed some 10,000 full-time agents with military rank, 2,500 of whom were assigned to the People's Army, and reportedly a quarter of the adult population as part time informers. Officers were generally career volunteers, recommended by loyal party members and subjected to careful political and psychological screening before finally being allowed to join the service. As elsewhere in communist Eastern Europe, they had an elite status and enjoyed many privileges designed to maintain their reliability and dedication to the party.

The Sigurimi included national headquarters and branches in each of Albania's 26 districts, and was organized into sections covering political control, censorship, public records, prison camps, internal security troops, physical security, counter-espionage, and foreign intelligence. The political control section verified the ideological correctness of party members and ordinary citizens, monitored private phone conversations and correspondence, and purged the party, government, military and secret forces of individuals closely associated with Yugoslavia, the Soviet Union and China, after Albania broke off with each of these countries. Unconfirmed reports claim that at least 170 Communist Party Politburo or Central Committee members were executed as a result of the investigations the Sigurimi carried out at various times. Among those to fall first was Koci Xoxe, the Interior Minister known as the Butcher of the Bourgeoisie, who in 1949 was tried for treason and executed, after Tito was thrown out of the Eastern bloc and Albania fell into the Stalinist line. The censorship section oversaw the press, radio, newspapers, cultural societies, schools and other organizations, the public records section administered government documents and statistics, including economic and social statistics handled as state secrets, the prison camps section was charged with the political reeducation of inmates in 14 prison camps throughout the country and the evaluation of the danger they posed to the society, the physical security section protected important party and government officials and installations, while the counterespionage section neutralized foreign intelligence operations in Albania and domestic movements opposed to the Communist Party. The foreign intelligence section maintained personnel abroad under the cover of foreign diplomatic missions, trade offices, and cultural centers to obtain intelligence about foreign capabilities and intentions that affected Albania's national security.[7]

The Sigurimi permeated Albanian society to the extent that every third citizen had either served time in labor camps or been interrogated by political police officers. The extent of control over people's lives was unmatched. One of the first unusual laws enacted was a complete ban on automobiles. No one without a permit was allowed to own one, and only two permits were issued for non-party members. Political power was consolidated in the hands of the Hoxha family, with First Lady Nexhmije Hoxha heading the Tirana Marxist-Leninist Institute, which decided on the official ideology of the day. After Hoxha's death, Ramiz Alia was unable or unwilling to maintain the totalitarian system of terror and repression that Hoxha had employed to maintain his grip on the country. Alia relaxed the most overt Stalinist controls over the population, instructed the Sigurimi to use more subtle, bureaucratic mechanisms, and allowed greater contact with the outside world, including easing restrictions to travel abroad.

Communist Albania also had a 7,000-strong Frontier Guard division organized into battalions along military lines, but subordinated to the Ministry of Internal Affairs until April 1991, when they were transferred to the Ministry of People's Defense. The Frontier Guards protected state borders and prevented criminals and smugglers from crossing them, but also stopped Albanians from leaving the country illegally. The People's Police was organized into five branches, including the economic police (which served as a guard force for state buildings, factories and construction projects), the communications police (which protected communication lines like bridges, railroads and the telephone and telegraph network), the detention police (which served as prison and labor camp guards), the fire police and the general police (which attended to traffic regulation and criminal investigation).

Making the communists pay

Let's now look at Albania's bizarre exit from communism. Simply put, Albania had an anti-communist revolution because everyone else was having one. In fact, as revolutions swept communist Europe in 1989, it appeared that Albania, isolated and alone, might have been able to resist the changes taking place. Albania, since 1976, had been the most isolated country in Europe, pursued an ultimately destructive policy of self-reliance, and largely seemed capable of continuing to go its own way. It is worth noting that it was only in December 1990, essentially a year later than elsewhere in the region, that events at the University of Tirana forced some radical changes in communist policies. The reasons for Albania's delayed revolution help us to better understand the issues of transitional justice.

In the first place, Albania had no dissident movement. Albania was only developing a dissident movement when collapse finally came. The anti-communist leaders and reform minded communists that emerged in 1990 and 1991 all had relatively solid communist credentials. Like Romania, we see elite reproduction, not elite replacement. That said, very few were willing to dig too deeply into the past and even fewer had any reason to call for a complete opening of the police files. However, they all had to work extra hard to prove their anti-communist credentials. The result was a highly politicized quest for justice. Albania's first multi-party elections in March 1991 were won easily by Albania's communists (known as the Party of Labor since 1948). The nascent Democratic Party, led by Sali Berisha and Gramoz Pashko, lacked adequate time to prepare and lacked strong connections to the villages where more than 65 per cent of Albanians lived. That said, de-communization was essentially delayed in 1991.[8] However, the communists faced mounting opposition from the cities in the vote's aftermath and conceded to forming a "national salvation" government with the Democratic Party. At its tenth, and its essentially last congress in June 1991, the communists did some house cleaning and re-named themselves the Socialist Party of Albania. The congress saw some relatively modest attacks on the past, but Ramiz Alia did not offer a significant attack on Hoxha's personality or legacy. That came from Dritero Agolli, one of Albania's best-known writers. As Elez Biberaj noted, the congress was a "humiliating defeat" for conservatives in the party.[9] With Fatos Nano elected at the new chairman, the party quickly dropped all references to Stalinism and communism and hoped to quietly join the mainstream of the European socialist left.

As the country drifted towards catastrophe in the summer of 1991, some very modest steps were taken. In July 1991, the Sigurimi was abolished and replaced by the National Information Service or NIS (*Sherbimi Informativ Kombetar* or SHIK.) Some Western observers believe that many of the officers and leaders of the NIS had served in the Sigurimi and that the basic structures of the two organizations were similar. Only former Sigurimi leaders were excluded from the new service. The new agency was prohibited from conducting unauthorized investigations and engaging in political activity. As the move was not accompanied by access to files or any substantive house cleaning, most assumed it was just a re-packaged Sigurimi, the more so since the service was never been effectively placed under parliamentary control.[10]

The first move against the old regime was the release of a report by Genc Ruli, the Democratic Party Minister of Finance in the coalition government, in July 1991. This document became the principal piece of evidence in the first trials against the former ruling families. Ruli's report, delivered in parliament and re-printed in the Democratic Party newspaper *Rilindja Demokritike*, is a fascinating document. It subsequently became the basis of the charges against members of the old regime. The report was essentially an audit of the often luxurious spending of the communist elite. It made clear that the communists were to be held to account not for their political actions but instead for economic crimes. Clearly, the country's new leaders felt that in a nation so stricken by poverty and shortages, the public would be more inclined to support actions that focused on financial abuses.

As former President Sali Berisha noted, there were practical reasons for choosing mundane economic issues over serious political ones. He suggested that the coalition government, which was essentially dominated by communists, forced certain compromises. More important, the judiciary was so stacked with communists that political charges would not stand a chance, and they needed time to develop a complete new court system amenable to serious charges. In his words, "If you want to ring a bell, you need a bell."[11] Lacking much else on the communist leadership, Ruli noted that the extra privileges were not based on law and that their perks were at odds with the reality outside their posh villas. Since most of what the communists did was in fact within the law, the best route for the new leaders was to catch them on preaching one thing – austerity – while practicing another – gluttony. Arben Imami, a former justice minister, also noted that "what happened in Albania was not a revolution of ideas, but a revolution based on economics. Since most Albanians lived in total misery, dismantling the system based on privilege seemed to have its advantages."[12] The former communist leaders, protected by countless laws they themselves had written, did not actually break any laws on the books. As Ramiz Alia noted, "law is law," and the communists did not break any laws.[13] In the words of former Constitutional Court Chairman Rustem Gjata, however, in terms of its impact on the lustration process, the decision to start investigation of the past with petty economic crimes was "a fatal mistake."[14]

Ruli's report was incredibly detailed citing all kinds of facts and figures on lavish consumption at a time when ordinary people went hungry. It noted, for example, that between September 1989 and September 1990 the family of the late Enver Hoxha had "2 tons of meat, 7 tons of salami, 523 liters of oil, 3.1 tons of butter, 321 liters of raki, alcoholic beverages and wine, 250 liters of beer, 5.3 tons of fruit and citrus products, 114 kilograms of olives ... and 1.8 kilograms of coffee." Greater abuse took place in the realm of medical treatment and holidays abroad. The report noted countless expensive trips abroad for members of the nomenklatura and their immediate relatives. For example, Hoxha's son, Sokol, spent 27 days out of Albania at a cost of $9,800.00. While the communist period was not devoid of economic progress, the country was far and away the poorest country in Europe. Aggressive plan targets, especially in agriculture, were hardly met, ordinary Albanians lacked access to basic necessities and they had not been allowed to exit the country. Moreover, when in 1991 the food situation has reached a critical point in Albania, the Italian Army began delivering much needed food aid through Operation Pelican. That said, the notion of living well while the population suffered was expected to strike a chord amongst the population.

Ruli's report led to the arrests of all members of the former Politburo. Hoxha's widow, Nexhmije, was arrested in December 1991 and was one of the first to face charges in January 1993. She received special attention in the report. She was ultimately jailed for minor offences related to her family's consumption. As Imholz noted, "No one doubted that the Hoxha family lived well and enjoyed goods unavailable to other Albanians, but making these charges the sole subject of a criminal proceeding seemed to trivialize the more serious abuses of the Hoxha regime."[15] The decision to make economic crimes the center piece of post-communist justice was based on the simple fact that it was easy and was more or less all the new leaders had on them. With the benefit of hindsight, one can say with certainty that the decision to move against the old elite based on economic crimes was a catastrophic blunder for two reasons: first, it alienated ordinary people who expected that communists would face justice and second it became nearly impossible after that to engage people when serious political charges were finally laid later.

In the wake of the Democratic Party's victory in the second post-communist elections of March 1992, justice for the old regime gained momentum despite the fact that Berisha was on record as saying he was prepared to leave the past to historians with his statement that "We are all guilty, we all jointly suffered." In the absence of serious public opinion surveys, it is hard to say just what the public wanted to do with members of the old regime. Given the harshness of Albanian Stalinism, it is likely that the public wanted to see the old elite in jail although people like party General Secretary Ramiz Alia insist that by avoiding bloodshed, the population for the most part admired him. Alia's legacy, and for the matter the legacy of Albania's communist leaders, is hardly good. Elez Biberaj was correct when he noted that "Alia will go down in history not as a distinguished leader but, like other Communist politicians in his position, as a leader incapable of embracing democratic change."[16]

By far the biggest single lobby for serious transitional justice was the class of former political prisoners who played key roles in the first Democratic Party government. As its sole raison d'être was anti-communism, the rhetoric of the Democratic Party at the outset was extremely inflammatory vis-à-vis the past, and one could only conclude that Albania was about to embark on a massive and unprecedented drive for justice. Spartak Ngjela, a founding member of the Democratic Party and a formerly politically persecuted person who spent ten years in the notorious Burrel prison, noted that one of the reasons more did not take place is because Berisha played a key role in moderating the calls for a tougher line on the former communists in 1991 and 1992.[17] Ngjela also seconded Berisha's suggestion that in 1991 and 1992, in the absence of an independent court, lustration was doomed to fail. In the minds of many of the formerly persecuted, the Democratic Party's top leadership were hardly untainted and it is doubtful former prisoners even trusted the party leadership. What one can discern in the early years of the Democratic Party is a group of former prisoners clamoring for justice and the party leadership, which more or less had solid communist credentials, holding them back. Lacking the skills in party machinations, generally uneducated and having spent most of their lives in prison, it is not surprising that the former prisoners lost the battle. In fact, what is interesting is that the formerly politically persecuted people ended up somewhat marginalized. Much to their chagrin, it was students from the University of Tirana who ended being heroes of democracy, not the people who went to jail for opposing the system.

With its solid majority in parliament after 1992, the Democratic Party undertook vast legislative changes. Hoxha's handpicked successor, Ramiz Alia, was arrested in September also on economic crimes. Alia suggests that he was jailed for two principal reasons: the first was personal because President Berisha wanted him in jail, and second, because Alia symbolized the past and the past had to go.[18] He found himself in jail with the entire aged Politburo. The vast majority were handed prison sentences based on the evidence outlined in the Ruli report at the end of 1993. Alia, along with two others, went to trial in March 1994. In addition to financial abuses set out in the Ruli report, some political charges were added based on events after the bombing of the Soviet Embassy in 1951, the abolition of religion in 1967 and a number of killings that took place along Albania's borders. All were guilty of financial abuses and of violating fundamental human rights like freedom of religion and freedom to travel. The trials against the old leadership failed to generate any kind of public enthusiasm. With the change in regime, the former ruling elite lost everything as everything they had belonged to the state. Outside their once inaccessible and lavish homes in downtown Tirana, it became clear that for the most part this was just a group of poor, almost pathetic, old men. There were no foreign bank accounts (not even domestic ones for that matter), no villas to go to, and no money other than their worthless pensions.

In addition to move against the top elite, the Democrats also conducted a massive purge of the civil sector. When other analysts suggest that Albania went further than most other countries in the former communist bloc, they are generally referring to the virtual emptying of this sector. On 3 December 1991, the coalition Socialist-Democratic Party government introduced Law 7526 "On Labor Relations," amending the country's labor code. The change, which was set out, in official parlance, as an attempt to strengthen reform, allowed the government to dismiss employees of state-owned firms or agencies without explanation or the right for appeal; indeed, no determinable criteria for replacement were set out, making an evaluation of the appropriateness of a dismissal nearly impossible. Human Rights Watch determined that this process was often done haphazardly, and that the vague terminology "allowed for political and personal favoritism to enter the process."[19] The Socialists suggested that about 250,000 people lost their jobs following the landslide Democratic Party victory in the March 1992 elections, and Human Rights Watch noted that many people who lost their jobs were merely Socialist sympathizers or their relatives with no connection at all to the old regime. It is likely that when the Socialists returned to power in 1997, a comparable number of people lost their positions. This purge–counter-purge aspect of Albanian political life cannot be confused with lustration. It is solely about vengeance and it goes a long way to explain why Albania's transition is so filled with catastrophes. On both sides of Albania's Democrat–Socialist divide, the politics of vengeance has done nothing to ensure reconciliation or to right past wrongs. It has served only to create in both parties thousands of militants and has stalled the process of creating a professional civil service. This process could hardly be called lustration. Pseudo-lustration would be more appropriate. The politicized fate of the civil service become so critical that after the elections in July 2005 which brought the Democratic Party back to power, Albania's President and incoming Prime Minister Sali Berisha stressed that the public sector did not face another devastating purge.

A major move, which is often wrapped up in the discussions of transitional justice, was the arrest in 1993 of Socialist Party Leader Fatos Nano. While this is not at all related to transitional justice as Nano was not charged with crimes related to the past, it sheds light on the nature of Albania's attempts to deal with the past. While Nano did hold high positions under the old regime, he was tried for economic crimes committed during 1991, the first year of transition, when he was Prime Minister. After a dubious trial he was subsequently jailed in 1994 for a total of 12 years. As Kathleen Imholz noted, Nano's sentencing compounded feelings of disillusionment, as it was longer than that given to the communist leaders.[20] While Berisha insisted that he acted because he owed it to the people to fight corruption, the agenda was primarily political: Nano's trial was more about crippling the country's main opposition force than in making sure crooks went to prison.

With Nano in jail, it was only in 1995, three years after they were elected, that the Democratic Party government introduced fundamental legislation that changed the focus from economic to political crimes. Timing is everything as this law is entirely political in purpose. In 1994, the Democratic Party put forward a new constitution, replacing what had been until then only a hodgepodge assortment of provisional constitutional laws and amendments. The new constitution would have provided for a centralized presidential republic in keeping with the type of administration Berisha had already established. No longer being able to muster the two-thirds parliamentary majority necessary to pass constitutional amendments, the Democratic Party put this crucial matter to a public referendum. The proposed constitution was soundly defeated by a vote of 59 percent against and 41 percent in favor, with a turnout of roughly 84 percent of eligible voters.[21] The loss generated a real fear that they could lose the elections due in 1996. As Gent Ibrahimi of the Tirana-based Institute for Policy and Legal Studies said, "the constitutional referendum was the first real election in Albania."[22] The first elections in 1991 hardly took place in a free and fair environment, and the elections of 1992 represented a vote against the horrors of the old regime rather than a vote for the Democratic Party. Until the referendum loss, the Democrats had really governed with impunity. The setback on the referendum sent a clear message: they were not invincible and staying in power might require extra measures. Most analysts conclude that the hasty introduction of legislation is directly linked to the impending elections. That said, the new law put everyone in one boat – old Politburo members along with reform-minded communists, who had been instrumental in bringing change in 1990 and 1991.

In late 1995, the People's Assembly passed Albania's first two lustration laws (together, the "Lustration Laws"): Law 8001 of 22 September 1995 *On Genocide and Crimes against Humanity Committed in Albania during Communist Rule for Political, Ideological or Religious Motives* (the "Genocide Law"), and Law 8043 of 30 November 1995 *On the Verification of the Moral Character of Officials and other Persons Connected with the Defense of the Democratic State*, subsequently amended pursuant to a Constitutional Court decision of 31 January 1996 (the "Verification Law").[23] Prima facie, the Lustration Laws seemed to be aimed at ensuring the democratic nature of the Albanian polity by restricting the entry of individuals with anti-democratic tendencies. However, in their context, scope, and implementation, it soon became evident that the Lustration Laws were being exploited by the Democratic Party to purge Albanian politics not of anti-democratic individuals, but rather of anti-Democratic Party individuals. Given how the Democratic Party had treated its opposition, an electoral loss spelled not just potential unemployment, but possibly a jail term. The new laws were not just written to keep certain groups from political power, but certain individuals in the Socialist and Social Democratic parties.

The Genocide Law

According to its preamble, the purpose of the Genocide Law was to assist and accelerate the prosecution of perpetrators of "crimes against humanity" committed under the auspices of the communist regime. The possibility of such prosecution was neither novel nor in contradiction with the Albanian law; crimes against humanity were listed as crimes under the communist-era penal code and therefore would have been indictable offences notwithstanding the Genocide Law. Rather than provide a statutory basis for prosecution, the Genocide Law embodied the government's intention and desire to pursue prosecution by charging the general prosecutor with commencing such proceedings "immediately and with priority."

The Genocide Law departed markedly from previous measures introduced by the post-communist Albanian government. The 1993–1994 criminal proceedings against former communists were based on minor charges of corruption and embezzlement arising out of the Ruli Report, while the Genocide Law explicitly called for the prosecution of more severe charges falling under the category of "crimes against humanity." In addition, the Genocide Law created a statutory basis for excluding persons associated with such acts from public office until 2002, whereas the only exclusions made previously had been of state employees, which were made arbitrarily and without reference to specific conduct under the communist regime. The government was quick to implement the Genocide Law. By January 1996, the general prosecutor had ordered the arrests of 24 former senior communist officials. Many of the accused had already been arrested and tried for lesser offences, but were now faced with much more serious punishment under the Genocide Law.[24]

Consider the case of Ramiz Alia, convicted on minor economic charges in 1994 and subsequently released less than one year later, after the introduction of a new penal code. Alia was rearrested in February 1996, this time under the auspices of the Genocide Law, on the charge that he had ordered the internment and imprisonment of thousands of citizens prior to 1991. The prosecutor later added further charges including: ordering the killing of people who attempted to leave the country; ordering troops and police to fire on the people who toppled the Hoxha monument in Tirana; ordering the arming of military students who subsequently killed some civilians; and ordering the shootings on 2 April 1991, in Shkoder, which left four dead. While Alia managed to flee the country in March 1997, before he was sentenced, others received sentences of anywhere from five years to life imprisonment.

The Genocide Law also provided for some political lustration. Article 3 stipulated that those persons convicted of being authors, conspirators or executors of crimes against humanity and had held certain positions prior to 31 March 1991 would be banned from being elected or nominated to leadership positions in government apparatuses, the judicial system, or the media until 2002.[25] Article 3 contains an enumeration of the pre-1991 positions that would trigger lustration under the Genocide Law, including former Party members, members of the People's Assembly, presidents of the Supreme Court of Justice, general prosecutors and Sigurimi full-time agents and part-time collaborators. Article 3 excludes those persons who had held an enumerated position, but had "acted against the official line and distanced themselves publicly."

Lustration under the Genocide Law was very limited; former communist officials would only have been banned from public office provided they were first convicted by the general prosecutor as the authors, conspirators or executors of a crime against humanity. Even in respect of those convicted, most had already been sentenced to dozens of years in jail, and could not have held political positions until long after 2002 anyway. Exceptions to this might include Haxhi Lleshi, chairman of the Presidium of the People's Assembly until 1982, and Manush Myftiu, former deputy Prime Minister and former Chairman of the Central Commission on Internal Exile. Both had been convicted for crimes against humanity but released on bail by the Court of Appeal on 24 July 1996 due to age and health considerations.[26] In their case, Article 3 did bar them from entering into postcommunist politics – but it is likely they would have stayed out of politics for the same reasons for which they were released from jail.

Political lustration could not then have been the primary purpose of the Genocide Law; a five-year ban from entering public office on someone serving a twelve year jail sentence was entirely illusory. Nor could one say that the Genocide Law aimed to bring the more infamous survivors of the old regime to justice. As former chairman of the Constitutional Court Rustem Gjata pointed out, the Democratic Party government could have prosecuted such individuals immediately following the 1992 elections, without introducing the Genocide Law. Genocide and crimes against humanity had been indictable offences under the old Albanian penal code, and, if anything, the evidence would have been fresher in 1992 than it was four years later when the prosecutions finally began.[27]

The Genocide Law did not therefore really serve a legal purpose; it did not effectively lustrate and was superfluous to genocide prosecutions. Rather, the law demonstrated to the public that the Democratic Party was now taking lustration seriously, identified the most well-known former communists and associated them with the Democratic Party's anti-lustration campaign, and provided an ideological prop for the law that would truly deal with lustration and file access, the Verification Law, introduced only two months later.

The Verification Law

The Verification Law provided for a committee (the "Verification Committee") responsible for screening potential and actual members of the government, police, judiciary, educational system and media in order to determine their affiliation with communist-era government organs and state police. To this end, the Verification Committee was granted exclusive rights to use the files of the former secret service Sigurimi and the Albanian Party of Labor (the Albanian communist party). As will be discussed later in this chapter, the Verification Law was the first Albanian law regulating the use of such files.

Article 1 of the Verification Law established an extensive list of positions that could be reviewed by the Verification Committee, including: member of parliament, President, member of central government, leaders of local governmental bodies, manager of banking, financial and insurance institutions, army officer, member of the secret services, chief of police, judge or state prosecutor, member of the diplomatic corps, director or rector of a school of higher education, or a director or editor in Albanian state radio or television. In a subsequent amendment, however, candidates for election to local councils or to the position of chairman of a commune were exempted from the scope of the Verification Law, while mayoral candidates and municipal prefects were still subject to the law. As a result, the number of prospective verifications on a local level dropped from 60,000 for 5,764 posts to just 800 for 64 posts.[28]

According to Article 2, the Verification Committee could screen actual or potential holders of the above-enumerated positions to determine if they had fell into one of roughly 20 categories of employment between 28 November 1944 and 31 March 1991. Such categories included, but were not limited to, members of the Politburo, the Central Committee, the government, the Presidential Council and the Supreme Court, officers, agents and collaborators of the state security apparatuses and foreign investigative services, officers of camps and prisons, and denouncers, investigators, prosecutors, and judges in political trials.

Following Article 4 of the same law, the Verification Committee included seven members: the chairman to be appointed by parliament, the vice-chairman and one member to be appointed by the Council of Ministers, and the remaining four members to be appointed by, respectively, the Minister of Justice, the Minister of the Interior, the Minister of Defense and the head of the National Information Service. Thus, of the seven members, all are directly or indirectly appointed by the government in power; none may be considered to be third party or minority representatives. Although, once appointed, the Verification Committee was theoretically independent, the composition thereof could be changed at will by parliament and the committee's actual freedom of action is debatable.[29] All meetings of the

Verification Committee were to be closed and its findings and decisions were not to be made public, unless the individual under review provided express consent for the release of the information. Where the individual under investigation was already holding a post in government and refused to step down on his own, the Verification Committee was authorized to release its findings and, as in the case of Rustem Gjata discussed later in this chapter, the government could then remove such an individual from office based on this information.

Although the individual under review was permitted to appeal a decision to the Court of Cassation within seven days of receiving such decision, the initial decision was to be made by a committee composed almost exclusively of individuals appointed by the Democratic Party. There was a general lack of public confidence that the "independent" agency was a responsible body, as it was purely in the hands of the governing party. Nine years later, Democratic Party members such as Sali Berisha and Spartak Ngjela acknowledged that the partisan nature of the Verification Committee had a significant negative impact on its effectiveness and reception by the public.[30]

Under Articles 7 and 9, any individual who wished to run in an election for a position listed in Article 1 had to first be reviewed by the Verification Committee. If the Verification Committee found that the candidate had held a position listed in Article 2, the candidate would be restricted from running for any Article 1 positions until 2002. If the candidate attempted to register before that date, the Verification Committee would open the candidate's dossier to the public and inform the Central Election Committee, which would then bar the candidate from the elections. Candidates for appointment to a position listed in Article 1 would, however, have the option of requesting a review by the Verification Committee – no mandatory review regime was established for appointments. Even Rustem Gjata, who had upheld the law in his capacity as Constitutional Court president, acknowledged that the process was selective and investigations were only carried out on requests from certain institutions, resulting in only partial, and thus flawed, implementation.[31] Many people with questionable communist pasts likely escaped scrutiny due to their political allegiance.

Pursuant to Article 7(c), an individual holding a position listed in Article 1 would also be subject to a review if so requested by their employer. Similarly, under Article 12, a political party leader would be subject to review if so requested by other members of the party leadership. In all other cases, individuals would only be examined by the Verification Committee if they explicitly requested such examination themselves. Individuals holding seats in parliament at the time the law came into effect were reviewed only if they chose to run in the June 1996 elections. Sali Berisha was not subject to a review at all, as Albanian Presidents are appointed by a three-fifths majority vote by members of parliament, rather than being elected by the public.

Shortly after the Verification Law was introduced, it became apparent that it would be applied to the advantage of the ruling Democratic Party and to the extreme detriment of the political opposition. After conducting closed-door reviews, the Verification Committee declared that 139 people should be barred from participating in the elections. Of these, 45 were members of the Socialist Party, 23 were Social Democrats, 11 were from the Democratic Alliance, 13 from the Republican Party, three from the Democratic Party, and the rest from minor parties. This represented just over 10 percent of the 1,180 candidates who eventually did participate in the May 1996 election in competition for 140 seats in parliament.[32] However, it is likely that those candidates who were barred included a disproportionate number of prominent opposition leaders. For instance, of the Socialist Party's eleven-member presidency, a total of seven were disqualified, including Fatos Nano, Servet Pëllumbi and Kastriot Islami. Other senior opposition leaders targeted by the Verification Law included Social Democratic Party leader Skendër Gjinushi and Democratic Alliance senior officials Preç Zogaj, Perikli Teta, and Ridvan Peshkëpia.[33] It is worth noting that because public disclosure required the assent of the investigated individuals, the names of barred candidates were generally not released to the public. Ordinary Albanians would never know the exact details of the accusations against barred candidates, nor would the Verification Committee make any statement on the truth of such accusations. Unless a barred candidate publicly protested his ineligibility for election, one could only surmise that a candidate had a communist past by the fact that he had been removed from the voter list.[34]

While, as mentioned, under Article 4 of the Verification Law it was possible to appeal to the Court of Cassation, only 57 individuals pursued this option, and the Court overturned just seven decisions. There were complaints that the time for appeal was too limited, and several decisions were made only after the time limit for registration in the elections had passed.[35] International observers such as Human Rights Watch/Helsinki and the Organization for Security and Cooperation of Europe's Office for Democratic Institutions and Human Rights (ODIHR) expressed further concerns, particularly regarding the composition of the Verification Committee and the secretive nature of the reviews. With six of seven members appointed by the Democratic Party, the objectivity of the Verification Committee would certainly be in question, and decisions would often be based on the interpretation of the Committee; what, for example is a "collaborator"? The Verification Law allows for individuals holding positions listed in Articles 2(a) and 2(b), members of government etc., to be exempted from lustration if they are shown to have "acted against the official line or distanced themselves publicly." However, due to the closed-door nature of the review process, it is not unlikely that the Verification Committee would fail to call witnesses or procure necessary evidence.[36]

The low ratio of Democratic Party candidates barred from the elections is also suspect. While it is possible that a lower proportion of Democratic Party members were affiliated with the communist regime, or that potential Democratic Party election candidates were warned by the party not to run if they had held a contested position within the former regime, it is also possible that the Verification Committee simply did not review all the Democratic Party candidates, or purposefully concealed some negative results. The opposition parties quickly manifested their dissatisfaction with the Lustration Laws; shortly after the Laws were introduced and the scope of their implementation became known, the Social Democrat Party brought a complaint to the Constitutional Court challenging Article 3 of the Genocide Law. At the same time, the Socialist Party brought a complaint challenging both laws. The Constitutional Court, under Rustem Gjata, rejected the complaints on 31 January 1996, introducing only some relatively minor amendments to the Verification Law.[37]

Interestingly enough, however, the Socialists did not protest publicly or openly suggest that the law caused problems for their electoral campaign. The ODIHR reported that "while the banning of candidates by the Verification Committee did place an extra burden on political parties in the election, and is an issue of concern for individual human rights, none of the parties complained that this caused insurmountable problems for their participation in the process."[38] This is perhaps understandable. If the Socialist Party were to attempt to challenge the law beyond raising the issue of its constitutionality, they might open themselves up to attacks from the Democratic Party and the international community for wanting to reintroduce communism. Moreover, they would have been reticent to draw attention to the fact that the Lustration Laws affected them more extensively than the Democratic Party, as this might have made the public suspicious that the Socialist Party did indeed have a higher proportion of ex-communists. Instead, the Socialist Party and other opposition parties framed their criticism of the Democratic Party in the context of the new electoral law recently introduced by Berisha, Law 8055 of 1 February 1996 *On Amendments to Law No 7556 On Elections to the People's Assembly of the Republic of Albania* (the "1996 Electoral Law"), which amended the 1992 electoral law by including not only specific wording implementing the Lustration Laws in the local and parliamentary elections, but also re-zoning changes and a reduction in the number of proportional seats.[39]

The 1996 Electoral Law was considered to be disadvantageous to the opposition parties for several reasons. The President delineated the new electoral zones without consultation with other political parties and only 45 days before the poll, while the shift of representation from a proportional to a majority system favored the larger parties (the Democratic Party and the Socialist Party) over the smaller ones.[40] Hours before the polls were scheduled to close on 26 May 1996, the Socialist Party, the Social Democrats, the Democratic Alliance and others boycotted the elections, citing flagrant election procedure violations and expressing continued dissatisfaction with the 1996 Electoral Law. However, as Biberaj points out, the boycott may have been to a large degree in response to the Lustration Laws.[41] There is reason to believe the action was premeditated, as Socialist Party representatives left their posts at the same time across Albania, a difficult feat in a country lacking adequate infrastructure and reliable means of communication, and most of the significant violations that were reported did not occur until counting had begun.[42] It is likely that the opposition parties did indeed feel the weight of the Lustration Laws, but used the 1996 Electoral Law and election procedure violations to mask their other concerns.

In fact, the opposition parties began to limit the extent to which the Lustration Laws were implemented at their earliest opportunity: 9 September 1996.

The Socialist Party was decimated in the 1996 election, which was widely deemed as fraudulent by the international community. The Democratic Party managed to secure 122 seats in the 140 seat legislature, the Socialists got only ten. Following the vote, the majority of the opposition publicly denounced the results and the Socialist members even refused to take their new seats in parliament.[43] Local elections were scheduled to take place in October 1996, and the Democratic Party faced significant international pressure to ensure that opposition parties participated. As part of a broad political reconciliation, Berisha held roundtable discussions with the opposition on 4 September, as a result of which, among other concessions, the Democratic Party introduced a law reading that candidates for local council or chair of a commune were exempted from the scope of the Verification Law, as mentioned above.[44] While this did relatively little to reduce the full scope of the Lustration Laws, political developments in Albania soon allowed the opposition to implement even further restrictions.

In summer and fall 1996, Albania saw a dramatic rise in public investment in several large pyramid companies. These companies had been active since the early 1990s, but by Fall 1996 they had reached a level of integration in the Albanian economy where many impoverished Albanians had become entirely dependent on their deposits therein. The government, for its part, had largely been supportive of the investment schemes and had even encouraged investment after the International Monetary Fund began to issue warnings of their stability after September 1996.[45] Beginning in November 1996, several pyramid schemes stopped making payments and declared bankruptcy, and, by mid-January 1997, all the large funds had collapsed. Civil unrest broke out in several southern cities and protesters set fire to government buildings, including police stations, city halls, courts and Democratic Party offices. Faced with the government's inability to cope with the economic fallout, the protests soon escalated to armed revolt and, on 2 March, Berisha declared a state of emergency. This was too late to quell the revolt, however, and armed gangs were soon able to take control of nearly half the country, threatening Tirana itself.

The Socialist Party, due to its pronounced hostility to the Democratic Party and its boycott of the new government, was embraced by the rebels, while blame for the collapse of the pyramid schemes was heaped upon President Berisha and the ruling Democratic Party. On 9 March 1997, faced with rebel demands for his resignation, Berisha agreed to form a "government of national reconciliation" with ten other political parties, appoint Socialist Bashkim Fino as Prime Minister, and hold new elections by June 1997.[46] The formation of a new government did not immediately ameliorate the situation. Armed bands roamed the country, criminal groups controlled many towns, and prison guards abandoned their posts across the country. Virtually all convicts, including Ramiz Alia and Fatos Nano, were able to walk out of their cells. Unfortunately, however, while Albania continued to spiral into chaos, the new coalition government could not agree on the terms of the new election. It was in this context that, on 9 May 1997, an OSCE mission led by Franz Vranitsky managed to broker a deal between the ten political parties. The six point "political contract" drafted at the time called for a new electoral law increasing proportional representation, the appointment of an international election coordinator and, more importantly, significant changes to the Lustration Laws.[47]

The changes took the form of two laws introduced on 13 May 1997, law 8215, which amended the Genocide Law, and law 8220, which amended the Verification Law. Under the new amendments, only former members of the ex-communist Politburo, former agents of secret police or foreign intelligence agencies, and individuals convicted of crimes against humanity could be lustrated. This drastically limited the scope of the Verification Law in particular; previously, for example, anyone who had been a minister in any communist government would have been barred. With such a limited application, the intended effect of the Verification Law, which for the Democratic Party was presumably to bar as many opposition members as possible from post-communist politics, had been seriously undermined.[48] The changes to the Verification law enabled the Constitutional Court and the Court of Cassation, no doubt expecting a Socialist victory, to clear many opposition candidates and allow them to participate in the June elections. Thus several opposition party leaders, including Fatos Nano and Social Democratic Party leader Skendër Gjinushi, were permitted to run for public office.[49]

A reversal of policy

The Socialists handily won the June 1997 elections, obtaining 101 of 155 parliamentary seats. Due to its pre-election coalition with the Socialists, the Social Democratic Party was able to obtain parliamentary representation and secure nine seats. The Democratic Party won only 24 seats. Fatos Nano, originally barred under the Verification Law, became the new prime minister. Moreover, the Socialist coalition controlled a two-thirds majority in parliament, and was given significant power to further alter the implementation of the Lustration Laws.[50] Shortly after its victory, the Socialists began to reorganize the central administration, judiciary, universities and state controlled media, widely replacing Democratic Party supporters with Socialists and recruits from the old guard. Although less systemic, this replacement campaign was virtually a mirror image of the Democratic Party bureaucratic purges that took place after 1992.[51] Whereas the Democratic Party had replaced many Socialists in an attempt to rid the state apparatus of supporters of the previous communist regime, the Socialists targeted supporters of the previous regime – without resorting to the pretext of lustration, however.

The new government moved quickly to strike down the effects of the Genocide Law. At the request of the newly appointed state prosecutors, Albanian courts re-examined the accusations of crimes against humanity that had been leveled under the Genocide Law against such former communist officials as Ramiz Alia, Hekuran Isai, and Simon Stefani, the latter two being former Politburo members. On 20 October 1997, the Supreme Court acquitted all the accused, ruling that they could not be held liable for actions that were not illegal at the time they were committed.[52] As Article 3 of the Genocide Law only barred those convicted of participating in genocide and crimes against humanity from running for office, all of the acquitted were eligible for participation in politics. As no further convictions were made under the Genocide Law for the remainder of its active life, the law essentially became a dead letter.

Under the new government, the Verification Law also underwent further changes. Shortly after the election, a new Verification Committee was appointed by the predominantly Socialist Party parliament, with Nafiz Bezhani as its chairman. At Bezhani's suggestion, on 15 January 1998 parliament changed the Verification Law by narrowing the scope of lustration even further. Most notably, the amendments altered the wording of the previous law which banned "officers" of the NIS and Interior Ministry from post-communist politics to include only "senior officers and leading functionaries," no longer called for the lustration of former communist judges and state prosecutors from civil service, and changed collaboration with the Sigurimi in general to include only collaboration with the Sigurimi in political trials and investigations. Bezhani launched a comprehensive review of the Socialist Party and the civil service, starting with the judiciary. On 28 January 1998, just two weeks after the changes were implemented, Bezhani announced that he had discovered the "spy" in the judiciary. This individual who, the Committee alleged, had collaborated both with the Yugoslavian and Albanian secret service, was none other than the staunch Democrat and Constitutional Court chairman, Rustem Gjata. Ironically, in 1996, Gjata had upheld both the Lustration Laws against well-grounded constitutional attacks. In a recent interview, Gjata still maintained that the Verification Law was good and fair – only its selective and biased implementation was problematic.[53] Of course, it is not clear to what extent this process was politicized, but it may not merely have been coincidental that the Socialist Party introduced a new constitution just seven months after Gjata's removal from the Constitutional Court.

By May 1998, Bezhani announced that the Committee had reviewed 3,000 members of civil service and had submitted the names of 81 for lustration, including only four members of parliament (two Socialists and two Democrats). As the Verification Law did not provide for members of parliament to be removed from office once elected, the latter retained their positions. It is not clear how many, if any, of these 81 individuals were Socialists, or how many, if any, were removed from their posts. After conducting the review, Bezhani happily announced that the entire Albanian government was "pure" and free of communist influence. There is no record of any further Verification Committee activity until 31 December 2001, when parliament quietly let the Verification Law expire.

File access

A distinct yet integral component of the transitional justice process is the issue of file access. There is no doubt that the Sigurimi maintained extensive files on their activities, victims and collaborators. Since one third of all citizens had been imprisoned or interrogated, not to mention those who were under surveillance, the archive must have been large. However, for reasons discussed below, the exact size and level of detail of the archive is not known.

In Albania, the first legislative attempt to regulate the use of Sigurimi files was made with the introduction of the Verification Law in 1995. Under this legal regime, only the Verification Committee was legally permitted to access the files. However, the partisan nature of the Committee resulted in only a selective review of the files, and even then, the files were generally only used for political purposes rather than disclosure to the public. Prior to the introduction of the law, the files had been used by individuals with connections in government to coerce or intimidate their political opponents. Smear campaigns and serious allegations were published in newspapers containing information that could only have been obtained through file access, and it was apparent that the files were being selectively opened and manipulated to the detriment or gain of a select few individuals.[54] When the Verification Law expired in 2001, so did the only piece of legislation providing for even limited access to the secret files. Since then, the question of access occasionally has surfaced and then quietly got shelved as though, in the words of journalist Ben Andoni, the process was "stopped by some invisible forces."[55]

There are several public figures who still openly push for file access. Ismail Kadare, Albania's best known contemporary writer, called for a complete opening of the files and he appeared to have the support of Albania's then President, Alfred Moisiu. The most recent public attempt to put the issue of file access back on the table was by three members of parliament in 2004. Nard Ndoka and Ilirjan Berzani of the New Democratic Party and Alfred Cako of the National Front Party, both small right-of-centre parties, tabled a bill for a complete, radical and unconditional opening of files. The proposed draft law also called for greater financial transparency and verification of wealth for politicians and public officials. Ndoka, Berzani, and Cako suggested that parliament still contained former members of the communist secret police and called for the opening of what they said were 300,000 extant files on former officers and collaborators.[56] The proposed scope of the draft law was similar to the Verification Law, but it varied most notably in that it called for a more nonpartisan verification committee, and required that *all* included state employees or officials be investigated, and that anyone with a past be dismissed immediately. However, both of the country's two major political forces, the Democratic and Socialist Parties, gave the law a cold shoulder and it died almost as soon as it was tabled. Some might hold up the failure of this law as evidence of the shadowy hand of former communists, pulling the strings of both major parties and preventing the unfortunate Albanian public from discovering the truth about their past.

For it would seem strange to suggest that in a country with a history of pervasive oppression, unjust imprisonment, exile and state murder, the public would not demand to know the identities and roles of their persecutors. Yet although the secret files have always remained closed to ordinary Albanians, there is no public clamor to see them opened, and does not appear to be on the forefront of public debate. A question thus presents itself: is it possible that Andoni's "invisible forces" are nothing more than public apathy? Sali Berisha noted that 15 years after the fall of communism, file access no longer has relevance for most Albanians, who would prefer to close that chapter of their lives. Berisha maintains that the class of politically persecuted is diminishing due to death and emigration and that the same holds true for former persecutors. Berisha also maintains that the top officials and the worst perpetrators never had files, that half the files were destroyed before 1992, and that the Sigurimi deliberately left behind only the files that would work in their favor.[57]

The communist government under Ramiz Alia certainly had ample opportunity to destroy or deliberately alter their files from December 1990 to March 1992. The public had good reason to suggest that this was done on several occasions; a June 1995 issue of *Tribuna Demokratia* reported that during his term as minister of internal affairs, Gramoz Ruci ordered the burning of thousands of incriminating secret service documents.[58] The string of illegal file misuses from 1992–1995 also seriously undermined public perceptions of the files' integrity. If politically connected individuals could gain access, who is to say they did not destroy their own files or alter those of their opponents? By the time the Verification Committee took control of the files, the public likely already viewed them with skepticism. The partisan composition of the Verification Committee, its selective review process, and the conflicting findings of its various incarnations did not improve matters either.[59] It would now be very difficult for any Albanian to take the literal content of the files seriously, let alone what a government organ chooses to filter and publish.

However, as Rustem Gjata noted, even if we assume that the files were left intact by the communists and that they were not altered in the subsequent 15 years of Democratic and Socialist Party rule, there remains an intrinsic problem in using the files to identify Sigurimi collaborators and agents. For, although the content of Sigurimi files may certainly be important, what is left out may be much more so. Gjata gave the example of an innocent young man, arrested and accused of a conspiracy to assassinate Hoxha that was fabricated by an overzealous investigator. The young man is intimidated, tortured, and faced with threats against his person and his family. Completely broken and fearing for his life, the young man confesses to whatever the investigator wants to hear, and invents a story of factory sabotage, incriminating his neighbors, his friends, anyone he can think of. The file, meanwhile, will indicate only that "X informed us that Y and Z were engaged in sabotage." The files will only record those facts that fit into the account of reality fabricated by the state, and there will be nothing on the record to testify to the actual circumstances of the confession. Are we to punish this young man as a police informer on the basis of his file, when in reality he was just an innocent victim of the system?[60] In a country where one third of the population had been interrogated by police or served time in a labor camp, the potential for such mistakes is immense.

Spartak Ngjela suggested a new approach to the issue, stating that Albania, if it elected a Democratic Party government in July 2005, would be at the forefront of a "new wave of lustration" but that this new wave had to be fundamentally different than the flawed experience that came before.[61] Ngjela and others think it is not too late for Albanians to be granted complete and unhindered access to files. He called for access that would not lead to punishment of individuals but merely on identification so that the public could simply be better informed. His point is a good one – arguing that the previous attempt had failed because it tried to impose a new morality in Albania without an independent agency. Only an impartial, equal, and non-judgmental approach to Albania's history can effectively dispel its ghosts.

Ngjela's optimism is reassuring, but as he himself admitted, the reality is that it is doubtful that Albania will be able to exhibit the requisite level of impartiality in the near future. It is much more likely that given all the potential pitfalls of opening the files, and the public's grave concerns concerning the integrity and completeness of the files, that the public will exclaim, as did Arben Imami, "enough is enough, let us move on," and Albania's failed attempt at file access will also be its last.[62]

Conclusion

Albania, like Romania, is a laggard in transitional justice. The process started but it always seemed to be driven by politics. In 1992, when the Democrats came to power, ordinary Albanian had high expectations in all respects but for certain they wanted justice for the past rulers. Despite an abundance of legislation, and firings in the public sector, there was no serious attempt to deal constructively with the communist past. Each and every step, from the changes to the labor law in 1991 to the Verification and Genocide Laws of 1995, was designed to serve political ends. As Arben Imami said, "lustration went wrong because it was always introduced to further other goals."[63] Moreover, by turning the process into a circus of sorts – with people first going to jail for drinking too much coffee – the process lost relevance to the Albanian people who saw only a repeat of Albanian history – out with old – in with the new. File access, which could have been relevant to many in the population, was never granted. Moreover, key issues of the communist past were never really subject to a national debate. What is most telling of this is the attitude of Albania's former communist rulers: for the most part, they appear utterly unrepentant and they appear to lack the ability to reflect in a detached way on the many mistakes of their 46 years of rule. In discussions with Ramiz Alia this is all too clear. He is still unable to understand the gross violations of rights that took place. Once in jail, Alia remarked that one of jailers was a formerly politically persecuted person, who told Alia that he spent his life in jail because of Alia's policies. Alia inquired as to what he had done to end up in jail. The man remarked that he had tried to flee the country. Alia said, "But you broke the law and you knew that."[64] For Alia and his collabora-tors it boiled down to the fact that the government adhered to the laws of the time. As to files, those that were made public were done so to serve political ends. Albania, like Romania, had countless reasons to deal with its communist past especially given the harshness of Stalinism. However, vested interests made this impossible. It is unlikely that another opportunity will present itself.

Notes

1 A. Barahona de Brito, C. Gonzalez-Enriquez and P. Aguilar, *The Politics of Memory: Transitional Justice in Democratizing Societies*, Oxford: Oxford University Press, 2001, p. 244.

2 K. Imholz, 'Can Albania Break the Chain: The 1993–1994 Trials of Former High Officials', *East European Constitutional Review*, 1995, vol. 4, 54.

3 Interview with Remzi Lani, Tirana, 23 June 2005.

4 N. Pano, 'Albania' in K. Dawisha and B. Parott (eds.) *Politics, Power and the Struggle for Democracy in South-East Europe*, Cambridge: Cambridge University Press, 1997, p. 291.

5 F. Abrahams, *Human Rights in Post-Communist Albania*, New York: Human Rights Watch, 1996, p. 33.

6 S. Courtois et al., *The Black Book of Communism. Crimes, Terror, Repression*, Cambridge: Harvard University Press, 1999, p. 397.

7 'A Country Study: Albania', US Library of Congress, 7 November 2005. Online. Available HTTP: http://lcweb2.loc.gov/frd/cs/altoc.html (accessed 23 January 2008).

8 For full election results see R. C. Austin, 'What Albania Adds to the Balkan Stew', *Orbis*, 1993, vol. 37, 263.

9 E. Biberaj, *Albania in Transition: The Rocky Road to Democracy*, Boulder: Westview Press, 1998, p. 105.

10 Pano, 'Albania', p. 316, and K. Kozara, 'Report on Freedom of Information in Albania', *In the Public Interest: Security Services in a Constitutional Democracy*, Helsinki Foundation for Human Rights, 1998. Online. Available HTTP: http://www.gwu.edu/~hurights/chapter4/secrets/foia_alb.html (accessed 23 January 2008).

11 Interview with Sali Berisha, Tirana, 23 June 2005.

12 Interview with Arben Imami, Tirana, 23 June 2005.

13 Interview with Ramiz Alia, Tirana, 17 November 2004.

14 Interview with Rustem Gjata, Tirana, 24 June 2005.

15 Imholz, 'Decommunization in Albania', p. 55.

16 Biberaj, *Albania in Transition*, p. 107.

17 Interview with Spartak Ngjela, Tirana, 21 June 2005.

18 Interview with Ramiz Alia, Tirana, 17 November 2004.

19 Abrahams, *Human rights in Post-Communist Albania*, p. 26.

20 K. Imholz, 'The Experience in Albania', paper presented as part of the conference on Disclosing Hidden History: Lustration in the Western Balkans, Belgrade, 2–4 July 2004, p. 38.

21 K. Imholz, 'States of Emergency as Pretexts for Gagging the Press: Word Play at Albania's Constitutional Court', *East European Constitutional Review*, 1997, vol. 6. Online. Available HTTP: www.law.nyu.edu/eecr/vol6num4/special/statesofemergency.html (accessed 23 January 2008).

22 Interview with Gent Ibrahimi, Tirana, 22 June 2005.

23 These were the first two laws on lustration, with the exception of Law 7666/1993, affecting only the certification of lawyers, which was struck down by the Constitutional Court. Unofficial English translations are reproduced in Abrahams, *Human rights in Post-Communist Albania*, pp. 140–149, and are available online at http://www.lustration.net/albania_documentation.pdf (accessed 23 January 2008).

24 Abrahams, *Human rights in Post-Communist Albania*, p. 41.

25 The (unofficial) translation in Abrahams, *Human Rights in Post-communist Albania*, reads 'perpetrators, promoters and implementers.' However, the wording 'authors, conspirators and executors' was used in an original English submission by the Albanian foreign minister to the Council of Europe and is not only clearer, but probably more accurate. See *Explanatory Note contained in a Note Verbale handed to the Secretary General at the time of deposit of the instrument of ratification of Treaty No. 009: Protocol to the Convention for the Protection of Human Rights and Fundamental Freedoms*, 2 October 1996. Online. Available HTTP: http://conventions.coe.int/Treaty/Commun/ListeDeclarations (accessed 23 January 2008).

26 Albanian Telegraph Agency, 'Nine Senior Ex Communists Face Trial', 29 July 1996. Online. Available HTTP: http://www.hri.org/news/balkans/ata/1996/96-07-30.ata.html#03 (accessed 23 January 2008).

27 Abrahams, *Human rights in Post-Communist Albania*, p. 37 footnote 59, and interview with Rustem Gjata, Tirana, 24 June 2005.
28 See discussion of Law 8151 of 9 September 1996 in *On Amendments to Law 7573 On Elections of the Organs of Local Authorities* in *Explanatory Note contained in a Note Verbale*.
29 Concerns over the committee's non-independence from the government were raised by the International Center against Censorship in a letter to then President Berisha. See 'Article 19 Expresses Concern over Lustration Law', *OMRI Daily Digest II*, 7 December 1995. Online. Available HTTP: http://www.hri.org/news/balkans/omri/1995/95-12-07.omri.html (accessed 23 January 2008).
30 Interviews with Spartak Ngjela, Tirana, 21 June 2005, and Sali Berisha, Tirana, 23 June 2005.
31 Interview with Rustem Gjata, Tirana, 24 June 2005.
32 Biberaj, *Albania in Transition*, p. 297.
33 Abrahams, *Human Rights in Post-Communist Albania*, p. 40, and Biberaj, *Albania in Transition*, p. 290.
34 *Albania Country Report on Human Rights Practices for 1996*, Washington, DC: U.S. Department of Justice, 30 January, 1997. Online. Available HTTP: http://www.state.gov/www/global/human_rights/1996_hrp_report/albania.html (accessed 23 January 2008), and Organization for Security and Cooperation in Europe, *The Albanian Parliamentary Elections of 1996*. Online. Available HTTP: http://www.csce.gov (accessed 23 January 2008).
35 *Albania Country Report on Human Rights Practices for 1996*.
36 Office for Democratic Institutions and Human Rights (ODIHR), *Final Report on Parliamentary Elections in Albania, 26 May and 2 June 1996*, 2 July 1996, p. 5. Online. Available HTTP: http://www.osce.org/documents/odihr/1996/07/1176_en.pdf (accessed 23 January 2008), and Abrahams, *Human Rights in Post-Communist Albania*, pp. 39–40.
37 Imholz, 'States of Emergency'.
38 ODIHR, *Final Report on Parliamentary Election in Albania*.
39 Biberaj, *Albania in Transition*, p. 289.
40 ODIHR, *Final Report on Parliamentary Election in Albania*, and OSCE, *The Albanian Parliamentary Elections of 1996*, p. 2.
41 Biberaj, *Albania in Transition*, p. 298.
42 Ibid., p. 299.
43 Ibid., pp. 297–298.
44 Ibid., p. 312. See also discussion of Law 8151 of 9 September 1996 in *On Amendments to Law 7573 On Elections of the Organs of Local Authorities* in *Explanatory Note contained in a Note Verbale*.
45 Biberaj, *Albania in Transition*, pp. 316–319, and C. Jarvis, 'The Rise and Fall of the Pyramid Schemes in Albania', *IMF Staff Papers*, 2000, vol. 47(1). Online. Available HTTP: http://www.imf.org/external/Pubs/FT/staffp/2000/00–01/jarvis.htm (accessed 23 January 2008).
46 Biberaj, *Albania in Transition*, pp. 319–325.
47 Ibid., p. 331.
48 K. Imholz, 'Albania', *East European Constitutional Review*, 1997, vol. 6. Online. Available HTTP: http://www.law.nyu.edu/eecr/vol6num2/constitutionwatch/albania.html (accessed 23 January 2008), and 'Albanian Parliament Softens Lustration Law', *RFE/RL Newsline*, 16 January 1998. Online. Available HTTP: http://www.hri.org/news/balkans/rferl/1998/98-01-16.rferl.html (accessed 23 January 2008).
49 Ibid. Also Biberaj, *Albania in Transition*, pp. 331–332.
50 Biberaj, *Albania in Transition*, pp. 335–337.
51 Ibid., pp. 352–353.

52 Ibid., p. 353.
53 Interview with Rustem Gjata, Tirana, 24 June 2005.
54 Biberaj, *Albania in Transition*, pp. 180–181.
55 B. Andoni, 'Are Albanians Afraid of Purity?', *Shekulli*, 10 December 2004.
56 *Gazeta Panorama*, 6 June 2005, p. 5. The text of the motion is available electronically
    at http://www.lustration.net/albania_documentation.pdf (accessed 23 January 2008).
57 Interview with Sali Berisha, Tirana, 23 June 2005.
58 Biberaj, *Albania in Transition*, pp. 180–181.
59 Interview with Gent Ibrahimi, Tirana, June 2005.
60 Interview with Rustem Gjata, Tirana, 24 June 2005.
61 Interview with Spartak Ngjela, Tirana, 21 June 2005. In those elections, the Demo-
    cratic Party won 55 seats, the Socialist Party 40, and other smaller political formation
    a total of 45. Sali Berisha of the Democratic Party became the new prime Minister in
    September 2005.
62 Interview with Arben Imami, Tirana, 24 June 2005.
63 Ibid.
64 Interview with Ramiz Alia, Tirana, 17 November 2005.

9   Slovenia

Tamara Kotar

Slovenia provides an interesting case study in transitional justice, because in that country swift and secure democratization was achieved while injustices of the communist past have yet to be dealt with. It may be that in order to ensure the continued vitality of the country's democracy, the Slovenian government should strive to ensure that people who committed crimes under the communist regime are unable to protect themselves through the use of their own political power. However, after almost two decades of post-communism, Slovenia has maintained a stable liberal democracy that has not been put into question due to lack of transitional justice measures. To be sure, there have been moments of political concern and public scandal regarding lustration and secret police file access. As of early 2008 there is no lustration legislation, and access to secret service files has been curtailed through a privacy law that protects even those public figures who may have grossly violated the law. There have not been any prominent trials launched against communist decision-makers and former secret spies. The fact that transitional justice was not dealt with in a comprehensive manner could speak to concerns with the rule of law, the state of the justice system, or simply the lack of public interest towards the subject.[1] The scandals that have surrounded lustration and file access issues, including the clandestine release of secret police file information in 2003, and the many unanswered questions related to lustration still periodically arouse public interest.

In order to offer a greater understanding of lustration and file access issues in post-communist times, this chapter first provides a brief background on Slovenian politics and on security services in the former Yugoslavia. Attempts and failures to engage in lustration and the absence of any plan or mechanism to deal with the secret police transgressions strike at the heart of transitional justice issues in Slovenia. These issues form the main part of the chapter. Although individuals have access to their own secret police files, the fact that the files of political and administrative leaders have not been publicly opened highlights the country's failure to face its communist past. Transitional justice in Slovenia is complicated by the fact that the same communist officials who ruled in the late 1980s were largely responsible for Slovenia's liberal-democratic transformation. They constituted a pro-democratic force, and their tolerance of non-state actors resulted in the successful liberal-democratic state Slovenia has become. While their work for an independent and democratic Slovenia is commendable, a minority believe that, in the interest of ensuring democratic governance, former communist officials who maintain political power should still answer for any criminal acts they or their associates may have committed during communist rule. On the other hand, failure to deal with the political past honestly and openly has informed the entrenchment of liberal democratic politics where discourse has moved beyond indictments for real or imagined political crimes to creating an environment of conflict and consensus. The ease with which Slovenians moved beyond the crimes of the past without the benefit of "truth and reconciliation" has also been aided by the fact that secret services were not as pervasive and the level of oppression in Slovenia and Yugoslavia was not as onerous as in other communist states.[2]

Yugoslavia and its secret political police

Socialist Yugoslavia was born in World War II from the ashes of the Kingdom of Yugoslavia. In the wake of extreme violence, both against the common enemies that occupied Yugoslavia and among its citizens, socialist Yugoslavia was established under the leadership of Marshal Josip Broz Tito. Following the "national liberation struggle" and the proletarian revolution, ethnic equality and federalism were promised in a multiethnic socialist federation under the slogan of "Brotherhood and Unity." Tito employed secret services to establish his control over the delicate balance of power between republics and nationalities. Note, however, that Tito's regime was less coercive than that of other communist states, and Slovenia enjoyed the least coercive environment of all Yugoslav republics. The republic was tucked away in the northernmost region of Yugoslavia, having a distinct language, a political history that included previous historical experience with parliamentary politics, and a modern leadership that sought to enhance its own power by usurping federal power. Slovenia's position and history allowed it to gain ever-greater protection from secret police coercion. However, Slovenia and Slovenians experienced the same organizational structure and general trends that characterized secret services in the larger Yugoslavia.[3]

Slovenia's first communist secret service was represented by the small *Varnostna Obveščevalna Služba* (VOS), which briefly functioned during World War II from 1941 to 1944. The VOS operated inside Slovenia's partisan community and was established by the Central Committee of the Communist Party of Slovenia in the summer of 1941. Three years later, when Slovenia's partisans joined the other partisan groups in Yugoslavia, the VOS was replaced by the all-Yugoslav Department for the Protection of the People (*Organizacija za Zaščito Naroda* or the OZNA). In 1946, the OZNA was in turn replaced by the centralized State Security Directorate (*Uprava Državne Bezbednosti* or the UDBa).[4] The communist state used the UDBa to persecute collaborators and partisan opponents. The directorate took part in massacres of suspected and actual collaborators at Kočevski Rog, Škofija Loca (Crngrob), Teharje, Ljubljana (Šentvid), and other locations. Rough estimates of the number of people executed by the UDBa in the 1946–1947 period are in the five figures, while estimates of the numbers of those held in concentration camps are in at least six figures.[5] After the Tito–Stalin split of 1948 the UDBa persecuted suspected "Cominformists", that is, party members and high-ranking military officials with allegedly pro-Soviet sympathies. According to some estimates, 50,000 people throughout Yugoslavia were investigated as alleged Cominformists.[6] The prison camp at Goli Otok was the most infamous internment site, but Stara Gradiska in Bosnia and Herzegovina and Sremska Mitrovica in the Serbia's region of Vojvodina also housed political prisoners. In 1950 alone the UDBa secretly reviewed more than 98,000 letters written by Slovenian citizens, and in the same year there were more than 24,000 registered UDBa collaborators in Slovenia (whose total population approximated only two million).[7] Nevertheless, repression greatly eased following the ideological shifts of the 1950s and 1960s.

Already in the early 1950s, for fear of decreased legitimacy in the face of poor economic indicators and growing social unrest, a new ideological focus emerged on the unique path of socialism that sought to facilitate long-term economic progress in Yugoslavia. By the mid-1960s, this unique path had been formalized through Workers' Self-Management, a social and economic institution that came to promote decentralization, a process that was denounced by communist authorities of neighboring countries. In this environment of decentralization and greater power devolved by the federal government to the republican leadership, all centralized Yugoslav institutions, including the secret political police, were progressively weakened. By the mid-to late-1960s, the Yugoslav secret police had become a force that was not as powerful and as ubiquitous as in other communist states. The seminal event in its abatement was Tito's dismissal of Vice-President Aleksander Ranković in 1966.

Ranković headed Serbia's wartime secret police, Yugoslavia's post war Interior Ministry, and the post-war secret police prior to his appointment as vice-president, a position in which he continued to maintain control of the UDBa. A staunch supporter of centralization, Ranković was removed from his post on charges of abusing his power.[8] During and even after his reign the UDBa heavily relied on Serbs or Montenegrins to staff the organization and its paramilitary units.[9] Tito, whose sympathies were increasingly with the supporters of decentralization, forced Ranković into retirement once he discovered that Ranković used the UDBa against the government and even bugged Tito's telephones. In 1966, after Ranković's fall, the UDBa, by then renamed the State Security Service (*Služba Državne Varnosti* or the SDV), was purged and dramatically decentralized at the republican level, with greater divisions between the services of different republics and less cooperation among them than before. The SDV retained its organizational structure and mission until 1991. The Yugoslav military police, on the other hand, remained a highly centralized organization, despite the fact that it was present in all constituent republics and it would made sense to work closely with the republican leadership. Ranković's activities were in part exposed by the Military Counterintelligence Service (*Kontraobveščajna Služba* or the KOS). The rivalry between the KOS and the UDBa extended to the anti-Cominformist struggle, during which the UDBa persecuted some members of the KOS. In return, in the wake of the Ranković scandal, the KOS participated in the purge of the UDBa. After Rankovic's fall, the influence of the Yugoslav People's Army's (*Jugosloven-ska narodna armija* or the JNA) and of its counterintelligence service (the KOS) strengthened.[10] The strengthening position of the JNA was evident in its enlarged responsibilities laid out in Article 240 of the 1974 Constitution. The JNA was entrusted with protecting Yugoslavia from external and internal enemies, as well as with protecting the constitution and the social order.

In the 1970s and the 1980s the secret services focused their attention on émigré organizations, their leaders, and their links to Yugoslavia. While still mindful of a pro-Soviet threat, it was Croatian, Kosovar (Albanian), Montenegrin, and Serbian organizations in Western states such as the United States, Canada, West Germany, Sweden, Austria, and France that primarily occupied the SDV. Security services were preoccupied by political unrest in Croatia in the early 1970s. Unrest intensi-fied during the Croatian Spring (1970–1972), when demands for autonomy were accompanied by nascent forms of nationalism. As a result, surveillance and infil-tration of émigré and dissident movements increased, and assassinations of sev-eral of their leaders were carried out. In 1972, the Croatian Spring was crushed by Tito with the help of a massive purge of the Croatian party leadership and the dis-missal of pro-liberalizing leaders in Slovenia and Serbia. To balance these repres-sive measures, Tito instituted the 1974 Constitution, which effectively established a quasi-confederation and strengthened regional economic and political powers at the expense of federal authorities precisely at a time when the economy began to falter and inter-republican rivalries became more pronounced. Article 173 of the 1974 Constitution called on citizens to report "hostile activities" to the SDV, thus promoting insecurity and distrust under the banner of "social self-protection."[11] The SDV officially operated at the federal level according to federally-issued instructions, but central authorities relied on the republican branches of the SDV for accurate reporting and for input to facilitate coordination at the federal level.

In 1980, Tito's death further exposed and exacerbated the economic and political problems of a federal arrangement in which progressively fewer people believed. In an environment of mounting crisis, it is not surprising that state secu-rity services "were becoming increasingly loyal to their own republic leaderships, and were already carefully filtering the information they passed on to the federal service."[12] The SDV in Slovenia estimated that by the late 1980s there had existed some 350 individuals with an anti-regime stance who sympathized with Western (liberal democratic) ideals and 150 others who sympathized with Eastern (Soviet) ideals. All of them were placed under close observation. The growing power of the republics ensured that the SDV reported these concerns directly to the repub-lican leaderships. In 1985, the Slovenian presidency "adopted a resolution ban-ning the SDV from acting against the republic's political authorities," and soon thereafter the resolution was extended to protect all those in leadership positions in Slovenia, including trade union officials. This happened precisely at the time when Slovenian authorities came into increasing conflict with federal authorities, and in these situations the SDV supported the republican authorities. It is worth nothing, however, that ultimately very little is known about the ties of the SDV with the Slovenian communist leadership, and about the structure of the SDV at the crucial time of transition.[13]

The KOS and the JNA, which still portrayed themselves as defenders of the socialist and federal Yugoslavia, were wary of the changes going on in Slovenia, so much so that on 25 March 1988 the Defence Council of Yugoslavia (*Svet Obroženih Sil* or the SFRJ) declared the liberalization in Slovenia as an "anti-revolutionary" activity that "challenged the constitutional order" that the JNA was tasked with defending. Reprints of the meeting minutes came into the hands of journalist Janez Janša, who was later arrested and tried with three others in relation to possessing (although not yet publishing) this secret information. The arrests and the reasons that led to them provoked what was known as the "Slovenian Spring" (1988), the civic protest and political change that marked the beginning of the end of communist and Yugoslav Slovenia. By the time the wars of Yugoslav succession broke out in 1991, the SDV in Slovenia, Croatia, and Bosnia and Herzegovina had severed ties with the Federal Secretariat of Internal Affairs.[14]

Subsequently, the secret services in Slovenia underwent a series of reforms. In 1991, they were renamed the *Varnostno Informativna Služb* (VIS), and four years later again renamed the Slovenian Intelligence and Security Agency (*Slovenska Obveščevalno-Varnostna Agencija* or the SOVA), an organization mandated to gather information for the strategic defense and economic stability of the new independent republic. It has been argued that the new security services retained the organizational structure of their communist predecessor. Critic Andrej Anžič noted that security services in Slovenia did not play a large role in establishing democracy, nor did they actively engage in pro-democratic reforms. Anžič's allegations were given credence by the first director of Slovenia's new secret services, Miha Brejc (1990–1993). Brejc recounted in his memoirs that the innermost circle of SDV officials, who were powerful in the communist-era secret services in Slovenia, remained influential in the post-communist secret services and used that power to advance their own economic advantages. This factor may have contributed to Slovenia's collective failure to come to terms with what secret services did in the communist era.[15]

Approaches to transitional justice

On the whole, member countries of the former Yugoslavia present a unique approach to transitional justice issues. To begin with, Yugoslavia was a communist federation when it broke apart, leaving disparate constituent units to deal with transitional justice in their own ways. Slovenia is one of the more interesting cases to emerge from the former Yugoslavia, and it is the easiest to compare with other Eastern European countries. It is a post-Yugoslav state that experienced a short ten-day war in 1991. The war did not interfere with the liberalizing and democratizing trends that had led the country out of Yugoslavia and by the middle of the 1990s firmly grounded it among consolidated democracies.

The liberalization and democratization demands emanating from the civil society in the face of increasingly reactionary pro-centralization and status-quo communist forces in other parts of the federation, most notably the leadership of the JNA and Slobodan Milošević, ensured that the Slovenian party had to choose sides. The Slovenian party chose reforms first by releasing in March 1989 a program calling for political pluralization, the so-called "Program of Renewal," then by enacting in October that year constitutional amendments that allowed for "disassociation" from Yugoslavia, and finally by legalizing in December 1989 a pluralist political system. During the first free multi-party parliamentary elections of April 1990, the two parties which gathered the most votes in the poll were both led by former communist officials.[16] The first President of the democratic Slovenia was the former leader of the League of Communists of Slovenia, Milan Kučan, who had also facilitated the liberalizing and democratizing reforms. However, it was a coalition of centre-right parties, collectively labeled the DEMOS, which came to control Slovenia's parliament, the National Assembly (*Državni Zbor*), for the following two years.[17] This dynamic ensured a post-communist party system where the communist elite maintained legitimacy together with significant political power.[18] In this smooth transition, several concessions were made to the centre-left forces. These concessions included an agenda free from lustration and other measures that would allow the country to deal with its secret police agents and their collaborators.[19]

On 25 June 1991, Slovenia declared its independence. At the northernmost edge of what was the Socialist Federal Republic of Yugoslavia, bordering Italy, Austria, Hungary, and Croatia, Slovenia was the most economically prosperous republic. It was the republic that led the drive for the federation's political and economic liberalization in the late 1980s and was, along with Croatia, the first of the former Yugoslav republics to declare its independence. By conventional measures, Slovenia remains one of the most successful transitional post-communist states. Since 1992, its GDP per capita and Human Development Index have been the highest among post-communist countries.[20] In the Corruption Perception Index, Slovenia ranks the lowest in the region.[21] Moreover, European Commissioner Romano Prodi commented on the ease of accession negotiations and the country's ability to implement the *aquis communitaire*.[22] However, because of lack of European Union requirements for enacting lustration and file access measures and lack of political will on the part of the republican leadership, transitional justice has been a largely neglected topic.

In general, Slovenia's centre-right parties (also known as the Spring Parties because of their rise during the Slovenian Spring events) have been and continue to be proponents of lustration and public access to secret police files, while the centre-left parties whose top positions are primarily filled by former communist era elite members have come out against these transitional justice methods. A centre-right coalition, the so-called DEMOS, gained power in 1990 but only two years later lost an election that was forced through a vote of no confidence. The centre-left Liberal Democrats of Slovenia (*Liberalna demokracija Slovenije* or the LDS) emerged from the communist-era League of Socialist Youth and came to dominate parliamentary politics for the better part of the first two decades of post-communism. The party won the 1992 general elections and lost power only twice in subsequent years. The December 1992 elections went ahead without any lustration prerequisites and, as a result, they resulted in a resounding victory for the former communists. Since 1992, centre-right governments have only held power for six months in 2000 and for the last four years, since the elections of November 2004. With each successive regime, there is less and less of a discussion on the crimes and human rights trespasses of the former communist secret police.

Coming to terms with lustration

With each passing year, lustration is becoming progressively less of a political and public concern in Slovenia. This is partly a result of the fact that each year there are progressively fewer political leaders and secret police members who gained expertise and experience during the communist era or who may have abused their power. Many of them have died, are very old or in poor health, and fewer of them have retained an interest in politics. There are also progressively fewer direct victims of the communist-era abuse of power, who could have a personal stake in calling for justice, truth, and redress. Rather surprisingly, however, it is at this very late moment that scholarly interest in transitional justice is blossoming, due to the benefit of access to historical records and the distance of objective calls for accountability.[23] Even at the onset of transition, lustration was treated in Slovenia as a historical curiosity and a political strategy more than a contemporary political exercise required to ensure liberal democracy. The Slovenian elite members already enjoyed the trust of the citizens, and the European Union did not impose any lustration requirements in view of the country's accession. Thus, in Slovenia lustration did not have the same urgency it had in other post-communist states. In addition, former communists maintained a strong political presence in Slovenian politics, creating little opportunity for lustration to make it onto the political agenda.

By contrast, centre-right parties called for screening laws and criminal proceedings against communist-era political leaders and other state authorities, but their demands were often portrayed as nothing more than additional political ammunition, a misguided quest for scandal and political power, or simple political infighting. While opinion polls indicated public distrust in the government, this sentiment did not readily translate into popular support for lustration.[24] Independent Slovenia's two shortest-lived governments were headed by centre-right parties, which remained committed to lustration. For example, in September 1990, within six months of the first free elections, the Slovenian Democratic Party leader Slavko Kmetič proposed the public denunciation of communist-era secret informers and collaborators who continued their political careers within that political formation. Given the large numbers of people involved, the potential for mistakes, and the general public apathy, the proposal was never seriously considered. Before the 1992 elections it was rumored that President Milan Kučan, Prime Minister France Bučar, Interior Minister Igor Bavčar, and the Secret Service Director Mihael Brejc agreed to discreetly suggest that known secret collaborators holding public office or high administrative posts withdraw from their posts. If it was indeed ever adopted, the agreement was never implemented. Some of the most notable attempts at enacting lustration laws included the UDBa Amendment, the Resolution on the Illegality of the Communist Totalitarian regime, and the Bill on the Suppression of Consequences Inflicted by the Communist Totalitarian Regime (also known as the Lustration Bill). We will discuss each one in turn.

The UDBa Amendment

The UDBa Amendment (*Udbovski Amandma*) to the parliamentary election law was intended to prevent secret service collaborators from taking seats in the Slovenian National Assembly. Proposed in July 1992, the amendment stated that prior to parliamentary elections and upon accepting a candidature each candidate would be required to sign a written declaration answering the following question: "Did you, in the era before elections of spring 1990, cooperate with the SDV?" Added to this was the question of whether the person ever cooperated with foreign intelligence services within and outside of Yugoslavia. The individuals who collaborated with the SDV or with other foreign secret services were prevented from running for the seat, while those who had gained a seat but falsely denied collaboration would loose it.[25] The written declaration was to be a public document registered with the State Elections Commission.

Those who supported the amendment argued that it prevented potential blackmail of and the continued abuse of power by former secret agents. Prime Minister Lojze Peterle remarked that the UDBa amendment would "fulfill an important and above all moral [requirement], which could come to transform society, on a cultural level."[26] Those who argued against it noted that it would be difficult to determine the nature of collaboration with any kind of precision, and that, even if a candidate had collaborated, he or she would most likely lie about it, since an admission would terminate that person's participation in the electoral campaign even before it began. France Bučar, then the President of the Slovenian National Assembly, reasoned that the passing of the UDBa amendment "would mean that we made the first step towards a quasi-fascist state," but gave no concrete reasons for such strong wording. Bučar further remarked that the UDBa in Slovenia never held the kind of influence that secret political police forces did in neighbouring communist countries. In his words, "Here, [the secret intelligence service] was always an instrument in the hands of the Communist Party and it never dominated the policy-making process."[27] When the amendment came to a vote in September 1992, it was rejected after failing to garner the required two thirds of the vote.

The DEMOS Coalition of 1990–1992 sought to deal with the crimes of the communist past, but it focused on the crimes committed during World War II and on the treatment of the *domobranci* (that is, the home guards, the domestic collaborationist forces allied with Nazi Germany and fascist Italy) rather than on a wider range of secret service persecution perpetrated throughout the communist era.[28] This limited focus did contribute to the rehabilitation of victims of post-World War II show trials and to a serious debate revolving around the roles of collaborators and partisan forces in the country. The DEMOS also ensured the restitution of property nationalized and abusively confiscated by the communist authorities after World War II.[29] However, the DEMOS and its successive governments failed to address the issues of transitional justice in terms of the victims of secret services in all successive periods of communist rule in Yugoslavia. They also did not address the problem of post-communist political leaders who may have abused their power in the previous communist regime. In 1992, a Parliamentary Commission for the Investigation of Post-War Mass-Murders, Dubious Trials and other Irregularities was set up. The commission operated until 1996 and was chaired by the Slovenian Democratic Party leader and Deputy Prime Minister Jože Pučnik. Its interim report due in 1996 was removed from the parliamentary agenda, but it was reproduced by the respected intellectual journal *Nova Revija*.[30] Focused on the immediate post-World War II period, the report concluded that the secret police issued 16,117 political convictions and 178 death sentences from 1945 to 1977, mostly in the early post-war years. In 1996, Pučnik published a book detailing the names and crimes of suspected OZNA collaborators and agents perpetrated from 1945 to 1950.[31] Since the report failed to convince the public of the need for lustration, Pučnik continued to blame former communists turned post-communist politicians, particularly Kučan and Drnovsek, for Slovenia's failure to come to terms with its communist past.[32]

In 1997, the centre-right forces brought lustration once again to the forefront of political debate just after they lost another parliamentary poll. In November, days before the presidential elections, two center-right politicians, Janez Janša of the Slovenian Democratic Party and Lojze Peterle of the Slovenian Christian Democrats, introduced in parliament two documents: the Resolution on the Illegality of the Communist Totalitarian Regime, and the Bill on the Suppression of Consequences Inflicted by the Communist Totalitarian Regime (also known as the Lustration Bill).[33] The first Defense Minister of independent Slovenia and a former journalist at the centre of the controversy that ignited the "Slovenian Spring," Janša had authored both documents. His position was that NATO's eastward expansion required Slovenia to directly confront the individuals with a questionable communist past in order to prove that the new member state could be trusted with sensitive NATO secrets. It could be hardly expected that people who had collaborated with the communist intelligence services, which were recognized for their disdain and hostility toward Western governments and Western organizations, could then turn around and claim they wholeheartedly supported Slovenia's efforts to accede to the NATO, their former archenemy. After Slovenia was not included in the first wave of NATO expansion into Central and Eastern Europe, the Spring Parties blamed the failure on lack of lustration, while their centre-left rivals condemned lustration for damaging the reputation of the "Republic of Slovenia as a state of law."[34] Given the timing of this debate and the well-known rivalry between Janša and Kučan, it is safe to conclude that centre-left parties saw the resolution as just another attempt to resurrect the lustration effort and as a ploy to damage Kučan's chances of re-election.

Janša had first accused Kučan of betraying Slovenia's national interests in the late 1980s. By 1994 Kučan and Janša's rivalry had grown into an open conflict.

In March that year, Janša was dismissed from his position as Defense Minister on charges that he tolerated under his command a special brigade whose members were indicted for engaging in criminal activities.[35] At the time of his dismissal, Janša was also accused of ordering wire taps on journalists investigating top politicians. In retaliation for his public humiliation, Janša revealed that the Slovenian government, with the knowledge of Kučan, had allowed weapons to be shipped from the Maribor Airport to Bosnian Muslims. Refusing to allow his dismissal to completely derail his political career, Janša went on the offensive, arguing that "the Udbomafia" (the term he coined to refer to the alleged unreformed communists) was powerful enough to endanger Slovenia's democracy. Despite his public accusations, in the 1996 elections his Democratic Party gained only 19 percent of the vote, while the Liberal Democrats, the country's leading centre-left party led by a number of prominent former communists, gained as much as 28 percent of the vote.[36] Searching for a platform with which to influence the presidential poll, Janša looked to lustration. After the presidential elections took place and following almost a full week of heated debates, on 26 November 1997 the lustration bill was rejected in a vote of 22 in favor and 57 against. Only 79 of the 90 members of the National Assembly were present for the vote, a fact indicating the relative lack of importance attached to the issue by legislators. Criticism of the bill included the potential for assigning collective guilt, the unclear provisions relative to what will happen to the individuals found guilty, and the proliferation of public offices to which the bill applied. Lustration was to affect members of the parliament and the government, lawyers, prosecutors, legal experts, mayors, editors, and journalists.[37]

The Resolution on the Illegality of the Communist Totalitarian regime, which also reached the floor of the parliament after the 1997 presidential elections, was a denunciation and an indictment of the former regime. It did not call for action against specific individuals or specific institutions, and, as such, it was fully supported by the Spring Parties. The resolution made reference to three successive periods of communism in Slovenia: a) the totalitarian system of early communism, b) the classical social-realist system, and c) the later one-party system with two faces (the so-called "socialism with a human face"). The resolution indicted the Communist Party of Slovenia for its responsibility in upholding a repressive regime, and argued that the neo-communist elite continued to influence Slovenia's political life, and that a delay in democratic development prevented the country from entering NATO in 1997. Proponents of the law deplored the fact that the Slovenian "parliament did not even adopt one law to condemn the former regime as illegitimate and to separated the communist-era good from the bad by principled means."[38] To ensure that that those who abused power during communist times would not have the opportunity to regain political power, the resolution proposed a seven-member Lustration Court to oversee the files of individuals entering national public office and to ensure they had not committed criminal-political sins in the communist period. Archival documents from all public institutions, particularly the former secret police, could be used as evidence.[39] Because many high ranking members of the centre-left parties had also been members of the

Communist Party they were not going to support this resolution. President Milan Kučan, for example, said that both the proposed lustration law and the Resolution on the Unlawful Activities of the Communist Totalitarian Regime were "politically and morally unjustified and harmful, legally impermissible" because they misrepresented Slovenia as having not broken "legally, politically or symbolically with the previous system of one-party rule, its failure to respect human and political rights, and its self-managing socialist economy."[40] To make his point, the President cited several laws that contributed to the break with the communist past: the Constitution, the Penal Code, the Law on Criminal Procedure, the Law on the Courts, the Law on Judicial Service, and the Law on Public Prosecutors. The resolution was narrowly rejected in a vote of 44 against and 42 in favour. The general public had little interest in the debates, as demonstrated by the Slovenian public opinion polls, which in 1998 found that 56.7 percent of respondents "did not hear" of the resolution.[41]

Following these defeats, the Spring Parties did not pursue lustration or legal measures to denounce the communist regime any further. In 2001, two anonymous documents labeled "for internal use only" – the Resolution for Demarcation between the Communist Regime and the Democratic Republic of Slovenia, and the Declaration of National Reconciliation – were circulated among deputies, but none were seriously debated. Under a new Law on Investigative Activities read in parliament in October 2002, the Social Democrats sought to lustrate post-communist secret services in order to exclude agents who had worked for the communist political police. When the Spring Parties came back to power in 2004, lustration was neither a part of their campaign promises nor on the government agenda, although Janez Janša, the most vocal proponent of access to secret files and lustration, became the head of the new government.[42]

Coming to terms with secret police file access

Lustration requires access to and information contained in the secret police files. Note, however, that the Yugoslav communist-era secret archive was initially housed in Belgrade, that is, outside the borders of independent Slovenia. By 1991 the majority of Slovenia's secret service archive had mysteriously disappeared, only to reappear in 2003 in a truncated form. Access to the remaining files was curtailed due to privacy laws that prohibited public disclosure of the contents of individual files, but allowed access to one's own files. This created a situation where even though it is known that files on numerous political and administrative leaders existed, baring self-exposure, the contents could not be made publicly known. Even when the records of some elected officials were publicly exposed, the reliability of the SDV collection and reporting placed the vast majority of the content of the files under a question mark. Beyond this, the general public has not clamored for enhanced access. Today, access is seen as serving the purposes of historical accuracy and curiosity rather than representing a requirement for liberal democratic transition.

Once transferred to Slovenia, the UDBa and later the SDV files were stored in the Central Active File of the Slovenian Ministry of Interior (*Republiškega*

Sekretariata za Notranje Zadeve Socialistične Republike Slovenije or the RSNZ), housed in the National Archives together with other materials compiled by the Ministry for Interior. Each one of over one million files was assigned a unique code. It further contained the person's name, surname, birth date, nationality, criminal offenses, and reasons for investigation (in the case of victims) or recruitment (in the case of collaborators or agents).[43] Secret files were created for a number of reasons, including suspected contact with the regime, status as a criminal offender, suspected opposition to the regime, or general surveillance. The files that garnered the most attention were those that dealt with collaborators of and persons of interest to the SDV.

The transfer of secret files from Belgrade to Ljubljana began as early as 1986. The first transport included some 74,000 files dealing with cases that occurred between 1945 and 1955. The steady transfer of files ensured that by 1989 the majority of secret files on or concerning Slovenians had been transferred to the Slovenian Archives, and stored in the Gotenica underground bunker.[44] Although Slovenia had access to the secret archive two years prior to the disintegration of the Yugoslav federation, in April 1990 the centre-right DEMOS governing coalition unexpectedly claimed that most files were nowhere to be found.[45] It is not known where and why the files transferred before 1990 disappeared, but credible reports concur in noting the fact that they were spirited away by unknown hands. According to Ljuba Dornik Šubelj of the Slovenian National Archives, only about 3,000 communist-era secret files on Slovenes remain. These files were transferred from Belgrade between 1991 and 2000. A separate archival fond included files on 860 deceased individuals and 2,000 other persons.[46] According to DEMOS politicians, the mysterious disappearance of files from 1989 to 1990 could be explained by the fact that the then still-ruling communists destroyed the files because of the incriminating evidence they contained. After winning the 1992 elections, the Liberal Democrats pledged to determine how and why did the files disappear, but the issue has remained unsolved. Access to the extant secret archive has been seriously restricted by the privacy laws.

The Personal Data Protection Act was enacted in 1990 and subsequently amended in 1999 and 2001, and again in 2004 in preparation for the country's accession to the European Union.[47] The act requires an individual's written consent for accessing personal data, thus barring access to communist-era secret files in the absence of express consent of the person for whom that file was compiled. Of course, few, if any, post-communist political luminaries and former secret collaborators are inclined to relinquish such privacy privileges effectively ensuring that their tainted past remains out of the public's sight for the near future. In 2001, the independent Inspectorate for Personal Data Protection Agency was established within the Ministry of Justice. Responsibility for privacy issues is now divided between the Inspectorate and the Human Rights Ombudsman, with the Ministry of Justice bearing responsibility for maintaining a database registry of consent for access to personal information. Several provisions of the Criminal Code also cover privacy issues, particularly Articles 149 to 152, 154, 225, and 242. For example, Article 149 prohibits unauthorized recording or image taking of individuals or their premises if this act entails a serious invasion of privacy, Article 152 specifies sanctions for the violation of dwellings through an unauthorized entry, Article 154 prohibits any use of data that is in breach of the law, while Article 242 sanctions the intrusion of an electronic database for personal or third party use.[48] However, it was not until 2003 that Slovenian authorities had to deal with an unprecedented violation of these laws in relation to the secret service files.

UDBa.net

In April 2003, the police and secret police files references to some one million Slovenes were published on-line. The files included the names of common criminals, secret police full-time agents, part-time collaborators and informers, and the victims who had been monitored by the UDBa. The UDBa web site (http://www. UDBa.net) included the name of the person, the secret service file number, the citizenship/nationality status, the names of the parents, the employment history, the criminal record, and the birth date of all those listed.[49] The problem with the information listed on the internet was the fact that the persons listed were not only secret agents, but also individuals who came in contact with the communist secret services for a variety of reasons. Among those named were prominent Slovenian politicians and public figures.

Of the one million files referenced on the UDBa.net database, only about one hundred thousand actually referred to the secret political police. The majority of files were organized under the title "person registered in criminal evidence" (*oseba je zabeležena v kazenski evidence*), while the next largest number of files fell under "criminal activities" (*kaznivo dejanje*), and the smallest number of files belonged to the category "SDV file" (*dosje SDV*). Most files in the Central Active Files refer to people who simply had or were suspected of having a run-in with the law, people considered part of preliminary evidence in an investigation that remained opened since the communist era, and individuals who had contact with the police or criminal investigators. Some SDV files contained subcategories of targets of investigation, agents and collaborators (which included sources and reservists who were state employees regularly called upon to provide information to the SDV). The number of collaborators rapidly diminished starting in 1966 when the reform of the intelligence services took place, so that by the 1980s there were only an estimated 1,000 collaborators.[50]

Even after the names of people who had SDV files were released, little was known about what information their actual files contained, a situation complicated by the disappearance of the majority of the secret archive. It is widely assumed that the most politically damaging files were removed or destroyed sometimes before 1990. Most of the files that remained did not contain incriminating evidence. Beyond that, there was no way to distinguish between files on informers, collaborators, agents, or victims of the secret services. Some claim to be able to distinguish between these categories by using the file number. However, no one is quite sure what the file number really means. Rumor has it that the SDV files catalogued under the numbers 60,000 to 69,999 indicate that the person worked as an agent of the secret police, the files containing the numbers 50,000 to 50,999 indicate official collaborators with the secret services, while number 55,000 indicates unofficial collaborators.[51] There were calls for an in-depth investigation of the files and file numbers disclosed on the internet, but such an evaluation was never completed.

Neither the secret services nor the government confirmed the authenticity of the UDBa.net list, but independent experts supported its authenticity. Historian Bozo Repe judged that the documents were genuine, while the Director of the National Archives, Vladimir Žumer, reported that UDBa.net had access to the majority, but not to all, of the secret files.[52] In addition, Leopold Vidmar, who oversaw part of the file transfer as former head of Slovenia's Department of Informatics' Sector for Primary Evidence, which organized access to the SDV and other criminal files by transferring reference information from a card index and paper based system to an electronic system, confirmed that the UDBa.net files were authentic.[53] Soon, it was confirmed that Slovenia's Honorary Consul for Australia and New Zealand, Dušan Lajovic, made the list public. Appointed by the Liberal Democrat leader Drnovšek, Lajovic supported the calls for lustration. Claiming that he obtained the information in 1991, Lajovic said that he withheld it for fear of jeopardizing Slovenia's accession into the European Union. But after the country secured an invitation to join the Union, Lajovic felt it was time to deal with the unresolved issue of secret collaboration among high state officials. In his book on the secret archive, released in 2003, Lajovic discussed the files of some 14,000 suspected former agents.[54]

In an effort to shed light on the way Lajovic accessed this sensitive information, the Oversight Commission of the Work of Security and Information Services (*Komisijo za nadzor nad delom varnostnih in obveščevalnih služb*) issued a report stating that up until 1986 UDBa paper files were issued with multiple copies on microfilm, with the implication that Lajovic could have accessed one of those microfilm copies. Marjan Antončič, a data protection expert working for the Ministry of Interior, confirmed that the UDBa.net data came from the microfilm copy of the files that originated in the late 1980s.[55] Created for cases of emergency, the microfilm copies were stored in various, still undisclosed, army locations. The Slovenian secret services and the police also initiated an investigation into how Lajovic obtained the files, but were not successful in finding the truth.

There has been speculation that the Police Chief Marko Pogorevc, the former secret service director Miha Brejc, or the Social Democrat leader Janez Janša might have provided the secret information to Lajovic. In August 2003, Lajovic revealed that on 24 June 1991 he received a microfilm from Jože Malnar, a secret service official. The microfilm contained all of the data that was later posted on the UDBa.net. Claiming to have no knowledge of what the microfilm really contained, Lajovic handed the microfilm over to an unnamed friend, who took it to the United States. The next year the microfilm arrived in Australia, where Lajovic used expert analysis to find out what information it really contained. Lajovic first believed that the secret documents would come out on their own, but in time, seeing that they continued to remain secret, he decided to publish a book about the communist secret police and at the same time post the information on the internet in the interest of "uncovering the barbarism of communist times" and of "rethinking those times."[56]

Despite Lajovic's research and the proven authenticity of the file references, the information contained on the UDBa.net and in Lajovic's book was incomplete and insufficient to launch lustration proceedings. It did not even generate renewed political support for lustration, although the secret files exposed on the UDBa.net referred to high profile center-left politicians such as the current President and former Prime Minister Janez Drnovšek (whose SDV file was file no. 0055000), former speaker of the National Assembly Borut Pahor (SDV file no. 0013588–00015), and former director of SOVA Miha (Mihael) Brejc (SDV file no. 0000198–18472). Drnovsek and Pahor denied working for the UDBa, arguing instead that they must have certainly been considered persons of interest because of their involvement in politics. In 2003, Pahor sent a written request to see his secret file to Prime Minister Anton Rop.[57] Some center-right politicians felt vindicated by the fact that high-profile politicians were on the list, and the Democratic Party leaders stated that the list proved that their call for lustration had been morally right all along.[58] While the Spring Parties had long sought the public release of the secret service files of post-communist politicians in the hope of discrediting their center-left rivals, the disclosure of the UDBa files proved that among the extant files were files on politicians representing other political formations, most notably the nationalist Slovenian National Party.

Commanding only four seats in the Slovenian parliament, the National Party broke up into factions after the UDBa site released the files that implicated National Party leader Zmago Jelinčič Plemeniti as an agent of the Yugoslav military counterintelligence. Jelinčič's inclusion on the list and the revelation of his military counterintelligence activity were compounded by his drive to destroy the SDV files in the early 1990s. In 1993, Jelinčič and his fellow party member Polonca Dobrajc proposed a bill that legislated the destruction of the communist secret files of agents and informers, but not victims, within six months of the bill's adoption. Two years later Jelinčič withdrew his proposal without explanation. Many suspect that his desire to destroy the secret archive was motivated by the fact that the files suggested that he was a long-time secret collaborator.[59]

Centre-right parties also felt vindicated by the length of the list. Lojze Peterle, former Prime Minister from 1990 to 1992, figured on the UDBa list along with People's Party member Janez Podobnik. Peterle admitted that "Janša was for the most part right" when he called for lustration, because the electronically-posted list "confirmed [the] fact that the Slovenian UDBa has a longer list [of collaborators] than Stasi," the feared East German communist secret political police.[60] Peterle nonchalantly explained his inclusion on the list by saying that he was "convinced that during the DEMOS [government] ... I was among the most eavesdropped on ... I was a person of interest ... [but] I never cooperated with the UDBa."[61] Supported by the Spring Parties, Lajovic also claimed that these documents should be revealed in the public interest. According to him, the public had the right to know this important information about their leading elected officials and, in the interest of ensuring and strengthening the rule of law, those who committed crimes must be held accountable. In reply, other politicians and local observers argued that making the files public endangered the rule of law because it infringed on privacy rights.[62]

In reaction to the release of the secret service file information on the UDBa. net, the Slovenian government took the extraordinary measure of immediately blocking access to the web site. The Inspectorate for Personal Data Protection ordered all Slovenian internet service providers to block access to the site. The inspectorate recalled its order a few days later, when it became clear that the site could not be shut down. Blocking access to it through the Slovenian internet service providers was not effective in preventing the dissemination of the information, and the order to block access was itself controversial. The site could not be shut down because it was registered in New York and operated from a server in Thailand.[63] The fact that these files contained names of people suspected of or charged with engaging in common criminal activities, being involved in or being tracked by the SDV speaks to privacy concerns, and as soon as the web site appeared the privacy laws were enforced.

Under the privacy laws, access to archived SDV material is blocked for a period of 75 years following its creation or for 10 years after the death of the individual on whom the file was compiled. Individuals may, however, have unrestricted access to their own files. The names of the full-time agents and part-time informers who contributed information to the files are removed prior to the opening of the file. Prior to and even after the UDBa affair, there were comparatively few requests from individuals for releasing information contained in their SDV files. It was estimated that the National Archives received between 50 and 100 applications every month to view files compiled by various branches of the Ministry of Interior, most of these requests falling under the category of legal and administrative rights for "Victims of Armed Violence" (*Žrtvah Vojnega Nasilja*). Only a handful of those requests dealt directly with the SDV.[64] Even after the UDBa affair, Slovenians were not clamoring to access their files, nor was there a renewed public call for lustration.

The publication of secret data on the UDBa.net was seen by the Commission for Oversight of Security and Intelligence Services (*Komisijo za Nadzor nad Delom Varnostnih in Obveščevalnih Služb*) as a violation of the rights of victims, agents and collaborators of the SDV.[65] In response to the scandal, the commission held a closed meeting and issued a secret report on the influence of the UDBa.net on Slovenian national security. During the session, the oversight commission sought the testimony on the meeting of the Historical Commission called by the Central Committee of the Slovenian Communist Party in May 1989, where allegedly there was some discussion on the fate of the SDV archives.[66] The fact that it took the UDBa.net affair to even bring this issue to the committee's attention speaks to the lack of interest in resolving those issues. However, as reported by Iztok Podbregar, the session focused on the privacy rights for the individuals who had SOVA and National Archive files.[67] Similarly, the lawsuit that Slovenia's public prosecutor launched against Lajovic centred on his illegal publication of personal data.

The prosecution's case was hampered by the fact that the data was provided over an internet account registered and housed in countries other than Slovenia. The UDBa affair highlighted Slovenia's failure to effect transitional justice. Debates over the right to public information on leading political and administrative figures versus these individuals' right to privacy will likely arise in the future.

Conclusion

Transitional justice involves reckoning with the communist past and strengthening the liberal democratic rule by seeking out, holding accountable, and bringing to justice those who committed crimes but were protected by their political and administrative positions in the previous regime. In Slovenia there is much speculation about but little sustained investigation into the role of current political and secret police elite members both in terms of the crimes some of them may have committed during the communist era and in terms of covering up those crimes in the post-communist era. Throughout the 1980s, Slovenians gained increasing trust in their communist leaders during the fight against Yugoslav centralization and the establishment of an independent state tolerating greater civil liberties. This translated into a post-communist state where it was not believed that the communist past would inhibit the liberal democratic transition. Yugoslavia, its federal institutions, and its leaders shouldered much of the blame for communist injustices, affording a type of instant lustration during Slovenia's independence, when Serbs were marginalized on the republic's political scene. This allowed Slovenes to focus on establishing an independent democracy without addressing lustration in political or administrative terms. The fact that political transition in Slovenia did not include transitional justice did not negatively impact democratization and political liberalization.

In a democracy where citizens have not called for transitional justice, the time for such measures may have passed, to the benefit of sustained democracy. At the same time, the lack of transitional justice may signal ambivalence and apathy in the face of issues that speak to the core of liberal democratic rule of law. If Slovenes do not seek accountability for the crimes of the communist era, what are they going to seek accountability for? During any era and in any state, it is in the interest of justice and the rule of law to ensure that people who commit crimes not shield themselves with political power. The fact that issues of transitional justice periodically arise in public scandals and are used as political ammunition speaks to the lingering distrust and instability caused by the failure to deal with the communist past honestly. However, the disappearance of the majority of secret police files may mean that Slovenians will never be able to deal with their political past fully and honestly.

Notes

1 For example, in its publication recording Slovenian public opinion from 1990–1998, Slovenia's respected Centre for the Study of Public Opinion and Mass Communication asked respondents in 1993 to record their ideas regarding required action for dealing

with the communist past. The survey asked if "the National Assembly should adopt a declaration [denouncing] the Communist Party of Slovenia as a criminal organization, which brought damage and crime to the nation." Of the 1,044 respondents 2.8 percent strongly agreed with the statement, 9.8 percent agreed in principle, 19 percent were undecided, 36.6 percent disagreed in principle, 16.7 percent strongly disagreed, and 15.2 percent did not know. In the 1994 survey in response to the following statement, "the National Council should adopt a declaration of the Communist Party of Slovenia as a criminal organization," of 1,023 respondents 3.9 percent strongly agreed, 7.8 percent agreed in principle, 19.8 percent were undecided, 23.2 percent disagreed in principle, 25.5 percent strongly disagreed, and 19.8 percent were undecided. In response to almost the same question in 1998, "the National Council should adopt a declaration of the Communist Party of Slovenia as a criminal organization, which brought harm and crime to the nation," on a scale of 1 to 5 (with 1 in agreement and 5 in disagreement) out of 1,011 respondents 6.9 percent chose number 1, 5.5 percent number 2, 11 percent number 3, 14.5 percent number 4, and 43.6 percent number 5. See N. Toš (ed.) *Vrednote v prehodu II, Slovensko javno mnenje 1990–1998*, Ljubljana: FDV-CJMMK, 1999, pp. 276, 370 and 871.

2 L. Plut-Pregelj, A. Gabrič, and B. Repe (eds.) *The Repluralization of Slovenia in the 1980s: New Revelations from Archival Records*, Seattle: The Donald W. Treadgold Papers, University of Washington, 2001; B. Repe, *Jutri je Nov Dan*, Ljbuljana: Modrijan, 2002, pp. 44–51; J. Poglajen, 'Obilna žetev hinavsega paragrapha', *Mladina*, 12 November 2003. Online. Available HTTP: http://www.mladina.si (accessed 20 January 2006); T. Bukovec, 'UDBa je udarila prek interneta', *Dnevnik*, 27 April 2003. Online. Available HTTP: http://www.dnevnik.si/novice/iskalnik?sel=advanced (accessed 20 January 2006); and A. Anžič, 'Obveščevalne službe-legalni in legitimni labirinti in izhodi', *Varstvoslovje*, 1 January 1999. Slovenia's liberal democracy was confirmed by the country's accession to the European Union in May 2004.

3 Communist Yugoslavia's secret services underwent several name changes. Initially, from 1941 to 1944 the Slovenian Communist secret services were known as the *Varnostna Obveščevalna Služba* (VOS). During the 1944–1946 period, they were replaced by the centralized Yugoslav *Organizacija za Zaščito Naroda* (OZNA). In 1946 the OZNA was renamed the *Uprava Državne Varnosti* (UDBa), which functioned until 1966, when it was in turn replaced by the *Služba Državne Varnosti* (SDV), active until 1991. Independent Slovenia's secret services were known as *Varnostno Informativna Služb* (VIS) from 1991 to 1995, and *Slovenska Obveščevalno-Varnostna Agencija* (SOVA) after 1995.

4 J. Tomasevich, *War and Revolution in Yugoslavia 1941–1945: Occupation and Collaboration*, Stanford: Stanford University Press, 2001, pp. 97 and 127; J. Gow and C. Carmichael, *Slovenia and the Slovenes: A small State and the New Europe*, London: Hurst, 2000, pp. 50 and 113; J. Pučnik, *Iz Archivov Slovenske politične policije*, Ljubljana: Založila Veda, 1996, pp. 13–86; J. R. Lampe, *Yugoslavia as History: Twice There was a Country*, New York: Cambridge University Press, 2000, p. 238; and M. Tanner, *Croatia: A Nation Forged in War*, New Haven: Yale University Press, 1997, p. 177.

5 Lampe, *Yugoslavia as History*, p. 238.

6 J. Pučnik, *Iz Archivov Slovenske Politične Policije*.

7 Z. Seliskar, *Zgodovina organov za notranje zadeve v Socialisticni Republiki Sloveniji*, Ljubljana: Mladinska knjiga, 1970, p. 145.

8 D. Cosic, *Piscevi zapisi 1951–1968*, Belgrade: Filip Visnjic, 2000, p. 263.

9 B. Allcock, J. J. Horton and M. Milovojević, *The role of the Yugoslav intelligence and security committee in Yugoslavia in Transition*, New York: Berg, 1992, pp. 204–207 and 234.

10 The Brioni Plenum of July 1966 entrenched the post-Ranković reforms, which had been implemented by 1967. These reforms included a KOS that that had greater influence over

civilian affairs. Tito came to rely on the internal discipline of KOS along with the army's philosophical dedication to the unified Yugoslavia that it was instrumental in establishing. B. Milosavljevic, 'Reform of the Police and Security Services in Serbia and Montenegro Attained Results or Betrayed Expectations', *Sourcebook on Security Sector Reform*, Geneva: Geneva Centre for the Democratic Control of Armed Forces, 2002. Online. Available HTTP: www.dcaf.ch, pp. 261 and 294 (accessed 18 January 2008).

11 'Ustav Savezne Republike Jugoslavije', *Službeni List*, Belgrade: Vlada Savezne Republike Jugoslavije, 1974.

12 J. Drnovšek, *Escape from Hell: The Truth of a President*, Ljubljana: Delo, 1996, p. 43.

13 B. Nežmah, 'Obračun z zogovina, zakaj se UDBa vrača kot zombi?', *Mladina*, 28 April 2003. Online. Available HTTP: http://www.mladina.si/tednik/200317/ (accessed 18 January 2007). Nežmah notes that there is still a critical lack of information on the structure and operations of secret services in Slovenia and Yugoslavia in the 1970s and 1980s. He called for the history of the UDBa (and SDV) to be written, detailing its organization, methods, employees, and the distribution of power. See I. Bavcar and J. Janša, 'Emigranti: Med represijo in kolaboracionizmom s SDV', *Mladina*, 19 February 1989. Online. Available HTTP: http://www.mladina.si/tednik/198907 (accessed 18 January 2007); 'Pregled opozicijkih sil v slovenia analiza republiškega sekertariata za notranje zadeve', *Republiškega sekertariata za notranje zadeve*, Ljubljana, 25 January 1979; *Archive RS dislocirana enota i fond Seje CK ZKS*, 14th session of the presidency CK ZKS, 29 January 1979; Milosavljevic, 'Reform of the Police and Security Services in Serbia and Montenegro', p. 262; Drnovšek, *Escape from Hell*, pp. 42–44; D. Fers, 'From Security and Intelligence Service to Slovenian Intelligence and Security Agency', *National Security and the Future*, 2003, vols. 1–2, 61–80; and 'The Act on National Protection', *National Gazette*, 1988, vol. 38, 8–20. In 1980 criticism of the regime was restricted in part because sensitivity in the face of Tito's death.

14 J. Janša, *The Making of he Slovenian State 1988–1992: The Collapse of Yugoslavia*, Ljubljana: Mladinska knjiga, 1994, p. 15; S. Basic Hrvatin, 'The Role of the Media in the Transition', in D. Fink-Hafner and J. R. Robbins (eds.) *Making a New Nation: The Formation of Slovenia*, Brookfield: Dartmouth, 1997, p. 270. The JLA was also wary because it had come under increasing criticism from the Slovenian media. For example, there was a spate of articles criticizing its sale of arms to Ethiopia. The SDV in Serbia and many members of the Federal Secretariat of Internal Affairs had fallen under the influence of Slobodan Milosevic.

15 A. Anžič, 'Parlamentarno nadzorstvo nad obeščevalno vanostnimi službami: Slovenske izkušnje', *Varstvoslovje*, 2000, vol 2, 85; Anžič, 'Obveščevalne službe-legalni', 129; and M. Šetinc, 'Zapisani, izrisani, zamolčani', *Mladina*, 6 May 2002. Online. Available HTTP: http://www.mladina.si/tednik/200218/ (accessed 10 January 2006). Also, M. Brejc, *Vmestni čas: varnostno informativna služba in nastanjane nove slvoenske države 1990–1993*, Ljubljana: Mladinska knjiga, 1994. Unfortunately, in his memoir Brejc does not often go beyond generalities, citing fear of potential lawsuits. A good English-language source is D. Fers, 'From Security and Intelligence Service to Slovene Intelligence and Security Agency', *National Security and the Future*, 2003, vol. 3, 61–80. Online. Available HTTP: http://hrcak.srce.hr/file/28815 (accessed 18 January 2008).

16 T. Hribar, 'Odločitev za Samostojnost', *Mladina*, 29 December 1989, p. 6. Online. Available HTTP: http://www.mladina.si/tednik/198951 (accessed 18 January 2006); and S. P. Ramet, 'Democratization in Slovenia—the Second Stage', in K. Dawisha and B. Parrot (eds.) *The Consolidation of Democracy in East-Central Europe*, New York: Cambridge University Press, 1997, p. 196.

17 In 1990, Kučan, received 44.4 percent of the vote in the first round and 58.6 percent of the vote in the second round of voting. In 1992, running as an independent, Kučan garnered 63.9 percent of the vote, and in 1997 again as an independent candidate he won 55.57

Slovenia 219

percent of the vote. I. Lukšič, *The Political System of the Republic of Slovenia: A Primer*, trans. by E. Johnson Debeljak, Ljubljana: Znanstveno in Publicisticno Sredisce, 2001, p. 14. Former head of the League of Communists of Slovenia, Milan Kučan, was elected President in 1990, a post he held until his term limit expired in 2002.

18 In a public opinion survey asking respondents "Which of the following factors primarily contributed to the independence of Slovenia," 34.2 percent of respondents picked as the number one reason "the Slovenian leadership in the previous regime which acted against central powers in Beograd." See Toš, *Vrednote v prehodu II*, pp. 276, 370 and 872.

19 'Interview with Anton Drobnič', *Delo Sobotna Priloga*, 15 October 1994. Online. Available HTTP: http://www.delo.si (accessed 10 March 2006).

20 Slovenia is ranked 27th in the 2007 Human Development Report, ahead of all other East European countries. See The United Nations Development Program, *The 2007/2008 Human Development Index Rankings*. Online. Available HTTP: http://hdr.undp.org/en/statistics/ (accessed 22 January 2008).

21 Estonia and Slovenia are both ranked at 31st place, ahead of other East European countries. Transparency International, *The 2004 Corruption Perception Index*. Online. Available HTTP: http://www.transparency.org (accessed 22 January 2008).

22 Interview with Romano Prodi, Ottawa, 15 December 2002.

23 M. Kaminski and M. Nalepa, 'Introduction', Judging Transitional Justice conference, University of California at Irvine, Centre for the Study of Democracy, 30–31 October 2004. Online. Available HTTP: http://www.democ.uci.edu (accessed 14 July 2006).

24 N. Toš, et. al., 'Slovensko Javno Mnenje', *Center za Raziskovanje Javnega Mnenja in Množičnih Komunikacija*, Ljubljana: FDV: CJMMK, 1994.

25 D. Starman, 'Zakon o volitvah v državni zbor', *Uradni list*, 2001, vol. 3, 1–3; and A. Zidar, *Lustracija: izločitev nasprotnikov demokracije z javnih položajev*, Ljubljana: Nova Revija, 1996, pp. 236–237.

26 The Editors, 'Volilna zakonodaja v mlinu parlamentarnih peripetij', *Delo*, 10 September 1992.

27 F. Bučar, 'Razpisal bom volitve', *Delo*, 10 September 1992; and I. Žajedla, 'Kako je padel udbovski amandma', *Slovenec*, 11 September 1992, p. 15.

28 The issue of how to mark the graves of Slovenia's collaborationist home guards and other collaborationists who died on Slovenian territory has been vigorously debated. Unsure on how to handle the problem, the government has begun to commemorate both sides of the war. D. Reindl, 'Mass Graves from the Communist Past Haunt Slovenia's Present', *Radio Free Europe Radio Liberty*, 29 November 2001. Online. Available HTTP: http://www.encyclopedia.com/doc/1G1-80342089.html (accessed 22 January 2008).

29 'The Law on Denationalization', *Uradni List*, 1991, no. 27, and *Uradni List*, 1993, no. 31.

30 Pucnik Commission, 'Porocilo o Raziskovanju povojnihsodnih procesov', *Nova Revija*, Ljubljana, January-March 2003, pp. 16–55.

31 Pučnik, *Iz Archivov Slovenske*.

32 V. Cokl, *Vecer*, 13 October 2001. Online. Available HTTP: http://www.vecer.si (accessed 18 January 2008).

33 J. Janša, 'Predlog Zakona o Odpravi Posledic Komunisticnega totalitarnega Rezima, 5 November 1997', *Uradni list*, 1997, no. 53, and J. Janša, 'Predlog resolucije o protiprvnem delovanju komunisticnega totalitarnega rezima, 5 November 1997', *Uradni list*, 1997, no. 52.

34 J. Poglajen, 'Dnevnik Parliament', *Dnevnik*, 11 November 2001. Online. Available HTTP: http://www.dnevnik.si/novice/iskalnik?sel=advanced (accessed 20 January 2006).

35 The brigade included the Ministry of Defence, the Republic of Slovenia Brigade, and the Special Brigade (*Ministrstvo za obrambo republike Slovenije* or the MORiS). In 1993 the brigade beat and arrested Milan Smolnikar, the former Ministry of Defence security agent.

36 Ramet, 'Democratization in Slovenia—the Second Stage', p. 213.

37 Kučan won 55.57 percent of the electorate, while the leading rightist candidate Janez Podobnik won only 18 percent. Lukšič, *The Political System of the Republic of Slovenia: A Primer*, p. 14
38 Janša, 'Predlog Zakona o Odpravi Posledic', no. 53.
39 Ibid.
40 M. Kučan, 'Opinion of the President of the Republic of Slovenia, Milan Kučan, on the Proposed Law on the Dismantling of the Consequences of the Communist Totalitarian Regime and on the Proposed Resolution on the Unlawful Activities of the Communist Totalitarian Regime', National Assembly of the Republic of Slovenia, Ljubljana, 26 November 1997. Online. Available HTTP: http://www2.gov.si/up-rs/uprs_ang.nsf (accessed 5 October 2006).
41 N. Toš, *Vrednote vPrehodu II*, p. 874.
42 J. Poglajen, 'Agentje med detective', *Dnevnik*, 23 October 2002. Online. Available HTTP: http://www.dnevnik.si/novice/iskalnik?sel=advanced (accessed 20 January 2006).
43 A. Žerdin, 'Sova v vašem računalniku', *Mladina*, 8 October 2001. Online. Available HTTP: http://www.mladina.si/tednik/200140/ (accessed 20 January 2006).
44 The Director of the Archives of the Republic of Slovenia Vladimir Žumer notes that in 1976 there were more than 1,000 meters of paper of numerous microfilms. Today, there are only 212 meters of microfilms. Of these files the National Archives authenticated 40,000, with an additional 60,000 concerning economic and political emigrants and 6,000 home guards. See Odmeve, TV Slovenia, 14 May 2003.
45 In 1990, Ljerka Bizilj was the first Slovenian journalist to gain access to secret police archives. She found that the SDV relied chiefly on electronic espionage, particularly bugging and wiretapping. L. Bizlij, *Cerkev v policijskih arhivih*, Ljubljana: Cankarjeva zalozba, 1990, p. 24.
46 TV aktualno, ATV, RTV Slovenija, 22 April 2003.
47 'Zakon o Varstvu Osebnih Podadkov, 15 July 2004', *Uradni list*, 2004, no. 34. The act was amended to be consonant with the European Union Data Protection Directive and the Convention for the Protection of Individuals with Regard to Automatic Processing of Personal Data (ETS no 108). See 'Directive 95/46/EC of the European Parliament and of the Council of 24 October 1995 on the protection of individuals with regard to the processing of personal data and on the free movement of such data', *Official Journal of the European Communities*, 23 November 1995, No. L 281/31. Online. Available HTTP: http://ec.europa.eu/justice_home/fsj/privacy/docs/95-46-ce/dir1995-46_part1_en.pdf (accessed 4 October 2006).
48 *Privacy and Human Rights 2003: Slovenia*, New York, 2003. Online. Available HTTP: http://www.privacyinternational.org/survey/phr2003/countries/slovenia.htm (accessed 20 January 2008).
49 The UDBa.net mentioned that the posted files had emanated from the RSNZ Central Active Files Prior to the release of information on UDBa.net. The centre-right affiliated magazine *Demokracija* published their list of the SDV reserve troops. Jože Pučnik had already published archive materials which originated before 1950.
50 Bukovec, 'UDBa je udarila prek interneta'.
51 M. Kovač, 'Konji, zanikrni mediji in pamento ljudstvo', *Mladina*, 28 April 2003. Online. Available HTTP: http://www.mladina.si/tednik/200140/ (accessed 2 February 2008); and The Editors, 'Nove razsežnosti afere', *Mladina*, 1 August 2003. Online. Available HTTP: http://www.mladina.si/tednik/200331/ (both accessed 20 January 2006).
52 Bukovec, 'UDBa je udarila prek interneta'.
53 The Editors, 'Udbino EVidenco sem spravil v računalnik', *Mladina,* 25 May 2003. Online. Available HTTP: http://www.mladina.si/tednik/200321/ (accessed 20 January 2006).
54 D. S. Lajovic, *Med svobodo in rdečo zvezdo*, Ljubljana: Nova obzorja, 2003, p. 14.
55 Z. Savin, 'UDBa in cenzura', *Mladina* (18 April 2003). Online. Available HTTP: http://www.mladina.si/tednik/200315/ (accessed 20 January 2006).

56 Lajovic, *Med svobodo in rdečo zvezdo*, p. 14.
57 Z. Savin, 'Odzivi na www.UDBa.net', *Mladina* (23 April 2003). Online. Available HTTP: http://www.mladina.si/tednik/200316/ (accessed 20 January 2006).
58 J. Sever, 'Usodna UDBa', *Mladina* (28 April 2003). Online. Available HTTP: http://www.mladina.si/tednik/200317/ (accessed 20 January 2006).
59 A. Zerdin, 'Udobski dosiji', *Mladina* (26 July 1993). Online. Available HTTP: http://www.mladina.si/tednik/200330/ (accessed 20 January 2006); and Z. Jelinčič and P. Dobrajc, 'Teze za zakon o uničenju dosjejev obveščevalnih služb 1993', *Drzavni zbor Republike Slovenije*, 1993, no. 211.
60 Sever, 'Usodna UDBa'.
61 U. Matoš, 'Politika z UDBa.net', *Mladina*, 26 May 2003. Online. Available HTTP: http://www.mladina.si/tednik/200321/ (accessed 20 January 2006).
62 G. Cerar and I. Mekina, 'Pravica do zasebnosti', *Mladina*, 5 May 2003. Online. Available HTTP: http://www.mladina.si/tednik/200318/ (accessed 20 January 2006).
63 The owner of the internet page was Srirama Associates Ltd. located in Thailand. In early 2008, the UDBa.net was a portal for mortgage, tax, travel, and other services.
64 M. Kovač, 'Konji, zanikrni mediji in pamento ljudstvo', *Mladina*, 26 April 2003. Online. Available HTTP: http://www.mladina.si/tednik/200317/ (accessed 20 January 2006).
65 The commission was set up in 1993. See Republic of Slovenia, 'Komisijo za nadzor nad delom varnostnih in obveščevalnih služb', *Uradni list*, 1993, no. 12.
66 On the agenda in the Oversight Committee meeting were the "problematic files of the SDV and evidence files on the Internet." Jozev Jerovsek presided, Minister for Internal Affairs Rado Bohinc and SOVA Director Iztok Podbregar came to provide background. See The Editors, 'V parlimentarni "tihi sobi" o uničenih dosjejih nekdanje SDV in aferi UDBa.net?', *Mladina*, 6 June 2003. Online. Available HTTP: http://www.mladina.si/tednik/200322/ (accessed 20 January 2006); and Komisija za nadzor nad dellom obvescevalnih in varnotnih sluzb, *zaprta seja*, 25 April 2003 and 13 May 2003.
67 The Editors, 'O aferi UDBa.net', *Mladina*, 24 April 2003. Online. Available HTTP: http://www.mladina.si/tednik/200316/ (accessed 20 January 2006).

10   The former Soviet Union

Lavinia Stan

Compared with its Eastern European satellites, the former Soviet Union had a surprisingly early start at transitional justice. As early as 1987, Mikhail Gorbachev's policy *glasnost* (openness) "shattered the hitherto unchallenged certainties of the past"[1] and helped to "remove the blank spots of history"[2] by allowing Soviet citizens to call for a reevaluation of the darkest moments of the communist past before citizens in Eastern Europe could even hope to do so. In its quest for transparency and legitimacy, some of the new party leaders distanced themselves from their predecessors by encouraging the public to denounce the abuses of past Soviet regimes. An important grassroots organization set up in 1987 was Memorial, concerned with history and political symbols, engaged in discovering and revealing the truth, and dedicated to preserving the memory of the victims of successive waves of Soviet repression. With over 120 regional chapters in Russia, Ukraine, Belarus, and the Baltic states, Memorial prepared *Books of Memory* including the names and biographies of victims in different regions. In total, the books present fewer than one million of the four million victims of the Great Terror, but they represent a powerful tool in keeping the memory of those sacrificed alive for future generations.[3] By 1991, when the Soviet Union disintegrated and the communist regime officially collapsed, citizens in those countries had become increasingly aware of Stalin's reign of terror and increasingly willing to openly recount their own harrowing personal accounts of life under the hammer and sickle.[4]

Early start did not guarantee long-term commitment to confront the memory of communist human rights abuses, sort the torturers from the tortured, hold communist decision-makers accountable for their actions, or allow citizens to know the details of secret political police operations directed against them. Indeed, with the notable exception of the three Baltic states – which effected lustration, secret file access, and court proceedings – the other republics of the former Soviet Union maintained a rather disappointing transitional justice record. The wave of social enthusiasm for reckoning with the communist past dissipated in the early 1990s, as these countries faced economic hardship and political instability, and the Soviet Union disintegrated. None of these republics brought communist party leaders and secret agents to justice, allowing instead these unsavory characters to control the post-communist political process. None of these countries publicly opened the collections of secret documents left at their disposal by KGB agents withdrawing to Moscow. And none saw it necessary to ban former communist decision-makers from post-communist politics. Parliaments in Russia, Ukraine, Georgia, and Moldova registered lustration proposals only to set them aside without any rigorous examination or to defeat them on moral, political or technical grounds.

A combination of factors accounts for the wide disparity between former Soviet republics, the uniqueness of the Baltic experience in the Soviet space, and the handicap of Russia, Ukraine, Belarus, Moldova, and the countries in the Caucasus and Central Asia relative to Eastern Europe in terms of reassessing the past. The controlled transitional justice encouraged by Gorbachev made a lasting imprint on successor republics by placing transitional justice on the shoulders of the society, not of the state, by privileging truth telling, not justice and redress, and by disconnecting political reforms from the need to reassess the past, to make a clear break with it, and to reign in secret intelligence services. Indeed, it was for the mass media and the civic groups to uncover instances of past abuse, document Stalinist repression, map the geography of the Gulag, and identify victims and victimizers. All these efforts were conducted under the tolerating but watchful eye of communist authorities of a reformist persuasion, who encouraged self-expression and public debate, while believing that glasnost should "function like a high-octane social fuel; it would rev up the existing institutions and enable them to perform better."[5] Revisiting the past was not meant to destroy the communist system, but to make it more viable and more competitive relative to its rival, democracy, and more legitimate in the eyes of the Soviet people and of the larger world. Probing the past was to be done only to the extent that it helped Gorbachev achieve such goals, without compelling him to change the system at its core, discard it in favor of democracy, or refashion the very institution that had been responsible for instilling fear, quashing dissent, and preventing citizens from speaking their mind. Indeed, the structure of the feared secret police was left untouched by Gorbachev, as was its special relationship with the dominant Communist Party. Truth telling never went so far as to encompass the very real and direct connection between Stalin's and Gorbachev's secret political police structures.

The vast majority of states employing transitional justice methods have been new democracies. Eastern European countries – even Hungary, which experienced "communism with a human face" – had to wait for the 1989 regime change to be able to revisit their recent past. The Soviet Union is a rare instance of a non-democracy seeking redress. True, Gorbachev's rule was more reformist and milder than that of Idi Amin, the dictator who, at the pressure of the international community, set up in 1974 the first truth commission to investigate the actions of his own government, with predictable results. For this reason, the process of coming to terms with the past had better chances to succeed in the Soviet Union than in Uganda. But one should be mindful of the fact that Gorbachev had no desire or willingness to pursue this path beyond his own limited, iconoclastic, short-term goals.[6]

Year 1991 marked the disintegration of the Soviet Union and the collapse of the communist regime in that part of the world, two distinct processes relevant for how transitional justice unfolded. With the exception of the Baltic states, the collapse of communism brought only limited regime change: the communist elite reproduced itself, asserting control over politics and economics, while the political police split into several intelligence services inheriting its personnel, methods, and goals. Elster pointed out this very fact, when he wrote that the Soviet Union's "most important moment of coming to terms with the past occurred during the process of destalinization, rather than in the later process of decommunization" that followed 1991, because "this was a within-regime change rather than a regime transition."[7] The disintegration of the Soviet colonial empire meant that successor republics remained dependent on Russia in more ways than they initially envisioned. Much of their post-Soviet politics has been conducted with Moscow in mind, sometimes in vocal opposition and defiance to their former master (as in the Baltic states), sometimes in silent submission to it (as in Central Asia), and yet at other times in search of a precarious and illusory middle ground (as in Moldova or Ukraine). The evacuation of most of the secret archive to Moscow meant that successor republics other than Russia could not employ public access to secret files as a method of reckoning with the recent past. The lack of direct access to the totality of the secret files has hampered the identification of former KGB collaborators, a process that is key to marginalizing them politically. Also, the fact that many former NKVD and KGB agents have Russian citizenship has impeded republican courts to bring these individuals to justice.

The many faces of the KGB

After the 1917 Revolution, Russia and then the Soviet Union had a succession of intelligence and security services protecting the country's leaders against domestic and external threats. Pre-communist elites were purged, opposition of any stripe was swiftly crushed, religious denominations and independent groups were disbanded, and torture, mass arrests and summary executions were widely employed. The Extraordinary Commission for Combating Counter-Revolution, Speculation and Sabotage (the Cheka) was set up under the leadership of Feliks Dzerzhinsky to defend the revolution and the Bolshevik leaders by any means possible. Cheka's three-man courts (*troikas*) carried out the extra-judicial reprisals associated with the Red Terror that led to the execution of between 100,000 and 500,000 people. In 1922 the Cheka was replaced by the State Political Administration (*Gosudarstvennoe Politicheskoe Upravlenie* or GRU), that in turn gave way in 1934 to the People's Commissariat for Internal Affairs (*Narodniy komissariat vnutrennikh del* or the NKVD), responsible for political repression during the Stalin era. The feared NKVD ran the Gulag system of forced labor and prison camps, conducted purges and mass extrajudicial executions, persecuted the *kulaks* (peasants) resisting collectivization and forced land confiscation, deported entire national groups, and set up the political police of satellite communist countries. Historians still debate the total numbers of those who died or were affected by the repression campaigns. It is estimated that around 8–12 million people were deported or interned in the Gulag in 1937–1938, and other seven million were executed between 1935 and 1945.[8]

After Stalin's death, the Committee for State Security (*Komitet Gosudarstvennoy Bezopasnosti* or the KGB) assumed domestic and external intelligence functions under the supervision of the Council of Ministers. While Stalin controlled security services single-handedly, his successors did it in a more collegial fashion. Russians still controlled the top KGB leadership, but efforts were made to recruit candidates from other ethnic groups. The scope of repression diminished as communism matured, the party leadership felt less threatened, and a social contract was forged with the population. As a result, the KGB was less inclined to use sheer force, arbitrary arrests and imprisonment to quell dissent, preferring instead to convince, misrepresent, and manipulate. Its responsibilities remained broad, ranging from the traditional missions of intelligence and counterintelligence to the regime's political security and control of all forms of expression. A measure of socialist legality was introduced in the activity of secret security services that continued, nevertheless, to operate in complete secrecy, answering to no one save top political leaders.[9] The Communist Party distanced itself from much of the legacy of Stalin, who was accused of past excesses, but this selective rewriting of history occurred without significant public participation.[10]

Thought to number 720,000 during the Soviet Union's heyday,[11] the KGB full-time officer corps developed in a closed, privileged and feared group of regime enforcers who together made up the most efficient secret organization of its time, and probably one of the best that ever existed. In the 1970s Yury Andropov reinvigorated the KGB and instilled a new sense of mission and pride following the partial exposure in the 1950s of the crimes committed by the secret police under Lenin and Stalin. In the 1980s, however, nepotism and entrepreneurialism threatened to compromise the quality of the information network. Nepotism was rampant among officers, who recruited and promoted their relatives regardless of their personal qualifications. Taking advantage of the weakness of the Soviet top political leadership, the KGB also pursued its own bureaucratic interest to a larger extent than it could under the all-controlling Stalin. Gorbachev encouraged the rehabilitation of exiled individuals, opened up Soviet history to public discussion and evaluation, but left the KGB structure intact.

As any other communist political police, the KGB employed a vast network of part-time collaborators drawn from all walks of life, an information network thought to number some 2.9 million across the Soviet Union, roughly one percent of the total population.[12] Following the 1983 Statute on the System of Agents and Trusted Persons of the Soviet KGB, secret collaborators could act as agents, residents, safe house owners or trustees. In 1954 the KGB was prohibited from monitoring and recruiting nomenklatura members such as the secretaries of party and Komsomol organizations, officials of the party apparatus, political officers of the Soviet armed forces, members of the Soviet legislature, and trade union officials. The KGB was free to recruit citizens outside the party as well as regular party members on the basis of misguided patriotism, financial rewards or coercion. As a result, the secret police succeeded in infiltrating its agents in the media, religious and academic circles, and public organizations.

In August 1991, the KGB, the Communist Party, and the Soviet Union became the major casualties of the failed coup d'etat. Shortly after the putsch was foiled, Vadim Bakatin became the KGB commander. "The most liberal chief of any

Moscow's secret services, before or since,"[13] Bakatin fired many hard-liners and broke up the monolithic KGB into separate services. As constituent republics declared their independence, the KGB made sure to transfer to Moscow most of the secret files it had diligently compiled on the citizens of those republics. In some cases, it left behind clues (in the form of cards, documents or photos) that could suggest collaboration on the part of republican elites, but provided insufficient information to sort villains from angels. In a desperate effort to salvage the Soviet intelligence structure, Moscow signed cooperation agreements with Armenia, Belarus, Kazakhstan, Kyrgyzstan, Moldova, Tajikistan, Turkmenistan, and Ukraine in 1992 and with Georgia in 1995. In all successor republics security services have retained considerable power not tempered by constitutions. Rather than being asked to observe the law and being placed under parliamentary oversight, secret services have been used by the government against the political opposition and the independent journalists. Instead of becoming democratic agencies, security services have retained most of the functions, operations and personnel of the KGB. The Committees on National Security of Turkmenistan, Tajikistan, and Kazakhstan, the State Security Committee of Belarus, the Information and Security Service of Moldova, the Azerbaijani National Security Ministry, the Security Service of Ukraine, and the National Security Services of Uzbekistan, Kyrgyzstan and Armenia have responsibilities for national security, intelligence and counterintelligence. Only the Kyrgyz security service is led by a civilian. In all successor republics, the President appoints the security service chief.[14]

In Russia, the new security services carried over the personnel and mission of the Soviet KGB. Successor to the KGB's notorious Second Chief Directorate, the Federal Security Service (*Federalnaya Sluzhba Bezopasnosti* or the FSB) takes care of domestic security missions and border protection. Increasingly, the FSB also handles intelligence activities in the former Soviet republics. This is possible because the FSB "has probably maintained at least part of the vast network of informers that covered what was once the USSR and is today the CIS, making FSB intelligence connection in the former Soviet republics a feasible prospect."[15] With recognized links to 80 countries and offices in 18 by the 1997, the FSB rivals with its notorious and feared predecessor.[16] Foreign intelligence is the purview of the Foreign Intelligence Service (*Sluzhba Vnesheny Razvedki* or the SVR), that grew from the KGB's First Chief Directorate. Military intelligence is carried out by the Main Intelligence Directorate (*Glavnoye Razvedyvatelnoye Upravleniye* or the GRU) of the armed forces general staff, the heir to the KGB's Third Chief Directorate. The praetorian Federal Protective Service (*Federalnaya Sluzhba Okhrany* or the FSO) guards and protects top state officials, while the Federal Agency for Government Communications and Information (*Federalnoye Agenstvo Pravitelstvennykh Svyazi i Informatsii* or the FAPSI) is responsible for the national computerized election system, the security of the banking system, and control of national telecommunication lines. The Ministry of Internal Affairs (*Ministerstvo Vnutrennikh Del* or the MVD) is involved in special operations, and criminal investigations. All these agencies are militarized. Rather than being civil servants, their personnel have military ranks.

The Russian President exercises direct control over the FSB, the SVR, and the FSO, using these bodies to preserve his power. Parliamentary oversight of security services is nonexistent. The legislative committees on security, formed mostly of former army and KGB officers, discuss exclusively non-strategic matters.[17] With so many former secret agents directly involved in politics, it is not surprising that the Russian parliament routinely supports the security community, regardless of the consequences such vote has for Russian democracy. Initially, the staff of all security services was significantly reduced. For example, FSB staff levels declined from 140,000 in 1993 to 80,000 in 1997, while SVR numbers shrank to about 15,000 in the early 1990s.[18] Since then, however, all services have employed a growing number of agents and have enlarged their leadership structures, a trend reflecting the disproportionate role they play in the country.[19] By 1995, for example, the Russian MVD was already twice as large as its Soviet predecessor, employing 1.7 million men, including 800,000 troops organized in 29 divisions and 10 military districts.[20]

Russia's forgotten past

In Russia, the high point of truth telling occurred during the late 1980s under Gorbachev, when small but meaningful efforts were made to investigate Stalin-era atrocities. As both his grandparents had been deported by Stalin to Siberian labor camps, Gorbachev had a personal stake in discrediting the era in which the Gulag system was created. His denunciation of communist repression echoed the famous 1956 secret speech in which Nikita Khrushchev spoke out against Stalinism. But Gorbachev's attempt to denounce Stalin, as Khrushchev's, did not commit state resources for the quest for truth, justice and retribution.[21]

The country found it impossible to go beyond the politics of memory and embrace lustration, launch court trials against communist leaders and KGB agents, and open secret archives. Opinion polls have suggested the Russian public takes a favorable view of intelligence and security services, and the dark communist past. Polls conducted in 2002 showed that Russians viewed KGB officers as highly intelligent, professional, and trustworthy. Whereas only one in five and one in three respondents trusted the Duma and the Federation Council, respectively, more than half of all respondents trusted the FSB.[22] In 2003, one in two respondents viewed Stalin's role in Soviet history as "probably" or "definitely" positive.[23] Since 1993 the New Russian Barometer surveys have consistently showed that the majority of Russians rate the pre-perestroika political and economic systems more highly than the current ones.[24]

After former KGB officer and FSB director Vladimir Putin assumed the Russian Presidency in 2000, the massive influx of former spies in the presidential administration, the government, and regional administrations has increased governmental hostility toward coming to terms with the communist past. Sociologist Olga Kryshtanovskaya estimated that the so-called *siloviki* account for 26 percent of Russia's senior political and economic elite. That figure jumps to 78 percent, if one includes the secret part-time informers, whose identity remains closely guarded. Many Russian luminaries, including former premier Mikhail Fradkov and Russian Orthodox Patriarch Aleksy II, apparently owe their careers to decade-long collaboration with the KGB. The group's core, led by Putin, includes some 6,000 agents promoted during his two presidential terms.[25] The *siloviki* form a network of like-minded professionals, "sharing common values, a common worldview, and common approaches to problem solving," and bent on avenging the humiliation they experienced in the years immediately following the 1991 failed coup.[26] The enhanced role of former KGB agents has given impetus to the glorification of KGB operations. Scores of books present the heroism of dedicated spies, who selflessly defended their country and their people against domestic and foreign enemies. The Russian national television stations regularly rerun Soviet-era movies devoted to the KGB's glorious struggle against Western "imperialist" intelligence agencies.[27]

Lustration has never been seriously discussed, although a lustration bill was proposed as early as 1992 by Galina Starovoytova, a human rights advocate and leader of the Democratic Russia reformist party. The proposal imposed temporary restrictions on the political activity of secretaries and members of the Communist Party federal and republican committees, secretaries of rayon, oblast and city party organizations, full-time activists of the territorial and industrial party organizations, regular KGB officers and reservists whose responsibilities included political surveillance and taking repressive measures, and KGB secret collaborators involved in domestic repression who had signed a collaboration pledge. These persons were excluded from positions of responsibility in the government, from the rayon and city to national level, in education and law firms, in radio, television and the press.[28] Starovoytova was assassinated in St. Petersburg in 1998, and her proposal was set aside. Another proposed banning of former party officials from a wide rage of public positions, including management positions in universities, secondary schools, and the media, was also defeated in parliament. After the 1991 coup, Yeltsin issued several decrees banning the Communist Party and confiscating its assets. The Constitutional Court ruled that local branches of the Communist Party, but not the national organization, could be reestablished. Instead of embracing lustration, parliament made it a criminal offense to publicly identify KGB collaborators, and even classified as a "state secret" the identity of SVR "confidential collaborators."[29]

Russian citizens have been denied access to the secret files compiled on them by the former KGB. In 1991, President Yeltsin ordered the transfer of KGB and party archives to the new Russian Committee on Archives (*Roskomarkhiv*), but made no effort to have his decree implemented. The committee began declassifying sections of the party archive to make them available to the public, but the KGB archives remained in the hands of the territorial branches of security services, that had vested interests in holding onto the files. In 1992, *Roskomarkhiv* allowed security services to delay transfer of most secret archives in exchange for receiving promptly the files on rehabilitated victims. That deal was a blow to those who hoped secret archives would be opened to the public as soon as possible. The following year, American historian Amy Knight was convinced that "it is unlikely that the KGB archives will be transferred over to the Russian repositories in the near future."[30] She was right.

Also in 1991, the Russian parliament set up the Commission on the Transfer of the CPSU and KGB Archives to State Use, and appointed leading democrats as commission members. The following year, the commission proposed that victims of police persecution have the right to prevent the publication of material of a personal nature, but not to restrict access to their files by researchers. The proposal was never implemented. Soon the commission and the KGB successor services were at odds. While the commission pressed for the transfer of secret documents to the *Roskomarkhiv*, security service representatives used every possible excuse to prevent the transfer. With the backing of the Yeltsin government, they refused to give up the operational archive describing police methods and containing the informer files. The conflict stemmed from strikingly different views. On the one hand, commission member Iurii Afanasev believed that the archive belonged to the Russian people and any decision regarding its fate should serve the needs of the society, because Russians deserve to know the truth about their past. On the other hand, security services considered the archive as property of a state entitled to keep it close in order to preserve its secrets and to defend national security.

Since 1991 selected individuals have accessed selected archival documents, but no transparent policy has been adopted to facilitate secret file access for ordinary Russians. True, "The Fundamentals of Legislation of the Russian Federation on the Archival Corpus of the Russian Federation and on the Archives" was passed by the Supreme Soviet and signed by President Yeltsin on 7 July 1993. This law guaranteed equal right of access to archives to everyone without exception, whether the person was a foreigner or a Russian citizen. The law established a 30-year limit on restrictions on access to documents classified as "secret" or "top secret."[31] But the logistics of granting access to citizens have never been worked out. In addition, large parts of the archives of the Communist Party (preserved in state archives such as Archive of the President of the Russian Federation, Russian State Archive of Contemporary History, Russian State Archive of Socio-Political History and State Archive of the Russian Federation) and including almost all documents of its Central Committee, remains classified.

Lack of transparency and a deficient catalogue system have obscured the true length and content of the party and KGB archives. It is known that the secret archives include documents of police persecution of innocent citizens throughout the Soviet period, police dossiers and agent files, records of secret surveillance and copies of denunciations, and records of criminal cases investigated by the political police from the 1920s onward. This latter collection alone contains protocols of arrests, interrogations and trials on four million cases of counter-revolutionary crimes. In comparison to the secret archive produced by the much smaller East German Stasi, the entire secret archive compiled by the monumental KGB and its Soviet predecessors could stretch for tens of linear miles and include billions of documents ranging from confiscated samizdat material and annual reports filed by the secret agents to information notes provided by and receipts for money allowances given out to various informers.[32] It is also known that even before the 1991 coup, KGB leaders began to destroy sensitive material. For example, in 1989 the Second Chief Directorate was instructed to dispose of all records of persons charged for "anti-Soviet agitation and propaganda" during the Brezhnev era. The following year, the KGB began destroying its 'operative' documents, a process that continued after the 1991 coup. The loss was catastrophic, and cannot be estimated with precision. The most sensitive material, that could taint the reputation of post-communist political leaders, might have already been "lost" by secret agents interested to use it as a future bargaining chip.

To date, Russian courts have heard no cases of former Communist Party officials or secret NKVD or KGB agents involved in human rights abuses during the Soviet era, although Russia had probably the bitterest record of political persecution, given its prolonged communist rule, whose start predated the advent of communism in other countries. Given the old age of the possible defendants, such court trials are becoming less feasible as time goes by. In a perverse turn of events, in 1995 the FSB brought charges against former KGB captain Viktor Orekov, who had spent seven years in a labor camp for warning dissidents of arrest.[33] Disillusioned with its country's loss of international standing, eroding living standards, and prolonged political instability, the resigned Russian public has seemingly forgotten or buried its recent past. It remains to be seen if future generations will be as willing to forgive communist torturers for their human rights trespasses.

Transitional justice in the Baltic States

Among former Soviet republics, Latvia, Lithuania, and Estonia stand apart because of their willingness to pursue transitional justice expeditiously and vigorously. In spite of the numerous hurdles they had to overcome in their quest for truth and justice, these three tiny republics succeeded in employing lustration, file access and court trials as transitional justice methods. Overall, however, the Baltic experience of coming to terms with communist human rights transgressions stands in sharp contrast to that of Eastern Europe. These latter countries could make their secret files available to the public because those files were produced by their own indigenous secret services. By contrast, the Baltic states fell within the jurisdiction of the Soviet KGB, which took with it a large part of the Estonian, Latvian, and, to a lesser extent, Lithuanian secret files, as the Soviet Union began to disintegrate and the KGB withdrew. Since the Baltic countries had no access to the bulk of the secret records, they had to identify collaborators by other means in order to understand the extent of the KGB's penetration of their societies. Soon after gaining independence, Estonia and Latvia asked collaborators to come forward and register themselves. Lithuania took longer to address the role of collaborators because there the Communist Party transformed into a major political force.[34]

All Baltic republics introduced bans on former KGB agents and collaborators holding high public office, mostly because the secret operatives had been directly responsible for the annexation of their territories by the USSR, and both during and immediately after the restoration of independence they posed direct threats to the sovereignty of these states.[35] Lithuania, where the Russians never constituted more than one-tenth of the total population, limited the role of former Soviet decision-makers only through lustration laws. It granted citizenship to every person irrespective of ethnic background wishing to accept it and residing permanently on the territory of Lithuania at the time of independence. By contrast, Latvia and Estonia adopted stringent citizenship laws that excluded from public life large segments of the population, mainly ethnic minorities considered untrustworthy because of their involvement with the former occupying power. While citizenship laws defined who qualified as citizens, the constitutions granted the right to vote and to be voted to citizens only. Lustration was not necessary for political advancement in either Estonia or Latvia because there "the reformed communist parties did not represent a serious challenge to anticommunist political forces."[36]

The problem of how to handle former KGB collaborators caused immediate concern following Lithuania's declaration of independence of March 1990. On 12 October 1991, the government banned former KGB officers and collaborators from holding positions in the local and national government for five years, while on 17 December parliament asked candidates to disclose their past connections to the KGB and the Communist Party.[37] Those holding such positions were required to resign by the end of the year. A special parliamentary commission chaired by deputy Balys Gajauskas was called to review the information contained in the available secret KGB files in order to ascertain past collaboration of elected representatives. The verdicts handed down by the commission could be appealed in the Supreme Court in the case of a deputy or in a regional court in the case of a local or regional councilor. If the verdict was upheld, the elected body had to suspend the mandate of the accused and organize a recall election within 30 days. During its investigations, the commission unmasked former premier Kazimira Pruskiene, deputies Vergilijus Cepaitis and Jakubas Minkevicius, and party leaders Vladimir Berezov and Eduardas Vilkas as former secret collaborators.[38] Despite a requirement that all candidates publicly disclose their past, presumably in order to prevent electors to vote in favor of untainted individuals, the October 1992 parliamentary elections were won by the successor to the Lithuanian Communist Party, the Lithuanian Democratic Labor Party.[39] Lustration was thus blocked.

The 1998 presidential election brought the issue of past collaboration with the KGB to the forefront. After independent deputy Audrius Butkevicius referred in parliament to a book by KGB General Vyacheslav Shironin, *Under Counterintelligence's Surveillance*, that alleged that presidential candidate Vytautas Landsbergis was a KGB informer, the chair of the parliamentary commission investigating parliament members' ties to foreign secret services interviewed four former KGB officers who all claimed that Landsbergis was a KGB informer in the late 1950s and early 1960s. This testimony was not supported by any documentation. After the minutes of the interviews were published in the press, Landsbergis denied the charge and his Homeland Unity (Conservative) allies pointed out that the father of independent presidential candidate Arturas Paulauskas was a KGB general. Following the scandal, parliament amended the Law on Presidential Elections to oblige candidates to inform the Electoral Commission about their cooperation "with the NKVD, NKGB, MGB, and KGB services of the USSR and former Soviet republics, as well as with similar services of other foreign states, about training received at the schools of these services or collaboration with those services." Collaboration did not disqualify a candidate from the electoral race, but that person had to inform voters about its nature, scope, and duration. If a candidate concealed pertinent information, the Electoral Commission could take legal action.[40]

In November 1998 a parliament not controlled by the former communists adopted the Law on the Registration, Recognition, Reporting and Protection of Identified Persons Who Secretly Collaborated with the Former Special Services of the USSR. Initiated by the ruling Conservatives, the law asked former KGB agents to register with and disclose their past activity to a special commission within 18 months of the law's adoption if they wished to have their identity protected. The names of former agents who concealed their past were made public, if their past collaboration was demonstrated. The law further barred former secret agents from practicing law, from working in the security services, the banking system, education, mass media, and private detective agencies, or from assuming management positions in state-owned firms for a ten-year period.[41] The Center for Research into People's Genocide and Resistance of Lithuania and the State Security Department could jointly recommend the suspension of lustration against former spies who revealed everything about their former links to the KGB. After considering the recommendation, a three-person commission appointed by the President of the Republic could make a favorable decision. Lustration procedures were suspended if that decision was confirmed by the President.

Instead of promulgating the law, President Valdas Adamkus asked, and deputies agreed, to postpone its implementation and instead allow the Constitutional Court to examine its constitutionality.[42] The court was unable to rule before the law went into effect on 1 January 1999.[43] When asked to appoint the members of the lustration commission the law provided for, President Adamkus chose to wait for the court's verdict. The commission was to decide which former KGB agents were exempt from the legislation.[44] Faced with the President's unwillingness to allow the launching of lustration proceedings, the government released a list of jobs from which former KGB employees were barred under the lustration law, and amended the Criminal Code to provide for fines for employers who refused to fire former KGB agents from those positions. The list included the Lithuanian Railways, the strategically important, state-run Ignalina Nuclear Power Plant and Klaipeda port, some electricity and energy suppliers, air traffic control, and communications, oil and gas utilities.[45]

In March 1999, the Constitutional Court found the lustration law constitutional,[46] but struck down the exemption provisions that empowered the President not to recommend the suspension of the lustration procedure and thus to restrict individual constitutional rights, a privilege enjoyed only by parliament, under the constitution. The court further rejected claims that lustration allowed for criminal sanctions to be meted out by non-judicial bodies, that it denied the presumption of innocence, and that it violated the constitutional right to a free choice of occupation because it excluded certain persons from certain positions. The court found the requirement for loyalty and credibility in connection to service in a state office "common and understandable," and extended this argument to positions in private enterprises and occupations such as private lawyer or notary. As observers noted, the court "expressed an extremely high level of deference to the legislature thus largely giving it *carte blanche* to determine any position in society – public or private – as being of sufficiently high importance to warrant the exclusion of ex-secret service persons."[47] The court decision allowed the lustration commission, which included representatives of the Lithuanian Genocide and Resistance Center and the Committee for National Security, to resume its work.[48] By November that year, the commission had investigated 303 cases, and ordered 87 people to resign their jobs. Five of the 20 persons who appealed in court won their cases.[49] Within the first 18 months of activity, the commission was approached by 1,500 former secret agents.[50] In virtue of the law, the Prosecutor-General suspended six prosecutors tied to the KGB.[51]

That month, dissatisfaction with the lustration legislation prompted parliament to adopt a new law providing for the registration of persons who confessed to their ties to Soviet secret services during the 1940–1990 period. Self-declared former KGB agents were guaranteed protection and confidentiality of their past, unless they were elected or nominated for the posts of President, deputy, member of national or local government, prosecutor and judge. Former secret agents had until 1 July 2000 to report their past to the special commission and complete a form at the Committee of National Security.[52] Observers hoped the law will set the historical record straight, but warned that from a practical viewpoint it came too late to limit the political and economic influence of former spies.[53] The law's implementation depended on the identification of former KGB spies. While some observers argued that this identification was impossible, given the fact that large portions of the former secret archive remained closed to Lithuanian authorities, others argued that the identities could be known either from the extant KGB files or from testimonials provided by victims and other collaborators.[54]

In 2005, a Lithuanian mass-media campaign alleged that more than 5,000 former KGB agents were still active politically, while the Committee on National Security estimated that the total of former KGB agents living in Lithuania reached some 15,000.[55] In response, parliament revisited the lustration issue when Liberal and Center Union deputies Algis Caplikas and Vytautas Cepas proposed the setting up of another parliamentary commission to finalize the prompt exploration of "the country's KGB problems."[56] Two years later, parliament accepted a new law allowing former KGB employees, reservists and informers to voluntarily register and acknowledge collaboration with Soviet secret services in order to have their identity protected. In October 2007, a new scandal irrupted when a former officer identified only as Damulis alleged that the Committee of National Security issued work permits for the Lithuanian Ministry of Foreign Affairs without consulting the Lustration Commission. The ministry defended itself by saying that it knew of no former KGB spies infiltrated within its ranks. Parliament launched investigations into the case, but instead of scrutinizing the activity of the Committee of

National Security, it dismissed the chair of the lustration commission for unclear reasons. No lustration cases have been examined since then.[57]

The Vilnius International Public Tribunal on the Evaluation of Communist Crimes held public hearings from June to September 2000 in the presence of experts from Latvia, Estonia, the United States, Slovakia, Albania, Bulgaria, Hungary, and Ukraine. The tribunal established that the communist regime of 1941–1953 engaged in genocide, as a result of which 444,200 fled to the West, 132,000 people were exiled, 20,000 were killed in the resistance movement, and 1,000 others were executed. The total loss of population amounted to some 780,000 individuals, more than one-third of Lithuania's total population of three million in 1939. Only a fraction of the Soviet-era victims still survive. In 2002, for example, the Union of Exiles and Prisoners, representing victims of communist repression, had some 15,400 members.[58]

Similar to Estonia and Lithuania, Latvia bans former KGB agents from local and national government, but lacks the political consensus to legislate the registration and self-identification of former collaborators.[59] Latvia effected lustration primarily through its elections laws. The 1994 law barred former Soviet secret agents and Communist Party members from running in general and local elections, while a 1995 law barred candidates who had remained active Communist Party members after 13 January 1991, Latvia's day of independence, presumably because party membership demonstrated loyalty to the Soviet communist regime more than to the newly independent Latvian democracy. That year, several Socialist Party candidates who opposed Latvia's declaration of independence were accused of covering up their past, while the Constitutional Court deemed the 1995 law inconsistent with Article 69 of the Latvian Constitution, which compelled the President "to proclaim laws passed by parliament not earlier than the seventh day and not later than the twenty-first day after the law has been adopted."[60] In November 1996 parliament adopted a new law restricting anyone associated with the communist regime from running in the March 1997 local elections. In spite of this plethora of legislative initiatives, lustration has remained limited by lack of sufficient evidence to unmask former secret agents.[61]

On 3 March 2000 the Riga City Zemgale District Court ruled that Social Democratic Workers' Party deputy Janis Adamsons had collaborated with the KGB while he served as a Soviet border guard political and intelligence officer from 1981 to 1992. The case was the first in which parliament considered to revoke a deputy's mandate on the basis of the lustration rule denying former KGB agents the right to serve as deputies. Parliament refused to revoke the mandate unless the court provided all relevant information proving Adamsons' involvement with the KGB. The past came to haunt Adamsons again before the 2002 general elections, when his name was excluded from the electoral party lists for the same reason. On 20 August 2002, the deputy lost his appeal to seek reelection when the Riga Central District Court found that the Election Commission acted properly when it struck his name from the ballot in virtue of the lustration rule preventing former KGB agents from running in elections.[62] After the Latvian Supreme Court upheld the decision, Adamsons petitioned the European Court of Human Rights.

The court heard his case alongside that of Tatjana Zhdanoka, the leader of the leftist For Human Rights in a United Latvia party and a former elected member of the Riga City Council, who had been barred from participating in the 2002 poll because she remained an active Communist Party member after 13 January 1991. Known as the "iron lady of the opposition," Zhdanoka has been a staunch defender of the rights of Latvia's Russian minority. In June 2004, the European Court ordered Latvia to pay 20,000 Euros to Zhdanoka. The European Parliament Election Law of January 2003 removed some restrictions, allowing Latvians who remained secret agents or Communist Party members after 13 January 1991 to run for the European Parliament. Adamsons' case, still pending before the European Court, will likely lead to a similar decision.[63]

Estonia reduced the political influence of former KGB secret agents and Soviet Communist Party leaders with the help of citizenship and lustration laws passed in 1995. The citizenship law denied Estonian citizenship to Russian ethnics, many of whom had occupied high-ranking positions in the Soviet communist system, and to anyone who had worked in the intelligence or security service of a foreign state. As of 8 June 1996, 41 persons were refused residence and work permits because they had a criminal record, were former KGB employees, or gave false information about themselves. Further restrictions were introduced by the lustration law, which required people who collaborated with the Nazi and Soviet security services or the Communist Party to register with the Estonian security service within a year. The information they supplied was confidential. Those who did not comply were banned from holding high public office until 2002. Local observers considered the lustration law a success, not because it stirred a catharsis of the society, but because it allowed collaborators to put the past behind them. As almost no KGB files were left in Estonia, the identification process was purely voluntary, but as many as 1153 former spies came forward. By 2004, the names of 250 former spies who concealed their past were published in the official journal, *Riigi Teataja*.[64]

Access to KGB files by ordinary citizens has been hampered by the 1991 transfer to Moscow of large segments of the KGB secret archives of Lithuania, Latvia and Estonia. Since then, Russian authorities have ignored pleas for the return of secret documents to the Baltic states, agreeing to turn over copies of only a limited number of secret files to Lithuania. Only the KGB knew how large the original secret archive was, what it consisted of, and which parts were transferred, removed or destroyed. As such, there is uncertainty regarding the collections left behind in the three independent republics. As Estonia has almost no secret archives at its disposal, the information concerning the actions of former Communist Party leaders and KGB agents is not available and incriminating material is believed to have been destroyed.

The Latvian Center for the Documentation of the Consequences of Totalitarianism keeps the 5,000 file cards the KGB left behind. Because the cards specify just the names of secret agents, additional data is needed to uncover the role of the informers and the reasons behind their collaboration. More importantly, the cards do not include the names of the Communist Party apparatchiks, whose files were normally destroyed. Because the archive is incomplete, in 1995 parliament rejected a proposal to permit public access to the KGB agent files.[65] In 2004 President Vaira Vike-Freiberga asked for the KGB files to remain closed until 2014.

In Lithuania, most of the files transferred to Moscow were located in the KGB headquarters in Vilnius, and were agent files detailing the activities of secret collaborators. The files in the provincial KGB branches in Lithuania, the files of the KGB victims, together with copies of the reports prepared for the KGB director, and highly detailed "work notebooks" remained largely intact and safeguarded.[66] The first shipment alone reportedly included 2,400 different boxes containing 31,241 screening files and 11,558 interrogation files. In November 1992, the Lithuanian parliament declared the KGB files to be part of the Lithuanian 'national heritage', barring their destruction or removal from the country.[67] Careful study of all these documents, some of them published in local newspapers, has disclosed the network of informers and agents active in Lithuania.

The Baltic republics brought to court several communist-era torturers. The majority of those convicted were former NKVD agents involved in the deportation of hundreds of thousands of Lithuanians, Latvians, and Estonians to Siberia in the 1940s. The first wave of deportations, targeting mostly political, business and military leaders, occurred in 1941. Almost 80 percent of those deportees died in exile. The second wave started in March 1949 and targeted mostly relatives of those deported in the early 1940s. One in five deportees belonging to this wave perished in Siberia before living conditions improved after Stalin's death in 1953. According to official estimates, 14,484 people were deported from Latvia in 1941 and an additional 40,000 in 1949.[68] Some 20,498 were deported from Estonia in 1949.[69] Because defendants were in their seventies and in poor health condition, and because the purpose of the trials was not to bring perpetrators to justice but to help surviving victims to overcome the past, sentences were shortened or pardoned. Note that no charges were laid against the Soviet Communist Party officials who masterminded the deportations.

Several individuals were convicted of Soviet-era deportations in Latvia and Estonia. The most significant trial was that of the 87-year-old Alfons Noviks, the head of the NKVD Latvian branch from 1940 to 1953, accused of helping organize the deportation of over 60,000 persons. Though he claimed to have followed orders and not remember the events, Noviks was sentenced to life imprisonment, but he died after spending just one year in prison. Another high-profile case was that of the 84-year-old Mikhail Farbtukh, a former NKVD agent who received a seven-year prison term for collecting information on potential "enemies of the state" slated for deportation. A medical panel recommended his release from prison on medical grounds and his lawyers asked for a presidential pardon, but Farbtukh remained in prison. The judges ruled he did not suffer from new ailments, a legal condition for early release, while the presidency pointed out that Latvian law requires that inmates serve at least half of their term before becoming eligible for presidential clemency. In 2001, the 80-year-old Nikolai Tess was convicted for signing in 1949 the deportation orders for 138 persons whose ages ranged from five months to 80 years. As Tess held a Russian passport, Russia criticized Latvia for launching court proceedings against "helpless ... disabled war veterans" who could not be held accountable for actions that were not illegal at the time under Soviet law.[70] In Estonia the first successful convictions related to Soviet-era deportations occurred in 1999 when two NKVD officers, the 78-year-old Johannes Klaassepp and the 80-year-old Vassili Beskov, were sentenced each to eight years jail time on probation for the deportation of 23 and 210 people, respectively, in 1949.[71] Other NKVD agents given prison terms were 79-year-old Mikhail Neverovsky, who was sentenced to four years in jail in 1999, and 81-year-old Yuri Karpov, who received an eight-year prison term.

Charges have also been laid against those responsible for the death of anticommunist resistance fighters after these countries' annexation by the Soviet Union. From 1944 to 1953, some 50,000 army officers fought Soviet invaders in Lithuania. Around 20,000 of them were killed in battles with the Soviet regular army and NKVD units. Small groups continued this fight up until 1956. In 1999, after much procrastination due to the defendants' refusal to show up in court, Lithuanian courts convicted Stalin-era NKVD agents Kiril Kurakin, Petras Bartasevicius, and Juozas Sakalys to sentences ranging from three to six years for murder and violence committed during the late 1940s. Court proceedings against 70 other individuals suspected of involvement in Soviet-era mass killings of Lithuanians were launched the following year, after Criminal Code amendments allowed individuals accused of genocide to be tried in absentia.[72] As a result, the courts sentenced former NKVD colonel Petras Raslanas in absentia to life imprisonment for participating in the June 1941 massacre of 76 Telsiai jail prisoners tortured and decapitated at the order of the NKVD in the face of advancing Nazi troops.[73] Raslanas denied the accusations, but instead of pleading his innocence he fled to Russia. Because Raslanas carried a Russian passport, Russia declined requests for his extradition. In 2005 Estonian courts convicted the 76-year-old Karl-Leonhard Paulov, who received an eight-year suspended prison term for shooting three anti-Soviet guerillas. Russian officials have strongly criticized Estonia for exacting revenge on an ailing, elderly man.[74] In Latvia, Vassily Kononov was convicted to a suspended prison term of 20 months for ordering the killing of nine civilians during World War II.

Lithuania became the first former Soviet republic to bring a former KGB agent to justice when Algis Klimaitis was arrested in 1992 following the publication in the local press of secret documents filed by an agent code-named "Kliugeris." The foreign affairs advisor to Prime Minister Pruskiene, Klimaitis alias Kliugeris was a leader of the Baltic Group in the European Parliament, in which capacity he sought to delay diplomatic recognition of independent Lithuania.[75] While all post-communist countries have used court trials rather sparingly, it is surprising to note that none of the Baltic states launched trials for crimes occurring between the deportations of the 1940s and the calls for independence of 1991.[76]

Limited transitional justice

In Moldova, Ukraine, and Georgia lustration proposals were introduced more than a decade after these republics gained independence, only to be rejected by parliaments reluctant to effect belated transitional justice. Secret archives have remained close to ordinary citizens, and no Communist Party official or KGB agent has been brought to trial for involvement in Soviet-era human rights abuses. As in other parts of the Soviet Union, the record of such abuses is long and troublesome, but of no immediate concern for the society or the political elite. Apart from occasional calls to ban the Communist Party, to remove communist symbols from the public space, or to recognize historical events as acts of genocide or crimes against humanity, the past has seemingly been forgotten and no longer divides these societies.

Ethnic conflict, regional cleavages, and the continued influence of Soviet elites have delayed the process of coming to terms with the past in these republics. In the early 1990s, Moldova faced violent conflict between its Romanian-speaking majority, desiring reunification with neighboring Romania, and its Russian-speaking groups, seeking rapprochement with Moscow. In the process, the predominantly Russian-speaking region of Transnistria gained de facto independence from Chisinau. Georgia was marred by political instability resulted from the separatist claims of South Ossetia and Abkhazia, loyal to Kremlin, and the war in the Russian republic of Chechnya, Georgia's northern neighbor. Ukraine has been divided between its prosperous Western regions and its economically disadvantaged eastern regions. Lustration would predominantly affect the eastern regions, where collaboration was widespread, and further increase tensions with that region's political elites. In addition, communist elites have remained highly influential in all three republics. In Moldova former Soviet Communist Party officials Petru Lucinschi and Vladimir Voronin have served as Presidents since 1996, and the Communist Party has retained a majority in parliament. In 1992, Gorbachev's Foreign Minister Eduard Shevardnadze became chairman of the Georgian state council, after Georgia's first democratically-elected President Zviad Gamsakhurdia was deposed in a military coup. Shevardnadze was elected in 1995 and 2000, but had to resign after the 2003 parliamentary election. In Ukraine, transitional justice was not in the cards as long as Leonid Kuchma, a former Soviet Communist Party leader, was President of the republic.

Moldova was the first of these republics to debate a lustration proposal, introduced in parliament in 2000 by deputies representing the Popular Party Christian Democrat, heir to the Popular Front, the artisan of Moldova's independence. The bill allowed Moldovans to access their NKVD and KGB secret files, and banned former secret agents from the presidency, parliament, cabinet, the judiciary, and mass-media. In presenting the bill, Christian Democrat deputy Stefan Secareanu lamented the fact that former spies were "in control of [important] economic sectors" and were "blackmailing" politicians with a tainted past. As though to confirm Secareanu's remark, on 31 May 2001 the Communist Party parliamentary majority rejected the bill that would have ended the political careers of many of its members.[77]

After the Orange Revolution of 2005, the new All Ukrainian Union "Fatherland" government drafted two lustration bills banning from public office Soviet-era Communist Party and Communist Youth Union leaders, collaborators of intelligence services of foreign countries, and individuals who participated in the rigging of the 2004 presidential poll.[78] Observers noted that neither legislative proposal had chances to be adopted. They were right. While insisting that Ukraine must know its Soviet past in depth, President Viktor Yushchenko declared that the time for lustration had passed because neither the Ukrainian people nor the political elite supported it.[79] Yushchenko's position was echoed by Justice Minister Roman Zvarych, who opposed lustration for violating human rights and threatened to ask the President to veto lustration, if parliament adopted it.[80] This opposition to lustration stemmed from the government's belief that the Orange Revolution gave it the mandate to remove Kuchma's supporters without resorting to a controversial method like lustration. In 2005 "a wide-ranging and unprecedented in its scale wave of dismissals of provincial and rayon-level governors, security chiefs, and administrators" was under way, a purge that also affected law enforcement agencies and other levels of government.[81]

In Georgia, Shevardnadze's successor, Mikheil Saakashvili, became the center of a public scandal when a Russian documentary alleged that he had served in the Russian border troops, a post typically requiring lifelong collaboration with the KGB. A number of political formations supported a lustration law designed to make public the agreements that Saakashvili reportedly signed with the KGB. In July 2005 the opposition Democratic Front introduced in parliament a lustration bill believed to be "tantamount to the condemnation of the Soviet regime" and to "a break with our Soviet legacy."[82] The bill barred former Communist Party leaders and KGB operatives from holding senior government posts in the presidential office, the cabinet, and the Defense and Interior Ministries. Electoral candidates had to make public their ties to Soviet authorities. On 16 February 2007, parliament rejected the proposal.[83]

Local observers do not waste time deploring the failure of lustration in these republics, since they believe that the removal of former secret agents is impossible without access to the secret KGB archives providing concrete proof of individual collaboration. Moldovan Christian Democrat leader Iurie Rosca argued that self-identification of former KGB agents is better than no identification at all, and revealed that in 2005 a Moldovan deputy told parliament he never belonged to the Soviet or Russian secret services.[84] Even when politicians disclose their past, the accuracy of their statements and the nature of their collaboration must be ascertained with the help of the archival record. In 1991, all three republics saw the better part of their KGB archives being moved to Moscow, but it is unclear how many and which secret files remain in Chisinau, Kyiv and Tbilissi. Some reports claim that the KGB left behind only material of little political and historical importance, but the stubbornness with which the secrecy of such meager archives has been defended suggests the contrary. In 1997 Shevardnadze opposed the opening of the local KGB archives on grounds that during the 70-year-long communist rule "tens of thousands" of ordinary Georgians were coerced to collaborate, and thus access to files would "reopen old wounds" and lead to "a new wave of resistance, mistrust and hatred."[85] In 2005 Olga Ginzburg, the head of the Ukrainian Archives Committee, defended the closing of Soviet-era archives on grounds that making public the names of those who participated in repressions could hurt their children and relatives.[86] In Moldova, the Information and Security Service continues to house valuable KGB materials documenting the repression against Moldova's once sizeable Jewish community.[87]

No transitional justice

Transitional justice has not been on the docket in the other former Soviet republics, where no lustration proposals made it in parliament. To date, Belarus, Armenia, Azerbaijan, and Central Asia have had no serious discussion on lustration, access to secret files or court trials. Not because these countries' human rights abuses of the Soviet era were less severe than in other corners of the communist world. Collectivization, deportations, Russification, and forced industrialization affected all these republics. During World War II the Caucasus lost and Central Asia received many national groups forcibly deported by Stalin to prevent "subversive" activity. Though depicted by Soviet historians as a minor event, the anti-Soviet Basmachi Rebellion that rocked Central Asia in the 1920s and the 1930s led to the death of many Turkmens, Kazakhs, Kyrgyz, and Uzbeks. As any other Soviet citizens, nationals in Belarus, Armenia, Azerbaijan, and Central Asian republics were placed under strict surveillance by the KGB, which harassed, intimidated and compiled secret files on those who criticized the communist regime, its leaders, and its policies.

An honest reevaluation of the past has been hampered by these republics' limited political change. The executive remains the most important policy maker, the separation of powers principle is not observed, and Soviet-era politicians and secret KGB agents retain considerable political influence and the force to block attempts to reconsider a political system with which they were once associated. In Belarus, all power rests with President Aleksandr Lukashenko, reelected thrice since 1994. The first elections organized by the independent Turkmenistan, Tajikistan, Uzbekistan, and Kazakhstan allowed Soviet Communist Party leaders to become Presidents. Even in Kyrgyzstan, where the Communist Party leader was defeated, President Askar Akayev eventually acquired the unsavory character traits of his Central Asian counterparts. None of these leaders has agreed to give up power peacefully, instead rigging elections and amending the constitution to allow them to run in as many polls as they want. Islam Karimov and Nursultan Nazarbayev continue to preside over Uzbekistan and Kazakhstan, Imomali Rakhmonov controls Tajikistan, while Saparmurat Niyazov ruled Turkmenistan with an iron fist until his untimely death in 2006. Akayev alone was overthrown in the Tulip Revolution of 2005 and forced into exile to Russia.

In addition, transitional justice efforts have been blocked by the fact that both Azerbaijan and Armenia have been rocked by violence related to the disputed region of Nagorno-Karabakh, part of Azerbaijan but claimed by Armenia. In response to a wave of violence in 1990 Moscow deployed police, secret police, and army forces to suppress the riots. By 1993 the conflict lessened and Russian forces withdrew. The following year Heydar Aliyev, former chief of the

Azerbaijani KGB branch and First Deputy Prime Minister of the Soviet Union, became President. Aliyev strengthened his control over military and security affairs by reforming the Ministry of Internal Affairs and creating a Defense Council reporting directly to the President.[88] In 2003 Ilham Aliyev succeeded his father as President. Given his father background, it is unlikely that the son will pry open the secrets of the Soviet past.

Conclusion

As this chapter contended, the successor republics of the former Soviet Union have adopted transitional justice to strikingly different degrees. On the one hand, there are the Baltic states, which enacted several rounds of lustration, convicted a number of former secret agents responsible for Soviet-era human rights abuses, and publicly opened the meager secret file collections left at their disposal. On the other hand, there are all the other former Soviet republics in Europe and Asia, which made no progress in reckoning with their communist past. Rather surprisingly, there are no successor republics situated between these two extremes of the spectrum running from sustained to no transitional justice, as though to prove that the past must be revisited as fully as possible or it must be completely buried.

Of all communist countries, the one that experienced communist repression the longest has also been the most reluctant to reassess it critically. This should not be surprising, given the fact that Russia was the country that made it its mission to export communism worldwide and to extol its many virtues, and it was the country that benefited the most from the perpetuation of both the communist system and the Soviet Union. Of all former Soviet republics, the ones that had a distinct pre-communist history and a Western political culture to fall back on were also the ones to pursue transitional justice most vigorously. This should also not be surprising, since the Baltic states felt the Soviet yoke the most in the form of forced mass deportations, summary executions, and the almost complete destruction of pre-communist elites.

Notes

1 W. Slater, 'Russia's Imagined History: Visions of the Soviet Past and the New "Russian Idea"', *Journal of Communist Studies and Transition Politics*, 1998, vol. 14, 71.
2 I. Takayuki (ed.) *Facing Up to the Past: Soviet Historiography under Perestroika*, Sapporo: Slavic Research Center, 1989, p. 209.
3 A. White, 'The Memorial Society in the Russian Provinces', *Europe–Asia Studies*, 1995, vol. 47, 1343–1366, K. Smith, *Remembering Stalin's Victims: Popular Memory and the End of the USSR*, Ithaca: Cornell University Press, 1996, and K. Smith, *Mythmaking in the New Russia: Politics and Memory during the Yeltsin Era*, Ithaca: Cornell University Press, 2002.
4 A. Hochschild, *The Unquiet Ghost. Russians Remember Stalin*, Boston: Houghton Mifflin Co., 2003.
5 N. Calhoun, *Dilemmas of Justice in Eastern Europe's Democratic Transitions*, New York: Palgrave Macmillan, 2004, p. 137.
6 Ibid, pp. 136–140.

7 J. Elster, *Closing the Books. Transitional Justice in Historical Perspective*, New York: Cambridge University Press, 2004, p. 67.
8 A. Applebaum, *Gulag: A History*, London: Penguin Books, 2003. For the recent debate on numbers, see R. Conquest, 'Excess Deaths and Camp Numbers: Some Comments', *Soviet Studies*, vol. 43, 1991, 949–952, R. Conquest, 'Victims of Stalinism: A Comment', *Europe–Asia Studies*, 1997, vol. 49, 1317–1319, R. Conquest, *The Great Terror*, New York: Macmillan, 1973, and R. Tucker, *Stalin in Power: The Revolution from Above, 1928–1941*, New York: W. W. Norton, 1990.
9 A. Knight, *Spies without Cloaks: The KGB's Successors*, Princeton: Princeton University Press, 1996.
10 B. Forest, J. Johnson and K. Till, 'Post-totalitarian National Identity: Public Memory in Germany and Russia', *Social and Cultural Geography*, 2004, vol. 5, 368.
11 Y. Albats and C. A. Fitzpatrick, *The State Within a State: The KGB and Its Hold on Russia – Past, Present and Future*, Farrar Straus Giroux, 1994, cited in R. Coalson, 'Russia: Why the Chekist Mind-set Matters', *RFE/RL Report*, 15 October 2007.
12 Ibid.
13 M. J. Waller, 'Russia's Security Services: A Checklist for Reform', *ISCIP-Perspective*, 1997, vol. 8. Online. Available HTTP: http://www.bu.edu/iscip/vol8/Waller.html (accessed 25 January 2008).
14 'A Country Study: Turkmenistan', US Library of Congress, 1996. Online. Available HTTP: http://lcweb2.loc.gov/frd/cs/tmtoc.html, 'A Country Study: Tajikistan', US Library of Congress, 1996. Online. Available HTTP: http://lcweb2.loc.gov/frd/cs/tjtoc.html, 'A Country Report: Uzbekistan', US Library of Congress, 1996. Online. Available HTTP: http://lcweb2.loc.gov/frd/cs/uztoc.html, 'A Country Study: Kazakhstan', US Library of Congress, 1996. Online. Available HTTP: http://lcweb2.loc.gov/frd/cs/kztoc.html, and 'A Country Report: Kyrgyzstan', US Library of Congress, 1996. Online. Available HTTP: http://lcweb2.loc.gov/frd/cs/kgtoc.html. All accessed on 15 December 2007.
15 M. Tsypkin, 'Russia's Failure', *Journal of Democracy*, 2006, vol. 17, 75.
16 P. Todd and J. Bloch, *Global Intelligence. The World's Secret Services Today*, London: Zed Books, 2004, p. 143.
17 In 2006, of the 29 members of the Duma committee of security eight were former KGB or FSB officers, eight had worked for the Ministry of Internal Affairs, four were army officers, and one was a Soviet-era prosecutor.
18 Todd and Bloch, *Global Intelligence*, pp. 137, 140, and 143.
19 V. Yasmann, 'The KGB Has Spawned A Large Set of Osspring', *Prism*, 26 May 1995. Online. Available HTTP: http://jamestown.org/publications_details.php?volume_id=1&issue_id=13&article_id=162 (accessed 15 December 2007).
20 Tsypkin, 'Russia's Failure', 76.
21 L. Beehner, 'Russia's Soviet Past still Haunts Relations with West', Council on Foreign Relations, 29 June 2007. Online. Available HTTP: http://www.cfr.org/publication/13697 (accessed 15 December 2007).
22 Tsypkin, 'Russia's Failure', 76.
23 VTsIOM Analytic Agency, *VTsIOM Nationwide Survey*, 28 February–3 March 2003. Online. Available HTTP: http://www.russiavotes.org/Mood_rus_cur.htm#395 (accessed 14 July 2004).
24 R. Rose, *A Decade of New Russia Barometer Surveys*, Glasgow: Center for Public Police, University of Strathclyde, 2002.
25 V. Yasmann, ''Siloviki' Take the Reigns in Post-Oligarchy Russia', *RFE/RL Newsline*, 18 September 2007.
26 Coalson, 'Russia: Why the Chekist Mind-set Matters'.
27 V. Yasmann, ''Spymania' Returns to Russia', *RFE/RL Reports*, 15 April 2004. The literature critical of security services also expanded. See, among others, A. Litvinenko,

The FSB Blows Up Russia, Pskov: Giness, 2001, and Idem, *The Criminal Group from the Lubyanka*, Pskov: Giness, 2002.

28 V. Yasmann, 'Legislation on Screening and State Security in Russia', *RFE/RL Research Report*, 1993, vol. 2, 11–16, reprinted in N. Kritz, ed, *Transitional Justice: How Emerging Democracies Reckon with Former Regimes*, Washington, DC: United States Institute for Peace, 1995, vol. 2, pp. 754–761.

29 Article 16 of the Law on Operative and Detective Activity of April 1992 banned the exposure of KGB agents. Article 17 of the Law on Federal Security Organs of the Russian Federation of April 1992 protected the covert status of secret collaborators. Article 19 of the Law on Foreign Intelligence of August 1992 stipulated that information about SVR's confidential collaborators was a state secret accessible only to authorized officers of the state. See also M. Ellis, 'Purging the Past: The Current State of Lustration Laws in the Former Communist Block', *Law and Contemporary Problems*, 1997, vol. 59, no. 4, 195.

30 A. Knight, 'The Fate of the KGB Archives', *Slavic Review*, 1993, vol. 52, 586.

31 V. Chernetsky, 'On the Russian Archives: An Interview with Sergei V. Mironenko', *Slavic Review*, 1993, vol. 52, 839–846.

32 P. Kennedy Grimsted, 'Increasing Reference Access to Post-1991 Russian Archives', *Slavic Review*, 1997, vol. 56, 733–734.

33 Todd and Bloch, *Global Intelligence*, p. 139.

34 A. Lobjakas, 'Lithuania: Parliament Asks KGB Collaborators To Confess', *RFE/RL Feature*, 8 February 2000.

35 W. Sadurski, '"Decommunization", "Lustration" and Constitutional Continuity: Dilemmas of Transitional Justice in Central Europe', *EUI Working Paper* No. 15/2003, 23–24.

36 E. Jaskovska and J.P. Moran, 'Justice or Politics? Criminal, Civil and Political Adjudication in the Newly Independent Baltic States', *Journal of Communist Studies and Transition Politics*, 2006, vol. 22, 498.

37 'Decree Banning KGB Employees and Informers from Government Positions' No. 418 of 12 October 1991, and 'Law on the Verification of Mandates of Those Deputies Accused of Consciously Collaborating with Special Services of Other States' No. I-2115 of 17 December 1991, in Kritz, *Transitional Justice*, vol. 3, pp. 427–431.

38 Kritz, *Transitional Justice*, vol. 2, p. 764.

39 Ellis, 'Purging the Past, p. 190.

40 'Lithuania', *East European Constitutional Review*, 1997, Vol. 6. Online. Available HTTP: http://www.law.nyu.edu/eecr/vol6num4/constitutionwatch/lithuania.html (accessed 21 December 2007).

41 'New Lustration Law Passes in Lithuania', *RFE/RL Newsline*, 24 November 1999.

42 'Adamkus Wants Constitutional Court to Rule on Lustration Law', *RFE/RL Newsline*, 13 July 1998, 'Lithuanian Lawmakers back Adamkus over Lustration Law', *RFE/RL Newsline*, 17 July 1998, and 'Lithuanian Conservatives not to Appeal to Court over Lustration Law', *RFE/RL Newsline*, 20 July 1998.

43 'Lustration Law Appealed in Constitutional Court', *RFE/RL Newsline*, 7 October 1998, and 'Lithuanian Lustration Law Goes into Effect', *RFE/RL Newsline*, 4 January 1999.

44 'Lithuanian President to Wait for Court Ruling on Lustration Law', *RFE/RL Newsline*, 11 January 1999.

45 'Lithuanian Government Publishes Lists of Jobs Off-Limits for Former KGB Employees', *RFE/RL Newsline*, 15 January 1999.

46 'Lithuanian Court Deems Lustration Law Constitutional', *RFE/RL Newsline*, 5 March 1999.

47 W. Sadurski, '"Decommunization', 'Lustration' and Constitutional Continuity: Dilemmas of Transitional Justice in Central Europe', *EUI Working Paper* no. 15/2003, pp. 23–24.

48 In 1988 the Lithuanian parliament created the State Center for the Enquiry of Genocide in Lithuania, which 10 years later became the Genocide and Resistance Center.

49 'Lithuania', *East European Constitutional Review*, 2000, vol. 9. Online. Available HTTP: http://www.law.nyu.edu/eecr/vol9num_onehalf/constitutionwatch/lithuania. html (accessed on 21 December 2007).

50 'Lithuanian Parliament Amends Lustration Law', *RFE/RL Newsline*, 23 April 1999.

51 'Six Lithuanian Prosecutors Suspended under Lustration Law', *RFE/RL Newsline*, 9 March 1999.

52 A. Lobjakas, 'Lithuania: Parliament Asks KGB Collaborators To Confess', *RFE/RL Feature*, 8 February 2000.

53 Ibid.

54 *RFE/RL Report*, 14 February 2000.

55 'Lithuanian Parliament Adopts Lustration Law's New Edition', *Eurasian Secret Services Daily Review*, 14 October 2007. Online. Available HTTP: http://www.axisglobe. com/article.asp?article=1406 (accessed 15 December 2007).

56 Jaskovska and Moran, 'Justice or Politics?', 497.

57 'In Lithuania, Uncertainty about State Security Department's Lustration Efforts', *RFE/RL Newsline*, 3 October 2007.

58 A. Prazauskas, 'Transitional Justice in a Post-Soviet Nation: The Case of Lithuania', pp. 4–5. Online. Available HTTP: http://igpa.nat.gov.tw/public/Attachment/782810245671. pdf (accessed 25 December 2007).

59 Lobjakas, 'Lithuania: Parliament Asks KGB Collaborators To Confess'.

60 'Constitution of the Republic of Latvia', 2003. Online. Available HTTP: http://www. servat.unibe.ch/icl/lg00000_.html (accessed 6 January 2008).

61 'Latvian Lustration Law Survives Court Challenge', *RFE/RL Newsline*, 31 August 2000.

62 'Court Says Latvian Lawmaker Was KGB Agent', *RFE/RL Newsline*, 13 March 2000, 'No Decision Taken on Revoking Latvian Deputy's Mandate', *RFE/RL Newsline*, 23 March 2000, 'Latvian Election News', *RFE/RL Newsline*, 20 August 2002, and 'Latvian Parliamentarian Loses Ballot Appeal', *RFE/RL Newsline*, 21 August 2002, and 'Plans to Sue', *RFE/RL Report*, 13 December 2002.

63 'Latvian MEP to Get E20,000 over Electoral Ban', *European Voice*, 24 June 2004. Online. Available HTTP: http://www.europeanvoice.com/archive/article.asp?id=20767 (accessed 6 January 2008), and D. Akule, 'Latvia Bars Candidates with a Communist Past from Elections', *Transitions Online*, 6–12 August 2002.

64 Ellies, 'Purging the Past', pp. 191–192, and Lobjakas, 'Lithuania: Parliament Asks KGB Collaborators To Confess'.

65 Ellies, 'Purging the Past', pp. 190–191.

66 J. Darski, 'Police Agents in the Transition Period', *Uncaptive Minds*, 1991–1992, vol. 4, 28–28, reprinted in Kritz, *Transitional Justice*, vol. 2, pp. 766–769.

67 Kritz, *Transitional Justice*, vol. 2, p. 765.

68 Jaskovska and Moran, 'Justice or Politics', 492. For Latvia, see also *Occupation of Latvia. Three Occupations 1940–1991. Soviet and Nazi Take-Overs and their Consequences*, Riga: Occupation Museum Foundation, 2005.

69 A. Kung, 'Communism and Crimes against Humanity in the Baltic States', April 1999. Online. Available HTTP: http://www.rel.ee/eng/communism_crimes.htm (accessed 26 December 2007). See also P. Polian, *Against Their Will: The History and Geography of Forced Migrations in the USSR*, Budapest: Central European University Press, 2004.

70 'A Riga District Court Has Rejected Pleas that a Jailed Ex-police Officer Be Freed', and 'Latvian Prosecutors Indicted Another Soviet-era Secret Policeman', *The Weekly Crier*. March-April 2001. Online. Available HTTP: http://www.balticsww.com/ wkcrier/0219_0409_01.htm (accessed 21 December 2007).

71 H. Jara, 'Dealing with the Past: The Case of Estonia', *Ulkopoliittinen Instituutti Working Paper* No. 15, 1999. Online. Available HTTP: http://www.up-fiia.fi/document. php?DOC_ID=69#wp15.php (accessed 10 March 2007).

72 'Lithuania', *East European Constitutional Review*, 1998, vol. 7. Online. Available HTTP: http://www.law.nyu.edu/eecr/vol7num4/index.html, 'Lithuania', *East European Constitutional Review*, 1999, vol. 8. Online. Available HTTP: http://www.law.nyu.edu/eecr/vol8num1–2/constitutionwatch/lithuania.html, 'Lithuania', *East European Constitutional Review*, 2000, vol. 9. Online. Available HTTP: http://www.law.nyu.edu/eecr/vol9num_onehalf/constitutionwatch/lithuania.html, and 'Lithuania', *East European Constitutional Review*, 2001, vol. 10. Online. Available HTTP: http://www.law.nyu.edu/eecr/vol10num2_3/constitutionwatch/lithuania.html. All accessed 21 December 2007.

73 Reports of Raslanas's involvement in the killings emerged as early as 1988, at a time when he held an important position in the Soviet Ministry for Religious Affairs in Vilnius. 'Soviet War Criminal in Office', *The Baltic Bulletin*, March 1988. Online. Available HTTP: http://www.lituanus.org/1988/88_3_08.htm (accessed 21 December 2007).

74 'A Riga District Court Has Rejected Pleas that a Jailed Ex-police Officer Be Freed', and 'Latvian Prosecutors Indicted Another Soviet-era Secret Policeman', *The Weekly Crier*. March–April 2001.

75 Kritz, *Transitional Justice*, vol. 2, p. 769.

76 M. Tarm, 'Stalinist Crimes Hunted in Baltics', The Associated Press, 18 March 1999. Online. Available HTTP: http://www.angelfire.com/tx/LABAS/issue13.html (accessed 26 December 2007).

77 'Moldovan Parliament Rejects Lustration Bill', *RFE/RL Newsline*, 1 June 2001.

78 This later provision responded to allegations that Russian secret services supported Viktor Yanukovych's presidential bid by unwisely poisoning Viktor Yushchenko, the candidate who won the poll. 'Justice Minister Zvarych Voices Protest against Lustration', 13 February 2005. Online. Available HTTP: http://blog.kievukraine.info/2005/02/justice-minister-zvarych-voices.html (accessed 15 December 2007).

79 'Press Release of the Embassy of Ukraine to the Republic of Estonia', 12 April 2005. Online. Available HTTP: http://home.uninet.ee/~embkura/Press-68.htm (accessed 15 December 2007).

80 S. Woehrel, 'Ukraine's Orange Revolution and U.S. Policy', CRS Report for Congress, 1 April 2005. Online. Available HTTP: http://fpc.state.gov/documents/organization/45452.pdf (accessed 15 December 2007), and 'Press Release of the Embassy of Ukraine in Estonia', 10 February 2005. Online. Available HTTP: http://home.uninet.ee/~embkura/Press-24.htm (accessed 15 December 2007).

81 'Ukraine – Governance Assessment', March 2006, p. 75. Online. Available HTTP: http://www.sigmaweb.org/dataoecd/46/63/37127312.pdf (accessed 15 December 2007).

82 'Ruling Majority Rejects Draft Law on Lustration', *Georgia Online*, 16 February 2007. Online. Available HTTP: http://www.civil.ge/eng/article.php?id=14644 (accessed 2 January 2008).

83 Georgian communists claimed that Zviad Gamsakhurdia and his supporters broke into the KGB building and stole secret documents. 'But Shelves Debate on Lustration', *RFE/RL Newsline*, 3 January 2007, 'And Draft Law on Lustration, Extension of Tax Break for Media', *RFE/RL Newsline*, 20 February 2007, and 'Georgia, Moldova and Bulgaria: Dismantling Communist Structures Is Hardly Extremist', *Demokratizatsiya*, 2001, p. 314. Online. Available HTTP: http://www.ariasking.com/files/DemSarishvili.pdf (accessed 15 December 2007). Also Z. Anjaparidze, 'Russian Film on Saakashvili Tests Georgian Democracy', *Eurasia Daily Monitor*, 4 October 2004. Online. Available HTTP: http://jamestown.org/publications_details.php?volume_id=401&issue_id=3093&article_id=2368629 (accessed 15 December 2007).

84 'Georgia, Moldova and Bulgaria', p. 314.

85 'Georgian President Opposes Lustration', *RFE/RL Newsline*, 9 December 1997.

86 N. Hyshnyak and O. Konashevych, 'Yushchenko: Why Should We Forget the History of Repressions?', BBC, 13 June 2007. Online. Available HTTP: http://orangeukraine. squarespace.com/long-articles/2007/7/6/yushchenko-why-should-we-forget-the-history-of-represssions.html (accessed 15 December 2007).

87 'Moldova Intel Enhances Ties to International Jewish Organizations', *Axis*, 10 February 2007. Online. Available HTTP: http://www.axisglobe.com/article.asp?article=1223 (accessed 15 December 2007).

88 'A Country Study: Azerbaijan', US Library of Congress, 1994. Online. Available HTTP: http://lcweb2.loc.gov/frd/cs/aztoc.html (accessed 16 December 2007).

11 Conclusion

Explaining country differences

Lavinia Stan

Post-communist countries have responded differently to their recent past by adopting screening and lustration programs, by prosecuting communist officials and secret agents, and by making secret archives available to the public at different times and to different degrees. This chapter seeks to answer important comparative questions. The first section assesses how countries have dealt with their communist dictatorial past by summarizing the experience with transitional justice in Eastern Europe and the former Soviet Union during the first stages of post-communist transformation, starting with the collapse of the Eastern European communist regimes in 1989 and ending in 2007, the year when Romania and Bulgaria were accepted into the European Union. Moreover, this section places each post-communist country on the continuum stretching from "forgiving and forgetting" to "prosecuting and punishing," depending on their progress in dealing with the past. The second section reports on the theories proposed to date to explain country differences, while the third section outlines a model that better explains why some countries have been leaders and other countries have been laggards with respect to the politics of memory. We argue that the theoretical frameworks proposed to date fail to fully explain why different post-communist countries have adopted different transitional justice processes at different times, and that the three factors we propose, taken together, can serve as more accurate predictors of post-communist efforts to seek truth and obtain justice.

A scorecard of post-communist transitional justice

In Eastern Europe and the former Soviet Union, concerns over the fate of the secret archives, the communist officials, the secret full-time agents, and their part-time collaborators were raised early on in the transition process by politicians, civic activists, and ordinary citizens alike. Indeed, the region's very exit from communism and its early steps toward democratization were marked by heated public debates on the need to find out the truth about the communist regime, to uncover the role of the hegemonic communist parties and their obedient security services, to vindicate the victims and their surviving families, to sort out villains from angels, to acknowledge and, whenever possible, to redress past human rights abuses. While these issues were viewed as equally important in Prague and Sofia,

Budapest and Warsaw, Tallinn, and Riga, the way each country addressed them has differed significantly. This section summarizes the progress to date of Eastern European countries and former Soviet Union republics in terms of three key areas of transitional justice.

The first to launch lustration were East Germany and Czechoslovakia, which also adopted the most radical programs of banning former communist officials and secret agents from a wide range of political and economic post-communist positions for extended periods of time (for 15 years in Germany, and indefinitely in the Czech Republic, but not Slovakia). These two Central European countries were shortly thereafter followed by Bulgaria and Albania, where lustration remained tied to loss of public office for individuals with proven links to the former Communist Party or to the intelligence services. At the same time, however, in these Balkan countries the scope of the ban was severely limited either to only a handful of positions (management posts in "scientific" research organizations in Bulgaria) or to a shorter period of time (until new elections were organized in Albania). Hungary and Poland launched lustration with considerable delay in 1994 and 1997, respectively, only after sustained political negotiations between the heirs of the Communist Party and the opposition forces considerably watered down the process to consist of screening without automatic loss of office. Working on the premise that the communist-era repression was masterminded by the party-state and was carried out by the secret services, which therefore had to be treated as two equally-responsible partners, the German and Czechoslovak lustration programs targeted both former party officials and spies. By contrast, the Hungarian and Polish variants tried to uncover only past ties to the domestic repression branches of the communist state security agencies, implicitly suggesting that the ruling parties or the military and counter-intelligence services were less guilty for their actions. These lustration programs further restricted investigations to elected and nominated post-communist politicians, but not the public administration and bureaucracy, and dissociated screening from vetting, the automatic loss of public office if a person's tainted past was established. Politicians were asked to admit to their past in statements kept hidden from the public eye, and only those persons found to have lied about their past (presumably to cover up past involvement in human rights abuses) were in danger of losing their posts.

Instead of losing its appeal, as some Western authors have predicted, lustration returned to the forefront of politics more than a decade after the collapse of the communist regimes. In 2001 Slovakia carried out limited vetting of selected categories of public officials in view of accession to the European Union, after having quietly allowed the Czechoslovak lustration law to expire in the early 1990s. In 2003, Serbia launched a limited lustration program, and the following year both Moldova and Ukraine discussed, but rejected, variants of vetting. In 2005 the Romanian Parliament was asked to discuss a number of lustration proposals directed against former Communist Party leaders and Securitate agents, but to date the house was unable to adopt any of these bills, despite extensive negotiations among members of the fragmented ruling coalition. Even more spectacular, in 2006 Poland renewed its commitment to publicly shame former communist

Table 11.1 Lustration in Eastern Europe and the former Soviet Union (1989–2007)

Country	Year of adoption	Law's main provisions
Albania	1995	Law on Genocide and Crimes against Humanity Committed during the Communist Regime for Political, Ideological and Religious Motives (the "Genocide Law") Persons convicted under the law of being authors, conspirators or executors of crimes against humanity and having held public office (members of the Politburo and Central Committee, ministers, members of Parliament, Supreme Court presidents, and agents and collaborators of Sigurimi) cannot hold selected positions in parliament, government, or mass media. *End of ban:* 2002.
	1995	Law on the Verification of the Moral Character of Officials and Other Persons Connected with the Defense of the Democratic State (the "Lustration Law") Public officials must be "cleared" by the Special Verification Commission before running in elections or being nominated to their posts. Anyone holding a position in one in 20 communist-era employment categories (including members of Politburo, Central Committee, government, Supreme Court, officers, agents and collaborators of Sigurimi, and denouncers, investigators, prosecutors, and judges in political trials) are barred from certain elected or appointed positions in government, education, the mass media, police, and the judiciary.
	1998	Amendments to the Genocide and Verification Laws Reduced the scope of lustration to former members of the Politburo, former secret police agents, and individuals convicted of crimes against humanity.
Bulgaria	1992	Law on Banks and Credit Activity Persons elected to the leading bodies of the Bulgarian Communist Party, the Communist Youth League, the Fatherland Front, the Union of the Active Fighters against Fascism and Capitalism, the Bulgarian Trade Unions, and the Bulgarian Agrarian People's Union, or appointed to a managerial full-time position in the Central Committee of the Bulgarian Communist Party, as well as officers and paid and unpaid associates of the State Security were banned from being elected and appointed to managerial positions in the banking sector. *End of ban:* 1997.
	1992	Law on the Temporary Introduction of Additional requirements for Members of Executive Bodies of Scientific Organizations and the Higher Certifying Commissions (the "Panev Law") Screened leaders of "scientific organizations" (such as research institutes and universities) for past links to the Communist Party leadership.

(continued on next page)

Table 11.1 (continued)

Country	Year of adoption	Law's main provisions
	1997	Law on Public Administration Prohibited members of the communist nomenklatura from taking high positions in the civil service. Lustration clauses revoked by the Constitutional Court in January 1998.
	2002	Law on Classified Information The State Commission on Information Security screens public servants who apply to work with NATO classified information, and issues clearance permits. The commission can deny clearance if the applicant was a State Security collaborator.
The Czech Republic	1991	Enforced the Czech and Slovak Federal Republic Screening Law no. 451/4 October 1991 Screening for past activity as StB agents and collaborators, Communist Party officials from the district level up, People's Militia members, political officers in Corps of National Security, members of purge committees in 1948 and 1968, students at KGB schools, and owners of StB "conspiration apartments." *Ban:* elected or appointed positions in federal and republican levels of government (with the exception of Member of Parliament), rank above colonel in the army, management positions in state-owned enterprises and joint stock companies, the official press agency, top positions in Czechoslovak, Czech and Slovak Radio and television, top academic positions, Supreme Court, judgeships and prosecutorial posts. *End of screening procedure or ban:* initially 1995, extended to 2000, then extended indefinitely.
(East) Germany	1990	German Unification Treaty Screening for past collaboration with the Stasi. *Ban:* Employers could request from the BStU information on an employee's prior involvement with the Stasi. Individual provinces and employers set the standard for what level of involvement with the Stasi would be grounds for dismissal. *End of screening procedure or ban:* Originally 28 December 2006, but extended until 2011 for individuals in leading positions in state and society (i.e., members of Parliament). Individuals involved with the Stasi files in an official capacity (i.e., archivists) may be vetted indefinitely.

Estonia	1995	Citizenship Law
		Denied Estonian citizenship (and the political rights that came with it) to current and former agents of intelligence and security services of a foreign state, and persons who have acted against the state of Estonia and its security. Ban upheld in 2004.
	1995	Lustration Law
		Required people who collaborated with the Nazi or Soviet security services or the Communist Party to register with the Estonian Security Service within a year. The registration statements are kept secret, except in cases involving crimes against humanity or if the registree is a member of Parliament or the president. Those who did not comply were banned from holding high public office until 2002.
Hungary	1994	Act XXIII on the Screening of Holders of Some Important Positions, Holders of Positions of Public Trust, and Opinion-Leading Public Figures
		Screening for past activity as agents of Main Division III/III (domestic repression)
		Screened categories: Parliament and government members; president and vice-presidents of the National Bank; ambassadors; army commanders; the presidents, vice-presidents and editors of the Hungarian Radio, Hungarian Television, and the Hungarian News Service; chiefs of police; presidents, deans, general directors, and department heads of state-owned universities and colleges; career judges; district attorneys; editors at daily newspapers and weekly magazines; and managers of state-owned banks, financial institutions, and insurance companies.
		End of screening procedure: 30 June 2000
	1996	Amendments to Act XXIII of 1994
		Screening of all public officials born before 14 February 1972, who take an oath before Parliament or the President of the Republic.
Latvia	1994	The Election Law on City and Town Councils, District Councils and Pagasts Councils
		Banned current and former salaried secret agents of the USSR, the Latvian SSR or other country's state security, intelligence or counterintelligence services, and persons who, after 13 January 1991, have been active in the Soviet Communist Party, the Working People's International Front of the Latvian SSR, the United Board of Working Bodies, the Organization of War and Labor Veterans, the All-Latvia Salvation Committee or its regional committees from running in local elections. Ban upheld in 2004.

(continued on next page)

Table 11.1 (continued)

Country	Year of adoption	Law's main provisions
	1994	**The Citizenship Law** Denied Latvian citizenship who: after 4 May 1990 have propagated fascist, chauvinist, national-socialist, communist or other totalitarian ideas; served in the armed forces, internal military forces, security service or police (militia) of some foreign state; have been employees, informers, agents or safehouse keepers of KGB or other foreign state security forces; after 13 January 1991 have worked against the Republic of Latvia in the Soviet Communist Party, the Working People's International Front of the Latvian SSR, the United Board of Working Bodies, the Organization of War and Labor Veterans, the All-Latvia Salvation Committee or its regional committees, or the Union of Communists of Latvia.
	1995	**The Saeima Election Law** Banned current and former salaried secret agents of the USSR, the Latvian SSR or other country's state security, intelligence or counterintelligence services, and persons who, after 13 January 1991, have been active in the Soviet Communist Party, the Working People's International Front of the Latvian SSR, the United Board of Working Bodies, the Organization of War and Labor Veterans, the All-Latvia Salvation Committee or its regional committees from running in local elections. Ban upheld in 1998, 2002, 2003, and 2006.
Lithuania	1991	**Decree Banning KGB Employees and Informers from Government Positions no. 418** Banned KGB agents and informers from being appointed as members of the Lithuanian government, state services, ministries and departments of public administration. Those holding such positions had to resign them no later than 1 October 1992. *End of ban:* 1996.
	1991	**Law on the Verification of Mandates of Those Deputies Accused of Consciously Collaborating with Special Services of Other States no. I-2115** Investigated accusations that elected members of the Lithuanian Parliament and of regional/city/municipal councils have collaborated with the KGB. If collaboration is established, a vote will be held to confirm or nullify the deputy's mandate.
	1999	**Lustration Law** Forces all KGB operatives to disclose past activity.

Poland	1997	**Lustration Law** Screening for past collaboration with Sluzba Biespiecenstwa Current public officials and candidates for those positions (including the President, members of Parliament and cabinet, judges and prosecutors, and persons appointed to senior posts by the President, the Prime Minister or the Prosecutor General) must give statements detailing their (non)collaboration. Only those who lied lose their public offices for ten years.
	2006	**Lustration Law** Screening for past collaboration with the SB (all directorates). Public figures, including senior officials, judges, teachers, journalists, diplomats, municipal officials, heads of state-owned companies, editors, publishers and school principals have to ask the IPN for certificates detailing their (non)collaboration with the SB. Records are made public. Public officials could be fired, if unveiled as former secret agents. Law took effect in March 2007, but was declared unconstitutional.
Romania	2006	Emergency Ordinance no. 16, amending Law no. 187 of 1999 on Access to One's Own File and the Unveiling of the Securitate as a Political Police (the 'Ticu Law') Screening for ties to the Securitate. The names of those uncovered as former secret agents or informers are made public. These persons do not have to resign their public office. In January 2008, the ordinance was declared unconstitutional.
Slovakia	1991	Czech and Slovak Federal Republic Screening Law no. 451/4 October 1991 Screening for past activity as StB agents and collaborators, Communist Party officials from the district level up, People's Militia members, political officers in Corps of National Security, members of purge committees in 1948 and 1968, students at KGB schools, and owners of StB 'conspiration apartments'. The law, which expired in 1996, was not enforced. *Ban*: elected or appointed positions in federal and republican levels of government (with the exception of Member of Parliament), rank above colonel in the army, management positions in state-owned enterprises and joint stock companies, the official press agency, top positions in Czechoslovak, Czech and Slovak Radio and television, top academic positions, Supreme Court, Judgeships, and prosecutorial posts.

spies, when it passed legislation that significantly enlarged the scope of the tooth-less lustration law of 1997. Of all Eastern European countries included here, only Slovenia has made no serious attempt to use lustration as a post-communist transitional justice method.

The situation in the former Soviet Union is somewhat different, in the sense that there lustration represented the exception, rather than the rule. The three Baltic states were the only ones to screen their post-communist political class for ties with the former communist intelligence services, whereas the other inde-pendent republics either did not consider lustration seriously or were unable to have it endorsed by their parliaments. The great silence regarding the need to vet the post-communist elite that has gripped Belarus and the republics of Central Asia and the Caucasus (Armenia and Azerbaijan) has its roots in these countries' inability to effect regime change at the moment of gaining their independence. Indeed, it could be argued that theirs was not a progress, but a regress, since the regimes they experienced after splitting up from the Soviet Union have been in many respects harsher, more dictatorial, and more oblivious to the need to observe fundamental human rights than the reformist Gorbachev rule they experi-enced as part of the Soviet Union. Not surprisingly, political elites dominated by Lukashenka, Karimov, Nazarbayev, Niyazov, Rakhmonov or Putin, and consti-tuted of individuals who started their careers in Soviet times in the Communist Party or the KGB, have had no desire to enact introspective measures that could block their personal political ascension. When current human rights abuses are rampant, societies are little inclined to investigate past abuses, regardless of how serious they were. Again, despite Western predictions that the appetite for lustra-tion will temper with time, Ukraine, Moldova and Georgia considered lustration laws more than a decade after they obtained their independence, not because vet-ting was expected to clean up the republican political elite from individuals with an unsavory past, but more because lustration reflected their deeply divided soci-eties, split between a commitment to maintain close ties to their former master, Moscow, and a desire to pursue a more independent road.

Even in the Baltic states lustration has been tainted by ethnic considerations. To a certain extent it was true that Russian-speaking ethnic minorities had been more vocal and enthusiastic supporters of the Soviet regime, and they had allowed themselves to be used as instruments of systematic Russification, repression, dis-crimination, and intimidation in more ways than one. But certainly not all Com-munist Party leaders and KGB full-time agents and part-time informers living and operating in Latvia, Lithuania, and Estonia from the mid-1940s to 1991 were ethnic Russians. For example, half of the Communist Party membership was ethnic Estonian, and there are reasons to believe that these numbers were replicated in the other Baltic states as well.[1] In addition, it is likely that the KGB employed vast networks of ethnic Estonian, Latvian and Lithuanian secret informers, since they could spy on Estonians, Latvians and Lithuanians better than Russians ever could. Why would citizens in these republics disclose their most inner thoughts to the occupying Russians, when they knew that the Russians were more likely to support the communist regime and their republics' forceful incorporation into the Soviet Union? Despite this reality, after declaring their independence from the Soviet Union the Baltic societies seemed almost exclusively preoccupied with rooting out non-Baltic Communist Party leaders and secret agents from the midst of their political elite. With the stroke of a pen, Russians were "lustrated" by being denied citizenship, and all the political rights that come with it. Whereas in Eastern Europe lustration entailed the loss of the right to be elected or nominated to public office, but not of the right to vote, in Estonia and Latvia lustration entailed losing both rights, because vetting was tied to citizenship. Since soon after independence the political slate was thus cleaned of non-Baltics through the citizenship laws, the focus of lustration remained tied to future appointments, and as a result vetting was carried out primarily through election laws. In Eastern Europe lustration aimed to prevent former communist decision-makers and secret spies to assume public office and at the same time to force current holders with tainted records to give up their posts. In the Baltic states, by contrast, lustration laws retained only the first goal, since the second had already been dealt with through the citizenship laws.

Overall post-communist Eastern Europe has been willing to open the secret archives compiled by its notorious state security services during the 1945–1989 period, although each state has shielded its most sensitive documents from public sight. This trend has placed the region far ahead of Western European countries, which continue to guard their secrets jealously. Among Eastern European countries, East Germany was the first to open the archives of Stasi (*Ministerium fur Staatssicherheit*) to the public, and to keep classified for reasons of "national security" the smallest number of secret police files, mostly related to the work of the military intelligence agencies. This manifest commitment to openness was matched only much later by other countries in the region, which were undecided as to the continuity between communist and post-communist intelligence services. The Czech Republic, Bulgaria, and Poland allowed partial access to selected secret files inherited from the *Statni Bezpesnost*, the *Komitet za Durzhavna Sigurnost*, and the *Sluzba Biespiecenstwa* in 1996 and 1997, more than five years after the Gauck Institute opened its doors. After 2000, Romanians, Slovakians, and Hungarians were allowed to read their own files compiled by *Departamentul Securitatii Statului*, the *Statni Bezpesnost* or Main Division III/III, but large sections of the secret archives, including the most sensitive files pertaining to the past of prominent post-communist politicians, have remained unavailable to the general public, although subject to illegal trafficking and truncated disclosure for short-term political gains. Albania and Slovenia have done little in this regard, despite the fact that periodically the civil society in those countries has called on the political class to declassify secret materials.[2] Access to secret files is ensured through independent governmental agencies recognized as custodians of the communist secret archives, and sometimes entrusted with the additional responsibility of publicly identifying former spies. Since their formation, most such agencies have struggled to keep themselves free of public scandal and political influence.

The experience of the former Soviet Union with access to communist-era secret files is unique. Whereas each Eastern European communist country had its

Table 11.2 Access to communist-era secret archives

Country	Time of adoption	Law's main provisions
Bulgaria	1997	Law on Opening Communist Secret Files Files of current high ranking communist officials (excluding Constitutional Court judges) were opened, and made public within one year. Public officials had one month to admit to past ties to the KDS.
	2006	Law on Access and Disclosure of Documents and Determining Connections of Bulgarian Citizens to the State Security and Army Intelligence Agencies Citizens have the right to read the secret files compiled on them, with the exception of files touching on issues of "national security," which remain classified.
The Czech Republic	1996	Act no. 140 on Access to Secret Files Citizens can view their own files, with the names of third-parties blackened out.
	2002	Act no. 107 Expanded file access. Adult citizens can access their own files and the files of StB collaborators, StB personnel files, and entries recorded with intelligence technology and monitoring.
	2004	Archive Act no. 499 Further expanded file access. Citizens can view files of anti-communist dissidents, including compromising information on them.
Estonia	1995	Law Citizens can read the files compiled on them, and also agent reports, mission statements by the secret police, observations on ordinary people, and the files of the arrestees. Citizens do not have access to the files of KGB agents. All secret KGB files dated prior to 1960 are available to the public. The law was revised in 2002.
Germany	1990	Law on the Securing and Use of Individual-Based Data of the former Ministry of State Security/Office for National Security Right to information without right to documents: citizens were informed by case worker of information contained in the secret files compiled on them, but not allowed to read or to have copies of the documents.

Country	Year	Law
	1992	Stasi Files Law Right to information with right to documents: citizens can read the secret files compiled on them, and request copies of documents. Documents compiled by the communist-era military intelligence remain classified.
Hungary	2003	Law Citizens can read the secret files compiled on them, and the records of people who spied on them. Files touching on "national security" issues remain classified.
Latvia	2007	Law Disclosed the contents of KGB files containing the names of former secret police agents.
Lithuania	2006	Law Opened the government's special archive, where all remaining KGB files are stored, to unlimited public access.
Poland	1997	Law on Access to Communist Secret Files Selected secret files were declassified. Historians and journalists had access to the files of some holders of public office. Citizens could access the files compiled on them by the SB.
	2006	Lustration Law Public access to files of current diplomats, government ministers, and members of Parliament was granted.
Romania	1999	Law no. 187 on Access to One's Own File and the Unveiling of the Securitate as a Political Police (the "Ticu Law") Citizens can read their own secret files, obtain copies of documents, and statements detailing their (non)collaboration with the Securitate. Files touching on "national security" issues remain classified.
Slovakia	2002	Act no. 553 on Access to Documents Concerning the Activities of the State Security Services between [18 April] 1939 and [31 December] 1989 and the Establishment of the National Memory Institute Slovak citizens and foreigners can access secret files containing information on them. Files of foreign nationals, those whose disclosure could pose a threat to human life and public interest, and the personal data of people persecuted by the former communist political police remain classified.

Table 11.3 Independent transitional justice agencies in Eastern Europe and the former Soviet Union

Country	Agency

Bulgaria	Commission on the Disclosure of Documents and Establishing Affiliation with the Former State Security and Intelligence Directorate with the General Staff (the "Andreev Commission"), created in 2001
	    7 members appointed to 5-year terms; 5 members elected by Parliament, and 2 by Council of Ministers
	Commission on the Disclosure of Affiliation with the Former State Security and Intelligence Directorate with the General Staff, created in 2001
	    5 members appointed to 5-year terms; chairman appointed by President of Bulgaria
	Commission on the Disclosure of Documents and Determining Connections of Bulgarian Citizens to the State Security and Army Intelligence Agencies, created in 2007
	    9 members elected to 5-year terms by the Parliament

The Czech Republic	Office for the Documentation and the Investigation of the Crimes of Communism in the Czech Republic (*Úřad dokumentace a vyšetrování Zločiň komunismu služby kriminální policie a vyšetrovái or UDV*), created in 1995, made part of the Czech Police in 2002
East Germany	Federal Commissioner for the Files of the State Security Service of the Former German Democratic Republic (*Bundesbeauftragte für die Unterlagen des Staatssicherheitsdienstes der ehemaligen Deutschen Demokratischen Republik* or BstU, the "Gauck Commission", later "Birthler Commission"), created in 1990
Estonia	State Commission on Examination of the Policies of Repression, created in 1993 International Commission for the Investigation of Crimes against Humanity, created in 1998 7 members appointed by the Estonian President. Released its reports in 2006.
Hungary	Institute for the History of the 1956 Revolution (*As 1956-os Magyar Forradalom Tortenetenek Dokumentacios es Kutatointezete Kozalapitvany*), created in 1989 The Office of History, created in 2001 Part of the Interior Ministry

Country	
Latvia	Commission for the Investigation of Totalitarian Regime Crimes, created in 1992, worked until 1996 Commission for the Assessment of the Crimes of Totalitarian Regimes (Latvia's "History Commission"), created in 1996 created by President of Latvia; worked in four different sub-commissions
Lithuania	Genocide and Resistance Research Center of Lithuania (*Lietuvos Gyventoju Genocido ir Rezistencijos Tyrimo Centras*), created in 1993. Includes the Lithuanian Genocide and Resistance Research Institute and the Lithuanian Genocide Victims Memorial Institute. International Commission for the Evaluation of the Crimes of the Nazi and Soviet Occupation Regimes in Lithuania (*Tarptautine Komisija Naciu ir Sovietinio okupaciniu rezimu nusikaltimams Lietuvoje ivertinti*), created in 1998
Poland	Institute for National Remembrance (*Instytut Pamieci Narodowej* or IPN), created in 2000 works in four departments: Commission for the Prosecution of Crimes against the Polish Nation; Office for Preservation and Dissemination of Archival Records; Public Education Office; and Vetting Office
Romania	National Council for the Study of Securitate Archives (*Consiliul National pentru Studiul Arhivelor Securității* or CNSAS), created in 2000 11 non-party members appointed to 6-year terms by political parties represented in Parliament
Slovakia	Institute of National Remembrance (*Ustav Pamati Naroda* or UPN), created in 2003

independent state security force, Soviet republics were all placed under the watchful eye of the *Komityet Gosudarstvennoy Bezopasnosti*, controlled by Moscow. The KGB was careful to ship to Russia the bulk of the secret files it had patiently archived in each Soviet republic as soon as the first calls for independence were heard. As a result, successor republics found it impossible to grant their citizens access to the files compiled on them by the Soviet secret police, since most files were located outside their borders. Estonia has almost no secret archive at its disposal, Latvia and Lithuania have incomplete records, the Moldovan archive has mysteriously disappeared on the road from Chisinau to Tiraspol to Moscow, while the fate of the KGB collections in Central Asia, the Caucasus, and Belarus remains unknown. Thus, even when political will was present, secret file access has been meager and partial at best. This is not to say that all former Soviet republics rushed to open their secret files. The Baltic states stand apart from other Soviet successor republics, because they alone have allowed citizens to pry open available secret documents. Russia houses the lion's share of the former KGB archive, but it denies citizens access to both the secret collections that pertain to its communist past and those that speak of the past of its former Soviet satellites. Such refusal is rooted in the many points of continuity linking the communist and post-communist intelligence services in terms of personnel, methods, and goals. Rather surprisingly, the Russian political establishment and the intelligence community display unflinching sympathy not only for late communism, the period of time when many of its members launched their public careers, but also for earlier stages of communism.[3]

Probably the slowest progress to date has been registered with regard to the criminal prosecution of former communist officials and secret agents for their participation in beatings, torture, murder and other gross violations of human rights. The burden of proof in prosecuting crimes committed, sometimes decades before investigations are launched, under a tightly secretive regime careful to cover up its tracks has taken a toll on trials as a method of reckoning with the communist past. Of all countries we studied, Romania has taken the lead, launching investigations and gathering evidence in close to one hundred different cases of human rights violations perpetrated during the Gheorghe Gheorghiu-Dej and Nicolae Ceausescu regimes and the bloody December 1989 revolution. However, in only a handful of cases did those investigations lead to court hearings resulting in the prosecution of those accused, and in even fewer cases did those who were found guilty serve jail time. East Germany and Poland rank second in terms of cases investigated in view of a trial, but there again in only very few cases were communist-era officials found guilty. All other countries have been laggards in this respect, because the statute of limitation was extended for most crimes except genocide and crimes against humanity or because by the time investigations were launched the accused were not able to stand trial for reasons of health. These results are consistent with developments in post-authoritarian countries in Latin America, Asia and Africa, where trials and court proceedings were limited in number.

Within the former Soviet bloc the Baltic states again constitute an exception, as they were the only ones to bring former secret agents to court for their involvement in human rights abuses. Since gaining their independence, Estonia, Latvia, and Lithuania have endeavored to hold NKVD agents responsible for facilitating the deportations of thousands of Estonian, Latvians and Lithuanians out of their homes in the years following these republics' annexation by the Soviet Union. Despite considerable efforts to hold these agents accountable, the number of cases heard by the courts has been rather small, while the number of those convicted has been even smaller, given the defendants advanced age and frail health condition. The determination with which the Baltic states have employed court proceedings as a transitional justice method markedly contrasts with the apathy of societies and the despondency of governments of other former Soviet republics, including Russia.

In terms of reckoning with the communist past, Eastern European countries and former Soviet republics stand together in clusters on the continuum stretching from "no transitional justice" to "vigorous transitional justice." As our analysis suggests, Albania, Slovakia, the former Yugoslav republic of Slovenia, Russia, Belarus, Ukraine, Moldova, Armenia, Azerbaijan, Georgia, and the Central Asian countries of Kazakhstan, Kyrgyzstan, Tajikistan, Turkmenistan, and Uzbekistan have been the least interested in reconsidering their past through lustration, file access, and trials. Reckoning with the recent past has not been a priority in the former Soviet republics just mentioned. Slovenia has registered very little progress in any of the three areas mentioned above, Slovakia conducted very limited purges only in 2001 and reluctantly prepared the ground for partial access to the secret archives two years later, whereas Albania has launched successive purges aimed less to address the past and more to weaken the opposition and provide the government a relative pre-electoral advantage. At the other end of the spectrum stands East Germany, which alone pursued transitional justice aggressively by employing all three methods at the beginning of the post-communist period. The Czech Republic comes closest behind East Germany, with early radical lustration leading to loss of jobs for a wide category of representatives of the old regime, but with delayed access to secret archives, and court proceedings that generally lacked stamina. This group of leaders is joined by Estonia, Latvia, and Lithuania, which enacted lustration through citizenship laws, electoral laws and screening laws in the first years following their declaration of independence, granted their citizens access to the meager collections of secret documents left behind, and pursued with considerable determination former NKVD agents responsible for the deportations of the late 1940s. Poland, Hungary and Romania stand somewhere between these two clusters of extreme cases. With the 2006 legislative amendments rekindling lustration, Poland has enjoyed a relative advantage over Hungary, which itself enjoys a relative advantage over Romania, a country where all methods of transitional justice were vigorously debated, but where lustration never enjoyed the unconditional support of any political formation, access to secret documents began in earnest only in 2006, and few cases ultimately went to court.

Thus, Eastern European countries and former Soviet republics can be divided into four main clusters, based on the severity and timing of their efforts to reckon with the past. Countries that adopted strong approaches to transitional justice pursued lustration, access to secret archives and court proceedings vigorously and quickly. Germany, the Czech Republic, and the three Baltic states belong to this category. Countries like Hungary and Poland, where transitional justice was either less radical in scope or delayed in time constitute a second category of mild transitional justice approaches. The two Balkan countries of Romania and Bulgaria have adopted weak approaches to transitional justice, addressing the past with the help of one or two of the methods outlined here (early court proceedings and late file access, but no lustration in Romania; early lustration, late file access and almost no court trials in Bulgaria). A fourth distinct category is formed by those countries that resisted attempts to reevaluate the past and seemingly followed a "forgive and forget" approach. Slovakia, Slovenia, Albania, and all Soviet successor republics (except Estonia, Latvia, and Lithuania) fit this description.

Explanations for country differences

The previous section established that post-communist countries approached the process of reckoning with the past in significantly different ways. What makes a country a leader or a laggard in reckoning with the past? This question has preoccupied a number of researchers, whose fine work is presented below. Explanations for country differences with regard to post-communist transitional justice refer to either the "politics of the past" or the "politics of the present." Let us discuss them in the order in which were first presented. Note that these explanations have focused on the countries of Eastern Europe, ignoring realities in the former Soviet Union.

In a seminal book published in 1991, *The Third Wave: Democracy in the Twentieth Century*, Samuel Huntington claimed that three main types of transition from authoritarian rule characterized the "third wave" of democratization, which included the Eastern European revolutions, and that the outcome of the "torturer problem" was predicted by the type of transition a society underwent in its effort to democratize.[4] In the Hungarian and Bulgarian transformations, Huntington argued, communist leaders took the lead and changed that regime into a democracy. In the East German and Romanian replacements, the communist government lost strength until it collapsed or was overthrown by revolutionary forces. Finally, in the transplacements that occurred in Poland and Czechoslovakia democracy was brought about in negotiations between weak political regimes and weak oppositional forces, because in those countries neither the regime nor the opposition was powerful enough to enforce its vision alone. Huntington considered that, in essence, "justice was a function of political power," and transitional justice was determined by transition type.[5] While officials of regimes that transformed themselves were able to declare amnesties to protect their position, and transplacements involved amnesty as part of the negotiated transition, officials in regimes that were replaced were not in a position to demand anything. Hence, of all types of transition Huntington identified replacements were most likely to result in the prosecution of authoritarian officials. Consistent with his prediction based on transition type, Huntington observed that "in Eastern Europe, apart from Romania and East Germany, the initial overall tendency was to forgive and forget."[6] The weaker an authoritarian regime was at the time of the transfer of power to democratic forces, the more likely officials and collaborators would be held accountable for their acts of oppression. In addition, Huntington insisted that transition must be swift, for transition type to translate into justice, and cautioned that "democratic justice cannot be summary justice of the sort meted out to the Ceausescus, but it also cannot be slow justice." That is because "the popular support and indignation necessary to make justice a political reality fade; the discredited groups associated with the authoritarian regime reestablish their legitimacy and influence. In new democratic regimes, justice comes quickly or it does not come at all."[7]

In an article published in 1994, John P. Moran replied to Huntington by arguing that the extent to which a communist country tolerated dissent and emigration determines the scope of transitional justice.[8] Borrowing Hirschman's psychological terms, Moran discussed the importance of "voice" and "exit" in explaining the appetite for vengeance in post-communist countries. He found that in Eastern Europe "the tendency to forgive and forget can be found in those countries – Poland, Hungary – where either exit and/or voice were allowed under the former regime. In countries where neither exit nor voice was allowed – Bulgaria and Czechoslovakia – calls for punishment predominated."[9] Thus, the more liberal the communist leaders, the more lenient the citizenry and the less willing to exclude them from post-communist politics and bring them to justice. By contrast, the more a regime silenced dissent and kept its citizens captive in the country, the more inclined the population to seek retribution and hold former communist officials accountable.

The "nature of the communist regime" factor accounts for the speed and resolve with which Czechoslovakia and East Germany, known for their harsh and restrictive communist dictatorship, adopted radical lustration programs soon after the regime change of 1989, and why Bulgaria was quick to adopt lustration laws, which unfortunately were deemed unconstitutional and therefore were never implemented. The factor further accounts for the reluctance of post-communist governments in Hungary and Poland, countries known for their milder versions of communism, to bar communist officials and secret spies from public life or bring them to justice. The Yugoslav "socialism with a human face" also explains why Slovenia was not interested in punishing communist officials through lustration, public identification or court proceedings. The same factor worked in Albania, where purges were launched soon after the regime change to a democratic system, although it alone cannot explain why those purges soon turned into political vendetta. The nature of the communist regime was also at work in Romania, where calls for sidelining former communist officials were voiced insistently during the December 1989 revolution and formed the core of the Timisoara Declaration of March 1990.

As in most post-communist countries transitional justice was supported by opposition forces, one would expect more radical lustration, more vigorous prosecution and more comprehensive access to secret archives in those countries where the dissidents and the anti-communist forces were unable to initiate serious talks with the communist officials. Unreformed communist regimes insulated from the opposition and the larger society robbed East Germany, Bulgaria, Romania, and Albania of the possibility to change the regime through round table talks. The communist leaders' radical, uncompromising stance encouraged their critics to adopt an equally inflexible position, and legitimized radical purges as just punishment for unrepentant tyrants. Conversely, in countries like Poland and Hungary where it obtained a regime change through negotiations with the communist leadership, the opposition was unwilling to punish them later, not because amnesty was specifically included in the final deal (as there is no evidence that was indeed the case in Poland or Hungary), but because it did not want such punishment to reflect badly on itself. If communist officials had to be brought to justice and politically marginalized for their involvement in serious human rights violations, opposition representatives should not have agreed to enter into negotiations with such unsavory characters in the first place.

More recent analyses moved away from Huntington's focus on transition type and Moran's focus on the communist past to emphasize the impact of post-communist political competition. Several explanations can be bundled together under "the politics of the present" category.

Helga Welsh was the first to consider the simultaneous impact of multiple determinants related to both the past and the present.[10] In an oft-cited 1996 article, she proposed that the "politics of the [post-communist] present" played a greater role than the nature of the communist regime or the exit from communism in determining a country's choice for or against lustration. She noted that the reasons for favoring lustration were related to the post-communist party struggle for political power, although calls for banning leaders and spies of the ancient regime almost always made reference to the communist past. For Welsh, "the weaker the electoral strength of the former communists, the easier it has been to move ahead with de-communization efforts." The trend resulted in significant country differences. Czechoslovakia could adopt radical lustration early on because the communist camp was weakened and delegitimized. "In Bulgaria and Romania, where former communists have continuously been able to garner substantial electoral support, issues of lustration and prosecution of crimes committed under communist rule have added to the already substantial political polarization."[11] Welsh discounted the possibility of countries enacting lustration as long as former communists controlled parliament, the body called to vote in favor of screening bills. As Szczerbiak suggested, "Welsh also factors in the possibility that lustration might continue to recur as an issue because it becomes politicized as attitudes toward the communist past become more sharply defined as part of the day-to-day political power struggle." That is, "the issue of attitudes towards the communist past would not necessarily disappear as time passed and could even become more salient as some politicians exploited it in an attempt to undermine their opponents' legitimacy."[12]

Building on Welsh's theory suggesting that a key factor explaining the progress of transitional justice was the electoral strength of the former communists,

Kieran Williams, Aleks Szczerbiak, and Brigid Fowler argued that the variables determining lustration legislation in Central Europe were the differing access of former opposition groups to power and their ability to put together a coalition supportive of lustration.[13] In their 2003 working paper, the three British researchers refined Welsh's theory by identifying the circumstances in which lustration can be instrumentalized as part of the political game, and specifying the motives animating advocates of screening procedures. They noted that countries that pursued lustration more vigorously – the Czech Republic, Hungary, and Poland – differed in terms of their communist experiences and transition type, but faced identical demands for lustration in the early 1990s. As they explained, "these demands were translated into legislation at different times, and varied considerably in the range of offices affected and the sanctions imposed." Because of pervasive networks of secret informers and continuous political prominence of un-repented communist leaders, "many of the political divisions in the newly-democratizing East European societies were expressed by reference to the old regime," and "attitudes to the past developed into an issue on which parties cooperate and compete."[14]

The three authors contended that the passage of a lustration bill depended on the ability of its most ardent advocates to persuade a heterogeneous parliamentary plurality that the safeguarding of democracy required it. Whereas Huntington and Moran believed that the past decided the timing and strength of transitional justice, Williams and his colleagues noted that none of the five "sources of the demand for lustration" they identified "had much to do with the nature of the preceding regime or the exit from it."[15] Whereas Welsh believed that support for lustration could mount primarily from within the ranks of the anti-communist opposition, Williams and his colleagues recognized lustration as a policy palatable to a range of political actors. Key to its adoption were justifications crossing the ideological divide to equally appeal to former communists and former dissidents. In all three countries, the authors pointed out, lustration bills were initiated by anti-communist opposition forces, but had to be modified to become acceptable to a sufficiently large parliamentary majority.

By 2004 several authors had proposed explanatory frameworks linking lustration to the communist past and/or post-communist politics. Without exception, they had focused their attention on the political negotiation leading up to the adoption of lustration laws. Nadya Nedelsky for the first time factored in the neglected implementation of lustration laws, recognizing that ex-communist countries face tremendous difficulties in enacting any kind of legislation, including legislation pertaining to lustration.[16] Rather than considering all East European countries or only those that pursued lustration more vigorously, Nedelsky employed one of those quasi-experimental research designs political scientists long for. The comparison of the Czech Republic and Slovakia, two countries that shared a common communist past, but had different post-communist experiences following the breakup of the federation in 1993, allowed Nedelsky to control for both the nature of the old regime and type of exit from communism.

Whereas Huntington and Moran considered the past, and Welsh, Williams, Szczerbiak, and Fowler considered the present as primary determinants of lustration,

Nedelsky drew a link between past and more recent developments by arguing that "struggles over transitional justice issues should not be considered exclusively as 'the politics of the present' or as 'the politics of the past'." For her, "a stronger influencing factor is represented by the level of the preceding regime's legitimacy, as indicated during the communist period by levels of societal cooptation, opposition or internal exile, and during the post-communist period by levels of elite re-legitimization and public interest in 'de-communization'."[17] Thus, "the lower levels of regime repression in Slovakia both reflected and produced a higher level of regime legitimacy than existed in the Czech lands." In addition, "the communist regime's higher level of legitimacy in Slovakia contributed to a lesser interest in transitional justice there than in the Czech lands." For Nedelsky then, the Czechs adopted lustration because they viewed the communist regime as less legitimate, and the post-communist government carrying it out as legitimate. By contrast, the Slovaks quietly left the lustration law to expire because of their acceptance of the communist regime and dissatisfaction with early post-communist rule. Nedelsky spelled out the mechanism translating regime legitimacy into lustration:

> The higher a society's view of the previous regime's legitimacy, the lower its motivation to pursue justice for its authorities and the higher the likelihood, in a democratic context, that it will allow elites associated with the former regime to return to the political stage. These elites, in turn, would not be particularly likely to support vigorous transitional justice. Therefore, the more quickly they regain power, the less likely a legal framework will be established to screen such elites out of the political sphere over time. Conversely, the lower the society's view of the previous regime's legitimacy, the more likely it is to have both an anti-communist counter-elite to offer an alternative to communist successor parties and to offer electoral support to this counter-elite. In turn, these elites would certainly be more likely than the communist successor elites to pursue "de-communization."[18]

Using Kitschelt, Nedelsky applied her theory to Poland, Hungary, and Romania, countries with different types of communist regimes that translated into different levels of regime legitimacy in the late communist and early post-communist periods. According to Kitschelt, Poland represented a mix of national-accommodative and bureaucratic authoritarian communism, Hungary was a national-accommodative regime, whereas Romania was a case of patrimonial communism. Patrimonial communist regimes used strong repression and strong cooptation into clientelist networks, and allowed for little elite turnover in post-communism. National-accommodative communism relied on cooptation, and ended in negotiations permitting communist parties to reinvent themselves as viable post-communist political actors. Last, bureaucratic-authoritarian communist regimes relied on repression, and ended in implosion, after which post-communist elites had little chance of reassuming an influential position.[19]

The most recent theoretical framework for explaining lustration was advanced by Monika Nalepa in 2005.[20] Her doctoral dissertation defended at Columbia

University tried to explain the puzzling behavior of Polish and Hungarian successors to Communist Parties, which first insisted on immunity from transitional justice as the price of supporting liberalization and democratization, and then implemented the very screening policies they raised initially against. In her study, Nalepa determined that when former communists anticipated losing power to anti-communist forces, as was the case in Hungary in 1994 and Poland in 1997, they tried to appease a pivotal median political party in order to prevent harsher legislation favored by hard-line anti-communists. Thus, she concluded, the former communists behaved rationally by initiating less punitive versions of transitional justice than their anti-communist rivals would. For the former communists, support for lustration was not the result of support for an honest reexamination of the communist past, but a pre-emptive strategy designed to protect their political careers from more radical policies.

A multivariate model

While informative, all these analytical frameworks have been affected by limitations. Being the first of its kind, Huntington's study received enormous attention but was placed at a serious disadvantage by the number of cases it rested on, the time span it investigated, as well as the methods of transitional justice it discussed. Contrary to his prediction, there seems to be no evidence for the fact that the politics of memory can be pursued during a limited window of opportunity immediately following the transition to democracy. The majority of Eastern European countries and former Soviet republics engaged in transitional justice some years after the post-communist political scene coalesced; a significant number of court trials were started with considerable delay due to the difficulties in gathering the needed evidence; and important laws allowing for lustration and file access were adopted close to a decade after the collapse of the communist regime. Huntington was also unable to assess the full importance of access to the secret file, a process which had barely begun by the time he formulated his theory.

Virtually all other theoretical framework rested on the examination of a subset of countries that were purposely selected because they shared some important characteristics (for example, they adopted "radical" transitional justice or they launched mild lustration with the help of the successors to the communist parties), or because they had pursued the politics of memory up by the time the authors took them into consideration. None of these authors was interested to find out why countries avoided confronting their past, although non-cases could tell us as much about the reasons for and against transitional justice. Further, none of these studies investigated all three main types of transitional justice processes in all countries of the former communist block, none looked at both the adoption and the implementation of relevant legislation, and none scrutinized the entire period of transition up to these countries' integration into the European Union.

While not arguing that transition type and levels of exit/voice are unimportant, we contend that a stronger predictor of transitional justice is the relative political power of communist successor parties and their former opposition. We move beyond these other authors' theoretical frameworks, however, by arguing that the dynamics of this competition, particularly regarding transitional justice, are strongly linked to the relationship between regime and opposition during the communist period. In a clear pattern throughout Eastern Europe, former communists voted against lustration and file access laws, while their opposition provided the impetus for them. We argue that the outcome of this struggle appears to have been strongly influenced by three interrelated factors: 1) the composition, orientation, and strength of the opposition, both before and after 1989, 2) the communist regime's dominant methods of ensuring societal compliance with its rule (repression and/or cooptation), and 3) the country's pre-communist level of experience with political pluralism. In countries with a pre-communist history of strong multi-party politics, and where communist-era opposition was comprised of some combination of dissidents, mass opposition movement members, and internally exiled technocrats, as in the Czech Republic, Poland, Hungary, and the Baltic states, one finds in the post-communist period a well-organized, well-educated, potentially powerful alternative elite. This elite's orientation toward communism's legitimacy is grounded in its experience under that regime, and transitional justice has been far more stringent where communist rule was enforced primarily through repression and ideological rigidity (as in the Czech Republic and East Germany in Eastern Europe, and Estonia, Latvia, and Lithuania in the former Soviet Union) than in those where it relied more on cooptation and allowed some level of reform (as in Poland, at times, and especially in Hungary). Where, on the other hand, organized opposition toward communism was very weak because of a combination of little pre-communist experience with political pluralism (Bulgaria, Romania, the Caucasus, and Central Asia) and, in the communist period, the regime's severe repression of any nascent counter-elite (Romania) and/or successful cooptation of many elites (Slovakia, Russia, Ukraine, and Belarus, and to some extent Romania), in the post-communist period we find a much weaker push toward transitional justice. In this group of cases, again, the former regime's behavior was important in shaping the opposition's post-communist orientation toward it, as transitional justice was pursued more vigorously and successfully where repression rather than cooptation was the primary method of ensuring societal compliance.

More broadly, however, in this second set of countries, communist-successor parties were able to consistently retain power longer after the 1989 revolutions and after the 1991 break-up of the Soviet Union than in the first-set countries. In addition, in these countries it was later that opposition parties gained sufficient electoral strength to adopt transitional justice legislation (or only to propose it, as it was the case in Ukraine, Georgia, and Moldova). Among second-set countries that adopted such legislation, the categories of former communist officials and secret policemen banned from politics were fewer and the list of state offices closed to them was shorter than in countries with more powerful opposition forces. Moreover, the later a country launched lustration and file access, the more tampered the archives, the harder to identify the individuals imvolved in past human rights abuses and the more disputed the official findings. We hypothesize, then, that the three factors that we identify are in combination a stronger predictor of 1) the year when lustration and file access laws gained parliamentary approval, 2) the comprehensiveness and stringency of the laws in terms of the social categories targeted and the implications for those who fall within them, and 3) the number of trials against former communist officials and political police agents, than transition type, exit/voice, and the "politics of the present," narrowly defined.

Our cases indicate the temporal distinctions used by the leading theories to distinguish themselves from one another (such as the past is primary or the transition decides everything or the present is now the most important) are actually misleading and unhelpful. Rather, the continuities between past, transitional and present factors transcend the dislocations of regime change in important ways. What we contend, then, is not only that none of the prevailing theories explains why each and every Eastern European country and former Soviet republic pursued or rejected transitional justice, but also that they limited themselves by suggesting that one particular time period is of paramount importance (the period they covered) and neglecting the integral relationships between time periods. Rather than being dissociated from each other, the past and the present are closely linked. The national specificity of the communist past led to a particular type of transition which in turn led to a specific post-communist political constellation that facilitated or prevented transitional justice. Drawing these observations together makes it difficult to argue that normative considerations of justice are entirely absent, because the past remains relevant almost two decades after the collapse of the communist regimes. At the same time, we can note that individual personalities of politicians assuming leading roles in speeding up or slowing down the transitional justice process, and awareness of developments and problems in neighboring countries make an imprint on how national elites approach the politics of memory. History is not destiny, but it matters a lot.

Notes

1 H. Jara, 'Dealing with the Past: The Case of Estonia', *Ulkopoliittinen Instituutti Working Paper* No. 15, 1999, p. 12. Online. Available HTTP: http://www.up-fiia.fi/document.php?DOC_ID=69#wp15.php (accessed 1 February 2008).
2 In 2006 the Albanian Parliament adopted a resolution calling for the opening of the secret Sigurimi archives.
3 Telling in this regard was Russia's refusal to shed light on the life of Pavlik Morozov, the 13-year-old who in 1932 reported on his estranged father to the NKVD. After his father was deported to the Gulag, Pavlik was murdered by his father's relatives.
4 S. P. Huntington, *The Third Wave: Democratization in the Late Twentieth Century*, London: University of Oklahoma Press, 1991.
5 Ibid.
6 Ibid.
7 Ibid.
8 J. Moran, 'The Communist Torturers of Eastern Europe: Prosecute and Punish or Forgive and Forget?', *Communist and Post-Communist Studies* 1994, vol. 27, 95–109, and A. O. Hirschmann, *Exit, Voice and Loyalty*, Cambridge: Harvard University Press, 1970.

9 Moran, 'The Communist Torturers of Eastern Europe', 101.
10 H. Welsh, 'Dealing with the Communist Past: Central and East European Experiences after 1990', *Europe-Asia Studies* 1996, vol. 48, 419–428.
11 Ibid., 422.
12 A. Szczerbiak, 'Dealing with the Communist Past or the Politics of the Present? Lustration in Post-Communist Poland', *Europe–Asia Studies* 2002, vol. 54, 553–572.
13 K. Williams, B. Fowler and A. Szczerbiak, 'Explaining Lustration in Central Europe: A 'Post-Communist Politics' Approach', *Democratization* 2005, vol. 12, 22–43. The paper was first published in March 2003 as Sussex European Institute Working Paper no. 62. Note that this analysis completely disregarded the Bulgarian and Albanian purges, which in many ways were more vigorous, and which affected more individuals, than the mild Hungarian or Polish lustration programs.
14 Ibid., 30.
15 Ibid.
16 N. Nedelsky, 'Divergent Responses to a Common Past: Transitional Justice in the Czech Republic and Slovakia', *Theory and Society* 2004, vol. 33, 65–115.
17 Ibid., 65.
18 Ibid., 88.
19 H. Kitschelt, Z. Mansfedova, R. Markowski, and G. Toka, *Post-Communist Party Systems: Competition, Representation and Inter-Party Cooperation*, Cambridge: Cambridge University Press, 1999, pp. 24–25.
20 M. Nalepa, 'The Power of Secret Information: Transitional Justice after Communism', Ph.D. Thesis defended at Columbia University, Department of Political Science, 2005.

Bibliography

'16 superagenti sred bivshite deputati I ministry ostanaha skriti', *Sega*, 15 April 2005.
'764 more StB officers ousted', *The Slovak Spectator*, 14 May 2007. Online. Available HTTP: http://www.spectator.sk (accessed 25 January 2008).
Abrahams, F., *Human Rights in Post-Communist Albania*, New York: Human Rights Watch, 1996.
Achter Tätigkeitsbericht des Bundesbeauftragten für die Unterlagen des Staatssicherheitsdienstes der ehemaligen Deutschen Demokratischen Republik, Berlin: BStU, 2007.
Act III of 2003. Online. Available HTTP: http://www.th.hu/html/en/acts/ABTL_4_2003_evi_III_tv_e.pdf (accessed 14 July 2007).
'The Act on National Protection', *National Gazette*, 1988, vol. 38, 8–20.
Adamičková, N. and M. Königová, 'Lustrace se rušit nebudou', *Právo*, 8 December 2005. Online. Available HTTP: http://pravo.newtonit.cz/default.asp?cache=617992 (accessed 8 February 2006).
'Adamkus Wants Constitutional Court to Rule on Lustration Law', *RFE/RL Newsline*, 13 July 1998.
Akule, D., 'Latvia Bars Candidates with a Communist Past from Elections', *Transitions Online*, 6–12 August 2002.
Albania Country Report on Human Rights Practices for 1996, Washington, D.C.: US Department of Justice, 30 January, 1997. Online. Available HTTP: http://www.state.gov/www/global/human_rights/1996_hrp_report/albania.html (accessed 23 January 2008).
'Albanian Parliament Softens Lustration Law', *RFE/RL Newsline*, 16 January 1998. Online. Available HTTP: http://www.hri.org/news/balkans/rferl/1998/98-01-16.rferl.html (accessed 23 January 2008).
Albanian Telegraph Agency, 'Nine Senior Ex Communists Face Trial', 29 July 1996. Online. Available HTTP: http://www.hri.org/news/balkans/ata/1996/96-07-30.ata.html#03 (accessed 23 January 2008).
Allcock, J. B., Horton, J., and Milovojević, M., *The role of the Yugoslav intelligence and security committee in Yugoslavia in Transition*, New York: Berg, 1992.
Alpha Research Agency, 'Representative Poll for Sofia, 18–20 July 1997', *Capital Weekly*, 1997, No. 30.
——, 'Representative Poll for Sofia, 2 September 1997', *Capital Weekly*, 1997, No. 45.
'And Draft Law on Lustration, Extension of Tax Break for Media', *RFE/RL Newsline*, 20 February 2007.
'And Prime Minister Condemns 'Collaboration' Tack in Politics', *RFE/RL Newsline*, 8 July 2002. Online. Available HTTP: http://www.rferl.org/newsline/2002/07/080702.asp (accessed 28 January 2008).

Andoni, B., 'Are Albanians Afraid of Purity?', *Shekulli*, 10 December 2004.

Andreev, M., 'Dekomunizatiata v Bulgaria', March 2002. Online. Available HTTP: http:// www.geocities.com/decommunization/Decommunization2/Andreev.htm (accessed 29 January 2008).

Anghelescu, A. and Artene, A., 'Chitac facut scapat', *Ziua*, 17 February 2004.

Anjaparidze, Z., 'Russian Film on Saakashvili Tests Georgian Democracy', *Eurasia Daily Monitor*, 4 October 2004. Online. Available HTTP: http://jamestown.org/publications_ details.php?volume_id=401&issue_id=3093&article_id=2368629 (accessed 15 December 2007).

'Another Former Hungarian Minister Admits Collaborating with Communist Secret Services', *RFE/RL Newsline*, 19 August 2002. Online. Available HTTP: http://www.rferl. org/newsline/2002/08/190802.asp (accessed 28 January 2008).

Anžič, A., 'Obveščevalne službe-legalni in legitimni labirinti in izhodi', *Varstvoslovje*, 1 January 1999.

——, 'Parlamentarno nadzorstvo nad obeščevalno vanostnimi službami: Slovenske izkušnje', *Varstvoslovje*, 2000, vol. 2, 10–20.

Appel, H., 'Anti-Communist Justice and Founding the Post-Communist Order: Lustration and Restitution in Central Europe', *East European Politics and Society*, 2005, vol. 19, 379–405.

Applebaum, A., *Gulag: A History*, London: Penguin Books, 2003.

Archive RS dislocirana enota i fond Seje CK ZKS, 14th session of the presidency CK ZKS, 29 January 1979.

Arendt, F. 'Die MfS-überprüfung im öffentlichen Dienst am Beispiel des Freistaates Sachsen', in J. Weber and M. Piazolo (eds.), *Eine Diktatur vor Gericht: Aufarbeitung von SED-Unrecht durch die Justiz,* Munich: Olzog, 1995, pp. 159–180.

Arnold, J., 'DDR-Vergangenheit und Schranken rechtsstaatlichen Strafrechts', in J. Arnold (ed.) *Strafrechtliche Auseinandersetzung mit Systemvergangenheit*, Baden-Baden: Nomos Verlagsgesellschaft, 2000, pp. 100–130.

——, 'Einschränkung des Rückwirkungsverbotes sowie sorgfältige Schuldprüfung be den Tötungsfällen an der DDR-Grenze' in J. Arnold (ed.) *Strafrechtliche Auseinandersetzung mit Systemvergangenheit*, Baden-Baden: Nomos Verlagsgesellschaft, 2000, pp. 131–146.

Artene, A., 'Dreptate pentru Ursu', *Ziua*, 15 July 2003.

'Article 19 Expresses Concern over Lustration Law', *OMRI Daily Digest II*, 7 December 1995. Online. Available HTTP: http://www.hri.org/news/balkans/omri/1995/95-12-07. omri.html (accessed 23 January 2008).

Ascherson, N., *The Polish August*, Harmondsworth: Penguin, 1981.

'As Medgyessy Commission Members Leak Intended Questions to Media', *RFE/RL Newsline*, 1 August 2002. Online. Available HTTP: http://www.rferl.org/newsline/ 2002/08/ 010802.asp (accessed 28 January 2008).

'As Poll Reiterates that Public Doesn't Care', *RFE/RL Newsline*, 24 September 2002. Online. Available HTTP: http://www.rferl.org/newsline/2002/09/240902.asp (accessed 28 January 2008).

Assenov, B., *Ot Shesto – za Shesto*, Sofia: Polygraf, 1994.

Associated Press, 13 February 2005.

'Auch Kanzler haben Rechte', *Der Tagesspiegel*, 21 June 2004, 10.

Austin, R. C., 'What Albania Adds to the Balkan Stew', *Orbis*, 1993, vol. 37, 259–279.

Bachmeier, R., 'Datenschutz und Umgang mit Stasi-Akten' in E. Benda, R. Bachmeier and P. Busse, *Persönlichkeitsschutz und Stasi-Akten*, Berlin: Broschürenreihe der Konrad-Adenauer-Stiftung, 2000, pp. 13–19.

Bača, I., 'Udavači, mate zelenú', *Národná obroda*, 12 February 2002.

Bacu, D., *Pitesti. Centru de reeducare studenteasca*, Hamilton: Cuvantul Romanesc, 1989.

Baev, J. and K. Grozev, *Bulgarian Intelligence & Security Services in the Cold War Years*. CD-ROM. Sofia: Cold War Research Group, 2005.

Barahona de Brito, A., Gonzalez-Enriquez, C. and Aguilar, P. (eds.) *The Politics of Memory. Transitional Justice in Democratizing Societies*, Oxford: Oxford University Press, 2001.

Barrett, E., Hack, P.and Munkacsi, A., 'Lustration in Hungary: An Evaluation of the Law, Its Implementation and Its Impact', paper presented at the American Association for the Advancement of Slavic Studies conference, Boston, 4–7 December 2004.

Basic Hrvatin, S., 'The Role of the Media in the Transition', in D. Fink-Hafner and J. R. Robbins (eds.) *Making a New Nation: The Formation of Slovenia*, Brookfield: Dartmouth, 1997, 267–277.

Bavcar, I. and Janša, J., 'Emigranti: Med represijo in kolaboracionizmom s SDV', *Mladina*, 19 February 1989. Online. Available HTTP: http://www.mladina.si/tednik/198907 (accessed 18 January 2007).

Becker, N., 'Strafprozesse gegen Funktionäre der ehemaligen DDR', *Neue Justiz*, 1998, vol. 7, 353–354.

Beehner, L., 'Russia's Soviet Past still Haunts Relations with West', Council on Foreign Relations, 29 June 2007. Online. Available HTTP: http://www.cfr.org/publication/13697 (accessed 15 December 2007).

Bekiarov, A., *Chetvurt Vek v UBO*, Sofia: Letopisi, 1990.

Benda, E., 'Persönlichkeitsschutz und Stasi-Akten', in E. Benda, R. Bachmeier and P. Busse, *Persönlichkeitsschutz und Stasi-Akten*, Berlin: Broschürenreihe der Konrad-Adenauer-Stiftung, 2000, pp. 5–12.

Biberaj, E., *Albania in Transition: The Rocky Road to Democracy*, Boulder: Westview Press, 1998.

Bickford, L., 'Transitional Justice', in D. Shelton (ed.) *The Encyclopedia of Genocide and Crimes against Humanity*, New York: MacMillan, 2004. Online. Available HTTP: http://www.ictj.org/static/TJApproaches/WhatisTJ/macmillan.TJ.eng.pdf (accessed 4 January 2008.

Birnbaum, R. and Rimscha, R. von, 'SPD und FDP kritisieren Stasi-Urteil', *Der Tagesspiegel*, 26 June 2004, 4.

'Birthler-Behörde in der Kritik', *Die Tageszeitung*, 13 August 2007.

'Birthler: Neue Impulse für die Aufarbeitung der SED-Diktatur durch novelliertes Stasi-Unterlagen-Gesetz', 15 December 2006. Pressemitteilung der BstU.

Bizlij, L., *Cerkev v policijskih arhivih*, Ljubljana: Cankarjeva zalozba, 1990.

Blažek, P. and P. Žáček, 'Czechoslovakia', in K. Persak and Ł. Kamiński (eds.) *A Handbook of the Communist Security Apparatus in East Central Europe 1944–1989*, Warsaw: Institute of National Remembrance, 2005, pp. 87–162.

Boed, R., 'An Evaluation of the Legality and Efficacy of Lustration as a Tool of Transitional Justice', *Columbia Journal of Transnational Law*, 1999, vol. 37, 357–402.

Borčin, J., 'Dokedy bude štát občanmi skrývat' spisy ŠtB?', *Národná obroda*, 21 February 2002.

Borneman, J., *Settling Accounts. Violence, Justice and Accountability in Postsocialist Europe*, Princeton: Princeton University Press, 1997.

Bota, V., 'Securitatea, invingator absolut in alegeri', *Evenimentul Zilei*, 18 March 2000.

Both, H., 'Rechtliche und sachliche Probleme bei Mitteilungen zur Überprüfung von Personen', in S. Suckut and J. Weber (eds.), *Stasi-Akten zwischen Politik und Zeitgeschichte: Eine Zwischenbilanz*, Munich: Olzog, 2003, pp. 291–308.

Brejc, M., *Vmestni čas: varnostno informativna služba in nastanjane nove slvoenske države 1990–1993*, Ljubljana: Mladinska knjiga, 1994.

Bruce, G., *Resistance with the People: Repression and Resistance in Eastern Germany*, Lanham: Rowman and Littlefield, 2003.

——, "Wir haben den Kontakt zu den Massen nie verloren:' Das Verhältnis zwischen Stasi und Gesellschaft am Beispiel der Kreise Perleberg und Gransee', in J. Gieseke (ed.), *Staatssicherheit und Gesellschaft*, Göttigen: Vandenhoeck & Ruprecht, 2007, pp. 365–379.

Bučar, F., 'Razpisal bom volitve', *Delo*, 10 September 1992.

Bukovec, T., 'UDBa je udarila prek interneta, *Dnevnik*, 27 April, 2003. Online. Available HTTP: http://www.dnevnik.si/novice/iskalnik?sel=advanced (accessed 20 January 2006).

Bulgaria, New York: Human Rights Watch, 1995. Online. Available HTTP: http://www. hrw.org/reports/1995/WR95/HELSINKI-04.htm (accessed 29 December 2007).

Bulgarian Communist Party Central Committee Resolution on Intensifying the Prevention of Criminal Activities, 14 January 1960, Bulgarian Communist Party Archives, Fond 1B, Record 64, File 264.

Bulgarian Communist Party Central Committee Secretariat Protocol B 8, *Guidelines for the Work and Activity of the Intelligence Department in the Committee for State Security (9 July 1963)*, Bulgarian Communist Party Archive, Fond 1B, Record 64, file 313.

Bulgarian Communist Party Central Committee Secretariat Resolution no. 6, *Guidelines for the Work and Activity of the Military Counter-intelligence in the Ministry of Interior (18 June 1963)*, Bulgarian Communist Party Archive, Fond 1B, Record 64, File 311.

Bulgarian Communist Party Central Committee Resolution on the Creation of the Sixth Department in the Committee for State Security (November 1967), Bulgarian Communist Party Archive, Fond 1 B, Record 64, File 368.

Bulgarian Communist Party Central Committee Politburo Resolution B 4, *Main Guidelines for Decree for the State Security (3 April 1974)*, Bulgarian Communist Party Archive, Fond 1B, Record 64, File 438.

Bulgarian Communist Party Central Committee Politburo *Resolution No. 17 of 27 June 1977 On Improvement of the Work for Prevention and Neutralization of the Activities of the Bulgarian Enemy Emigration*, Bulgarian Communist Party Archive, Fond 1B, Record 64, file 504, p. 23.

Bulgarian Ministry of Interior, *Ordinance on the Recruitment and Utilization of State Security Secret Informers and Reliable Persons. 11 April 1989*. Online. Available at HTTP: http://www.geocities.com/decommunization/Communism/Bulgaria/Documents/MVR1989.htm (accessed 10 March 2005).

Bundesbeauftragte Marianne Birthler anlässlich der Vorstellung des 6. Tätigkeitsberichtes am 12.9.2003', 12 September 2003. Pressemitteilung der BStU.

'But Opposition Will Submit Own Amendments', *RFE/RL Newsline*, 24 June 2002. Online. Available HTTP: http://www.rferl.org/newsline/2002/06/240602.asp (accessed 28 January 2008).

'But Shelves Debate on Lustration', *RFE/RL Newsline*, 3 January 2007.

Calhoun, N., 'The Ideological Dilemma of Lustration in Poland', *East European Politics and Societies* 2002, vol. 16, 494–520.

——, *Dilemmas of Justice in Eastern Europe's Democratic Transitions*, New York: Palgrave Macmillan, 2004.

Castex, M., *Un mensonge gros comme le siecle: Roumanie, histoire d'une manipulation*, Paris: A Michel, 1990.

Ceausescu, M. M., *Nu regret, nu ma jelesc, nu strig*, Bucharest: Editura Meditatii, 2004.

Cerar G. and I. Mekina, 'Pravica do zasebnosti', *Mladina*, 5 May 2003. Online. Available HTTP: http://www.mladina.si/tednik/200318/ (accessed 20 January 2006).

'Check uncovers 15 former secret police collaborators at Czech police headquarters', *Radio Prague News*, 18 April 2007. Online. Available HTTP: http://www.radio.cz/en/news/90506#5 (accessed 26 January 2008).

Chernetsky, V., 'On the Russian Archives: An Interview with Sergei V. Mironenko', *Slavic Review*, 1993, vol. 52, 839–846.

Chureshki, S., *Pravoslavieto I Komunizmut v Bulgaria, 1944–1960*, Sofia: Prosveta, 2004.

Ciuceanu, R., *Potcoava fara noroc*, Bucharest: Meridiane, 1994.

——, *Pecetea diavolului*, Bucharest: Institutul National pentru Studiul Totalitarismului, 2002.

Coalson, R., 'Russia: Why the Chekist Mind-set Matters', *RFE/RL Report*, 15 October 2007.

Cokl, V., *Vecer*, 13 October 2001. Online. Available HTTP: http://www.vecer.si (accessed 18 January 2008).

'Collaboration Issue Backfires on Hungarian Opposition Leader', *RFE/RL Newsline*, 8 July 2002. Online. Available HTTP: http://www.rferl.org/newsline/2002/07/080702.asp (accessed 28 January 2008).

'Collaborators Revealed', *Uncaptive Minds*, 1991, vol. 4, 8–12.

Commission for Revelation of Documents and Determining Connections of Bulgarian Citizens to the State Security and the Army Intelligence Agencies, *Resolution no. 7*, 19 July 2007. Online. Available HTTP: http://www.comdos.bg/pub/7.pdf (accessed 3 February 2008).

Commission for Revelation of Documents and Determining Connections of Bulgarian Citizens to the State Security and the Army Intelligence Agencies, *Resolution no. 14*, 4 September 2007. Online. Available HTTP: http://www.comdos.bg/pub/14.pdf (accessed 3 February 2008).

'Communist Secret Files to be Opened with Caution', *RFE/RL Report*, 13 June 2000. Online. Available HTTP: http://www.ukrweekly.com/Archive/2000/300006.shtml (accessed 28 January 2008).

Conquest, R., *The Great Terror*, New York: Macmillan, 1973.

——, 'Excess Deaths and Camp Numbers: Some Comments', *Soviet Studies*, vol. 43, 1991, 949–952.

——, 'Victims of Stalinism: A Comment', *Europe-Asia Studies*, 1997, vol. 49, 1317–1319.

Constante, L., *The Silent Escape. Three Thousand Days in Romanian Prisons*, Berkeley: University of California P ress, 1995.

'Constitution of the Republic of Latvia', 2003. Online. Available HTTP: http://www.servat.unibe.ch/icl/lg00000_.html (accessed 6 January 2008).

'Constitutional Court Decision on the Law on Banks and Credit Activity No. 8 of 27 July 1992' in N. Kritz (ed.) *Transitional Justice: How Emerging Democracies Reckon with Former Regimes*, Washington, D.C.: United States Institute of Peace Press, 1995, vol. 3, pp. 294–295.

Coposu, C., *Confessions*, Boulder: East European Monographs, 1998.

Corbeanu, N., *Vara transfugului*, Bucharest: Humanitas, 2002.

Corpas, I., *Secvente din fostele inchisori politice*, Bucharest: Humanitas, 2003.

Cosic, D., *Piscevi zapisi 1951–1968*, Belgrade: Filip Visnjic, 2000.

'A Country Report: Kyrgyzstan', US Library of Congress, 1996. Online. Available HTTP: http://lcweb2.loc.gov/frd/cs/kgtoc.html (accessed 15 December 2007).

'A Country Report: Uzbekistan', US Library of Congress, 1996. Online. Available HTTP: http://lcweb2.loc.gov/frd/cs/uztoc.html (accessed 15 December 2007).

'A Country Study: Albania', US Library of Congress, 7 November 2005. Online. Available HTTP: http://lcweb2.loc.gov/frd/cs/altoc.html (accessed 23 January 2008).

'A Country Study: Azerbaijan', US Library of Congress, 1994. Online. Available HTTP: http://lcweb2.loc.gov/frd/cs/aztoc.html (accessed 16 December 2007).

'A Country Study: Kazakhstan', US Library of Congress, 1996. Online. Available HTTP: http://lcweb2.loc.gov/frd/cs/kztoc.html (accessed 15 December 2007).

'A Country Study: Tajikistan', US Library of Congress, 1996. Online. Available HTTP: http://lcweb2.loc.gov/frd/cs/tjtoc.html (accessed 15 December 2007).

'A Country Study: Turkmenistan', US Library of Congress, 1996. Online. Available HTTP: http://lcweb2.loc.gov/frd/cs/tmtoc.html (accessed 15 December 2007).

'Court Says Latvian Lawmaker Was KGB Agent', *RFE/RL Newsline*, 13 March 2000.

Courtois, S. et al., *The Black Book of Communism. Crimes, Terror, Repression*, Cambridge: Harvard University Press, 1999.

Cubeddu, G., 'From a Distant Country, to spy close up', *30Days in the Church and the World*, 2005, vol. 8. Online. Available HTTP: http://www.30giorni.it/us/articolo. asp?id=9211 (accessed 28 December 2007).

'Czech Informers' Names Published', *BBC News*, 20 March 2003. Online. Available HTTP: http://news.bbc.co.uk/2/hi/europe/2868701.stm (accessed 27 January 2008).

Czech Ministry of the Interior, 'Zpřistupnění svazků vzniklých činností bývalé ŠtB'. Online. Available HTTP: http://www.mvcr.cz/agenda/labyrint/svazky.html (accessed 28 January 2008).

Dale, G. *The East German Revolution of 1989*, Manchester: Manchester University Press, 2006.

Darski, J., 'Police Agents in the Transition Period', *Uncaptive Minds*, 1991–1992, vol. 4, 28–28

Dastych, D. M., 'Better Late than Never: Retarded De-communization in Poland', *The Gazette*, 9 January 2007. Online. Available HTTP: http://www.axisglobe.com/article. asp?article=1192 (accessed 28 January 2008).

——, 'No 'Zero Option' But a Shake Up', Online. Available HTTP: http://www.fas.org/ irp/world/poland/dastych.html (accessed 28 December 2007).

David, R., 'Lustration Laws in Action: The Motives and Evaluation of Lustration Policy in the Czech Republic and Poland (1981–2001)', *Law and Social Inquiry*, 2003, vol. 28, 387–439.

Dawisha, K. (ed.) *The Consolidation of Democracy in East-Central Europe*, Cambridge: Cambridge University Press, 1997.

'Decree Banning KGB Employees and Informers from Government Positions' No. 418 of 12 October 1991, and 'Law on the Verification of Mandates of Those Deputies Accused of Consciously Collaborating with Special Services of Other States' No. I-2115 of 17 December 1991, in Kritz, N. (ed.), *Transitional Justice: How New Democracies Reckon with Their Authoritarian Past*, Washington, D.C.: US Institute for Peace, 1995, vol. 3, pp. 427–431.

'Decree no. 1670 for State Security', *State Gazette* [Sofia], No. 65, 20 August 1974.

Deegan-Krause, K., 'From Another Dimension: Public Opinion and Party Competition in Slovakia and the Czech Republic', paper presented at the American Political Science Association conference, Boston, 5 September 1998. Online. Available

HTTP: http://www.la.wayne.edu/polisci/kdk/papers/apsa1998p.htm (accessed 28 January 2008).

Deletant, D., *Ceausescu and the Securitate: Coercion and Dissent in Romania, 1965–1989*, London: Hurst, 1995.

——, 'Romania', in K. Persak and L. Kaminski (eds.) *A Handbook of the Communist Security Apparatus in East Central Europe. 1944–1989*, Warsaw: Institute of National Remembrance, 2005, pp. 285–328.

Dennis, M., *The Stasi: Myth and Reality*, London: Pearson, 2003.

Diaconescu, I., *Dupa temnita*, Bucharest: Nemira, 2003.

——, *Temnita, destinul generatiei noastre*, Bucharest: Nemira, 2003.

'Directive 95/46/EC of the European Parliament and of the Council of 24 October 1995 on the protection of individuals with regard to the processing of personal data and on the free movement of such data', *Official Journal of the European Communities*, 23 November 1995, No. L 281/31. Online. Available HTTP: http://ec.europa.eu/justice_home/fsj/privacy/docs/95–46-ce/dir1995–46_part1_en.pdf (accessed 4 October 2006).

Dobre, F., Banu, F., Duica, C., Moldovan, S. B. and Taranu, L., *Trupele de Securitate (1949–1989)*, Bucharest: Nemira, 2004.

'Documentul APCE considera ca exista forte populiste care mizeaza pe formarea unui sentiment de nostalgie pentru fostele regimuri', *Cotidianul*, 12 August 2003.

Dritter Tätigkeitsbericht der Bundesbeauftragten für die Unterlagen des Staatssicherheitsdienstes der ehemaligen Deutschen Demokratischen Republik, Berlin: BStU, 1997.

Drnovšek, J., *Escape from Hell: The Truth of a President*, Ljubljana: Delo, 1996.

Dudek, A. and Paczkowski, A., 'Poland', in K. Persak and L. Kaminski (eds.) *A Handbook of the Communist Security Apparatus in East Central Europe, 1944–1989*, Warsaw: Institute of National Remembrance, 2005, pp. 221–286.

Ďurišková, P., 'Eštebákom hrozia problémy', *Pravda*, 30 October 2001. Online. Available HTTP: http://www.pravda.sk/dennik/2001/10/30/slovensko/01/article.5566.html (accessed 29 March 2002).

The Editors, 'Volilna zakonodaja v mlinu parlamentarnih peripetij', *Delo*, 10 September 1992.

——, 'O aferi UDBa.net', *Mladina*, 24 April 2003. Online. Available HTTP: http://www.mladina.si/tednik/200316/ (accessed 20 January 2006).

——, 'Udbino EVidenco sem spravil v računalnik', *Mladina,* 25 May 2003. Online. Available HTTP: http://www.mladina.si/tednik/200321/ (accessed 20 January 2006).

——, 'V parlimentarni "tihi sobi" o uničenih dosjejih nekdanje SDV in aferi UDBa.net?', *Mladina*, 6 June 2003. Online. Available HTTP: http://www.mladina.si/tednik/200322/ (accessed 20 January 2006).

——, 'Nove razsežnosti afere', *Mladina*, 1 August 2003. Online. Available HTTP: http://www.mladina.si/tednik/200331/ (accessed 20 January 2006).

'Eight Parties Believe Collaboration with StB is No Crime', CTK, 31 January 1991.

Ellis, M., 'Purging the Past: The Current State of Lustration Laws in the Former Communist Block', *Law and Contemporary Problems* 1996, vol. 59, 181–196.

Elster, J., 'Coming to Terms with the Past: A Framework for the Study of Justice in the Transition to Democracy', *Archives Europeenes de Sociologie* 1998, vol. 39, 9–13.

——, *Closing the Books. Transitional Justice in Historical Perspective*, New York: Cambridge University Press, 2004.

Encheva, E., 'Temida si razigrava konia s Brigo Asparoukhov', *Sega*, 10 July 2003.

Erinnerungspolitisches Konzeptes zu den Gedenkstätten der SED-Diktatur in Berlin. Online. Available HTTP: http://www.havemann-gesellschaft.de/info193.htm (accessed 22 January 2008).

Erster Tätigkeitsbericht des Bundesbeauftragten für die Unterlagen des Staatssicherheits-dienstes der ehemaligen Deutschen Demokratischen Republik, Berlin: BStU, 1993.

Explanatory Note contained in a Note Verbale handed to the Secretary General at the time of deposit of the instrument of ratification of Treaty No. 009: Protocol to the Convention for the Protection of Human Rights and Fundamental Freedoms, 2 October 1996. Online. Available HTTP: http://conventions.coe.int/Treaty/Commun/ListeDeclarations (accessed 23 January 2008).

Eyal, G., *The Origins of Postcommunist Elites: From Prague Spring to the Breakup of Czechoslovakia*, Minneapolis: University of Minnesota Press, 2003.

Eyal, J., 'Why Romania Could not Avoid Bloodshed?', in G. Prins (ed.) *Spring in Winter: The 1989 Revolutions*, Manchester: University of Manchester Press, 1990, pp. 139–160.

Fati, S., 'Ultimul meci prezidential', *Evenimentul Zilei*, 10 December 2004.

Fers, D., 'From Security and Intelligence Service to Slovenian Intelligence and Security Agency', *National Security and the Future*, 2003, vols. 1–2, 61–80. Online. Available HTTP: http://hrcak.srce.hr/file/28815 (accessed 18 January 2008).

Fisher, M. E., 'The New Leaders and the Opposition', in D. Nelson (ed.) *Romania after Tyranny*, Boulder: Westview, 1992, pp. 45–65.

Fisher, S., 'Slovak Parliament Approves Anti-Communist Law', *OMRI Daily Digest*, 5 February 1996. Online. Available HTTP: http://archive.tol.cz/omri/restricted/article.php3?id=4117 (accessed 28 January 2008).

Fitzpatrick, S. and Gellately, R. (eds.) *Accusatory Practices. Denunciation in Modern European History, 1789–1989*, Chicago: University of Chicago Press, 1997.

Flueras, T., 'Tovarasi domni', *Evenimentul Zilei*, 27 July 2004.

Forced Labor, Psychiatric Repression of Dissent, Persecution of Religious Believers, Ethnic Discrimination and Persecution, Law and the Suppression of Human Rights in Romania, New York: Amnesty International USA, 1978.

Forest, B., Johnson, J. and Till, K., 'Post-totalitarian National Identity: Public Memory in Germany and Russia', *Social and Cultural Geography*, 2004, vol. 5, 357–380.

'Former Hard-line Communist Sentenced for Role in 1968 Invasion', *Radio Prague*, 9 June 2003. Online. Available HTTP: http://archiv.radio.cz/ (accessed DATE).

'Former Hungarian Ministers React to 'Magyar Hirlap' Revelations', *RFE/RL Newsline*, 27 August 2002. Online. Available HTTP: http://www.rferl.org/newsline/2002/08/270802.asp (accessed 28 January 2008).

'Former Polish PM Refuses to Sign Lustration Document, *RFE/RL Newsline*, 26 April 2007. Online. Available HTTP: http://www.rferl.org/newsline/2007/04/260407.asp (accessed 28 January 2008).

'Former Solidarity Leader Cleared of Violating Polish Lustration Law', *RFE/RL Newsline*, 3 October 2002. Online. Available HTTP: http://www.rferl.org/newsline/2002/10/031002.asp (accessed 28 January 2008).

Freeman, J., 'Security Services Still Distrusted', *Transition*, 21 March 1997.

Fricke, K. W., "Das StUG ist auch ein Aufklärungsgesetz:' Interview mit Marianne Birthler', *Deutschland Archiv*, 2001, vol. 34, 12–21.

Fünfter Tätigkeitsbericht des Bundesbeauftragten für die Unterlagen des Staatssicherheits-dienstes der ehemaligen Deutschen Demokratischen Republik, Berlin: BStU, 2001.

Gallagher, T., *Romania after Ceausescu: The Politics of Intolerance*, Edinburgh: Edinburgh University Press, 1995.

Galloway, G. and Wylie, B., *Downfall: The Ceausescus and the Romanian Revolution*, London: Futura, 1991.

Garstka, H., 'Stasi-Unterlagen-Gesetz (StUG) – Bewährung oder Mißachtung der informationellen Selbstbestimmung', in T. Hollitzer (ed.) *Einblick in das Herrschaftswissen einer Diktatur – Chance oder Fluch?* Opladen: Westdeutscher Verlag, 1996, 153–158.

——, "Freiheit für meine Akte': Die Öffnung der Archive – Das Gesetz der Volkskammer über die Sicherung der Nutzung der personenbezogenen Daten des ehemaligen MfS/AfNS', in D. Unverhau (ed.) *Das Stasi-Unterlagen-Gesetz im Lichte von Datenschutz und Archivgesetzgebung*, Münster: LIT, 1998, 43–49.

Garton Ash, T., *The File. A Personal History*, New York: Vintage Books, 1997.

——, *History of the Present: Essays, Sketches and Dispatches from Europe in the 1990s*, London: Vintage, 2001.

Gauck, J., 'Dealing with a Stasi Past', *Daedalus*, 1994, vol. 123, 277–284.

——, 'Das Erbe der Stasi-Akten', *German Studies Review*, 1994, vol. 17, 187–198.

——, 'The German Way of Dealing with a Stasi Past', in M. Mertes, S. Muller and H. A. Winkler (eds.) *In Search of Germany*, London: Transaction Publishers, 1996, pp. 295–302.

——, 'Die politische Aufklärung nicht beschädigen', in T. Hollitzer (ed.) *Wie weiter mit der Aufarbeitung? 10 Jahre Stasi-Unterlagen-Gesetz*, Leipzig: Evangelische Verlagsanstalt, 2002, pp. 19–28.

Gazeta Panorama, 6 June 2005.

Genov, N. and Krasteva, A., *Recent Social Trends in Bulgaria, 1960–1995*, Montreal: McGill-Queen's University Press, 2001.

Gentle, P., 'Letter from Poland', Radio Polonia, 8 February 2005.

Georgescu, A., *In the Beginning Was the End*, Brasov: Aspera, 2004.

Georgescu, T., 'Legea ii protejeaza pe ofiterii de Securitate', *Evenimentul Zilei*, 14 February 2001.

'Georgia, Moldova and Bulgaria: Dismantling Communist Structures Is Hardly Extremist', *Demokratizatsiya*, 2001. Online. Available HTTP: http://www.ariasking.com/files/DemSarishvili.pdf (accessed 15 December 2007).

'Georgian President Opposes Lustration', *RFE/RL Newsline*, 9 December 1997.

Gerson, P., 'Dunagate's Waters Run Deep', *The Budapest Sun*, 9 March 2000.

'Ghosts of Communist Past Haunt the Present', Bratislava: IPS/GIN, 25 January 2005. Online. Available HTTP: http://ins.onlinedemocracy.ca/index.php?name=News&file=article&sid=4600&theme=Printer (accessed 28 January 2008).

Gieseke, J., *Die hauptamtlichen Mitarbeiter der Staatssicherheit*, Berlin: Ch. Links, 2000.

Giurescu, C. C., *Five Years and Two Months in the Sighet Penitentiary (May 7, 1950–July 5, 1955)*, Boulder: East European Monographs, 1994.

Golebiewska, D., Brycki, G. and Sochacki, W., 'A Mixed Bag of Communist Trials', *World Press Review* 1996, vol. 43. Online. Available HTTP: http://scilib.univ.kiev.ua/doc.php?5779544 (accessed 28 December 2007).

'Government Sees Public Naming of StB Collaborators as Imprudent', CTK, 24 May 1991.

Gow, J. and Carmichael, C., *Slovenia and the Slovenes: A small State and the New Europe*, London: Hurst, 2000.

Green, P., 'Czech Communists Face Treason Charge in '68 Soviet Invasion', *New York Times*, 20 December 2001, Online. Available HTTP: http://query.nytimes.com/gst/fullpage.html?res=9807E2DA133EF933A15751C1A9679C8B63&scp=1&sq=Czech+Communists+Face+Treason+Charge+in+%9268+Soviet+Invasion%92&st=nyt (accessed 28 January 2008).

Grindel, R. 'Ist die Stasibehörde noch nötig? Nein!', *Die Tageszeitung*, 15 August 2007.

Grzelak, P., *Wojna o lustracje*, Warsaw: Trio, 2005.

Gyárfašová, O., 'Fenomén ŠtB v širšom Kontexte', *Kritika & Kontext*, 2001, vol. 2–3.

Haas, M., 'Vor zehn Jahren: Kontroverse Debatte um die Öffnung der Stasi-Akten', *Deutschland Archiv*, 2000, vol. 33, 998–1000.

Guidelines for the Work and Activity of the Ministry of Interior (November 1962), Bulgarian Communist Party Archive, Fond 1B, Record 64, file 302.

Hall, R. A., 'The Uses of Adversity: The Staged War Theory and the Romanian Revolution of December 1989', *East European Politics and Societies* 1999, vol. 13, 501–542.

Halmai, G. and Lane Scheppele, K. 'Living Well Is the Best Revenge: the Hungarian Approach to Judging the Past', in J. A. McAdam (ed.) *Transitional Justice and the Rule of Law*, Notre Dame: University of Notre Dame Press, 1997, pp. 155–184.

Harris, F., '"Velvet Justice' for Traitors Who Crushed 1968 Prague Spring', *The Telegraph*, 23 August 1998. Online. Available HTTP: http://www.telegraph.co.uk/html Content.jhtml;jsessionid=V5SUIAXYEKSMTQFIQMGCFF4AVCBQUIV0?html=/archive/1998/08/23/wcze23.html (accessed 28 January 2008).

Hay, M., 'Grappling with the Past: The Truth and Reconciliation Committee of South Africa', *Accord. African Journal on Conflict Resolution* 1, 1999, 29–51.

Hayner, P. B., *Unspeakable Truths. Facing the Challenge of Truth Commissions*, New York: Routledge, 2001.

'Hearing on Missing File Delayed in Hungary', *RFE/RL Newsline*, 24 September 2002. Online. Available HTTP: http://www.rferl.org/newsline/2002/09/240902.asp (accessed 28 January 2008).

Hirschmann, A. O., *Exit, Voice and Loyalty*, Cambridge: Harvard University Press, 1970.

'Historiker und Medien kritisieren Stasi-Aktenurteil', *Der Tagesspiegel*, 25 June 2004, 4.

Hochschild, A., *The Unquiet Ghost. Russians Remember Stalin*, Boston: Houghton Mifflin Co., 2003.

Hollitzer, T., *Wir leben jedenfalls von Montag zu Montag: Zur Auflösung der Staatssicherheit in Leipzig*, Berlin: BStU, 2000.

Honigsbaum, M., 'Who (or What) Was Georgi Markov?', *The Spectator*, 12 September 1998. Online. Available HTTP: http://findarticles.com/p/articles/mi_qa3724/is_199809/ai_n8808324 (accessed 29 December 2007).

Horne, C. M. and Levy, M., 'Does Lustration Promote Trustworthy Governance? An Exploration of the Experience of Central and Eastern Europe', October 2002. Online. Available HTTP: http://www.colbud.hu/honesty-trust/horne/pub01.html, pp. 24–25 (accessed 7 June 2006).

Hribar, T., 'Odločitev za Samostojnost', *Mladina*, 29 December 1989, p. 6. Online. Available HTTP: http://www.mladina.si/tednik/198951 (accessed 18 January 2006).

Hristov, H., *Sekretnoto delo za lagerite*, Sofia: Ivan Vazov, 1999.

——, *Durzavna Sigurnost sreshtu Bulgarskata emigrazia*, Sofia: Ivan Vazov, 2000.

——, 'Prestupleniata po vreme na komunisticheskija rezhim i opitite za tiahnoto razsledvane sled 10 Noemvri 1989', paper presented at the International Trial of Communism conference, Koprivshtitza, Bulgaria, 24–26 September 2004. Online. Available HTTP http://www.geocities.com/decommunization/Articles/Hristov4.htm (accessed 29 January 2008).

——, *Ubiite "Skitnik". Bulgarskata I britanskata durzavna politika po sluchaia Georgi Markov*, Sofia: Ciela, 2005.

——, 'The Bulgarian Gulag', *Vagabond*, no date. Online. Available HTTP: http://www.vagabond-bg.com/?page=business&sub=11&open_news=535 (accessed 29 December 2007).

'Hundreds Demonstrate in Support of Hungarian Radio Chairwoman', *RFE/RL Newsline*, 14 October 2003. Online. Available HTTP: http://www.rferl.org/newsline/2003/10/141003. asp (accessed 28 January 2008).

'Hungarian Coalition Parties Propose Reducing Scope of Vetting Process', *RFE/RL Newsline*, 26 September 2006. Online. Available HTTP: http://www.rferl.org/newsline/2006/09/260906.asp (accessed 28 January 2008).

'Hungarian Former Prime Minister Invites Media to Committee Hearings', *RFE/RL Newsline*, 31 July 2002. Online. Available HTTP: http://www.rferl.org/newsline/2002/07/310702. asp (accessed 28 January 2008).

'Hungarian Government Publicizes Proposed Amendments to Law on Former Agents, *RFE/RL Newsline*, 24 June 2002. Online. Available HTTP: http://www.rferl.org/newsline/2002/06/240602.asp (accessed 28 January 2008).

'Hungarian "Medgyessy Commission" Chairman Says Bullet Is "A Message"', *RFE/RL Newsline*, 8 August 2002. Online. Available HTTP: http://www.rferl.org/newsline/2002/08/080802. asp (accessed 28 January 2008).

'Hungarian National Bank Governor Slams Mecs Commission', *RFE/RL Newsline*, 15 August 2002. Online. Available HTTP: http://www.rferl.org/newsline/2002/08/150802. asp (accessed 28 January 2008).

'Hungarian Opposition Criticizes Vetting Bills', *RFE/RL Newsline*, 12 September 2006. Online. Available HTTP: http://www.rferl.org/newsline/2006/09/120906.asp (accessed 28 January 2008).

'Hungarian Opposition Walks Out of Commission Hearings', *RFE/RL Newsline*, 6 August 2002. Online. Available HTTP: http://www.rferl.org/newsline/2002/08/060802.asp (accessed 28 January 2008).

'Hungarian Parliamentary Committees Approve Vetting Bills', *RFE/RL Newsline*, 11 July 2002.

'Hungarian Parliament Sets Up Two Investigative Commissions', *RFE/RL Newsline*, 10 July 2002. Online. Available HTTP: http://www.rferl.org/newsline/2002/07/100702.asp (accessed 28 January 2008).

'Hungarian Parliament Weakens Secret-Agent Bill', *RFE/RL Newsline*, 11 December 2002.

'Hungarian Police Investigate Whether Newspaper Violated State-Secrecy Laws', *RFE/RL Newsline*, 23 August 2002. Online. Available HTTP: http://www.rferl.org/newsline/2002/08/230802.asp (accessed 28 January 2008).

'Hungarian Premier Admits to Communist Secret Service Past', *RFE/RL Newsline*, 19 June 2002. Online. Available HTTP: http://www.rferl.org/newsline/2002/06/190602.asp (accessed 28 January 2008).

'Hungarian Premier Apologizes to Electorate', *RFE/RL Newsline*, 24 June 2002. Online. Available HTTP: http://www.rferl.org/newsline/2002/06/240602.asp (accessed 28 January 2008).

'Hungarian Premier Pledges to Expose Informers', *RFE/RL Newsline*, 20 June 2002. Online. Available HTTP: http://www.rferl.org/newsline/2002/06/200602.asp (accessed 28 January 2008).

'Hungarian President Vows Not to Intervene in Medgyessy Affair', *RFE/RL Newsline*, 2 July 2002. Online. Available HTTP: http://www.rferl.org/newsline/2002/07/020702.asp (accessed 28 January 2008).

'Hungarian Radio Chairwoman Denies Counterespionage Links', *RFE/RL Newsline*, 15 October 2003. Online. Available HTTP: http://www.rferl.org/newsline/2003/10/151003. asp (accessed 28 January 2008).

'Hungarian Radio Chairwoman Listed as 'Unpaid Agent'', *RFE/RL Newsline*, 8 October 2003. Online. Available HTTP: http://www.rferl.org/newsline/2003/10/081003.asp (accessed 28 January 2008).

'Hungarian Radio Chairwoman's Communist-Era Operator Steps Out of Shadow', *RFE/RL Newsline*, 27 October 2003. Online. Available HTTP: http://www.rferl.org/newsline/2003/10/271003.asp (accessed 28 January 2008).

'Hungarian Radio Chairwoman Vows to Sue Over Reports of Spying', *RFE/RL Newsline*, 26 September 2003. Online. Available HTTP: http://www.rferl.org/newsline/2003/09/260903.asp (accessed 28 January 2008).

'Hungarian Radio Chairwoman Was "Secret" Agent, Not "Social"', *RFE/RL Newsline*, 9 October 2003. Online. Available HTTP: http://www.rferl.org/newsline/2003/10/091003.asp (accessed 28 January 2008).

'Hungarian Socialists Insist on Amending Vetting Bill', *RFE/RL Newsline*, 10 September 2006. Online. Available HTTP: http://www.rferl.org/newsline/2006/09/110906.asp (accessed 28 January 2008).

'Hungary', *East European Constitutional Review* 2002, vol. 11, pp. 24–25.

'Hungary: Constitutional Court Decision on the Statute of Limitations, No. 2086/A/1991/14, 5 March 1992', in Kritz, N. (ed.), *Transitional Justice: How New Democracies Reckon with Their Authoritarian Past*, Washington, D.C.: US Institute for Peace, vol. 3, pp. 629–640.

'Hungary: Law on the Background Checks to be Conducted on Individuals Holding Certain Important Positions. Law no. 23, 8 May 1994', in N. Kritz (ed.) *Transitional Justice: How New Democracies Reckon with Their Authoritarian Past*, Washington, D.C.: US Institute for Peace, vol. 3, 1995, pp. 418–425.

'Hungary's Fidesz-Era Ministers Deny Links with Communist-Era Secret Services, *RFE/RL Newsline*, 1 August 2002. Online. Available HTTP: http://www.rferl.org/newsline/2002/08/010802.asp (accessed 28 January 2008).

'Hungary to Open Spy Files', *Deutsche Welle*, 9 December 2004. Online. Available HTTP: http://www.dw-world.de/dw/article/0,1564,1423227,00.html (accessed 28 January 2008).

Huntington, S. P., *The Third Wave: Democratization in the Twentieth Century*, Oklahoma: University of Oklahoma Press, 1991.

Hussain, A., 'Civil and Political Rights, Including the Question of Freedom of Expression. Report of the Special Rapporteur on the protection and promotion of the right to freedom of opinion and expression', United Nations Economic and Social Council, Commission on Human Rights, 29 January 1999. Online. Available HTTP: http://www.unhchr.ch/Huridocda/Huridoca.nsf/0/16583a84ba1b3ae5802568bd004e80f7?Opendocument (accessed 4 January 2008).

Hyshnyak, N. and Konashevych, O., 'Yushchenko: Why Should We Forget the History of Repressions?', BBC, 13 June 2007. Online. Available HTTP: http://orangeukraine.squarespace.com/long-articles/2007/7/6/yushchenko-why-should-we-forget-the-history-of-represssions.html (accessed 15 December 2007).

Ierunca, V., *Fenomenul Pitesti*, Bucharest: Humanitas, 1990.

Imholz, K., 'Can Albania Break the Chain: The 1993–1994 Trials of Former High Officials', *East European Constitutional Review*, 1995, vol. 4, 54–60.

——, 'States of Emergency as Pretexts for Gagging the Press: Word Play at Albania's Constitutional Court', *East European Constitutional Review*, 1997, vol. 6. Online. Available HTTP: www.law.nyu.edu/eecr/vol6num4/special/statesofemergency.html (accessed 23 January 2008).

——, 'Albania', *East European Constitutional Review*, 1997, vol. 6. Online. Available HTTP: http://www.law.nyu.edu/eecr/vol6num2/constitutionwatch/albania.html (accessed 23 January 2008).

——, 'The Experience in Albania', paper presented as part of the conference on Disclosing Hidden History: Lustration in the Western Balkans, Belgrade, 2–4 July 2004.

'In Lithuania, Uncertainty about State Security Department's Lustration Efforts', *RFE/RL Newsline*, 3 October 2007.

'Interview with Anton Drobnič', *Delo Sobotna Priloga*, 15 October 1994. Online. Available HTTP: http://www.delo.si (accessed 10 March 2006).

Ioanid, I., *Inchisoarea noastra cea de toate zilele*, Bucharest: Humanitas, 1999.

Ioanid, R., *The Ransom of the Jews: The Story of Extraordinary Secret Bargain between Romania and Israel*, Chicago: Ivan R. Dee, 2005.

Ionescu, D., 'Old Practices Persist in Romanian Justice', *Report on Eastern Europe*, 9 March 1990, 44–48.

Ivanov, D., *Shesti Otdel*, Sofia: Trud, 2004.

Jahntz, B., 'Die juristische Aufarbeitung der SED-Herrschaft', in S. Suckut and J. Weber (eds.), *Stasi-Akten zwischen Politik und Zeitgeschichte: Eine Zwischenbilanz*, Munich: Olzog, 2003, pp. 309–335.

'Jan Ordynski's conversation with professor Leon Kieres, the chairman of the Institute of National Remembrance. Honor Means Facing the Truth', *Rzeczpospolita*, 2 September 2002.

Janik, B., 'Otvorenie Pandorej skrinky vyvoláva v česku obavy', *Národná obroda*, 11 February 2002. Online. Available HTTP: http://195.168.40.176/20020211/08_006.html (accessed 1 April 2002).

——, 'Havel podpísal zákon o sprístupení zväzkov ŠtB', *Pravda,* 14 March 2002. Online. Available HTTP: http://www.pravda.sk/spravy/2002/03/14/svet/article.34918.html (accessed 29 March 2002).

Janša, J., *The Making of he Slovenian State 1988–1992: The Collapse of Yugoslavia*, Ljubljana: Mladinska knjiga, 1994.

——, 'Predlog resolucije o protiprvnem delovanju komunisticnega totalitarnega rezima, 5 November 1997', *Uradni list,* 1997, no. 52.

——, 'Predlog Zakona o Odpravi Posledic Komunisticnega totalitarnega Rezima, 5 November 1997', *Uradni list*, 1997, no. 53.

Jara, H., 'Dealing with the Past: The Case of Estonia', *Ulkopoliittinen Instituutti Working Paper* No. 15, 1999. Online. Available HTTP: http://www.up-fiia.fi/document.php?DOC_ID=69#wp15.php (accessed 10 March 2007).

Jarvis, C., 'The Rise and Fall of the Pyramid Schemes in Albania', *IMF Staff Papers*, 2000, vol. 47(1). Online. Available HTTP: http://www.imf.org/external/Pubs/FT/staffp/2000/00–01/jarvis.htm (accessed 23 January 2008).

Jaskovska, E. and Moran, J. P., 'Justice or Politics? Criminal, Civil and Political Adjudication in the Newly Independent Baltic States', *Journal of Communist Studies and Transition Politics*, 2006, vol. 22, 485–506.

Jelinčič Z. and P. Dobrajc, 'Teze za zakon o uničenju dosjejev obveščevalnih služb 1993', *Drzavni zbor Republike Slovenije*, 1993, no. 211, 15–25.

Jochen Winters, P., 'Erich Mielke – der falsche Prozeß?', *Deutschland Archiv*, 1993, vol. 26, 1347–1350.

——, 'Der Mielke-Prozeß', in J. Weber and M. Piazolo (eds.), *Eine Diktatur vor Gericht: Aufarbeitung von SED-Unrecht durch die Justiz,* Munich: Olzog, 1995, pp. 101–113.

'Justice Minister Zvarych Voices Protest against Lustration', 13 February 2005. Online. Available HTTP: http://blog.kievukraine.info/2005/02/justice-minister-zvarych-voices. html (accessed 15 December 2007).

Kalkandzieva, D., *Bulgarskata Pravoslavna Zurkva I Durzavata 1944–1953*, Sofia: Albatros, 1997.

Kaminski M. and M. Nalepa, 'Introduction', Judging Transitional Justice conference, University of California at Irvine, Centre for the Study of Democracy, 30–31 October 2004. Online. Available HTTP: http://www.democ.uci.edu (accessed 14 July 2006).

Karadzov, K., 'Simeon se otkaza ot Brigadir na sluzbite', *Sega*, 16 October 2003.

Karpinski, J. 'The Mystery of 'O'', *Transition*, 14 June 1996, 3–4.

——, 'Polish Security Services and the Oleksy Case', *Transition*, 1 November 1996, 9–13.

——, 'Politicians and the Past', *Uncaptive Minds* 1992, vol. 5, pp. 99–106.

Karsai, L. 'Crime and Punishment: People's Courts, Revolutionary Legality, and the Hungarian Holocaust', *East Central Europe* 2004, vol. 4. Online. Available HTTP: http://sipa.columbia.edu/regional/ece (accessed 12 June 2006).

B. Kenety, 'Top Communist, Aged 80, Begins Prison Sentence for Radio 'Sabotage' which Aided 1968 Soviet-led Invasion', *Radio Prague*, 9 August 2004. Online. Available HTTP: http://www.radio.cz/print/en/56873 (accessed 28 January 2008).

Kenez, P., *Hungary from the Nazis to the Soviets. The Establishment of the Communist Regime in Hungary, 1944–1948*, New York: Cambridge University Press, 2006.

Kennedy Grimsted, P., 'Increasing Reference Access to Post-1991 Russian Archives', *Slavic Review*, 1997, vol. 56, 733–734.

Kiss, C., 'The Misuses of Manipulation: The Failure of Transitional Justice in Post-Communist Hungary', *Europe-Asia Studies*, 2006, vol. 58, 925–940.

Kitschelt, H., Mansfedova, Z., Markowski, R., and Toka, G., *Post-Communist Party Systems: Competition, Representation and Inter-Party Cooperation*, Cambridge: Cambridge University Press, 1999.

Knight, A., 'The Fate of the KGB Archives', *Slavic Review*, 1993, vol. 52, 582–586.

——, *Spies without Cloaks: The KGB's Successors*, Princeton: Princeton University Press, 1996.

Komisija za nadzor nad dellom obvescevalnih in varnotnih sluzb, *zaprta seja*, 25 April 2003 and 13 May 2003.

Korecký, M., 'Havlův podpis odtajnil agenty ŠtB', *Lidové noviny*, 14 March 2002. Online. Available HTTP: http://www.lidovky.cz/tisk.asp?c=L063A01A&r=atitulni (accessed 25 March 2002).

Kostov, P., 'Tainite na Durzavna sigurnost', *Sega*, 27 February – 7 March 2001.

Kovač, M., 'Konji, zanikrni mediji in pamento ljudstvo', *Mladina*, 26 April 2003. Online. Available HTTP: http://www.mladina.si/tednik/200317/ (accessed 20 January 2006).

Kowalczuk, I.-S., 'Was den Stasi-Unterlagen im Bundesarchiv droht', *Frankfurter Allgemeine Zeitung*, 8 January 2005.

Kozara, K., 'Report on Freedom of Information in Albania', *In the Public Interest: Security Services in a Constitutional Democracy*, Helsinki Foundation for Human Rights, 1998. Online. Available HTTP: http://www.gwu.edu/~hurights/chapter4/secrets/foia_alb.html (accessed 23 January 2008).

Kraus, M., 'Settling Accounts: Postcommunist Czechoslovakia', in N. Kritz (ed.) *Transitional Justice: How Emerging Democracies Reckon with Former Regimes*, vol. II, Washington, D.C.: United States Institute of Peace, 1995, pp. 542–544.

Kritz, N. (ed.), *Transitional Justice: How New Democracies Reckon with Their Authoritarian Past*, Washington, D.C.: US Institute for Peace, 3 vols, 1995.

Kubosova, L. 'Slovakia: Pandora's Box Online', *Transitions Online*, 16–22 November 2004. Online. Available HTTP: http://www.ciaonet.org/pbei/tol/tol_2004/nov16–nov22/nov16-nov22e.html (accessed 28 January 2008).

Kučan, M., 'Opinion of the President of the Republic of Slovenia, Milan Kučan, on the Proposed Law on the Dismantling of the Consequences of the Communist Totalitarian Regime and on the Proposed Resolution on the Unlawful Activities of the Communist Totalitarian Regime', National Assembly of the Republic of Slovenia, Ljubljana, 26 November 1997. Online. Available HTTP: http://www2.gov.si/up-rs/uprs_ang.nsf (accessed 5 October 2006).

Kundera, M., *The Book of Laughter and Forgetting*, New York: Knopf, 1980.

Kung, A., 'Communism and Crimes against Humanity in the Baltic States', April 1999. Online. Available HTTP: http://www.rel.ee/eng/communism_crimes.htm (accessed 26 December 2007).

J. Kunicová and M. Nalepa, 'Coming to Terms With the Past: Strategic Institutional Choice in Post-Communist Europe', January 2006. Online. Available HTTP: http://www.sscnet.ucla.edu/polisci/cpworkshop/papers/Kunicova.pdf (accessed 28 January 2008).

Lajovic, D. S., *Med svobodo in rdečo zvezdo*, Ljubljana: Nova obzorja, 2003.

Lampe, J. R., *Yugoslavia as History: Twice There was a Country*, New York: Cambridge University Press, 2000.

Lamper, I., 'Respekt Weekly Roundup Nov 26th', *Respekt Weekly Roundup*, 28 November 2005. Online. Available HTTP: http://www.prague.tv/articles/respekt/respekt-26-11-2005 (accessed 28 January 2008).

'Langoš predkladá zákon o zločinoch nacizmu a kommunizmu', *Pravda*, 12 October 2001. Online. Available HTTP: http://www.pravda.sk/spravy/2001/10/12/slovensko/article.669.html (accessed 29 March 2002).

'Latvian Election News', *RFE/RL Newsline*, 20 August 2002.

'Latvian Lustration Law Survives Court Challenge', *RFE/RL Newsline*, 31 August 2000.

'Latvian MEP to Get E20,000 over Electoral Ban', *European Voice*, 24 June 2004. Online. Available HTTP: http://www.europeanvoice.com/archive/article.asp?id=20767 (accessed 6 January 2008).

'Latvian Parliamentarian Loses Ballot Appeal', *RFE/RL Newsline*, 21 August 2002.

'Latvian Prosecutors Indicted Another Soviet-era Secret Policeman', *The Weekly Crier*. March-April 2001. Online. Available HTTP: http://www.balticsww.com/wkcrier/0219_0409_01.htm (accessed 21 December 2007).

'Law for Temporary Introduction of Some Additional Requirements for the Members of the Executive Bodies of Scientific Organizations and the Higher Certifying Commission', *State Gazette*, 1992, No. 104, reprinted in N. Kritz (ed.), *Transitional Justice: How Emerging Democracies Reckon with Former Regimes*, Washington, D.C.: United States Institute of Peace Press, 1995, vol. 3, pp. 296–299.

'The Law on Access to the Archives of the Former State Security and General Staff Intelligence Department', *State Gazette* [Sofia], 1997, No. 63.

'Law on Banks and Credit Activity of 18 March 1992', in N. Kritz (ed.), *Transitional Justice: How Emerging Democracies Reckon with Former Regimes*, Washington, D.C.: United States Institute of Peace Press, 1995, vol. 3, p. 293.

'The Law on Classified Information', *State Gazette* [Sofia], 2002, No. 45.

'The Law on Denationalization', *Uradni List*, 1991, no. 27.

'The Law on Denationalization', *Uradni List*, 1993, no. 31.

'The Law on the Election of Members of Parliament, Municipal Councilors and Mayors', *State Gazette* [Sofia], 2001, No. 24.

'The Law on Radio and Television', *State Gazette* [Sofia], 1998, No. 138.

'Legea lustratiei uitata', *Ziua*, 3 March 2004.

Lesná, L., 'Eighteen years after the revolution, no justice', *The Slovak Spectator*, 19 November 2007. Online. Available HTTP: http://www.spectator.sk (accessed 25 January 2008).

Levant, C., 'Surse din Parchetul General dezvaluie: Informatii clasificate, pe mina tortionarilor lui Ursu', *Evenimentul Zilei*, 10 November 2003.

Levesque, J., *The Enigma of 1989: The USSR and the Liberation of Eastern Europe*, Berkeley: University of California Press, 1997.

Liiceanu, A., *Ranile memoriei. Nucsoara si rezistanta din munti*, Bucharest: Polirom, 2003.

Lindenberger, T., 'Everyday History: New Approaches to the History of the Post-War Germanies', in C. Kleßmann (ed.) *The Divided Past*, New York: Berg, 2001, pp. 43–67.

Linz, J. and Stepan, A., *Problems of Democratic Transition and Consolidation: Southern Europe, South America and Post-Communist Europe*, Baltimore: Johns Hopkins University Press, 1996.

'Lithuania', *East European Constitutional Review*, 1997, vol. 6–2001, vol. 10. Online. Available HTTP: http://www.law.nyu.edu/eecr (accessed 21 December 2007).

'Lithuanian Conservatives not to Appeal to Court over Lustration Law', *RFE/RL Newsline*, 20 July 1998.

'Lithuanian Court Deems Lustration Law Constitutional', *RFE/RL Newsline*, 5 March 1999.

'Lithuanian Government Publishes Lists of Jobs Off-Limits for Former KGB Employees', *RFE/RL Newsline*, 15 January 1999.

'Lithuanian Lawmakers back Adamkus over Lustration Law', *RFE/RL Newsline*, 17 July 1998.

'[Lithuanian] Lustration Law Appealed in Constitutional Court', *RFE/RL Newsline*, 7 October 1998.

'Lithuanian Lustration Law Goes into Effect', *RFE/RL Newsline*, 4 January 1999.

'Lithuanian Parliament Adopts Lustration Law's New Edition', *Eurasian Secret Services Daily Review*, 14 October 2007. Online. Available HTTP: http://www.axisglobe.com/article.asp?article=1406 (accessed 15 December 2007).

'Lithuanian Parliament Amends Lustration Law', *RFE/RL Newsline*, 23 April 1999.

'Lithuanian President to Wait for Court Ruling on Lustration Law', *RFE/RL Newsline*, 11 January 1999.

Litvinenko, A., *The FSB Blows Up Russia*, Pskov: Giness, 2001.

——, *The Criminal Group from the Lubyanka*, Pskov: Giness, 2002.

Lobjakas, A., 'Lithuania: Parliament Asks KGB Collaborators To Confess', *RFE/RL Feature*, 8 February 2000.

Los, M. and Zybertowicz, A., *Privatizing the Police-State. The Case of Poland*, London: Palgrave MacMillan, 2000.

Los, M., 'Reshaping of Elites and the Privatization of Security: The Case of Poland', *Journal of Power Institutions in Post-Soviet Societies* 2005, vol. 2. Online. Available HTTP: http://www.pipss.org/document351.html (accessed 28 December 2007).

Loupan, V., *La révolution n'a pas eu lieu ... Roumanie l'histoire d'un coup d'état*, Paris: R. Laffont, 1990.

Lukšič, I., *The Political System of the Republic of Slovenia: A Primer*, trans. by E. Johnson Debeljak, Ljubljana: Znanstveno in Publicisticno Sredisce, 2001.

'Lustrace zrušme v roce 2009, říká docent Zdeněk Koudelka', *Právo*, 28 December 2005. Online. Available HTTP: http://www.pravo.newtonit.cz/default.asp?cache=822124 (accessed 8 February 2006).

'Lustration Laws Further Valid, Lower House Decides', *CTK/Prague Daily Monitor*, 27 December 2005. Online. Available HTTP: http://www.praguemonitor.com (accessed 23 March 2006).

Luxmoore, J., 'Poland Fears Its Judas Files', *The Tablet*, 7 August 1999. Online. Available http://www.thetablet.co.uk (accessed 3 June 2005).

Maddrell, P., 'The Revolution Made Law: The Work Since 2001 of the Federal Commissioner for the Records of the State Security Service of the Former German Democratic Republic', *Cold War History* 4, 2004, vol. 4, 153–162.

Magierescu, E., *Moara Dracilor. Amintiri despre Pitesti*, Alba Iulia: no publisher, 1994.

The Main Guidelines for the Work and Activities of the Ministry of Interior (November 1962), Bulgarian Communist Party Archive, Fond 1B, Record 64, file 302.

Matoš, U., 'Politika z UDBa.net', *Mladina*, 26 May 2003. Online. Available HTTP: http://www.mladina.si/tednik/200321/ (accessed 20 January 2006).

McAdams, A. J., 'The Honecker Trial: The East German Past and the German Future', *The Review of Politics*, 1996, vol. 58, 53–80.

——, *Judging the Past in Unified Germany*, Cambridge: Cambridge University Press, 2001.

McKinsey, K., 'Czech Republic: Documenting Crimes of the Communist Past', *Radio Free Europe/Radio Liberty*, 9 July 1998. Online. Available HTTP: http://www.b-info.com/places/Bulgaria/news/98–07/jul09b.rfe (accessed 28 January 2008).

Meshkova, P. and Sharlanov, D., *Bulgarskata gilotina. Tainite mehanismi na Narodnia sad*, Sofia: Democracy Agency, 1994.

Michnik, A., 'Editorial', *Gazeta Wyborcza*, 25–26 September 1993, p. 1.

Michnik, A., Tischner, J. and Zakowski, J., *Miedzy panem a plebanem*, Cracow: Znak, 1995.

Miller, B., *Narratives of Guilt and Compliance in Unified Germany*, New York: Routledge, 1999.

Miller, J., 'Settling Accounts with a Secret Police: The German Law on the Stasi Records', *Europe-Asia Studies*, 1998, vol. 50, 305–330.

Milosavljevic, B., 'Reform of the Police and Security Services in Serbia and Montenegro Attained Results or Betrayed Expectations', *Sourcebook on Security Sector Reform*, Geneva: Geneva Centre for the Democratic Control of Armed Forces, 2002. Online. Available HTTP: www.dcaf.ch (accessed 18 January 2008).

'Ministrul de Interne nu este de acord cu Babiuc', *Evenimentul Zilei*, 21 July 1999.

Ministry of Interior Report of 1966. Bulgarian Communist Party Archive, Fond 1B, Record 64, file 359.

Mite, V., 'Poland: Tough Lustration Law Divides Society', *RFE/RL Reports*, 23 March 2007. Online. Available HTTP: http://www.rferl.org/featuresarticle/2007/03/38d9250c-4dd3–49fc-8e44-d2f21f83a190.html (accessed 28 January 2008).

'Moldova Intel Enhances Ties to International Jewish Organizations', *Axis*, 10 February 2007. Online. Available HTTP: http://www.axisglobe.com/article.asp?article=1223 (accessed 15 December 2007).

'Moldovan Parliament Rejects Lustration Bill', *RFE/RL Newsline*, 1 June 2001.

Moran, J., 'The Communist Torturers of Eastern Europe: Prosecute and Punish or Forgive and Forget?', *Communist and Post-Communist Studies* 1994, vol. 27, 95–109.

Morvai, K., 'Retroactive Justice Based on International Law: A Recent Decision by the Hungarian Constitutional Court', *East European Constitutional Review*, 1993–1994, vols. 3–4, 32–34.

Mousakov, A., *Shesto*, Sofia: Reporter, 1991.

Müller-Enbergs, H., *Inoffizielle Mitarbeiter des Ministeriums für Staatssicherheit*, Berlin: Ch. Links, 2001.

Müller-Neuhof, J., 'Vorteil Kohl', *Der Tagesspiegel*, 24 June 2004, 4.

Mungiu-Pippidi, A., and Althabe, G., *Secera si buldozerul. Scornicesti si Nucsoara. Mecanisme de aservire a taranului roman*, Bucharest: Polirom, 2002.

Naegele, J., 'Czech Republic: Bill Would Open Communist Secret Police Files to General Public', *Radio Free Europe/Radio Liberty*, 13 February 2002. Online. Available HTTP: http://www.rferl.org/features/2002/02/13022002085655.asp (accessed 28 January 2008).

Nalepa, M., 'The Power of Secret Information: Transitional Justice after Communism', PhD Thesis defended at Columbia University, Department of Political Science, 2005.

Navara, L. and D. Steiner, 'Havlův podpis odmekl archivy ŠtB', *Mladá fronta dnes/idnes*, 14 March 2002. Online. Available HTTP: http://zpravy.idnes.cz/havluv-podpis-odemkl-archivy-stb-d46-/domaci.asp?c=A020208_213018_domaci_pol (accessed 28 January 2008).

Nedelchev, M., 'Disidentstvoto v Bulgaria v konteksta na obshtata antikomunisticheska saprotiva i na mnogoobraznite formi na nesaglasie s komunisticheskata sistema', *The Democratic Review*, 2002, no. 49. Online. Available HTTP: http://dem-pr.hit. bg/2002_2/2002_2_10.html (accessed 31 January 2008).

Nedelsky, N., 'Divergent Responses to a Common Past: Transitional Justice in the Czech Republic and Slovakia', *Theory and Society* 2004, vol. 33, 65–115.

'New Lustration Law Passes in Lithuania', *RFE/RL Newsline*, 24 November 1999.

Nežmah, B., 'Obračun z zogovina, zakaj se UDBa vrača kot zombi?', *Mladina*, 28 April 2003. Online. Available HTTP: http://www.mladina.si/tednik/200317/ (accessed 18 January 2007).

Nicholson, T., 'Nation's Memory Institute Evicted', *The Slovak Spectator,* 8–14 January 2007. Online. Available HTTP: http://www.slovakspectator.sk (accessed 1 August 2007).

Nicolaescu, S., *Revolutia, inceputul adevarului: un raport personal*, Bucharest: Editura Topaz, 1995.

——, *Cartea revolutiei romane din decembrie '89*, Bucharest: Editura Ion Cristoiu, 2000.

Nikolov, J., 'Durzavna Sigurnost – maikata na bulgaskite spezsluzbi', *Capital Weekly*, 2001, No. 1.

'No Decision Taken on Revoking Latvian Deputy's Mandate', *RFE/RL Newsline*, 23 March 2000.

'Norme ale umilirii', *Cotidianul*, 13 March 2004.

'Nume celebre pe lista colaboratorilor serviciilor secrete comuniste ungare', *Cotidianul*, 12 February 2005.

Nyyssonen, H., 'Salami Reconstructed. 'Goulash Communism' and Political Culture in Hungary', *Cahiers du Monde Russe* 2006, vol. 47, 153–172.

Obrman, J., 'New Minister Dissolves State Security', *RFE/RL Report on Eastern Europe*, 16 February 1990, 10–14.

——, 'Slovak Politician Accused of Secret Police Ties', *RFE/RL Research Report*, 12 April 1992, 13–17.

Occupation of Latvia. Three Occupations 1940–1991. Soviet and Nazi Take-Overs and their Consequences, Riga: Occupation Museum Foundation, 2005.

Odmeve, TV Slovenia, 14 May 2003.

Ognianov. L., *Durzavno-politicheskata sistema na Bulgaria 1944–1948*, Sofia: Bulgarian Academy of Sciences, 1993.

Oltay, E., 'Hungary's Screening Law', in N. Kritz (ed.) *Transitional Justice: How New Democracies Reckon with Their Authoritarian Past*, Washington, D.C.: US Institute for Peace, vol. 2, 1995, pp. 665–668.

O'Donnell, G. and Schmitter, P. C., *Transitions from Authoritarian Rule: Tentative Conclusions about Uncertain Democracies*, Baltimore: Johns Hopkins University Press, 1991.

Office for Democratic Institutions and Human Rights (ODIHR), *Final Report on Parliamentary Elections in Albania, 26 May and 2 June 1996*, 2 July 1996. Online. Available HTTP: http://www.osce.org/documents/odihr/1996/07/1176_en.pdf (accessed 23 January 2008).

The Office for the Documentation and the Investigation of the Crimes of Communism (ÚDV), 'Information about Cases', 1 January 2008. Online. Available HTTP: http://www.mvcr.cz/policie/udv/english/pripady/index.html (accessed 27 January 2008).

Omar, D., 'Introduction to the Truth and Reconciliation Committee', in H. R. Botman and R. M. Petersen (eds.), *To Remember and to Heal*, Cape Town: Human and Rousseau, 1996, pp. 24–36.

Oprea, C., 'MApN refuza sa plateasca despagubiri in dosarul Timisoara 1989', *Evenimentul Zilei*, 18 July 1999.

Oprea, M. and Olaru, S., *The Day We Won't Forget. 15 November 1987, Brasov*, Bucharest: Polirom, 2003.

Organization for Security and Cooperation in Europe, *The Albanian Parliamentary Elections of 1996*. Online. Available HTTP: http://www.csce.gov (accessed 23 January 2008).

'Orosz označil Langošov zákon o pamäti národa za právny galimatiaš', *Pravda*, 17 October 2001. Online. Available HTTP: http://www.pravda.sk/spravy/2001/10/17/slovensko/article.900.html (accessed 29 March 2002).

Osiatynski, W., 'Agent Walesa?', *East European Constitutional Review* 1992, vol. 1, 28–30.

Pacepa, I. M., *The Red Horizons. Chronicles of a Communist Spy Chief*, Washington: Regnery Gateway, 1987.

Palata, L., 'Split Decision', *Transitions on Line*, 14 August 2000. Online. Available HTTP: http://www.tol.cz (accessed 5 June 2006).

Pano, N., 'Albania' in K. Dawisha and B. Parott (eds.) *Politics, Power and the Struggle for Democracy in South-East Europe*, Cambridge: Cambridge University Press, 1997, pp. 285–352.

Pataki, J., 'Dealing with Hungarian Communists' Crimes', *RFE/RL Research Report*, 28 February 1992.

Patrascu Buse, E., *Lumea pierduta*, Bucharest: Humanitas, 2003.

Persak, K. and Kaminski, L., *A Handbook of the Communist Security Apparatus in East Central Europe, 1944–1989*, Warsaw: Institute of National Remembrance, 2005.

Pingel-Schliemann, S., *Zersetzen: Strategie einer Diktatur*, Berlin: Robert Havelmann Gesellschaft, 2002.

Pithart, P., 'Towards a Shared Freedom, 1968–1989', in J. Musil (ed.) *The End of Czechoslovakia*, Budapest: Central European University, 1995, pp. 201–222.

Pitkin, J., 'Ruml Case Revives 'Lustration' Disputes: Influence of Former Communists Ruffles Political Feathers', *The Prague Post*, 13 June 2001. Online. Available HTTP: http://www.praguepost.cz/news061301f.html (accessed 28 January 2008).

'Plans to Sue', *RFE/RL Report*, 13 December 2002.

Plut-Pregelj, L., A. Gabrič, and B. Repe (eds.) *The Repluralization of Slovenia in the 1980s: New Revelations from Archival Records*, Seattle: The Donald W. Treadgold Papers, University of Washington, 2001.

Poglajen, J., 'Dnevnik Parliament', *Dnevnik,* 11 November 2001. Online. Available HTTP: http://www.dnevnik.si/novice/iskalnik?sel=advanced (accessed 20 January 2006).

——, 'Agentje med detective', *Dnevnik,* 23 October 2002. Online. Available HTTP: http://www.dnevnik.si/novice/iskalnik?sel=advanced (accessed 20 January 2006).

——, 'Obilna žetev hinavsega paragrapha', *Mladina,* 12 November 2003. Online. Available HTTP: http://www.mladina.si (accessed 20 January 2006).

'Poland', *East European Constitutional Review* 1997, vol. 6, 1998, vol. 7. and 1999, vol. 8. Online. Available HTTP: http://www.law.nyu.edu/eecr (accessed 28 December 2007)

'Poland. Dirty Hands', *Transitions on Line,* 6 September 1999. Online. Available HTTP: http://www.tol.cz/look/TOLrus/article.tpl?IdLanguage=1&IdPublication=4&NrIssue=2&NrSection=7&NrArticle=8363 (accessed 5 June 2006).

'Poland in Uproar over Leak of Spy Files', *The Guardian,* 5 February 2005. Online. Available HTTP: http://www.guardian.co.uk/international/story/0,3604,1406281,00.html (accessed 28 January 2008).

'Poland's Presidential Hopeful Admits Collaboration with Communist Secret Services', *RFE/RL Newsline,* 18 July 2000. Online. Available HTTP: http://www.rferl.org/newsline/2000/07/180700.asp (accessed 28 January 2008).

'Poland's Speaker Offers to Resign His Post', *New York Times,* 30 December 2004. Online. Available HTTP: http://www.nytimes.com/2004/12/30/international/europe/30poland.html (accessed 28 January 2008).

'Poland's EU Campaign Chief Admits Spying for Communist Secret Services', *RFE/RL Newsline,* 30 August 2002. Online. Available HTTP: http://www.rferl.org/newsline/2002/08/300802.asp (accessed 28 January 2008).

Polian, P., *Against Their Will: The History and Geography of Forced Migrations in the USSR,* Budapest: Central European University Press, 2004.

'Polish Deputy Minister Resigns before Lustration Verdict', *RFE/RL Newsline,* 8 June 1999. Online. Available HTTP: http://www.rferl.org/newsline/1999/07/080799.asp (accessed 28 January 2008).

'Polish Deputy Premier Resigns over Lustration', *RFE/RL Newsline,* 3 September 1999. Online. Available HTTP: http://www.rferl.org/newsline/1999/09/030999.asp (accessed 28 January 2008).

'Polish Parliament Condemns Communist Rule', *RFE/RL Newsline,* 11 June 1998. Online. Available HTTP: http://www.rferl.org/newsline/1998/06/4-SEE/see-110698.asp (accessed 28 January 2008).

'Polish Parliament Forms Commissions', *RFE/RL Newsline,* 25 October 2001. Online. Available HTTP: http://www.rferl.org/newsline/2001/10/251001.asp (accessed 28 January 2008).

Polish President Cleared of Secret Police Links', *CNN,* 10 August 2000.

'Polish President Signs Amended Lustration Law', *RFE/RL Newsline,* 16 October 2002. Online. Available HTTP: http://www.rferl.org/newsline/2002/10/161002.asp (accessed 28 January 2008).

'Polish Secret Services Blamed for Infringements over President's Lustration', *RFE/RL Newsline,* 1 August 2000. Online. Available HTTP: http://www.rferl.org/newsline/2000/08/010800.asp (accessed 28 January 2008).

'Poll: most Czechs of opinion country has not come to terms with StB collaborators', Radio Prague, 16 November 2007. Online. Available HTTP: http://www.radio.cz/print/en/news/97688 (accessed 26 January 2008).

Portocala, R., *Autopsie d'un coup d'état roumain: au pays du mensonge triomphant,* Paris:Calman-Levy, 1990.

The Position of Fidesz – Hungarian Civic Union on the Opening of Former State Security Files, 17 March 2005.

Prazauskas, A., 'Transitional Justice in a Post-Soviet Nation: The Case of Lithuania', pp. 4–5. Online. Available HTTP: http://igpa.nat.gov.tw/public/Attachment/782810245671. pdf (accessed 25 December 2007).

'Pregled opozicijkih sil v slovenia analiza republiškega sekertariata za notranje zadeve', *Republiškega sekertariata za notranje zadeve*, Ljubljana, 25 January 1979.

Pressemitteilung *Die MfS-Unterlagen zu Dr. Helmut Kohl werden morgen herausgegeben*, 23 March 2005.

'Press Release of the Embassy of Ukraine in Estonia', 10 February and 12 April 2005. Online. Available HTTP: http://home.uninet.ee/~embkura/Press-24.htm and http://home. uninet.ee/~embkura/Press-68.htm (accessed 15 December 2007).

Press Survey, CTK, 23 March 1991.

Privacy and Human Rights 2003: Slovenia, New York, 2003. Online. Available HTTP: http://www.privacyinternational.org/survey/phr2003/countries/slovenia.htm (accessed 20 January 2008).

'Pro-Fidesz Daily Says Hungarian Premier Was Secret Police Agent', *RFE/RL Newsline*, 18 June 2002. Online. Available HTTP: http://www.rferl.org/newsline/2002/06/180602. asp (accessed 28 January 2008).

Prŭcha, V., 'Economic Development and Relations, 1918–1989', in Musil, *The End of Czechoslovakia*, Budapest: Central European University, 1995, pp. 40–76.

Pučnik, J., *Iz Archivov Slovenske politične policije*, Ljubljana: Založila Veda, 1996.

Purvis, A., 'The Reckoning. How Accusations of Communist-Era Collaboration Are Shaking up Central Europe', *Time Europe*, 4 April 2005.

——, 'Dredging Up Bad Memories', *Time Europe*, 4 April 2005. Online. Available HTTP: http://www.time.com/time/magazine/article/0,9171,1042420,00.html (accessed 28 January 2008).

Putnam, R., *Making Democracy Work. Civic Traditions in Modern Italy*, Princeton: Princeton University Press, 1993.

Radicova, I., 'The Velvet Divorce', *Uncaptive Minds*, 1993, vol. 6, 51–2.

Rainer, J. M., 'Opening the Archives of the Communist Secret Police – the Experience of Hungary', paper presented at the Congress of Historical Sciences, Oslo, Norway, 6–13 August 2000. Online. Available HTTP: http://www.rev.hu/archivum/rmj_oslo_00_eng_ long.html (accessed 6 June 2006).

Ramet, S. P., 'Democratization in Slovenia—the Second Stage', in K. Dawisha and B. Parrot (eds.) *Politics, Power and the Struggle for Democracy in South-East Europe*, New York: Cambridge University Press, 1997, pp. 189–225.

Ratesh, N., *Romania: The Entangled Revolution*, New York: Praeger, 1991.

Raykov, E., 'Tunkiat led po patia kam tainite na NATO', *Sega*, 14 June 2004.

'Recursul la discurs', *22*, 1998, no. 45, 5–8.

Reindl, D., 'Mass Graves from the Communist Past Haunt Slovenia's Present', *Radio Free Europe Radio Liberty*, 29 November 2001. Online. Available HTTP: http://www. encyclopedia.com/doc/1G1-80342089.html (accessed 22 January 2008).

Repe, B., *Jutri je Nov Dan*, Ljbuljana: Modrijan, 2002.

Republic of Slovenia, 'Komisijo za nadzor nad delom varnostnih in obveščevalnih služb', *Uradni list*, 1993, no. 12.

'Resolution of the National Assembly regarding information for the organization, methods and means in the implementation of the specific tasks of the institutions of the State security as well as regarding information by agents, collected by those institutions', *State Gazette* [Sofia], 1994, No. 86.

'A Riga District Court Has Rejected Pleas that a Jailed Ex-police Officer Be Freed', *The Weekly Crier*. March–April 2001. Online. Available HTTP: http://www.balticsww.com/wkcrier/0219_0409_01.htm (accessed 21 December 2007).

Robers, N., *Joachim Gauck: Die Biografie einer Institution*, Berlin: Henschel, 2000.

'Romania', *East European Constitutional Review* 1999, vol. 8, 15–16.

Romanian 'Hot Line Affair' Probed by Prosecutor-General', *RFE/RL Newsline*, 28 March 2000. Online. Available HTTP: http://www.rferl.org/newsline/2000/03/280300.asp (accessed 28 January 2008).

Roper, S., 'The Romanian Revolution from a Theoretical Viewpoint', *Communist and Post-Communist Studies* 1994, vol. 27, 401–410.

Rose, R., *A Decade of New Russia Barometer Surveys*, Glasgow: Center for Public Police, University of Strathclyde, 2002.

Rosenberg, T., *The Haunted Land: Facing Europe's Ghosts after Communism*, New York: Vintage Books, 1995.

Roskin, M. G., *The Rebirth of East Europe*, Upper Saddle River, NJ: Prentice-Hall, 2002, 4th edition.

'Ruling Majority Rejects Draft Law on Lustration', *Georgia Online*, 16 February 2007. Online. Available HTTP: http://www.civil.ge/eng/article.php?id=14644 (accessed 2 January 2008).

Rzeczpospolita, 21 January 1992.

Sabbat-Swidlicka, A., 'Crisis in the Polish Justice Ministry', *RFE/RL Research Report* 1993, vol. 2, 15–19.

——, 'Former Security Officials Arrested', *Report on Eastern Europe*, 26 October 1990, pp. 18–21.

——, 'Poland: A Year of Three Governments', *RRF/RL Research Report* 1993, vol. 2, 102–107.

Sadurski, W., "De-communization', 'Lustration' and Constitutional Continuity: Dilemmas of Transitional Justice in Central Europe', *EUI Working Paper LAW* 15, 2005. Online. Available HTTP: http://cadmus.eui.eu/dspace/bitstream/1814/1869/2/law03–15.pdf (accessed 4 January 2008).

Samuelli, A., *Woman Behind Bars in Romania*, London: Frank Cass, 1997.

Sararu, D., and Stanculescu, V., *Generalul Revolutiei cu piciorul in gips*, Bucharest: Rao, 2005.

Savin, Z., 'UDBa in cenzura', *Mladina* (18 April 2003). Online. Available HTTP: http://www.mladina.si/tednik/200315/ (accessed 20 January 2006).

——, 'Odzivi na www.UDBa.net', *Mladina* (23 April 2003). Online. Available HTTP: http://www.mladina.si/tednik/200316/ (accessed 20 January 2006).

Schaefgen, C., 'Der Honecker-Prozeß', in J. Weber and M. Piazolo (eds.), *Eine Diktatur vor Gericht: Aufarbeitung von SED-Unrecht durch die Justiz,* Munich: Olzog, 1995, pp. 89–100.

Schulhofer, S. J., Rosendelf, M., Teitel, R., and Errera, R., 'Dilemmas of Justice' in Kritz, N. (ed.), *Transitional Justice: How New Democracies Reckon with Their Authoritarian Past*, Washington, D.C.: US Institute for Peace, vol. 1, 1995, pp. 146–153.

'Screening Commission Wants Names of StB Agents Made Public', CTK, 22 May 1991.

Sechster Tätigkeitsbericht der Bundesbeauftragten für die Unterlagen des Staatssicherheitsdienstes der ehemaligen Deutschen Demokratischen Republik, Berlin: BStU, 2003.

'Sedinta solemna comuna a Camerei Deputatilor si Senatului of 22 December 1997', *Monitorul Oficial al Romaniei, partea a II-a*, 12 January 1998.

Seliskar, Z., *Zgodovina organov za notranje zadeve v Socialisticni Republiki Sloveniji*, Ljubljana: Mladinska knjiga, 1970.

Šetinc, M., 'Zapisani, izrisani, zamolčani', *Mladina*, 8 May 2002. Online. Available HTTP: http://www.mladina.si/tednik/200218/ (accessed 10 January 2006).

Sever, J., 'Usodna UDBa', *Mladina* (28 April 2003). Online. Available HTTP: http://www.mladina.si/tednik/200317/ (accessed 20 January 2006).

Shafir, M., 'The Isolation of Romania and the Fall of Nicolae Ceausescu', *Report on Eastern Europe*, 5 January 1990, 28–32.

Siani-Davies, P., *The Romanian Revolution of December 1989*, Ithaca: Cornell University Press, 2005.

Siegerjustiz? Berlin: Kai Homilius Verlag, 2003.

Sislin, J., 'Revolution Betrayed? Romania and the National Salvation Front', *Studies in Comparative Communism* 1991, vol. 29, 395–412.

'Six Lithuanian Prosecutors Suspended under Lustration Law', *RFE/RL Newsline*, 9 March 1999.

Skalnik Leff, C., *National Conflict in Czechoslovakia: The Making and Remaking of a State, 1918–1987*, Princeton: Princeton University Press, 1988.

Skilling, H. G., *Charter 77 and Human Rights in Czechoslovakia*, London: Allen and Unwin, 1981.

Slater, W., 'Russia's Imagined History: Visions of the Soviet Past and the New 'Russian Idea'', *Journal of Communist Studies and Transition Politics*, 1998, vol. 14, 69–86.

'SLD Parliamentary Caucus Leader Cleared of Lustration Lie', *RFE/RL Newsline*, 31 July 2002. Online. Available HTTP: http://www.rferl.org/newsline/2002/07/310702.asp (accessed 28 January 2008).

'Slota indifferent to National Memory Institute', *The Slovak Spectator*, 25 September 2006. Online. Available HTTP: http://www.spectator.sk (accessed 25 January 2007).

'Slovak Parliament Overrides Presidential Veto', *RFE/RL Newsline*, 21 August 2002. Online. Available HTTP: http://www.rferl.org/newsline/2002/08/3-CEE/cee-210802. asp (accessed 28 January 2008).

'Slovak Supreme Court Returns Bilak Case to Prosecution', *RFE/RL Newsline*, 13 March 2002. Online. Available HTTP: http://www.hri.org/news/balkans/rferl/2002/02-03-13. rferl.html (accessed 28 January 2008).

Smith, K., *Remembering Stalin's Victims: Popular Memory and the End of the USSR*, Ithaca: Cornell University Press, 1996.

——, *Mythmaking in the New Russia: Politics and Memory during the Yeltsin Era*, Ithaca: Cornell University Press, 2002.

Social Research and Analysis Previs Consult Agency, 'Research on Media Coverage of Declassification of Files, 15–31 October 2004', Bulgarian Telegraph Agency, 2 November 2004.

'Soviet Disarray: Jail for 2 in Chenobyl Case', Reuters, 13 December 1991. Online. Available HTTP: http://query.nytimes.com/gst/fullpage.html?res=9D0CEFD91E3BF930A25751C1A967958260 (accessed 29 December 2007).

'Soviet War Criminal in Office', *The Baltic Bulletin*, March 1988. Online. Available HTTP: http://www.lituanus.org/1988/88_3_08.htm (accessed 21 December 2007).

Soyinka, W., *The Burden of Memory. The Muse of Forgiveness*, Oxford: Oxford University Press, 1999.

'So zverejnením zväzkov ŠtB slovenskí umelci súhlasa', *Sme*, 25 November 2004. Online. Available HTTP: http://www.sme.sk/clanok.asp?cl=1835468 (accessed 28 January 2008).

'Spies Caught in the Web', *Time Europe*, 24 March 2003. Online. Available HTTP: http://www.time.com/time/magazine/article/0,9171,433236,00.html (accessed 28 January 2008).

Spiewak, P., *Pamic po komunizmie*, Gdans: Slowo/Obraz/Terytoria, 2005.

'Sprawozdanie Komisji Nadzwyczajnej do Zbadania Dzialalnosci MSW z dzialalnosci w okresie X Kadencji Sejmu RP (1989–1991)', *Druk* 1104, 25 September 1991.

Sprawozdanie stenograficzne Sejmu PRL, 24 August 1989, pp. 84–86, 29 September 1989, pp. 84–87, 13 October 1989, pp. 89–93, and 30 December 1989, pp. 134–143.

Sprawozdanie stenograficzne Sejmu RP, 17 May 1993, p. 137, and 4 February 1994, pp. 24–25.

Stan, L., 'Access to Securitate Files: The Trials and Tribulations of a Romanian Law', *Eastern European Politics and Society* 2002, vol. 16, 55–90.

——, 'Moral Cleansing Romanian Style', *Problems of Post-Communism* 2002, vol. 49, 55–90.

——, 'Spies, Files and Lies: Explaining the Failure of Access to Securitate Files', *Communist and Post-Communist Studies* 2004, vol. 37, 341–359.

——, 'Inside the Securitate Archives', Washington, D.C.: Cold War History Project, Woodrow Wilson Center, February 2005. Online. Available HTTP: http://www.wilsoncenter.org/index.cfm?topic_id=1409&fuseaction=topics.item&news_id=109979 (accessed 29 December 2007).

——, 'The Opposition Takes Charge: The Romanian General Elections of 2004', *Problems of Post-Communism* 2005, vol. 52, 3–15.

——, 'Lustration in Romania: The Story of a Failure', *Studia politica* 2006, vol. 6, 135–156.

——, 'The Politics of Memory in Poland: Lustration, File Access and Court Proceedings', *Studies in Post-Communism Occasional Paper* 2006, no. 10. Online. Available HTTP: http://www.stfx.ca/pinstitutes/cpcs/studies-in-post-communism/Stan2006.pdf (accessed 28 December 2007).

——, 'The Roof over Our Head: Property Restitution in Romania', *Journal of Communist Studies and Transition Politics* 2006, vol. 22, 1–17.

——, 'Transition, Justice and Transitional Justice in Poland', *Studia Politica: The Romanian Political Science Review* 2006, vol. 6, 257–284.

——, 'Goulash Justice for Goulash Communism? Explaining Transitional Justice in Hungary', *Studia Politica: The Romanian Political Science Review* 2007, vol. 7, 269–292.

Stanislav, M., 'Osvieženie pamäti', *Pravda*, 7 November 2001. Online. Available HTTP: http://www.pravda.sk/dennik/2001/11/07/nazory/01/article.2819.html (accessed 29 March 2002).

Stankov, D., *Sled dalgi godini mulchanie. 42 godini v bulgarskoto razuznavane*, Sofia: Hristo Botev, 2001.

Starman, D., 'Zakon o volitvah v državni zbor', *Uradni list*, 2001, vol. 3, 1–3.

'Statement der Bundesbeauftragen Marianne Birthler', 3 August 2004. Pressemitteilung der BStU.

The Stenographic Notes of the Talks between Comrade Todor Zhivkov and Comrade Leonid Brezhnev at the Voden Residence, 20 September 1973, Bulgarian Communist Party Archive, Fond 378-B, File 360.

Stoica, I., 'Chitac si Stanculescu dibleaza puscaria', *Evenimentul Zilei*, 23 March 2004.

Summary of the Talks between Todor Zhikov and John Whitehead, US Undersecretary of State, Sofia, 4 February 1987, Bulgarian Communist Party Archive, Fond 1B, Record 60, File 392.

'Sudut v Strasbourg othvarli molbata na bulgaski turzi sreshtu Bulgaria', *Mediapool* (28 April 2005). Online. Available HTTP: http://www.mediapool.bg/show/?storyid=104376 (accessed 29 January 2008).

Sustrova, P., 'The Lustration Controversy', *Uncaptive Minds*, 1992, vol. 5, 129–134.

Szczerbiak, A., 'Dealing with the Communist Past or the Politics of the Present? Lustration in Post-Communist Poland', *Europe-Asia Studies* 2002, vol. 54, 559–572.

Szostkiewicz, A., 'The Time for De-communization Has Past', *The Warsaw Voice*, 28 June 1998.

Takayuki, I. (ed.), *Facing Up to the Past: Soviet Historiography under Perestroika*, Sapporo: Slavic Research Center, 1989.

Tanase, S., *Anatomia mistificarii*, Bucharest: Humanitas, 2003.

Tanner, M., *Croatia: A Nation Forged in War*, New Haven: Yale University Press, 1997.

Tarm, M., 'Stalinist Crimes Hunted in Baltics', The Associated Press, 18 March 1999. Online. Available HTTP: http://www.angelfire.com/tx/LABAS/issue13.html (accessed 26 December 2007).

Teitel, R., 'Paradoxes in the Revolution of the Rule of Law', *Yale Journal of International Law* 1994, vol. 19, 239–247.

——, *Transitional Justice*, Oxford: Oxford University Press, 2002.

'Ten Collaborators of Former Secret Police in Federal Parliament', CTK, 22 March 1991.

Tepeshanov, C., *Otrovata*, Sofia: Meridian Press, 1993.

'The Timisoara Declaration', *Report on Eastern Europe*, 6 April 1990, 41–45.

Thierse, W., 'Ist die Stasibehörde noch nötig? Ja!', *Die Tageszeitung*, 15 August 2007.

'The Three Lives of Helena Brus', *Sunday Telegraph*, 6 December 1998. Online. Available HTTP: http://www.anneapplebaum.com/communism/1998/12_06_tel_brus.html (accessed 28 January 2008).

Tismaneanu, V., *Fantasies of Salvation. Democracy, Nationalism and Myth in Post-Communist Europe*, Princeton: Princeton University Press, 1998.

Todd, P. and Bloch, J., *Global Intelligence. The World's Secret Services Today*, London: Zed Books, 2004.

Tomasevich, J., *War and Revolution in Yugoslavia 1941–1945: Occupation and Collaboration*, Stanford: Stanford University Press, 2001.

Toš, N. et. al., 'Slovensko Javno Mnenje', *Center za Raziskovanje Javnega Mnenja in Množičnih Komunikacija*, Ljubljana: FDV: CJMMK, 1994.

Toš, N. (ed.), *Vrednote v prehodu II, Slovensko javno mnenje 1990–1998*, Ljubljana: FDV-CJMMK, 1999.

Transparency International, *The 2004 Corruption Perception Index*. Online. Available HTTP: http://www.transparency.org (accessed 22 January 2008).

Troncota, C., 'Noua politica in domeniul institutiei securitatii regimului communist din 'Romania, 1965–1989', *Arhivele totalitarismului* 2001, vols. 32–33, 112–133.

Tsypkin, M., 'Russia's Failure', *Journal of Democracy*, 2006, vol. 17, 72–85.

Tucker, R., *Stalin in Power: The Revolution from Above, 1928–1941*, New York: W. W. Norton, 1990.

TV aktualno, ATV, RTV Slovenija, 22 April 2003.

'Two Former StB Officers Charged with Torture', CTK, 14 September 2005.

Tylová, K. and P. Kolář, 'Paroubek chce konec lustrací', *Lidové noviny*, 24 November 2005. Online. Available HTTP: http://www.lidovky.cz/paroubek-zruseni-lustraci-pocka-do3-/ln_domov.asp?c=A051124_144702_ln_domov_lvv (accessed 28 January 2008).

Uhl, P., 'Několik argementů pro Havla', *Právo*, 11 March 2002, p. 7. Online. Available HTTP: http://pravo.newtonit.cz/tisk.asp?cache=797095 (accessed 25 March 2002).

Uitz, R., 'Missed Opportunities for Coming to Terms with the Communist Past: The Hungarian Saga of Lustration and Access to Secret Service Files', paper presented at the American Association for the Advancement of Slavic Studies conference, Salt Lake City, 3–6 November 2005.

'Ukraine – Governance Assessment', March 2006, p. 75. Online. Available HTTP: http://www.sigmaweb.org/dataoecd/46/63/37127312.pdf (accessed 15 December 2007).

Ullmann, W., 'Das Stasi-Unterlagen-Gesetz. Eine Demokratie-initiative der Friedlichen Revolution', in S. Suckut and J. Weber (eds.) *Stasi-Akten zwischen Politik und Zeitgeschichte: Eine Zwischenbilanz*, Munich: Olzog, 2003, 45–66.

United Nations Development Program, *The 2007/2008 Human Development Index Rankings*. Online. Available HTTP: http://hdr.undp.org/en/statistics/ (accessed 22 January 2008).

Ursachi, R., 'Is the Trial of Communism a Criminal Trial?', paper presented at the Society for Romanian Studies congress, Constanta, Romania, 25–28 June 2007.

Ursachi, R. and Grosescu, R., 'Les processus pénaux et la gestion du passé dictatorial. Le cas de la Roumanie postcommuniste', unpublished paper, 2007.

Ústav pamäti národa, 'Disclosure'. Online. Available HTTP: http://www.upn.gov.sk/?page=disclosure (accessed 28 January 2008).

'Ustav Savezne Republike Jugoslavije', *Službeni List*, Belgrade: Vlada Savezne Republike Jugoslavije, 1974.

'Ustawa z dnia 18 października 2006 r. o ujawnianiu informacji o dokumentach organów bezpieczeństwa państwa z lat 1944–1990 oraz treści tych dokumentów'. Online. Available HTTP: http://www.abc.com.pl/serwis/du/2006/1592.htm (accessed 27 March 2007).

Vagovič, M., 'Tiene minulosti', *Pravda*, 2 November 2001. Online. Available HTTP: http://www.pravda.sk/dennik/2001/11/02/nazory/01/article.5309.html (accessed 29 March 2002).

——, 'Najvišší čas diskuovat' o zločinoch komunistckého režimu', *Pravda*, 16 November 2001. Online. Available HTTP: http://www.pravda.sk/dennik/2001/11/16/slovensko/01/article.14559.html (accessed 29 March 2002).

Vaksberg, T., 'Ne brumbar, a kosher zentrali', *Capital Weekly*, 2000, No. 33.

——, *Tehnologia na zloto*, documentary movie, Bulgarian national TV, 2001.

——, 'Tehnologia na zloto', *Sega Daily* (5–7 February 2001).

Valery-Grossu, N., *Binecuvintata fii, inchisoare*, Bucharest: Univers, 2002.

Vavro, P., 'Preverení', *Národná obroda*, 22 February 2002.

Velinger, J., 'Asanace – the Communists' Infamous Clearance Operation – Left Indelible Stain on Dissidents' Lives', *Radio Prague*, 31 August 2004. Online. Available HTTP: http://www.radio.cz/en/article/57645 (accessed 28 January 2008).

Vera, N. and Georgescu, T., 'Punctul opt de la Timisoara in Legea Electorala', *Evenimentul Zilei*, 10 March 1999.

Verdery, K. and Kligman, G., 'Romania after Ceausescu: Post-Communist Communism?', in I. Banac (ed.) *Eastern Europe in Revolution*, Ithaca: Cornell University Press, 1992, pp. 117–147.

Vernichten oder Offenlegen? Zur Entstehung des Stasi-Unterlagen-Gesetzes, Berlin: BStU, 1997.

'Vetting Denied to Medgyessy Commission Experts', *RFE/RL Newsline*, 15 August 2002. Online. Available HTTP: http://www.rferl.org/newsline/2002/08/150802.asp (accessed 28 January 2008).

'Vetting of Parliament a Necessary Purge, Civic Movement', CTK, 22 March 1991.

VTsIOM Analytic Agency, *VTsIOM Nationwide Survey*, 28 February-3 March 2003. Online. Available HTTP: http://www.russiavotes.org/Mood_rus_cur.htm#395 (accessed 14 July 2004).

Vinton, L., 'Poland's Government Crisis: An End in Sight?', *RFE/RL Research Report* 1992, vol. 1, 16–20.

Walicki, A., 'Transitional Justice and the Political Struggles of Post-Communist Poland', in J. A. McAdams (ed.) *Transitional Justice and the Rule of Law in New Democracies*, South Bend: University of Notre Dame, 1997, pp. 193–196.

Waller, M. J., 'Russia's Security Services: A Checklist for Reform', *ISCIP-Perspective*, 1997, vol. 8. Online. Available HTTP: http://www.bu.edu/iscip/vol8/Waller.html (accessed 25 January 2008).

'Warsaw Court Sentences Stalinist-Era Torturers', *RFE/RL Daily Digest*, 11 March 1996. Online. Available HTTP: http://www.rferl.org/features/1996/03/f.ru.96031317083328. asp (accessed 28 January 2008).

Weberling, J., *Stasi–Unterlagen-Gesetz: Kommentar*, Berlin: Carl Heymanns Verlag, 1993.

Welsh, H., 'Dealing with the Communist Past: Central and East European Experiences after 1990', *Europe-Asia Studies* 1996, vol. 48, 419–428.

Weydenthal, J. B. de., 'Inquiry into the Murder of Father Popieluszko Reopened', *Report on Eastern Europe*, 17 August 1990, pp. 12–15.

White, A., 'The Memorial Society in the Russian Provinces', *Europe-Asia Studies*, 1995, vol. 47, 1343–1366.

Williams, K., 'The StB in Czechoslovakia, 1945–89', in K. Williams and D. Deletant, *Security Intelligence Services in New Democracies: The Czech Republic, Slovakia and Romania*, New York: Palgrave, 2001, pp. 24–54.

Williams, K., Fowler, B., and Szczerbiak, A., 'Explaining Lustration in Central Europe: A 'Post-Communist Politics' Approach', *Democratization* 2005, vol. 12, 22–43.

'Who Says He Needs Time to deal with Revelation', *RFE/RL Newsline*, 8 July 2002. Online. Available HTTP: http://www.rferl.org/newsline/2002/07/080702.asp (accessed 28 January 2008).

Woehrel, S., 'Ukraine's Orange Revolution and U.S. Policy', CRS Report for Congress, 1 April 2005. Online. Available HTTP: http://fpc.state.gov/documents/organization/45452. pdf (accessed 15 December 2007).

Wolek, A. 'Lustracja jako walka o reguly polityki I proba wzmacniania legitymizacji nowych demokracji', *Studia Polityczne* 2004, vol. 15, 147–173.

Wong, T. E. M. 'The Truth and Reconciliation Commission. A Brief Analysis', unpublished paper, 1996.

Yasmann, V., 'The KGB Has Spawned A Large Set of Osspring', *Prism*, 26 May 1995. Online. Available HTTP: http://jamestown.org/publications_details.php?volume_id=1&issue_id=13&article_id=162 (accessed 15 December 2007).

——, 'Legislation on Screening and State Security in Russia', *RFE/RL Research Report*, 1993, vol. 2, 11–16, reprinted in N. Kritz, ed, *Transitional Justice: How Emerging Democracies Reckon with Former Regimes*, Washington, D.C.: United States Institute for Peace, 1995, vol. 2, pp. 754–761.

——, '"Siloviki" Take the Reigns in Post-Oligarchy Russia', *RFE/RL Newsline*, 18 September 2007.

——, '"Spymania" Returns to Russia', *RFE/RL Reports*, 15 April 2004.

Young, J. E., *The Texture of Memory: Holocaust Memorials and Meaning*, New Haven: Yale University Press, 1993.

Žajedla, I., 'Kako je padel udbovski amandma', *Slovenec*, 11 September 1992.

'Zakon o Varstvu Osebnih Podadkov, 15 July 2004', *Uradni list*, 2004, no. 34.

Zalaquett, J., 'Introduction to the English Edition', in The Chilean National Commission on Truth and Reconciliation, *Report of the Chilean National Commission on Truth and Reconciliation*, trans. P. Berryman, South Bend: University of Notre Dame Press, 1993, pp. xxi–xxii.

Žerdin, A., 'Udobski dosiji', *Mladina* (26 July 1993). Online. Available HTTP: http://www.mladina.si/tednik/200330/ (accessed 20 January 2006).

——, 'Sova v vašem računalniku', *Mladina*, 8 October 2001. Online. Available HTTP: http://www.mladina.si (accessed 20 January 2006).

Zidar, A., *Lustracija: izločitev nasprotnikov demokracije z javnih položajev*, Ljubljana: Nova Revija, 1996.

Živnerová, L., 'Podporíte odtajnenie zväzkov ŠtB v parlamente?', *Národna obroda*, 30 October 2001.

Zlobina, K., 'Slovensko: impresie a depresie', *Listy*, 1978, vol. 8, 1–12.

Zweiter Tätigkeitsbericht des Bundesbeauftragten für die Unterlagen des Staatssicherheitsdienstes der ehemaligen Deutschen Demokratischen Republik, Berlin: BStU, 1995.

Index